Weaving the Tapestry of Moral Judgement

Christian Ethics in a Plural World

John A. Harrod

EPWORTH

British Library Cataloguing in Publication data

A catalogue record for this book is available
from the British Library

978 0 7162 0618 7

First published in 2007
by Epworth
4 John Wesley Road
Werrington
Peterborough PE4 6ZP

Typeset by Regent Typesetting, London
Printed and bound in Great Britain by
William Clowes Ltd, Beccles, Suffolk

Contents

To Rosalie,
Paul and Natasha,
Stella and Mark

also to
James, Francesca and Daniel
with the hope that their generation will be given what is needed
to respond adequately to the issues discussed in this book

Preface

Ethics is a keenly debated and hotly contested field. The last 30 years or so has a seen a vast increase in the literature, especially that of moral philosophers, who tend now to see their brief much more widely than did their forebears. Ethics is even more contested when, as in this book, 'secular' and 'Christian' ethics are seen as creative dialogue partners, rather than as clashing like tectonic plates.

This book – inevitably selective in the topics discussed – seeks to survey part of that field and some of the issues. It is not a text book in the sense of simply surveying impartially the literature, the history of debate, and the various options available for discussion. It argues its own case too much for that, while also leaving many issues unresolved and for readers to make their own judgement. The emphasis is more on wrestling with issues than on cataloguing who among the great and the good have said this or that. At the same time, I hope this book will be of interest to A-Level students, undergraduates and others studying the subject, as well as to ministers and clergy and the general reader. I hope, in particular, it will be of value to study groups within the churches. Because of the position it takes, it may be of some interest also to the specialist.

The decision to write a book like this is to adopt a high-risk strategy. The challenge is to be economical without being thin, simple without being simplistic, and to summarize without distorting. Inevitably, I have touched on many areas where my competence is only sketchy. Such are the perils of a book of this genre. I hope my errors are not too grave and too serious.

I write from within the Christian tradition, while cherishing the hope that what I suggest concerning religion and belief in God might make sense to people of other faiths. When I speak of a 'Christian' position I do this not in order to be exclusive but because I have no right to speak for others.

If I write from within the Christian tradition I write also as a white British male, asking what might be offered from that perspective to the wider world context. I hope I am mindful of the resources and stringent challenges of the world Church. A book, however, that sought to adopt as its basic stance a world Church perspective would have been another kind of book and not one I am competent to write.

The main body of writing was completed during a period of sabbatical leave. I am deeply grateful to the Partnership for Theological Education in Manchester for permitting this, and especially to my two immediate colleagues Dr Jane Craske and Dr Andrew Pratt for the additional burdens they have willingly and generously carried. My thanks are due also to Dr Natalie Watson of Epworth Press for advice and encouragement. A number of people have read drafts of chapters and given me the benefit of their comments. For these I am deeply grateful. I remain myself, of course, fully responsible for errors and shortcomings, and this means I can save them the embarrassment of mentioning their names! I am also immensely grateful to my wife Rosalie, for uncomplainingly putting up with a much distracted husband and for being generously supportive.

I have tried to avoid wherever possible technical language, and when it is used it is generally explained in the text. Words and concepts in the text, however, which have a double asterisk (thus**) are given further explanation in the Glossary.

Part I

An Approach to Ethics

Introduction: Why Bother with Ethics?

The Ten Commandments, given a certain prominence in the Christian tradition, presuppose a society much simpler than our own. In our global village we face agonizing dilemmas, many of which did not, in their worst nightmares, trouble the editors of the book of Exodus. Is it ethical to abort an unborn human because identified, say, as Down's syndrome? Is it ethical to use human embryos for medical research? What pattern of consumption is consistent not only with social justice but also with care for the environment? What economic and political structures give a right balance between efficient wealth creation, its just distribution, environmental responsibility and freedom? Do I have a right to determine my own death through seeking medically assisted dying when my quality of life is no longer acceptable? Is it permissible to test drugs on animals and to use animals in other ways in medical research? In extreme cases, might torture be permissible – say to gain information as to the whereabouts of a terrorist bomb? Is it ethical to possess and to threaten to use nuclear weapons, even though their use will be immoral, when the intention behind possessing and threatening to use them is to prevent their use, believing we best prevent their use by so possessing them? The list of searching ethical questions could be continued for many pages.

I have described these issues as ethical, but what is it that makes an issue an ethical or moral one? What characterizes a choice as a *moral* choice? In this book, the words 'ethical' and 'moral' are used interchangeably. Suppose I am planting cabbages, and I take from the tool shed a dibber rather than a trowel? Is my choice of the dibber a *moral* choice? And if not, why not? What is it that makes an issue a moral one?

The attempt to give a summary answer to this question is a perilous undertaking. There is the danger that we give an answer too simple and reductionist, leaving out much from our rich ethical tradition. On the other hand, some summary answer must be attempted otherwise our discussion has no focus. A two-stranded approach to this question is taken in this book. First, a matter has an ethical dimension when it *impinges upon our well-being in our sharing of a common life*. Ethics is about discovering what leads to our mutual well-being, flourishing or enhancement. A fundamental fact about humanity is that we are relational beings. We are related to one another. This is expressed in the notion of *mutual* well-being within the human community, but we are also related to the earth and to other living things.

My choice of the dibber rather than the trowel is in itself hardly a moral one, but I can imagine a background that would make it so. Suppose cabbages planted with a dibber develop a more confined root system that stimulates the production of toxic chemicals in the leaves, thus damaging my children's health. Or suppose that by buying the dibber I support an unscrupulous tool manufacturer who exploits its labour force. Then the issue becomes a moral one because my choice has implications for people's well-being. Because our actions impinge upon our well-being to a greater or lesser extent, there is no clear and absolute dividing line between judgements that are moral ones and those that are not. The one shades off gradually into the other.[1] This approach to ethics may thus blur the boundaries marking off so-called 'moral issues', but that is no bad thing. Life's concerns are not easily or helpfully divided up into neat compartments.

For much of the time we can get along quite well in ethics by appealing to this one criterion, that of our mutual well-being, and to this alone. Some have found it sufficient as the one overarching conception in ethics. Sometimes, however, our ethical intuitions suggest that this criterion, although central, is not always alone adequate. The second strand derives from the insight that we cannot avoid fundamental, although tricky and controversial questions concerning *what a human person is*. What is it that gives our lives meaning, purpose, direction and significance? Is there a basic human 'nature' and are there common human needs, which guide our ethics? Even those who insist that meanings and direction in life are entirely what *we give it*, through *our choice*, may still work with some implicit response to such a question.[2] Moral judgements are not made discreetly and in isolation from this wider context of understanding. Thus, our understanding of what constitutes human well-being feeds on some conception of what it is to be a human person.

Bringing these two strands together then, ethics is about *discovering our mutual well-being, and discovering appropriate relationships, given the kind of creatures human beings are*. These fundamental notions are, of course, very general and there will be no easy consensus as to how they are filled out. But at least they give our study a sufficient focus to get the argument started. I will argue later that other concepts in the rich vocabulary of ethics – duty, obligation, virtue, human rights, justice and so forth – may be understood as giving substance to, and receiving rationale from, this basic understanding of what ethics is about. This basic understanding serves as a kind of portmanteau bag to hold together these more focused concepts of ethics.

The book, therefore, is about making moral judgements. The word 'judgement' is used in preference to 'choice' or 'decision' because it carries a strong hint of reflection and rationality. Pejorative overtones of the 'judgemental' are emphatically not intended. At the same time, there is a subversive theme within this book. Ethics is indeed about making judgements as to how to act, but ethics is not simply about 'doing'. It is also about 'being'. Alongside the approach to ethics that puts the emphasis upon making judgements over specific moral issues, there is the approach that puts the emphasis on the manner of people we are. The emphasis may be more on the 'good life' and 'being good' than on seeking over a particular matter to identify the right action. Alongside the question 'What must I do?', there should be another question, 'What sort of person do I seek to be?'

These approaches, however, are not alternatives. They are complementary. If some approaches to ethics show little interest in the kind of people we are, provided our actions are right, so an ethic that concentrates overmuch on our 'being' can leave us ill equipped to wrestle with specific moral dilemmas, or worse still neglectful of our duties because we are too busy cultivating our souls.

In this book I wish – if the metaphor is not too stale or even pretentious – to 'swim against the stream' in four ways.

First, I argue that ethics is a mature 'secular' discipline and that we can get along quite well without theology. This follows from my claim that questions of ethics and morality are questions about what leads to our mutual well-being. We can ask what leads to and what constitutes our mutual flourishing simply as human beings, and on the basis of a basic shared experience of being human. There can, therefore, be a public debate and a public consensus on ethics that does not require any reference to theology. In this first part of the book I ask how far we can get in thinking about ethics without appeal to theology, and the truth is that we can get a very long way indeed. I thus swim against the stream of those in the Church who dismiss 'secular ethics', claiming that Christians have special expertise in the area and that ethics proper is a private Christian party to which only Christians are invited, there being no other decent party in town.

At the same time, however, I argue that what is essentially a human concern may be importantly nuanced, and sometimes radically reshaped, when the insights of Christian faith are brought to bear. At one level ethics is autonomous.** At another level, our ethical and religious convictions may coexist in a mutually enriching relationship. For this reason, I also swim against the stream of those who wish to keep religion out of ethics. Contemporary literature is full of serious ethical indictments against religion. Many reject religion for reasons that are partly ethical. Religion is the enemy of the good life. Some even go as far as to say that the very profession of religious faith manifests a serious moral failing. My argument is that many of the criticisms are spot on – but against a distortion or caricature of Christian faith, be it a caricature exemplified by far too many Christians. A more subtle understanding of how religion impinges on ethics avoids (even if it learns from and is humbled by) these criticisms. This will be explored in the second part of the book.

I also swim against the stream of those who claim that 'everything is relative'. For this view our ethical stances have no validity beyond being our own choices or the perspective of our culture. My argument is that we can make good sense of the claim that there are universally valid values and obligations that hold 'as such', and not just because I or the tradition in which I stand says so. A few sentences earlier I spoke of doing ethics as human beings, but is there any human being apart from a specific cultural setting? Clearly there is not, but that does not mean there can be no progress at all in seeking a common point of view. We will explore this further in the next and subsequent chapters.

While resisting extreme relativism, I wish nonetheless, fourthly, to swim against the stream of those who claim too much certainty. I resist total scepticism but a good measure of ambiguity still remains. Broadly speaking, the more we move towards identifying 'general' values, obligations and virtues, the greater the confidence we have. Uncertainty and ambiguity attach more to applying and balancing these in the rough and tumble of the real world – in so far as we can understand the 'real' world. This is not a book about mathematics or regular verbs. It is a book about ethics and the good life. In contrast to mathematics and regular verbs, the whole area is riddled with un-certainty. We sometimes face genuine dilemmas: that is, questions that do not admit of an 'answer', manifestly 'the correct one', free from ambiguity. As Richard Hare remarked, there is no 'Cartesian' system of morals, by which he meant a system that is demonstrably correct and worked out cleanly from foundation principles.[3] Ambiguity and uncertainty abound. But that does not mean that anything goes, that we cannot distinguish a better from a worse argument, or distinguish judgements that are more responsible from those less so. The ethical 'sea' may be stormy and perilous and our charts sketchy. Nevertheless, we can still do our best to avoid the rocks and steer as steady a course as possible. This basic stance will nuance much of the argument of this book.

In arguing against these four positions I am clearly going to make some enemies. Whether or not I persuade some to be friends is for the reader to judge.

There is another question lurking in the background. Why bother with ethics or morality at all? Why not 'eat, drink and be merry' and dismiss Ethics as a county next to Kent? A willing volunteer for a house-to-house charity collection is challenged on the doorstep: '*Why should I? Why should I give of my hard-earned money for someone on the other side of the world whom I will never meet?*' It is a variation of the age-old question: '*Why should I act morally when it is not in my own interest?*' There are really two questions here, the one of rational justification and the other of motivation. What can be said to the person who will not be put out for the sake of others? And what can we say to *ourselves* when *we* are that person?

This is another question that will occupy our attention, even if it may not be clear what sort of question it is, or what might serve as a satisfactory answer. There is, however, a hint of the beginning of some response in our argument so far. Ethics is not about extraneous demands that have neither rhyme nor reason. Ethics is about discovering our mutual well-being, and so the question, 'Why bother about ethics?' strips down to the question, 'Why bother about our well-being?' It is not clear what force this question is supposed to have. Let us imagine a person says they have no desire that their life should flourish. They tell us they have no interest in having even their most worthy yearnings satisfied. We might be inclined to think they are having us on. It is not clear that such a position is psychologically conceivable or rationally plausible. Certainly, the question 'Why should I bother about *anyone else's* well-being?' has force. It is not clear, however, what force there is in the question 'Why should I bother about *my own* well-being?' Maybe the reasons why this second question lacks force can help us to tackle the first. This will occupy us later – and especially in Chapter 9.

The most sombre diagnosis of the current situation is that there can be no consensus on how we should live. It is, therefore, all up to individual choice. All we can agree on is that we agree to differ, and to give one another freedom to differ. This is the stance of one strand of modern liberalism, and especially when the adjective 'postmodern'** is thrown in for good measure. It follows that Christian values cannot connect with the wider world, so the emphasis must be on Christians living within their own distinctive church culture. Despite its laudable emphasis on freedom and toleration, this is not a very satisfying option. My argument is that the situation is more hopeful than this. We can continue to debate moral issues in the public forum, and Christian thought may contribute to this debate without losing its theological integrity and yet also in a way that may be heard.

Notes

1 Geoffrey J. Warnock, *The Object of Morality*, London, Methuen, 1971, pp. 1–2. Also Bernard Williams, *Ethics and the Limits of Philosophy*, London, Fontana, Collins, 1985, pp. 7 and 9.

2 Thus, Karl Popper maintained that 'life has no meaning' but that we may give it meaning. *The Open Society and Its Enemies*, London, Routledge & Kegan Paul, fourth edition 1962, Volume 2, p. 278.

3 R. M. Hare, *The Language of Morals*, Oxford, 1952, p. 38. 'Cartesian' is the adjective derived from René Descartes, the seventeenth-century French philosopher.

Ethics: A Humanistic Approach

2.1 Introduction

My claim, then, is that ethics concerns what serves *our mutual flourishing or well-being.* Reflecting on what this involves will lead us to consider also *what constitutes human need, what a human person is, and what is their 'nature' and 'end'.* In particular human beings exist in relationship and so ethics asks about what are *appropriate relationships*, with one another, with the earth and other creatures, and, for the theist with God. In this chapter I explore further some of what all this might involve.

Well-being and flourishing are ambitious ideals, and in some contexts all we can hope for is to hang on, and try to make life as tolerable as possible. Thus, less ambitiously and more realistically, ethics may be little more than a constraint on our malevolence and an appeal to widen our sympathies a little. If talk of human well-being sounds too ambitious – or even in some contexts insensitive – we could follow Geoffrey Warnock and speak instead of the 'amelioration of the human predicament' as being the 'object of morality'.[1] This, however, might, by contrast, be too cautious. In reality, we need the hope of the former concept, together with the caution and realism of the latter. That said, sometimes we can do more than simply eliminate the bad. We can also nurture the good. If we can set our sights too high, we can also set them too low.

We need to ask about responsibilities towards the environment and to animals (see Chapter 14), but the prime focus of morality upon the human can hardly be denied. In speaking of our well-being I do not imply a superficial hedonism,** still less an individualistic one. I do not deny the goal will involve sacrifice. Neither do I imply that well-being for one is identical to well-being for another. On the contrary, part of well-being involves the freedom to give the general notion a particular and individual expression. But at least this focus can get the discussion started. Fundamental notions such as liberty, justice, rights, duties and virtues help us to fill out what is involved in enhancing human life, and the criterion of our mutual enhancement gives these notions a rational underpinning. The reality is that, far from offering free vouchers for the supermarket of hedonism, the quest of ethics to discover what constitutes our mutual flourishing is intensely demanding and searching; and that is precisely because it seeks a 'depth' beyond easy superficialities.

The above paragraphs hint that there are dangers in a focus on well-being or flourishing as the controlling notion in ethics. It is worth pausing for a moment on some of these. The notion can be too ambitious, perhaps even encouraging the greed of modern culture, combined with a hint that we have a right to have all our wants satisfied. Talk of well-being thus becomes therapy for the affluent. Are we in danger of committing the same mistake as those who thought the kingdom of God can be built on earth? Suffering, want and the tragic are too much part of the human condition. There are limits to what can be realistically hoped for. This needs to be acknowledged, but at the same time all this means is that the concept has to be nuanced and qualified. Notions such as 'realism' and 'simplicity' and, above all, the virtue of patience, help to do this. Moreover, it is important to be alert to the fact that a focus on our mutual well-being can become intrusive and paternalistic. A zeal for our mutual flourishing can become crusading and we forget that people have a right to freedom and space to discover what it means for them. Concepts such as 'freedom' and 'rights' thus help to protect the individual from the excessive zeal of others, and the enjoyment of such freedoms and rights is part of what constitutes our flourishing.

All this cautious vigilance and judgement. The reality is, however, *all* concepts we use in ethics have their dangers. This is true of modern favourites such as 'rights' and 'liberty'. It is true also of Christian favourites such as 'love'. We have to use these concepts, but at the same time we need our wits about us when using them.

Can we give some broad content to the notion of human well-being? It is here that we return to the suggestion that ethics is guided by some conception of human nature, human need or some sense of purpose or goal for our lives. We will return to this again and again, and especially in sections 3.10 and 5.3–5.5. We should not be so sophisticated that we overlook what is basic and obvious. Human beings have certain needs. If these needs are satisfied, life can be full and rich. If none of these needs is satisfied, then life can be miserable. There is the need for food, shelter, health care and intellectual stimulus. There is the need for love and relationships of trust, loyalty and mutual delight. We have sexual needs. We may add the need to be creative and to have opportunity to delight in the beautiful, and to explore this fascinating world. Our dignity and rights need to be honoured in a just and free society. We need communities to belong to. We need freedom to take appropriate control of our own lives. We need to be loved, understood and valued, although not smothered by a goodwill that becomes intrusive, patronizing or meddling.

Admittedly, this last paragraph betrays at points a certain 'western' slant, for example in its emphasis on freedom. People and cultures are different and each will put together their own characteristic package. But all cultures have to recognize certain human needs and there are parameters outside of which it does not make sense to speak of humans flourishing. A number of writers have thus found in a basic commonality of human need a platform on which to base rationality in ethics and on which to have a sensible debate within the public realm, while still allowing for individual and contextual colouring. Because of a basic givenness about being human, the question 'How should we live?' cannot admit of *any* answer. Thus, Martha Nussbaum speaks of common human experiences – mortality, the body's capacities and needs, our capacity for pain, frustration and joy, our capacity for love, imagination, creativity and play, our intellectual capacities and our relatedness.[2] Such a list should, of course, be seen as being only indicative. A similar approach is found in Philippa Foot and John Finnis.[3]

Of course, the needs of one may differ from the needs of another; and one of our needs is to have that respected. There *may* be some broad gender differences, and certainly people are formed differently in different cultures. It also makes sense to claim we sometimes have a moral obligation to resist some perceived need. But such a moral perception derives from a profounder grasp of what our mutual well-being entails. We may have to ask what our 'real' needs are and which are manufactured. Our consumer society brings amazing blessings, but a 'shopaholic' acquisitiveness can be life diminishing, as well as irresponsible and complacent about justice. Not only do different people flourish differently, but people in different cultures are formed differently, so what constitutes flourishing may be differently nuanced. There are lots of issues here to debate. But at least we have an agenda for sensible discussion. Human beings are not like ball bearings. Human life is miserable or rich, depending on whether or not we are able to enjoy relationships of love and loyalty, on whether or not we can enjoy creativity, on whether or not our rights and dignity are honoured, on whether or not we can enjoy that which is beautiful, on whether or not we have a fair share of the earth's bounty, and so forth. And we do not need a blueprint on to which everyone is pressed whether they like it or not. This was the grave mistake of classical utilitarianism.** A commitment to human flourishing includes the recognition that people may flourish in different ways.

We do not live in isolation. We depend upon one another in society. In this there is almost infinite potential for good and ill. No one can seriously argue that a life of total self-sufficient individualism is the ideal for our flourishing. Yet our capacity to damage and oppress one another is horrific. Ethics concerns, negatively, protecting others from our folly. Positively it concerns discovering how we enhance one another's lives. It follows that ethics is about discovering those values and commitments, those social structures and institutions, those obligations and ways of living and relating, that serve our mutual well-being as we live together in society. This is why imagination and sympathy are so important in ethics. It follows that moral claims are not extraneous and alien demands. Moral claims nourish and sustain us both as individuals and in our corporate life and warn us against harm. For this reason, there is no ultimate and irresolvable conflict between morality and our 'deepest' needs and wants. This approach resonates with the claim that reason enables us to recognize moral claims, and the further belief that moral claims relate to our nature, that is the kind of creatures human beings are.

2.2 Reasons

If all this begins to make sense, it is simply not true, as some Christians claim, that our ethics are all at sea unless based on some 'religious authority', even if such a basis could be sustained. Neither is it true, as some secularists claim, that 'everything is relative'. The criterion of human well-being or flourishing gives our ethics a sufficient foundation and a place in the forum of public debate.

It is worth spelling this out a bit more. In the criterion of human well-being we locate the *rationality* of ethics. Ethics is not about weird intuitions on the one hand or subjective feelings on the other. It is not about obeying 'inscrutable oughts'. Ethics is about thinking through what serves our mutual well-being. This we can probe rationally and discuss in the public forum. We can test it against the bar of experience. Presupposed in all this is a basic commonality in human experience, despite immense cultural and individual differences. It is for this reason that we can take historic texts that are culturally remote and yet still engage with them, to say nothing of poems and novels that probe the many and varied dimensions of human experience.

There is a humanistic belligerence about this approach that is worth underlining. First, it claims the right and responsibility to think through our own reasoned response to ethical issues in the light of these criteria. 'Authorities' may stimulate and resource, but they may not dictate, still less impose alien and life-diminishing demands.

Second, it is because of their focus on our well-being that moral claims are experienced as being compelling or indeed overriding. Why do we care so deeply about moral issues? Why is it that we argue passionately about them and tend to regard moral considerations as having trumps? How do we account for the strong sense that the moral quest is about discerning and discovering and not about inventing? My suggestion is that all this is so because there is nothing more important for us than that which serves our common well-being. We are no longer trading in authoritarian demands, which we blindly obey. We discern for ourselves what serves our mutual good. And because we care deeply about what serves our mutual good we can make our judgements our own and so enjoy the dignity of a proper autonomy. It follows that the criteria for judging the right and the good are humanistic. Subject to qualification regarding an environmental ethic and our responsibilities towards animals (see Chapter 14), any claim concerning the right and the good must receive a rationale in terms of its contribution to our well-being. If a moral prescription is life diminishing, then our ethics has gone astray. Even masochists are interested in their well-being. It is only that they seek it in an odd way and probably in a way that ultimately diminishes rather than serves it.

There is, of course, nothing new in my proposal. Very broadly speaking it is in continuity with the moral philosophy of Aristotle, and that of Thomas Aquinas, whose discussion of the good life in the *Summa Theologiae* engages heavily with Aristotle. Furthermore, the dominant strand in biblical ethics sees the law of God as *for our good*.[4] The 'good' and the 'well' coincide. For the Psalmist, the law of the Lord is our delight, and those who meditate on it are like trees planted by the waters.[5]

2.3 Two approaches in moral philosophy

A focus on human well-being as the fundamental criterion of ethics helps us to see why two important traditions of twentieth-century moral philosophy went astray. Oddly, these two traditions did not see the essence of ethics in this way. The reason is probably twofold. First, because of a preoccupation with the *genre* rather than the *substance* of ethical discourse, and secondly because of obeisance before a philosophical dogma that was current at the time. This is the dogma (and I speak somewhat loosely) that there is no link between a 'fact' and a 'value'. To take 'facts' concerning human need and flourishing as the basis for ethics is to commit the fatal logical error of trying to find a bridge from a 'fact' to a 'value'. This idea in various forms had become part of the air that moral philosophers breathed. Kant had protested against an ethic derived from facts about human nature.[6] Hume had noted a logical distinction between 'is' statements and 'ought' statements,[7] and G. E. Moore had noted that the statement 'This is good' cannot be equivalent to a statement such as 'This leads to our flour-ishing'.[8] Moore is correct in so far as the former statement is evalu-ative while the latter is descriptive. But that does not forbid us from saying that the things we evaluate as good are also, and for that rea-son, those that lead to our mutual well-being. Mainly for these two reasons, Philippa Foot felt herself to be speaking controversially when in a 1958 paper she revisited the common-sense belief that morality might actually have something to do with human need and human well-being![9] A continuing sense of being innovatory is evident even 50 years later.[10]

We consider, then, two schools of thought in British moral philoso-phy. One American, C. L. Stevenson, is given a walk-on part. The first of these is generally called 'intuitionism'. It is not easy to distinguish between what intuitionists really thought, and what their opponents may have caricatured them as thinking. Furthermore, the language they used was somewhat slippery and how it is to be understood is not always clear. In essence, however, the intuitionist's approach went something like this. Through some kind of 'sixth moral sense' or 'intu-ition' we are immediately aware of fundamental moral values and claims. Just as we 'see' that two plus two equals four, and just as we 'see' that there cannot be square circles, so likewise we 'see' that some things are good or bad or obligatory. For example, if I contemplate gratuitous cruelty inflicted on children, or if I witness a brutal rape, then I know immediately these acts are morally wrong. The intuition is immediate and compelling. It is self-justifying. It requires no defence or explanation.

The intuitionists were widely criticized. What is the status and reli-ability of this way of knowing by 'intuition'? How do we resolve dis-agreement when all we have are conflicting intuitions? And suppose it be held that just as the universe is populated by chairs and tables so it is also populated by moral values and obligations existing in some kind of 'moral space' apprehended by 'intuition', then is not the whole notion exceedingly odd? Thus, J. L. Mackie appealed to an 'argument from queerness' in his critique of this approach.[11]

The fundamental claim of the intuitionists is that we simply 'see' that certain actions are right or wrong, or that certain states of affairs are good. My suggestion is that this makes some sense if what is 'seen' serves our mutual flourishing since, for humans, nothing else could be more significant or compelling. This is what intuitionists are 'seeing' – not some mysterious realm of 'value' or 'moral claim' in some kind of moral dimension 'out there'. The 'seeing' is immediate and compelling because humans are bound to care passionately about human well-being and human harm. This is confirmed by the fact, as Sidgwick observed,[12] that what is intuited in fact always serves human enhancement! No intuitionist ever intuited that it is our solemn obligation to murder, pillage and rape.

This throws light on a further difficulty with intuitionism, widely commented upon. Why should we bother about these intuitions? What is the basis of their authority over us? Why should weird moral claims existing in some weird moral realm and perceived through some weird moral intuition have any claim on us?[13] How is it that the 'calm and indolent judgements of the understanding' are able to 'excite passions' as David Hume puts it?[14] Again, this problem is solved if we see that our moral 'intuitions' are about what nourishes us both individually and corporately, and likewise what damages and diminishes us. This reminds us that in ethics we do not rely on some special 'moral sense'. We engage our whole being – reason and emotion and all else – in discerning what serves and constitutes our well-being.

We are thus led to a second tradition of moral philosophy – emotivism. At the time when intuitionism was being widely critiqued, A. J. Ayer published in 1947 *Language, Truth and Logic*. Ayer tries to sweep the universe clean of mystery. Speaking somewhat loosely his position is this. Apart from the truths of logic and mathematics, the only knowledge we have, and indeed the only knowledge claim that makes sense, is knowledge derived from what we can see, touch, hear, smell and taste. Knowledge therefore of poached eggs, gladioli and spiral nebulae, is okay. Suppose, however, I say it is my obligation to do this, or that you were right to have done that, or that this state of affairs is evil? If these claims are understood as being in some sense quasi-factual, then what I say is meaningless. We can make no sense of purported truth claims that are not claims about what we can see, hear, smell, touch or taste. It follows that the *factual* content of the statement, 'You acted wrongly in doing this' is simply 'You did this'.[15]

Ayer, however, must give us some account of what we are doing when we use moral language. Moral utterances are not in any way truth claims, or claims that can be justified rationally. Moral utterances merely express approval or disapproval, together with the attempt to urge others to feel similar disapproval or approval. This was the notorious 'emotive' theory of ethics. At the same time C. L. Stevenson in America developed a similar approach.[16] It is, of course, only a modern version of an ancient theme. Hume, for example, had said that morality is 'more properly felt than judg'd of'.[17]

Moral utterances, then, are nothing more than expressions of feeling. Such feelings have no validity or rationality since feelings are merely feelings. I may enjoy kippers and you may loathe them. But we cannot say the taste of kippers is pleasant as such. It is pleasant to some and loathsome to others. Strictly speaking, we do not disagree about the taste of kippers; we merely differ. We cannot discuss rationally whether or not kippers taste pleasant. It is simply a matter of individual taste.

Alarm bells ring when we think of ethics in a similar way. Is my 'feeling' of utter outrage when I contemplate the Holocaust of the same genre as my dislike of the taste of kippers? The approach trivializes ethics. It fails to give weight to the deep conviction that our moral stances are not invented by us. Our moral stances are in some way required of us. There are some 'objective' moral standards that we recognize as commending themselves to us, and as making a claim upon us. Of course we feel passionately about ethical matters. But a moral stance is not constituted by the feeling. The feeling is parasitic upon the judgement that in some sense the ethical stance is inherently rational and appropriate.

The strength of Ayer's approach is that it locates ethical inquiry in the arena of human response rather than in factual knowledge of what is 'out there'. To think of moral values and obligations as 'out there', part of the fabric of the world but apprehended through some kind of sixth moral sense, is to court confusion because we are using the wrong categories of thought. It is rather like trying to describe a game of football in terms of the language of cricket, or if, ignorant of chess, we think that talk of the queen taking the bishop has something to do with Buckingham or Lambeth Palaces.

This is the strength of Ayer's approach. The weakness is that he speaks of 'feeling'. We can agree with his insistence that the language of ethics is the language of evaluation rather than of description. But the evaluation has greater gravitas than a feeling. It is about that which leads to our mutual well-being, and that is why ethics has both a rationality and an overriding significance.

2.4 Swimming against the stream of relativism and scepticism

In the last chapter I said I was seeking to 'swim against the stream' of relativism and scepticism. The criterion of human well-being helps us maintain a measure of confidence when faced with these caustic challenges. So far I have been working under an implicit assumption. Ethics is about a vision of that which is right and good 'as such'. This is so not just for me and my culture but for humankind in general. Ethics has a rationale which we can publicly investigate. Ethics is about recognizing rather than inventing. Cultural contexts differ and basic values may be expressed in different ways, but we are still concerned with universal claims. Thus, slavery violates a basic human right not just in the modern world but also in ancient Athens and Rome; the presumption of innocence before the law is a basic requirement of natural justice, even if not recognized by a particular state; torture is wrong whatever political or legal system we belong to; the genocide of the Jews was a monstrous evil; enforced female genital mutilation is wrong, even if it is the cultural norm. Certain character traits ought to be universally admired, or deplored, even if some of the former are more appropriate in some cultural settings than in others.

It follows from all this that we may hope for at least some common ground in tackling ethical issues and some success in seeking a common vision of the good life. Ethics properly belongs to the forum of public debate. There are many things, however, that cause this confidence to wobble.

2.4.1 Pluralism

The first is pluralism. By pluralism I mean the simple historical and sociological fact that there are radical disagreements over ethics. There is a difference between the virtues outlined by Paul in Galatians 5.22 and Colossians 3.12 and those embraced by the Samurai. There is difference between the western view that well-being presupposes an appropriate freedom and self-determination, and those for whom well-being is found within a tight social structure where place and role are determined. Aristotle regarded humility as a vice, while for Christianity it is a virtue. When in Rome do as Rome does. But what about when Rome turns nasty? There is radical pluralism in the Church – for example, the seemingly incompatible paradigms of the 'evangelical' for whom ethics is about obeying the injunctions of Scripture, as they are perceived to be, and 'liberals' whose approach to making moral judgements is more broadly based.

Pluralism would not be a problem if there were – as is generally the case with the natural sciences – publicly recognized means for resolving disagreement. But how do we resolve disagreement in ethics? Faced with seemingly irresolvable differences, it is easy to lose nerve and concede that everything is relative. This is the response of 'emotivism' – an approach to ethics that has emerged in many forms throughout history. As we have just seen, its most modern form is associated with A. J. Ayer and C. L. Stevenson.[18] Ethical utterances express only feelings of approval or disapproval. They have no validity beyond being a person's feeling, and presumably Hitler's feelings were neither more nor less appropriate in any objective sense, however strongly my feelings may differ. Feelings do not have the transparency, coherence or rationale required for them to be usefully discussed in the public arena.

And it gets worse. Pluralism is not simply a matter of disagreement over the same questions. There is disagreement about the nature of the question and the concepts used. Different cultures and epochs may have radically different paradigms. The notion of 'honour', for example, has a central place in feudal systems, but it is almost unintelligible for many today. Notions of 'duty' and 'obligation' may be central to one moral outlook but almost unintelligible to another.

2.4.2 *Relativism*

Pluralism as I have defined it merely catalogues differences and disagreements. Pluralism may encourage a relativism that sees the human mind as so formed by and relative to its culture, language and life experience, that there can be no cross-cultural debate. No ethic has universal validity because each has its particular cultural location.

The world is thus rather like a kaleidoscope and the picture we see will depend on our language, culture, and generally on that complicated mishmash of things that makes up our 'way of seeing'. Instead of there being a 'meta-narrative', which we can all own, there are rather many differing 'truths', each reflecting different perspectives. The western humanist, the western liberal Christian, the Islamic fundamentalist, the progressive Muslim, the Japanese Samurai, the Nazi SS officer, those of the Christian 'right', will each have their minds formed by their culture. 'This is wrong' always has a particular cultural location. What it really means is, for example, 'Actually we don't do this in Guildford.'

2.4.3 *Ideology*

There is, however, nothing neutral about the way in which our moral consciousness is formed. Our culture is infused with struggle for power and privilege and the desire to preserve and legitimize power and privilege. Marx used the word 'ideology' to describe a belief system that is rooted in and validates the power of a particular class, so defined by its access to economic power. Those who adopt this ideology are not necessarily consciously dishonest or self-seeking. It is simply that their mental paradigm is formed in this way. The ideology has become internalized.[19]

We are therefore urged to ask: Whose ethics is it?[20] And whose interest is being served by it? If Marx exposed how 'bourgeois ethics' buttressed and validated the privilege of the bourgeoisie, feminists have argued that many value beliefs support the privilege and dominance of males. How strange that it is males who write books claiming leadership and priesthood should be male![21] And if women agree, then they have only internalized their oppression. How odd that it is heterosexuals – often married heterosexuals – who insist that the gay must remain celibate! Is there a dimension of ideology here? If gay people remain celibate, then the pre-eminence of heterosexual marriage as the norm for human coupling is maintained. Moreover, if heterosexuals can put the spotlight on the lifestyles of the gay community, their own lives can maybe escape scrutiny. Male opposition to abortion may reinforce male desire to keep women out of the workplace, while support for abortion may reinforce male desire for sex without responsibility.

Such a perspective might criticize the Church for wielding power by attacking people where they are most vulnerable, namely, over their sexuality. Impute and internalize guilt and shame over sex and people are in the grip of the power of priest or pastor. This is not to suggest each priest and pastor is deliberately intent on a power trip. The critique is of the culture and institution, and priest and pastor may be as much as others the victims of their formation. The system has sucked them in.

And so, scratch the veneer of ethics and we find power politics underneath.

2.5   A sufficient restored confidence?

Talk then of moral values is mere humbug. Everything is relative. At best ethics does nothing more than express particular customs and particular attitudes. At worst it is an attempt to validate power and privilege. The radical implications of all this need to be recognized. If all the above is true, then while I may object strongly to the Holocaust or the Soviet gulag, my protest has no validity, rationale or coherence beyond it being my protest. Immediately I claim more, I refuse to concede that the objections are fatal. There is no problem about some playing Rugby League and others playing Rugby Union. It is simply a matter of culture or preference. But there does seem a problem about saying that while it is wrong for us to murder babies it was okay in Ancient Sparta, or that it is okay in some countries to torture political dissidents, or deny education to women, since that is their culture. The problem is in seeing differing ethics as being like the differences between Rugby Union and Rugby League. All this contravenes the deep conviction that ethics is about universally valid claims, urging that which is fitting for and required of all human beings.

How do we respond to these charges? It would be foolish and unconvincing to respond with a total rejection. Ethical pluralism is a fact. Cultural relativity is a fact. It is also a fact that many of our ethical beliefs betray a disingenuous attempt to reinforce and validate our own prejudice, privilege or power. All this counsels vigilance, openness, self-criticism and self-awareness. Total scepticism, however, need not follow. It need not follow either that we have no hope of making value claims that have a rationale such as to commend themselves to our common humanity, and not simply to those whose culture, language or upbringing makes them see things in a particular way.

The human mind, it may be argued, its 'way of seeing', the paradigms in terms of which it sees the world, is determined by things such as language and culture. If by 'determined' we mean something like 'deeply formed' this is obviously true. We are to a large extent the products of the tradition in which we stand. But are we so totally determined that our minds are simply like computer programs made of meat? It does seem the whole enterprise of ethical judgement (as well as indeed any claim to knowledge or rational thought) implies some capacity to transcend a particular context and reflect critically. Indeed, in the very act of asserting the truth of total relativism I presuppose a more objective stance outside it.

Immanuel Kant and Richard Hare represent a moral philosophy that claims to be trans-cultural. Hare used the definite article in the title of his earliest book, *The Language of Morals*.[22] Alasdair MacIntyre, by contrast, has drawn our attention to the inculturalization of all moral traditions. He instances the fact that certain virtues were appropriate to Homer's society, others to the Athenian city state, and others to the military culture of Sparta.[23] Does this lead to total scepticism? A lot was written on this question a generation ago. It was argued that the differences are not in fact as radical as sometimes appears since sometimes the same basic value may be expressed in different ways in different cultural contexts. Different social and economic conditions tend to throw up different mixes. Boundaries may be drawn widely or narrowly and we can understand why. Again, differences can sometimes be overcome if they are seen as expressing complementary values which may be balanced in a wider synthesis.[24]

There is no reason for a total loss of nerve. Certainly, there is no justification in presuming 'God's eye view', but there is no reason either for complete scepticism.[25] We should learn from these challenges the importance of humility and openness. Relativism should not be confronted by ethical colonialism. To reject total relativism is not to embrace the hegemony of western liberalism. Am I so sure that my moral vision is clear and straight? Maybe it is distorted by my impoverished culture and blind to that impoverishment. In dialogue with the values of other cultures we become more self-aware. Being both open and critical we together look for a clearer vision. The point of debate, and especially the study of cultures different from our own, is to enlarge our understanding. For example, in contemporary Britain the dominant culture is one of sexual voyeurism and the celebration of the sexually charged perfect naked body. By contrast, there is the modesty of Islamic culture of which the *hijab* may be, among other things, a token.[26] Can we say one is right and the other wrong? The hope is that in the dialogue between the two a more balanced stance is found, learning from the insights and distortions of each. In both traditions dress ideally can affirm in different ways the dignity, identity and self-respect of a person. [27]

What is in fact remarkable is not the amount of ethical difference but rather the extent of agreement. Indeed, disagreements presuppose some consensus, otherwise we would not be addressing the same subject. 'There is a background of agreement ... that makes moral disagreement intelligible.'[28] Furthermore, we see more agreement if we consult the marginalized and oppressed than if we consult the powerful and privileged – and for obvious reasons. When it is protested that those with 'western values' should not from their standpoint criticize governments that torture or imprison without trial, it is usually not the imprisoned or the tortured who voice the protest. Yes, we are all situated in particular locations in history and culture, but we can study, experience, empathize with and learn from other cultures. Historic texts are not totally unintelligible. We can engage with them. In our global village there is no reason to retreat into our local cultures. The ideal is an enriched cosmopolitan vision.

These general considerations may engender a measure of restored confidence. This restored confidence is based fundamentally on the conviction that ethics is about exploring what serves our mutual well-being or flourishing. There are parameters beyond which it does not make sense to speak of such flourishing, and despite all the personal and cultural colouring we can explore together what it might mean. It follows that ethics has a sufficient rationale for it to inspire some confidence and be a proper subject for public debate.

2.6 Conclusion

Alasdair MacIntyre's *After Virtue* is often cited as adding fuel to the flames of scepticism. It is true that the book is devoid of any trumpeted confidence and he exposes the inadequacy of much modern moral philosophy. But the book nonetheless gives ground for modest confidence.

For European history until the modern period, he maintains, a classical scheme of morality reigned with roots in both Aristotle and Christian theology. The scheme was broadly supported by Maimonodies in the Jewish, and Ibn Rushd in the Islamic tradition. The scheme envisaged some natural 'end' of humanity as 'humanity as it could be if it realised its essence'. As we are now we do not realize this end or essence, but morality is about *moving towards it*. Decision making and the cultivation of virtues thus order, correct and channel us in that direction. The scheme is essentially the same whether the vision be seen as expressing our own inherent nature or end, as expressing the divine law, or as expressing the divine invitation to 'glorify God and enjoy God for ever'. Usually the latter only confirms what reason discovers as the former.[29]

For most modern thinkers this scheme has broken down. The elimination of any notion of human nature, essence or end leaves ethics without foundation and all other attempts to find an alternative base for morality have failed. Kant failed to find a basis in reason alone, Hume failed to find a basis in natural sentiments, and so forth. Without this underlying rationale, however, today's moral language uses orphaned fragments from the past without coherence or justification. Nietzsche clearly recognized this. Without any rational justification there are no constraints on individual will. This individual will can therefore be as egotistical as it chooses.

'Emotivism' is in this tradition. A person's ethical stance expresses their preference or feeling and has no validity beyond that. Confronting these academic denials, however, there is the strong protest: surely whatever anyone may feel, it is *inherently wrong* to send Jews to the gas chamber, to force genital mutilation on young girls, and so forth. The fact that western liberal academic 'emotivists' would never dream of choosing or feeling preference for these things does not prevent others from doing so.

MacIntyre's position is that if we are to refute Nietzsche and later emotivism we need *something like the reappropriation of the Aristotelian tradition*.[30] I agree with this conclusion in so far as in this book I seek to explore ethics through an investigation of what constitutes human well-being, within the context of an investigation of our 'nature' or 'end'. This can make sense simply as a human enquiry. In the first part of this book we confine ourselves to this human enquiry while in the second part I claim Christian theology brings rich further insight and resonance.

Notes

1 Geoffrey J. Warnock, *The Object of Morality*, London, Methuen, 1971, p. 16.

2 Martha Nussbaum, *Love's Knowledge*, Oxford, 1990, pp. 95–6, 389–90.

3 John Finnis, *Natural Law and Natural Rights*, Clarendon, Oxford, 1980, pp. 86ff.; Philippa Foot, 'Moral Belief' and 'Goodness and Choice' in *Virtues and Vices*, Oxford, Blackwell, 1978. Also *Natural Goodness*, Oxford, 2001.

4 E.g. Deuteronomy 5.29, 10.13, 12.28.

5 Psalms 1.2–3.

6 Immanuel Kant, *Groundwork of the Metaphysics of Morals* (1785), translation by H. J. Paton, *The Moral Law*, London, Hutchinson, 1948, pp. 54ff.

7 David Hume, *Treatise of Human Nature* (1739) III.I.I, ed. L. A. Selby-Bigge (1888), Oxford, pp. 468–9.

8 George E. Moore, *Principia Ethica*, Cambridge, 1903, pp. 37ff.

9 'Moral Beliefs' (1958), reprinted in Philippa Foot, *Virtues and Vices*, pp. 120ff.

10 Philippa Foot, *Natural Goodness*, pp. 5ff.

11 John L. Mackie, *Ethics: Inventing Right and Wrong*, Harmondsworth, Penguin, 1977, p. 38.

12 Henry Sidgwick, *The Methods of Ethics*, Cambridge, Seventh edition 1907, e.g. pp. 496–5.

13 Thus P. H. Nowell-Smith, *Ethics*, Harmondsworth, Penguin, 1954, p. 41.

14 Hume, *Treatise of Human Nature* (1739), III.I.I, p. 457.

15 A. J. Ayer, *Language, Truth and Logic*, London, Gollancz, 1947, p. 107.

16 C. L. Stevenson, *Ethics of Language*, New Haven, 1944.

17 Hume, *Treatise of Human Nature*, III.I.II, p. 470.

18 Ayer, *Language, Truth and Logic*; Stevenson, *Ethics and Language*.

19 Karl Marx in T. B. Bottomore and Maximilien Rubel (eds), *Karl Marx: Selected Writings*, Harmondsworth, Pelican, 1963, pp. 82ff.

20 Alasdair MacIntyre, *Whose Justice? Which Rationality?*, London, Duckworth, 1988.

21 David Pawson, *Leadership is Male*, London, Highland Books, 1988; Graham Leonard, 'The Ordination of Women', *Epworth Review* 11.1, January 1984; Eric L. Mascall, *Woman Priests*, London, Church Literature Association, 1977; P. Moore (ed.), *Man, Woman and Priesthood*, London, SPCK, 1978.

22 R. M. Hare, *The Language of Morals*, Oxford, 1952.

23 Alasdair MacIntyre, *After Virtue*, London, Duckworth, 1985, pp. 121ff.

24 E.g. A. C. Ewing, *Ethics*, London, English University Press, 1953, pp. 127ff.; Morris Ginsberg, *On the Diversity of Morals*, London, Heinemann, 1956, pp. 101ff.

25 Jeffrey Stout, *Ethics After Babel*, Cambridge, James Clarke, 1988, pp. 3, 15.

26 The *hijab* may symbolize a number of different things. It may betoken the male subjection of women, but it may also betoken the self-esteem of Muslim identity, sometimes over and against the power of a dominant culture. See Sa'Diyya Shaikh in Omid Safi (ed.), *Progressive Muslims*, Oxford, One World, 2003, pp. 151–4.

27 Zaym Kassam, 'Islamic Ethics and Gender Issues' in J. Runzo and Nancy Martin, *Ethics in the World Religions*, Oxford, One World, 2001, p. 19.

28 Stout, *Ethics After Babel*, p. 43.

29 MacIntyre, *After Virtue*, p. 53.

30 MacIntyre, *After Virtue*, p. 259. This was developed in later books: *Whose Justice? Which Rationality*, London, Duckworth, 1988 and *Three Rival Versions of Moral Inquiry*, London, Duckworth, 1990.

3

The Tapestry of Moral Judgement

3.1 Introduction

My claim then is that the vision of what nourishes our common life together, and of what serves our well-being and flourishing, is the central
guide to our ethics. This resonates with the related claim that ethics
is about our relationships with one another. Wholesome relationships
nourish our lives. Subject to our later discussion of responsibilities arising out of our relationship towards the environment and to animals,
it is difficult to understand how an ethical claim could *make sense*,
or have any *persuasiveness*, if it did not serve our well-being. This
is a defiantly humanistic approach. Morality is for us and not we for
morality! It is our solemn moral obligation always to walk past trees
to the left but never to the right.[1] Every morning it is my duty to touch
my left shoulder with my right thumb. It is immoral to marry someone
whose name begins with the same letter as your own. It is difficult even
to make sense of these weird claims. Why is this? It is because none of
them has a rationale in terms of what contributes to our good.

Discovering what serves our mutual well-being, and discovering
wholesome relationships, is a delicately nuanced task. It is like weaving a tapestry in which we give proper place to different threads and
colours. A balanced thinking is aware of the different shades and different threads if the picture is to be full, rich and pleasing to the eye.
To express a similar point, Dorothy Emmet used the metaphor of the
moral 'prism' giving different colours.[2]

In this chapter we look at some traditional strands of ethical thought
and suggest they might be seen, in their positive and constructive insights, as offering different threads, stitches and colours for the tapestry. They can all be analysed in terms of helping us explore what might
be taken into account in discovering what nourishes our common well-
being. Becoming aware of these different strands helps to tutor us in
the art of moral judgement. Moral judgements can become distorted
when there is an insufficient awareness of the many strands, threads
and colours, or where there is an injudicious balance between them.
What follows is a good selection, but I do not list all that we might find
in the sewing box.

It has been argued that there might be a gender difference in how we approach moral matters.[3] This may be so, at least in terms of how some cultures mould people, but the position of this book is that we can reflect critically upon, and benefit from, all resources for moral judgement, even if some may have an identifiable gender location. If men and women tend sometimes to have a different focus, then these differing resources, critically evaluated, can be shared.

Four brief comments may be made at this stage. First, the approaches we consider in this chapter are best seen, not as alternatives, but rather as each contributing valuable insight for 'weaving the tapestry' of moral judgement. Second, it is true that people will stand within a moral tradition, or a number of interrelated traditions. Indeed, each of these approaches constitutes its own tradition, and Part 2 will focus on the Christian tradition within which people may locate their lives and think about ethics. My claim is that we can and should still step back and reflect critically and, at least to a degree, transcend a particular tradition so as to engage with others. Third, I do not wish to give the impression that there is a long and laboured process of ethical pondering every time we make a judgement. Often we act out of habit and intuitively. At least sometimes, however, we should reflect on what we are doing. That is what the study of ethics is all about. Finally, it is true that much ethical insight and inspiration is found in novels, poetry and stories. These can inspire the will more than reflective analysis. The biblical writers knew that well. Critical reflection, however, remains important. The best of stories can lead us astray if the head is not also engaged. The 'emotivists' claimed ethics is about our feelings. Ethical language had 'emotive force' as the emotivists tried to get others to feel as they did. They totally missed the element of rational reflection. If ethics were really about getting others to feel as they did, and nothing more, they would have been better employed telling stories than thumping tables.

In the light of these introductory observations we now consider a good selection of the resources that are available in the tradition of reflection on ethics for weaving the tapestry of moral judgement.

3.2 The consequences of what we do

Things we do have consequences. If I fire a gun, I may kill someone. If I buy Traidcraft coffee, I may further fair trade. If I commit adultery, I may devastate not a few people's lives.

'Consequentialist' approaches to ethics put the spotlight on the consequences of choice. The right choice is the one that leads to wholesome consequences. No serious ethicist can ignore this dimension. But how are consequences taken into account? What consequences do we judge to be good? And what do we do if desirable consequences conflict or are incommensurable?

'Utilitarianism'**, associated with Jeremy Bentham and John Stuart Mill, is a famous brand of consequentialism. A study of utilitarianism's insights and blind spots helps identify some of the strands of the tapestry we weave when making moral judgements. Utilitarianism maintains that there is only one thing that is good in itself, and worth seeking for its own sake. This is happiness, or its synonym pleasure. It is pleasure and pleasure alone that constitutes our well-being and flourishing. Moral judgements, then, are about judging in each instance what behaviour leads to the 'greatest possible happiness of the greatest possible number'. As proposed by Bentham, utilitarianism was primarily about social policy and legislation and, as such, it was laudably egalitarian. In public policy everyone counts as one and no one as more than one.[4] It is, however, often repackaged as a guide to individual moral judgement. It is as such that we will consider it.

It is notoriously difficult to predict with accuracy the effects of our actions as any history of social policy, or any war, will show. And how do we measure 'pleasure'? Bentham's attempt to balance dimensions of pleasure (intensity, duration, propinquity, purity, fecundity, etc.) verges on the laughable. Furthermore, as people are different, comparing their pleasure and pain is a perilous task. There is a lack of realism in utilitarianism's endeavour to calculate all this. The criticisms, however, are not fatal to a basic consequentialism. It is equally counter-intuitive to discount the consequence of what we do. That said, we can hardly overstress how fallible is any prediction or calculus. Once an action feeds into the mishmash of cause and effect it can, as the literature of tragedy reminds us, have all kinds of unintended consequences.

Utilitarianism expresses a refreshing insistence that morality is about serving humanity, and not the other way round. It is difficult, nonetheless, to sustain the claim that the only thing that has intrinsic value is pleasure. Pleasure is certainly *a* good but not the *only* good. Relationships of loyalty, mutual respect and delight, intellectual enquiry, creativity, enjoyment of beauty, and such like, are good 'in themselves'. They are not merely extrinsically good because they lead to pleasure. Yes they do so lead – but only because they have *value in their own right*. Furthermore, some of these intrinsic goods may co-exist in some tension with the good of happiness. Intellectual enquiry, for example, brings its frustrations and feelings of dislocation. There is a great deal in human life – including altruism and self-sacrifice – which is not adequately described in hedonistic terms. The utilitarians were not pleasure hogs. But the caricature has value in pointing to an underlying failure of the utilitarian to do justice to its fundamental insight. 'Better to be a Socrates dissatisfied than a fool satisfied.' John Stuart Mill spoke of the intrinsic superiority of certain types of pleasure and in this acknowledgement fatally wounded his own professed claim that pleasure alone has value in itself.[5] This also implies that what constitutes our flourishing is not necessarily what we want at any moment.

There is in fact something odd about seeking pleasure *directly*. The things mentioned in the last paragraph are sought *for their own sake*, as constitutive of our well-being. The pleasure they give depends on their value for their own sake. If our aim is happiness we often fail to find it. We are more likely to find it if we pursue other goals for their intrinsic worth. This was the theme taken up by 'ideal' utilitarianism.[6] Such things are 'good for their own sake', however, *because they are good for us* – they contribute to our flourishing. This is the insight of the utilitarian tradition that must be preserved.

Essentially, utilitarianism has as its aim the promotion of our communal well-being; but it understands well-being in a very limited way. 'Pleasure' is too superficial a notion to express the rich depth of what we mean by 'flourishing'. It is better to see our flourishing as much more richly constituted such as was hinted at above. We must not, however, in moments of undue enthusiasm impose our vision of flourishing on others. Utilitarianism was in danger of dragooning people into the pursuit of happiness when some might have had more profound goals.[7] At the crudest level, football and gardening are, to different people sheer delight and mild torture. We need then to throw in the constraint of respecting people's proper autonomy in discovering their well-being, even though there will be common themes since we share a basic common humanity.

Notoriously, in its emphasis on 'the greatest possible happiness of the greatest possible number', utilitarianism neglects completely a principle of justice and fairness. What if the happiness of the majority is gained at the expense of injustice or deprivation for the minority? Thus, Mill acknowledged the danger of the majority exercising a tyranny over the minority.[8] Utilitarian theories of punishment allow punishments to be excessive and unjust in order to heighten the deterrent affect. 'It is expedient that one should die for the people.' 'You are hanged, not because you stole, but to deter others from stealing.' Utilitarianism – through its neglect of justice and fairness – thus draws our attention to the tension between justice for the individual and what is good for the majority. Another example is the policy of maintaining low inflation through tolerating a pool of unemployed. The greater economic good is at the expense of an underclass. The law of 'diminishing marginal utility', whereby my Rolex watch gives me less happiness than does release from starvation for you, gives the utilitarian some resource for safeguarding justice for the minority, but not as robustly as a commitment to justice.

Utilitarianism appears to expect us to act with complete impartiality. Everyone is to count equally in our calculation. But how realistic, or even desirable, is this commitment to the 'general welfare of all'? Utilitarianism raises the question of the boundaries of our moral concern. There may be times when such wide considerations force themselves upon us. But that is different from saying they are always part of our calculations, still less that everyone counts equally. Moreover, practicalities aside, it raises – if by default – the question of the special obligations we have to family, friends, colleagues and such like. Marriage and family life can indeed become an excuse for an extended selfishness. Marriage can become selfishness for two. But surely my own mother, my own wife, my own son and daughter, my own colleagues, have a *special* claim upon me – a point lost on Mrs Jellyby in *Bleak House* – even if not necessarily in every instance an overriding one. Mill, who was aware of the difficulties with an over-simplistic utilitarianism, at least implicitly seems to acknowledge this.[9] Furthermore, to make a promise is to accept an obligation that stands in tension with utilitarian impartiality. For strict utilitarianism, *betrayal* makes no sense since the notion of betrayal presupposes a promise, contract, covenant or some special obligation. Justice and a respect for rights do indeed demand no one should, in principle, be excluded from my moral concern. But that is very far from saying everyone is to count equally.

There can be a moral earnestness about utilitarianism that seems too demanding, too serious and too oppressive. We are always morally 'on duty' fervently calculating at every point what contribution our behaviour makes to the greater good. This is too heavy a burden to bear, and may be paternalistic towards those who are the beneficiaries, or victims, of our ferocious goodwill. No distinction is made between the permissible, the obligatory and the supererogatory**. It is one thing to *honour* a value, but there can be an excessive zeal in *promoting* it, still more in thinking it is our duty to maximize promotion at every moment. We cannot take time off and enjoy play, for when we are at play we are not labouring for the greatest possible happiness of the greatest possible number. Lovers are indeed permitted a kiss, but only with 'an eye to the common weal' – to plagiarize John Austin.[10] Furthermore, one of the values we seek is delivery from being incessant calculators. Apart from anything else, that is to take ourselves and our responsibilities too seriously.

To be fair, few utilitarians have drawn these conclusions. Austin's delicious witticism was in fact part of a defence of utilitarianism as offering simply a means for judging the goodness of consequences, not as a demand that we deliberate at every moment. But despite intentions, the dangers are real and it is important to be aware of them.

Yes, we do need to take into account the consequences of our action, and we need some notion of the ends we seek. This is an important thread in the tapestry. But the tapestry is dull if it is the only one. The strengths and weaknesses of utilitarianism, in its historical reality and in its caricature, and of consequentialism generally, in the insights and in the things overlooked, point to important strands in the tapestry of moral judgement.

A more focused conclusion can be drawn at this stage in the argument. There is within utilitarianism a mindset which sometimes longs for certainty and simplicity, the right action always being identified by clear calculation. Such simplicity and certainty eludes us, however, even when we allow utilitarianism's simple creed that pleasure is the only intrinsic good. How do I balance this source of pleasure with that source of pleasure? How do I balance Anthea's pleasure with Simon's? If we throw in the further complication that pleasure is not the only end we seek, together with considerations of justice and the special claims certain people make upon us, then the whole area becomes very messy. Generally speaking, ethics is as much about messiness as clarity. We need to think as clearly as we can, but in the end there is a limit to the precision we can find. Ethics is more about making the most responsible judgement we can as we juggle competing claims, wrestling with incommensurable values, and using ethical concepts which tend to be elusive and fuzzy at the edges. We try to sort it out as well as we can, but we cannot expect mathematical precision. This is a perspective on ethics that I will return to again and again.

3.3 The common point of view

This approach to ethics has served as the fundamental perspective for many moral philosophers, for example Immanuel Kant and R. M. Hare. It is fundamental also for Peter Singer, although he would more readily draw additional insight from elsewhere. Very broadly speaking, the 'Golden Rule' is in this tradition, the 'rule' that invites us to do to others as we would wish them to do to us – a 'rule' which, incidentally, is not original to Jesus. We find something like it in most ethical traditions.

For this perspective we seek in ethics a 'common point of view'. This involves two things at least:

First, we put ourselves in the other person's shoes and ask if we would be willing to be on the receiving end of our actions and choices. This involves imagination and sympathy. R. M. Hare wondered if the bear baiter had ever reflected on what it is like to be a bear.[11] The principle does need some fine tuning. If I have no interest in music I may be quite prepared to be on the receiving end of my opposition to public funding for orchestras. It follows that properly to think of myself in the other person's shoes, I must imagine myself with their feelings, needs and interests, rather than my own.[12]

Second, I have to ask if I can seriously countenance the principles underlying my choices being 'universalized' – that is adopted by everyone.[13] My indifference to someone's need, my disregard of the environment, my stealing from the firm, may not be noticed, and will certainly make little difference. But what if *everyone* behaved like this? Can I really wish that everyone should be guided by the principles I adopt myself? Kant famously argued that I cannot reasonably lie for selfish gain. I gain from lying only because people assume I am telling the truth. By lying I undermine the expectation of truth telling from which I seek through deception to benefit.[14]

In making ethical judgements, then, we seek the 'universal' or 'common' point of view. We imagine ourselves as impartial observers disallowing special privilege or self-interest. If I give a reason for acting, then someone else must be able to see the point. There is a discounting of unwarranted personal self-interest in favour of a fundamental fairness. In such a discounting of privilege and partiality, this approach is a close cousin of utilitarianism. In contrast, however, this approach has the advantage of tending to focus on a person's own interests. Everyone's interests should be considered. This is a valuable counterbalance to the danger of a paternalism that imposes upon others some restricted blueprint concerning what our well-being involves. We will see later that John Rawls adopts such a method in his treatment of the idea of justice (3.9).

What, however, counts as good from such a common point of view? On what grounds do we will that the principle guiding our action be adopted by everyone? Are impartiality and fairness sufficient guides in themselves? What does it mean to give equal consideration to each person's interests? These questions put down valuable markers, but again we find that precision eludes us. We need other strands in the tapestry alongside the one that invites us to take a common point of view.

3.4 Rights

A consequentialist ethic tends to leapfrog over the individual and ask what action leads to the greater common good. The problem is, as we have seen, the greater good may be at the expense of the individual, or a group weaker than another having power. The greater good needs to be balanced against the demands of justice and fairness. A person's claim to 'rights' puts the brake upon consequentialist zeal. Consequentialism may focus upon the good of the majority, but 'rights' language centres upon the individual and their due, protecting the individual from the neglect, intrusion or tyranny of the many. The pursuit of the common good must not be allowed to be so totally unfettered that the claims of the individual – especially those of a minority – are ignored. 'Rights' language is very much to the fore in the individualistic cultures of the West, and received impetus from the massive violation of human dignity in the communitarian regimes of Nazism and Communism.

Some claims to a 'right' seem well grounded. The right to the presumption of innocence before the law is a good example. John Locke was strongly influential in popularizing 'rights' language. He spoke of a right to life, liberty and property.[15] The American Constitution spoke of the 'pursuit of happiness' as a right and the French revolution added to Locke's list the right to security and the right to resist tyranny – implied also in the regicide of Charles I. Of course there are *legal* rights conferred by law – such as the right a police officer may have to use firearms. We are speaking here, however, of rights we have a *moral obligation* to recognize (sometimes called 'natural' or 'human' rights) whatever the law of the state says. In Locke's day rights tended to be asserted over and against the state. The right to life, liberty and property expressed the right to live as one chooses, enjoying the fruits of one's labour, unmolested by the state. Now it is common to assert rights that the state should honour – like the right to health care or education.

This development leads to other questions. Does a woman have a right to a child? Do a gay or lesbian couple have a right to equal consideration as adoptive parents? Claims to rights suffer from endless expansion. There is certainly a problem in justifying the ever-increasing and sophisticated rights that we claim. An uncritical use of rights language can get out of hand or even become silly, often making claims upon society, which society cannot be expected to meet. Baroness Warnock has asked if the UNICEF *Charter of Children's Rights* implies it is a right for every child to be born into an affluent family.[16] This, however, is utterly unrealistic.

At worst, claims to 'rights' pander to extravagant self-indulgence. My preoccupation with my rights can undermine generosity and charity. We have a 'right' to be protected from harm, and a 'right' to have all our wants satisfied. 'Rights' language can become confrontational. Through it I assert my 'rights' over and against others. I become isolated and lacking in trust. I speak of 'my' rights, regardless of broader social goals and regardless of my obligations. 'Rights' language, considered in isolation, can easily become distorted, *but only when considered in isolation.* We guard against isolation when we speak also of duty, generosity and the things we hold in common. Sometimes we may elect to waive a right or not insist upon it. Moreover, rights are reciprocal. I have rights, but then so also have others. Balanced against insight and commitment expressed in other concepts – such as duty, virtue, justice and the common good – rights language has the value of protecting the individual against the neglect or exploitation of the collective. Individuals are always in danger of being marginalized and oppressed. The language of 'rights' protects the individual; indeed, such language has often been used to draw attention to groups that are oppressed. We see this in Mary Wollstonecraft's classic *Vindication of the Rights of Woman* (1792). Furthermore, 'rights' language is seen as necessary when zealous social reformers, in their impatience to build a utopia, end up neglecting people. This is not to suggest the assertion of a right has trumps in all contexts. But its *prima facie* claim has serious weight.

Some writers place the language of 'rights' within the context of a bleak individualism. There is no consensus in society about anything, and so we must all create our own haven of private meaning, our 'right' to do this being protected from the encroachments of others. There is no agreed goal to human life and no common good. All we can agree on is to agree to differ. It is not necessary, however, to accept this bleak picture in order to see the value of the language of rights. Historically rights language is more deeply rooted in the reality of tyranny and oppression than in ethical scepticism. State, religion, culture and community can exercise an oppressive imperial power. We should indeed balance the language of rights with the language of community and role and obligation, but likewise the community can become oppressive and duties and roles can exercise their own subtle tyrannies. If there is not the complementary focus on the well-being and freedoms of the individual, the community's tyranny receives no challenge. All this is guarded by the language of rights. If we are weaving a tapestry we do not have to choose between the orange thread and the purple. We can have both.

For this reason, we can sympathize with the easy baptism of 'rights' language into Christian thought despite a certain 'secular' origin. 'Rights' language focuses upon the worth and dignity of the individual as made in the image of God. Some Christians are suspicious of 'rights' language because the concept is said to be not 'biblical' or not found in classic Christian traditions. But although the *concept* may not often be found, what it expresses is ubiquitous and central – namely the dignity and claims of the person. Furthermore, the language of rights tends to focus on the marginalized and the oppressed – a dominant biblical theme. Internationally, the language of rights places constraint on governments – especially those tempted to oppression. 'Rights' language becomes a weapon on behalf of those suffering through injustice.[17]

'Rights' language may also challenge a Christian tendency to commend an unreserved giving to others, with no thought for self, a self-sacrifice for the sake of others totally unqualified, together with a radical rejection of self-protection. Christians, however, are called to love their neighbour *as* themselves, not *instead* of themselves. We have a 'right' to be ourselves nourished, alongside our commitment to others. We can fully give only if we are first fed ourselves. Furthermore, my neighbour has a 'right' to have their wish that I also be nourished taken seriously!

Much of our life is played out in close relationship with family, friends, neighbours and colleagues. The language of rights is not inappropriate here, but it comes into its own when we deal with the stranger. There may be no real contact with the stranger but we recognize their rights. Here there is stringency in the language of rights. Others have rights – they belong to everyone by virtue of our common humanity. I must recognize the rights of those in Taiwan or Angola even if I know no one there. Alongside that stringency, however, there is also gentleness. Utilitarianism, Christianity and Buddhism have all attempted to widen the circle of our moral commitment. We are rightly so challenged but it is unrealistic to expect that we can treat everyone equally as our neighbour. The burden would be intolerable, and maybe our neighbourliness would not be welcome. The stranger may wish no more than that their rights be recognized. For the rest they wish to get on with their lives unencumbered by our crusading goodwill.

'Rights' language is not the only thread in the tapestry, but it is an important one. The language becomes distorted only when we fail to balance it with other insights.

On the notion of animal rights see 14.2.

3.5 Duties and obligations

We may treat the notions of 'duty' and 'obligation' as synonymous. If I have a duty, it is incumbent upon me to act in a certain way – and this, in the last analysis, derives from my commitment to our mutual well-being within the human community. If I have rights, I also have duties, and this includes the duty to honour the rights of others. That said, the correlation between one person's 'right' and another's 'duty' is messy. After all, I cannot possibly cope with the deluge of duties that might conceivably follow from the rights of six billion people. Your 'right' does not automatically confer a duty upon me, but sometimes it may do. There has to be judgement as to when it does and when such a claim is unreasonable and unrealistic. Furthermore, in order to make sense of the notion of a 'duty', we do not have always to couple it with a 'right'. The language of 'duty' can break free. Likewise, a new-born baby and someone with advanced Alzheimer's disease have rights – but hardly duties.

The natural habitat of the language of 'duty' is that of specific relationships with others, relationships which make claims upon me. The fact that the other person is my parent, wife, son, daughter, colleague, employer or employee, places upon me certain obligations. In all kinds of ways we are bound together and our membership of groups – nations, churches, companies, professions, hospitals, schools, clubs – confers privileges but also makes claims. The act of making a promise forges a special relationship, which imposes the strong *prima facie* obligation to keep it. If we recognized no obligations arising out of our relationships, it is difficult to see how any decency would survive, and yet it is this decency that is essential to a life worth living.

If the language of duty has its natural habitat within contractual relationships can it roam further afield? We may talk of our duty towards humankind as a whole. We may say we have a duty to care for the earth. This language makes sense and we should not veto it out of deference to a tidy theory that confines the language of duty to our more particular relationships. In any case, even in this broad territory we can see such duties as deriving from our special relationship with those of our own species and the one earth, which we share.

Reflection on the correlation and lack of correlation between 'rights' and 'duties' helps us to see how important it is to struggle to balance different strands in the tapestry. If we put exclusive stress on 'rights', we can end up becoming demanding, confrontational and blind to our obligations. If we put all the stress on 'duties' people can become 'doormats', worn out by excessive demands and lacking nourishment. Their own well-being should be honoured as much as their duties towards others. Much tyranny has been exercised by an undue emphasis on 'duties' – especially the duties the weak owe to the strong. In the Indian culture, the *Universal Declaration of Human Rights* has not been universally welcomed because it lacks a correlative emphasis on duties. At the same time, some in Indian society have seen the declaration as offering protection to those of lower caste where people traditionally had stronger duties than rights. What is impressive about New Testament passages such Colossians 3.18—4.1 is that they take the conventional language of the obligations of the underdogs and add to it reciprocal obligations of the top dogs. Such passages easily read today as hierarchical and non-egalitarian but in their historical context they were revolutionary.

3.6 The act itself

Suppose security forces catch up with a terrorist cell planning to detonate a large bomb in central London. Where and when, however, is not known. They have reason to believe the bomb has been planted and that detonation is imminent. They locate and arrest one of the gang. He refuses to talk. The security forces seek permission from the Home Secretary to use torture.

After a branding and the loss of two toenails he cracks. The information is given and the bomb located and defused. Are there any circumstances in which torture is permissible? The UN *Universal Declaration of Human Rights* of 1948 appears to regard the right not to be tortured as being unqualified and absolute.[18] But *in extremis* does the strong prospect of saving a thousand lives justify even torture? May we sometimes lay aside the 'Pauline principle' and do evil for the sake of the greater good? Does the end sometimes justify the means?

It could be argued that torture is ruled out even here on strict consequentialist grounds. Torture only hardens the terrorist, provoking worse atrocities. If security forces play fair and civilized they may lose more battles, but the attacks will not escalate. And what if they get the wrong person? Would the hoped-for saving of life justify torturing the innocent? Of course, we need a working definition of what constitutes torture. The category clearly describes branding, the removal of toenails, or the use of an electric drill on the knee. But what about sleep deprivation or repeated 'waterboarding' – the immersing of the head in water until on the verge of drowning? States denying they use torture can insist they speak the truth because they raise the threshold of definition, using not torture but only 'coercive interrogation'.

Let us set aside consequences. There are approaches to ethics that deliberately bracket consequences and concentrate on *the act itself.* Some acts are our duty 'in themselves', and others are intrinsically evil 'in themselves'. Some acts are not merely right or wrong 'extrinsically' because they lead to good or harm. They are rather right or wrong 'intrinsically' – in themselves.

To illustrate. When a surgeon attacks with a knife, this intrusion is hardly right 'in itself'. Surgery is not an end in itself. The surgeon's act is only extrinsically right because it leads to some other good beyond itself. By contrast, visiting the patient later, the surgeon is courteous and attentive. The surgeon also honours a promise to a trainee to discuss some complicated procedure. In contrast to the act of wielding the knife, these acts of courtesy, attention and keeping a promise are right not merely because they lead to wholesome consequences. They are right 'in themselves'.

Ethics is concerned not only with the consequences of an act, but also with the act itself. Consequentialism** in its pure form has no interest in the act alone, except in so far as it leads to maximal good. If a consequentialist approach to ethics asks about the consequences of what we do, a 'deontological'** approach asks about *the act itself.* ('Deontological' meaning 'of the being of' or 'of the nature of'.) Sometimes this is analysed in terms of the 'right' and the 'good'. For consequentialism the 'good' refers to a state of affairs. An action is 'right' if it leads to 'good'. For deontologists, by contrast, some actions are right or evil in themselves and not simply because of their desirable or undesirable consequences.

Things like surgery, taking cod liver oil and practising our scales are right only because of some greater good to which they lead. By contrast, promise keeping and truth telling are right in themselves. Likewise, the wrongness of violating human rights, terrorizing, stealing, torturing, murdering, etc.[19] To return to our illustration, a consequentialist might argue torture is sometimes permitted if the suffering it prevents is sufficient to counterbalance the violation of the person tortured, against which there is, of course, a massive onus. But the strict deontologist could argue it is always wrong to torture anyone – whatever the consequences. A person is protected against torture by an absolute prohibition, and not simply by a massive onus. There are some actions that are always wrong, no matter what suffering they might prevent or what good they might produce. 'The goodness of the ultimate consequences does not guarantee the rightness of the action which produced them. The two realms are not only distinct for the deontologist, but the right is prior to the good.'[20] Suppose – as with the tragic case of Mary and Jodi in 2000 – we terminate the life of one conjoined twin, Mary, in order to allow Jodi to live. There has been a deliberate termination of the life of Mary, but her life was not viable anyway. A consequentialist might deem this justified. The strict deontologist, however, might argue the termination was wrong. A life has been ended *through a deliberate act.* This is morally culpable in the way in which *allowing* both to die would not have been. Better two natural deaths than one murder, even if the murder of a non-viable twin leads to the prevention of the natural death of the other.

It is quite a tangled web! Can we make progress in sorting it out?

First, pure deontologism can encourage a very narrowly focused view of the moral life. We attend to simple duties and we avoid simple wrong actions. This hardly scales the height of moral virtue or moral responsibility. Furthermore, there may be self-indulgence in a simple and uncompromising deontological stance. I carefully guard my own moral rectitude. I do not step on slippery slopes or get my hands dirty. I shun compromise. I always fulfil my obligations in what may be a fairly narrow area. But by failing to get my hands dirty I ignore what is my prime duty – struggling in the messy ambiguity of the world to minimize suffering and maximize flourishing. I self-indulgently cultivate the tidy garden of my own moral uprightness and neglect responsibility for the wilderness beyond. My own avoidance of wrongdoing is what is paramount. Whatever *may happen*, what is important is *what I do*.[21] This concern is not far from the critique of some of the Pharisees in the New Testament. Whatever insights deontologism may have, this is a danger to be watched.

We see here complementary strengths and weaknesses in consequentialism and deontologism. For the latter, the area of our moral duty is often carefully prescribed. Unlike the consequentialist, who may demand that we calculate fervently at every point to ensure we are maximizing good, the deontologist is more relaxed. There is at worst the hint that provided we avoid a few evil deeds and fulfil a few simple obligations, for the rest we may eat, drink and be merry. Deontologism tends not to concern itself with the whole of life.[22] F. H. Bradley considers the person who speaks of 'my station and its duties'. But what of the world beyond my station?[23] If consequentialism is all inclusive in its concern, placing too heavy a burden on us, does the deontologist let us off too lightly? Christian tradition has also wrestled with this tension. While taking seriously our obligations and commitments it has generally avoided the stressful zeal of a utilitarian obliged at every moment to calculate maximum good. Each person has their own vocation, but final responsibility for the world is God's and not ours. There are burdens and yokes, but not more than we can reasonably bear.

None of this, however, prohibits the deontologist from having a prominent thread in the tapestry. The fundamental questions are: What sorts of things are right or wrong in themselves? How are they to be identified and justified? It seems the most persuasive answer to the second is implicit in the former. As we have seen, deontologists tend to focus on things like truth telling, promise keeping, honouring rights, refraining from exploitation, torture, abuse, etc. The examples are invariably to do with *how we treat people*. What it boils down to is *honouring and attending to the person*. This or that person has a claim upon me that is over and against consequentialist considerations. A person is not a means but an end. Acts are right in themselves because they express commitment to and respect for persons. It is acts violating the person that are ruled out. Our flourishing is served and constituted by relationships of decency, respect and sensitivity, such as are expressed by elementary obligations we have toward one another.

My suggestion, therefore, is that the true insight in deontologism protects the individual from tyranny, injustice, exploitation, abuse and neglect. Such a tyranny is a danger when there is an exclusive focus upon the wider public good. The contribution of deontologism is thus related to 'rights' language. I must not get so carried away with my zeal for seeking the most beneficial consequences of my action that I forget that certain acts are my duty, or are wrong in themselves. Such duties arise out of my obligation to the dignity and rights of particular people. I must not allow zeal for utopia to allow the neglect of basic truth telling and integrity. These 'deontological' duties express an honouring of people, and their needs and rights, and particularly those people to whom I am specially bound. Deontologism, in taking seriously our specific duties, gives us a space for decency and integrity in our personal dealings, which consequentialism in its strict and impartial calculus easily denies us. Our attention to such duties does not simply lead to good beyond themselves. Rather, their fulfilment constitutes good in itself in terms of personal dealings of integrity and decency.

We conclude that deontologism is correct in saying that certain actions are morally right or morally wrong *in themselves*. This leads, however, to the very difficult question: Are such actions right or wrong in *all conceivable circumstances*? In the 1930s Sir David Ross spoke helpfully of a distinction between the *prima facie** and the *actual*. We may certainly say of deontological rights and wrongs such as we have instanced that their rightness or wrongness is at least *prima facie*. In other words, they are *normally* right or wrong and, if we judge otherwise in a particular case, the burden of proof is upon us. There is a massive onus against departing from the norm. Sometimes, however, what we judge to be the *actual* may diverge from the *prima facie*.[24]

There is no difficulty in seeing how this may sometimes be the case. Duties conflict and there may also be a conflict between a *prima facie* duty and some wider goal. A judgement has to be made as to a proper balance. Deontologists seem bound to compromise the absoluteness of at least some duties when there is such a tension. Suppose I borrow a knife and promise to return it? In the meantime, I discover the owner is a murderer who needs the knife to dispatch the next victim. This rather twee example is Plato's, and Plato responds by saying that the obligation to prevent a murder is stronger than and overrules the obligation to keep such a promise.[25] Plato's response has stood the test of time, and we can think of other examples. My promise to meet you at the tea shop at 4.00 p.m. is overruled by the obligation to help another rambler who has strained an ankle. But even here the *prima facie* obligation to honour the promise remains, and I have a consequent obligation to explain why I let you down. Much of life involves juggling competing demands. How do I balance my duty to my employer with my duty to my family? How do I balance my commitment to supporting someone in need with a proper duty to care for myself? Interrogated about the 'hideous tie so kindly meant,'[26] I wrestle with a tension between the obligation to tell the truth and the obligation to be diplomatic and sensitive to another's feelings. It is too simplistic, however, to say all this is only a matter of asking about maximum beneficial consequences. Deontologism reminds us of particular duties arising out of our respect for persons, or out of particular commitments, and these have to be held in tension with a commitment to the wider good.

Are there some duties, however, that are not simply *prima facie* but instead *binding in all conceivable circumstances*? And if this is so, is it because of some mysterious 'moral absolute' or because pragmatically we cannot conceive of instances when some higher obligation or good might overrule? The obligation not to engage in torture seems to be an agonizingly difficult borderline case. There is nothing unreasonable in the insistence that such a violation of another person is never justified.[27] On the other hand, it is not obvious that we are guilty of moral depravity if we allow that in extreme cases even torture might be justified. Needless to say, in the genteel world of Cambridge in the 1930s Ross found no need to wrestle with this kind of menacing dilemma.

What about rape? Can I conceive of instances when the massive onus against rape is overruled? Sadistic Gestapo jailer to captured resistance leader: 'Unless you rape your compatriot for my voyeuristic pleasure the SS will massacre a whole village.' Does he concede to the blackmail or insist integrity demands that he refuses? It seems there is no one obviously correct response to such a dilemma – mercifully faced only rarely. The ethicist cannot sweep the world clean of dilemma and tragedy.

Nearer home, killing another person is a key example. There are few obligations as strong as that to honour the right of another person to life, and yet many accept killing is justifiable in the case of last-resort self-defence, when fighting a just war, and for some *in extremis* as a punishment. The example of taking another person's life alerts us to a further complication. In our discussion so far we have assumed that certain 'acts' may be identified by some tight common definition. Such an assumption might be behind the example of the compelled 'rape' in the Gestapo prison. As such, 'acts' are standardly packaged and parachuted into the infinitely varied terrain of real life situations. An act, however, cannot be defined in advance apart from the context, which gives it its character. Acts of killing another person do not conform to a common definition. There is a difference – ethically significant for many – between killing in a just war and killing in an armed robbery. We express this by the language we use. The concept of 'murder' is a value word reserved for particular kinds of killing. Likewise, despite the massive onus placed upon us to be truthful, the character of a 'lie' varies enormously. Again, as Aquinas stated, there is a difference between stealing from the poor for selfish gain and a mother stealing

from the indifferent rich to feed her starving children.[28] Moral concepts
are 'open textured' or 'analogous'. 'Proportionalism'** in Roman Catholic moral theology does not say 'evil acts' may sometimes be justified
by the end. It says rather that we cannot judge an act as being evil in
advance of taking into account its specific character in a specific situation. General moral guidelines can only be applied in specific cases
with the addition of a judgement that cannot easily be codified.[29] An
act must be correctly described before it can be evaluated.[30]

These issues are relevant to a consideration of John Paul II's encyclical *Veritatis Splendor*. John Paul allows the general point that 'positive moral precepts' have to be applied to a 'specific situation ... in view
of other duties which may be more important or more urgent'. He thus
seems to allow in some instances a 'proportionalism' that maintains
we cannot formulate an 'absolute prohibition' since the good life is
about balancing (finding a 'proportion' between) conflicting obligations or values and a responsible assessment of the goods involved in
the concrete situation.[31] This, however, is not always the case. Certain
behaviour is 'intrinsically evil' and there can be no 'legitimate exception'.[32] Some acts are always forbidden. They are not merely *prima
facie* wrong. They are '*intrinsically evil*' whatever the context. There
thus exist 'acts which *per se* and in themselves, independent of circumstances, are always seriously wrong by reason of their object'. On the
whole the Pope is siding with Roman Catholic moral theologians, such
as John Finnis and Germain Grisez, who reject the 'proportionalism'
of others, such as Bruno Schuller and Richard McCormick.[33]

This category of the 'intrinsically evil' comprises 'whatever is hostile
to life – homicide, genocide, torture, slavery, degrading conditions of
work', and such like. John Paul here exemplifies a typical deontological stance with its welcome emphasis on the evil of violating human
dignity. 'The unconditional respect due to the insistent demands of
the personal dignity of every person' demands that we in all instances
'prohibit without exception actions which are intrinsically evil'.[34]

As our discussion has indicated, there is an extremely strong case
for saying this of things such as rape and torture. Those who make
up text book dilemmas when even rape might be justifiable, happily
speak of instances mercifully rare. What is much more controversial is
what is further included in John Paul's list. In addition to the examples
already given, there is also abortion and voluntary euthanasia, thereby
begging the question in an area acutely debated, as we will see later
in 16.2 and 16.4. 'Contraceptive practices' are also 'intrinsically evil',
as is any sexual expression not vaginally penetrative. The list includes
'homicide', which presumably means *unjustified* taking of life. Homicide is thus wrong by definition, since homicide is defined as unlaw-
ful killing. ('Murder' might be a better translation of the Latin *homo-*

cidium.[35]) John Paul allows military force in some circumstances. Why is a 'proportional' approach taken to killing in a just war, but not over voluntary euthanasia and abortion? This is not to suggest we can be blasé about abortion or voluntary euthanasia, but the debate cannot be foreclosed before it begins.[36]

In conclusion, it seems difficult to deny that certain deontological duties – such as the obligation to keep a promise or tell the truth – are only *prima facie*. They indicate with regard to broad categories of acts where the burden of proof lies. To say there may be occasions when a higher obligation has trumps is, however, in no way to downplay the strong requirement that truth telling and loyalty to promises are the norm. There may also be some duties that are absolute in all circumstances, such as the absolute duty not to torture. The essential point is that, alongside and balancing our focus on the wider good, there is also respect for the rights and dignity of each person. The strength of deontologism is that it asserts this over and against consequences. When I lie, when I break a promise, when I steal, when I abuse, I am dishonouring a person. Even if the consequence is the maximization of the common good, I am still riding roughshod over the dignity of the person. The honouring of another person is an intrinsic good. It is something that is good in itself, and not simply because of some good beyond itself and to which it might lead. This is the truth to which deontologists bear an important if sometimes a rather foggy witness.

3.7 Rules and conventions

The above section reminds us that a 'popular' understanding of Christian ethics may see the Christian life in terms of obeying moral rules, normally expressed in a negative way: Thou shalt not lie, thou shalt not steal, and, of course, thou shalt not have sex before the legal wedding!

It is easy to see the limitations of this approach. Contexts vary and each situation has its own delicate nuances. It is difficult to see how life's complexity and richness can be covered by a list of slick prohibitions. Perhaps more to the point, simply by obeying rules we hardly scale the heights of moral maturity. Rules may save us from the worst of our folly, but moral maturity is more positively about discerning what is most rich and nourishing in our life together. Do we refrain from adultery because the rule forbids it, or because of a commitment to fidelity and decency in human relationships? And if we have this commitment, it follows that fidelity is about much more than avoiding adultery. Furthermore, if we have this commitment, do we still need the rule? Moral maturity is about nuanced judgement and finding a richness of which rules tell us nothing.

It need not follow that rules have no value. Maybe they constitute a modest thread in the tapestry. Rules can be seen as a deposit account accrued from past moral experience. They may indicate what is *usually* right or wrong, where the *onus* lies, or where the burden of proof falls. 'Thou shalt not lie' is thus only a rule of thumb. It does not mean it is always incumbent upon us to tell the truth. In some situations there may be a tension between truth telling and sensitivity to a person's feelings. Such sensitivity can be patronizing and paternalistic, but not necessarily always. This is the 'hideous tie so kindly meant' dilemma. There remains, however, a strong presumption in favour of truth telling. This point needs to be further nuanced by our earlier insistence that when we speak of a 'lie' or a 'theft', say, we are speaking of broad categories of action only. The specific character of an act is determined by the context. A lie told to the Gestapo is not the same kind of act as a lie told to my wife.

Furthermore, while we must avoid paternalism, and must not underestimate the capacity of our neighbours to grow into moral maturity, there may be some – especially those still growing up – for whom rules provide a useful guide to the broad contours of morality. The rules give us a lift in developing a mature moral judgement which enables us increasingly to dispense with them. Rembrandt did not need to paint by numbers, but then not everyone is a Rembrandt. At the same time, maturity in moral judgement is very much more widespread than artistic genius.

We must not forget either the reality of generally accepted social norms which provide both support and a context of expectation. Sometimes this can be narrow and oppressive. But such rules of behaviour and social mores have value in encouraging the good life and protecting those for whom the winds of autonomy and choice are a bit too strong. The general expectations and mores of society can provide a supportive framework for responsible living. Their absence in some countries makes it more difficult for those in business, say, to abide by reasonable standards of business ethics.

As we will note later there is cogency in the concern that the abandonment of many norms governing sexual behaviour, leaving a 'free for all' of autonomous choice is a mixed blessing (15.2 and 15.3).

The reality is that we do not engage in the ethical equivalent of reinventing the wheel every time we make a moral judgement. Most of the time we follow convention and accepted practice, and such convention provides a supportive context of expectation, as well as a deep reservoir of moral wisdom. Kant was commenting upon this kind of convention when he invited us to act only in such a way as we can will that the maxim of our action becomes a universal law.[37] If I lie for personal advantage, I cannot will that my action be universalized since I can gain personal advantage from a lie only if the convention of truth telling is assumed. By lying for personal gain I undermine the convention and expectation and we are all the losers. Kant was wrong in suggesting this means telling the truth is always our obligation, or in implying the broad category of 'lie' cannot be subdivided in ways that are ethically significant, but he was surely right in saying there is thereby a massive onus placed upon us to honour the obligation to be truthful. Much ethical wisdom is woven into the fabric of our societies, with their conventions and expectations. The same is the case with social institutions, such as – to give wildly differing examples – marriage and professional associations with their codes of practice. Morality cannot be about slavishly following convention on all occasions. After all, convention is not so easily defined or so monolithic as to permit this, and even if it is, it has sometimes to be challenged. Judgement and argument must check convention, develop it, and sometimes prophetically challenge it. Nevertheless, moral judgement involves a delicately nuanced interplay between personal moral judgement and proper regard for the conventions and expectations that are woven into the fabric of our cultures.[38]

3.8 The person: virtues and vices

3.8.1 Introduction

An uncomplicated and stripped-down consequentialism will have no interest as such in the *person* who acts. The interest will be rather in the *consequence* of the act. There is no difference between Mother Teresa and Hitler provided what they do leads to the desired results. Moreover, in so far as a utilitarianism pressed to extremes has such an interest, the person is a calculating machine focusing exclusively on the maximal good for all, leaving no space for leisure, friendship and fun[39] – a pretty dull sort of guy. Suppose, however, we put the spotlight now, not on *what we do* but rather on ourselves, on *what kind of a person we are*?

This raises the question of motivation. Suppose I visit my rich uncle in hospital because I genuinely care for his well-being? This seems laudable. But suppose I do it with an eye to an inheritance? This is devious, self-centred and lacks integrity. Suppose I perfect my musical performance out of a desire to beat a competitor. My motivation may not reach the height of moral virtue, but it is not obvious that a suitably house-trained competitiveness has no place in the good life. Of course, we are capable of mammoth self-delusion. We may convince ourselves that our motives are pure, when in fact they are not. We may act supposedly generously, but in fact in order to wield power, or in order to enjoy the buzz of being resourceful and generous.

Kant famously spoke of two grocers. Both were scrupulous in ensuring that they charged their customers fairly, but their motives were different. The one's motive was self-serving. Honesty is good for business. A dishonest grocer will lose customers. The other, by contrast, acted honestly because it was his *duty* so to act. Both grocers acted *in accordance with* duty, but only one *for the sake of* duty. Kant's argument is that the only laudable motivation is that which does 'duty for duty's sake'.[40] What Kant meant by this is unclear and, whatever the meaning, it is not obvious he was right. Suppose I act well towards someone because I delight in them, because I genuinely wish them to flourish, because of natural sympathy and goodwill, and because I am grateful for what they mean to me? This complex of motivation seems laudable. But it is not clear that I am acting 'for the sake of duty' in Kant's terms. A person, bad tempered and impetuous, who out of duty checks her behaviour, is morally praiseworthy, but arguably less so than someone for whom the check is unnecessary because of a compassionate and sensitive character. Kant's view on this is unclear, despite Paton's defence against Schiller who made this sort of criticism.[41] When Kant spoke of a *motive* he may have meant a *reason*, in the sense of rational justification, rather than a psychological impulse. There does seem to be some sort of difference between a *reason* for acting and a *motive* for acting, but the notions overlap and interpenetrate. Suppose I forgive someone *partly* because I believe God has forgiven me. This is a reason for acting and yet it may also kindle the motivation through inspiring the will.

The prime issue here, however, is not what Kant might have thought. The point is that Kant draws our attention to motivation as a legitimate area of interest in ethics, complicated as it might be. But more broadly than that, the discussion has shifted from *the act and its consequences to the person who acts*.

We thus move into the broader territory of the *kind of people we are*. Much ethical debate is focused on resolving dilemmas, on making 'moral decisions'. The rapid development of medical ethics is dilemma focused. 'Virtue ethics' shifts the focus. For 'virtue ethics' the spotlight is not so much on discrete acts, or 'moral decisions', wrestling with moral quandaries, and still less on moral rules. The spotlight is rather upon the person, and nurturing personal qualities such as decency, integrity, compassion, and a host of other things. People who are generous and compassionate in their disposition will be inclined to behave with generosity and compassion. Recent virtue ethics leapfrogs over much modern moral philosophy with its stress on duty, 'moral decisions' and analysing the genre of moral concepts, and finds inspiration in the stress on the kind of persons we are in Aristotle and Aquinas.[42]

The focus here is less on discovering the right solution to an ethical dilemma. It is rather more on nurturing people of mature character. There is a hint that those mature in virtues will not go far wrong. Implicit also is the insistence that *persons of character* have intrinsic value, and not merely acts and their consequences. Moreover, there is suspicion of the idea that there is always one correct answer to every ethical dilemma, and that we will discover it if we only wrestle with our moral quandary hard enough. The ethical life is more about living with uncertainty, but facing uncertainty and unresolved tensions with integrity and responsibility. Moreover, virtues are not merely instrumental in leading to good beyond themselves. On the contrary, much of what is involved in human flourishing is constituted by cultivating lives of virtue. Virtue may not guarantee our well-being, but it is an important constituent of it.

There is an interesting contrast here with more 'conservative' trends in the Church, which have fastened more tightly upon rules governing behaviour. In Protestantism we see this in the writings of Stott and Gumbel,[43] particularly over sexual ethics, and in Catholicism in *Veritatis Splendor* with its focus on avoiding acts which are 'intrinsically evil'[44] (see 15.3 and 15.4). That said, 'virtue ethics' have deep biblical as well as classical roots. The Wisdom literature speaks of different types of character, and the prophetic literature has the insight that inner disposition may have priority over legalistic obedience. The metaphor of the good tree producing good fruit is in this tradition and Paul has many lists of character traits. The beatitudes, as well as the Psalmist, speak of dispositions of the heart.[45] The Christian tradition with its ideals of sanctity follows on from this.

Suppose, then, the focus of the good life is not only on doing this and avoiding that, but also on maintaining in all contexts and relationships certain qualities of character, or, more traditionally, 'virtues'. It is not primarily that one avoids doing the wrong thing, occasionally also doing a few right things. Rather, one is a good person. There is undoubtedly important insight here.

3.8.2 The 'cardinal virtues'

Can we be specific about virtues or qualities of character we admire? Rooted in Aristotle, clarified by Cicero, and canonized by Augustine and Aquinas, the western tradition gives us four 'cardinal' virtues – *temperance*, *fortitude*, *justice* and *prudence*. At first sight this seems an odd foursome, but a little reflection reveals the reasons why these have been identified. The sense of oddness may be due to the fact that

I have used the traditional labels. *Self-restraint*, *steadfastness*, *fairness* and *judgement* might be better descriptions for modern ears. For a start, we humans desire things. Sometimes the desire is overwhelming. A rich chocolate pudding laced by double cream is immediately compelling, and there is nothing wrong with an occasional treat, but it is bad to have two a day. Sexual pleasure can be noble and nourishing within a relationship of tenderness and mutual delight, but it can become insatiable, feeding the obsession by poring over pornography. The virtue of *temperance* or self-control helps me watch over and channel properly my desires. The reality is that we are buffeted all the time with desires and impulses, and sometimes very strong ones. Without some ability to monitor, restrain and direct our desires, we can make no claim to moral maturity. A person who is controlled by an overwhelming desire for wealth, say, lacks the virtue of temperance.

Allied to this, the virtue of *fortitude* gives us the strength and commitment required. There may be an element of inner moral struggle as we battle with impulses and desires. The moral struggle is praiseworthy precisely because it has as its goal the control of feelings and desires, thus leaving the moral struggle behind. The virtues of temperance and fortitude allow us to find an appropriate balance and proportion between conflicting desires and conflicting demands. More generally, any mature character has to be loyal to commitments and thus to show the steadfastness – sometimes very costly – expressed in the traditional virtue of fortitude or courage. All this is not unrelated to Aristotle's doctrine of the 'Mean'. This is not to be understood as 'moderation in all things'. Outrage over the Holocaust should not be moderate. The doctrine of the mean is rather about finding an *appropriate* response in each situation. 'Persistence' might be another suitable synonym for this traditional virtue.

Fortitude and temperance are self-regarding virtues. They are virtues whereby we govern desires and inclinations. *Justice*, however, concerns our relations with others. For Plato the concept of justice is synonymous with that of morality itself. For Aristotle it becomes more specific. Justice is about how we deal with one another. The concept of justice is for us heavily nuanced after centuries of analysis and new applications. We will look at some of these later (3.9). As a classic 'cardinal virtue', justice is fundamentally about fairness, equity and decency in dealing with others. As such, it opens up the way for later analyses of legal and distributive justice. These notions of justice presuppose a commitment to a justice in personal dealings, with its commitment to fairness and non-malevolence. When I keep faith with promises, when I honour the truth, when I am committed to the protection of the innocent, I am showing justice. Justice seeks a balance between the good of the community and the good of the individual. Justice requires that people should not be treated unequally unless there are differences that justify this. For Aristotle, being a slave and being a woman were relevant differences. For Aquinas, a fundamental equality before God sows the seeds of challenging this, even if Christians were slow to see the implications.

Finally, there is *prudence*, not to be misunderstood as timid caution. *Judgement* might be a better word. This is called an 'intellectual' virtue, and with good reason. Prudence – or wisdom or judgement – is the capacity to judge the appropriate response in complicated situations. Moral principles may be general and vague. Individual situations are specific. In the rough and tumble of our complicated world the ideal is rarely within our grasp. We struggle with competing demands, intractable dilemmas and the deep-seated institutionalization of greed, power abuse and privilege. Yet a commitment to the good life demands we cannot give up the struggle. Prudence asks what is realistic and realizable. Prudence looks at the whole picture and makes an informed and wise judgement as to what manner of life and behaviour is appropriate.

It could be protested that Jesus did not display overmuch of prudence when he 'set his face towards Jerusalem'. In one sense, seen as a refutation of an emphasis on prudence, this remark misses the point. But in another sense, we need to be open to its challenge. It misses the point because the special vocation of Jesus should not be seen without further ado as a model for everyone. It may also be allowed that some are called to a 'special vocation' to live in a radically counter cultural way. The witness of the pacifist or of those who withdraw from mainstream society, as do some religious, may have their place. We have already noted a Christian acknowledgement of the special vocation of some. But for most their vocation is to live in the world of politics, earning a living, bringing up children, and prudence is required in judging how integrity and a commitment to the good life finds a balance between conflicting ideals, and a conflict between the ideal and the realizable. In many ways Reinhold Niebuhr's ethic is a brilliant exposition of the intellectual virtue of prudence.[46] Prudence is required in assessing whether or not a particular war is just. Prudence is required in the struggle for the most realistic mix between proper freedom, the efficient creation of wealth, and its just distribution. The critics of the pacifist and the socialist may claim they lack prudence. (See Chapters 12 and 13.)

3.8.3 Other virtues

The identification of the four cardinal virtues has stood the test of time. We are to be critically aware of our desires and impulses, to exercise restraint, and to find the appropriate balance and expression. We are to have the steadfastness to do this and to persist. In our dealings with others we are to be fair, considerate and non-malevolent. Wisdom allows us to judge appropriate responses in our day-to-day living. This is a very broad brush, but the four cardinal virtues give us a good framework for moral judgement and for understanding the nature of maturity in moral character.

There is no value, however, in limiting the virtues to these four. A rich vision demands a rich language. Differently named virtues communicate delicate nuances. We prize a rich variety of character dispositions and qualities. There is no way in which we can offer a complete list, and anyway that would be undesirable because closed lists shut us off from further insight. A rough *indicative* list of other virtues may, however, be given. *Integrity* speaks of a fundamental honesty, a commitment to truthfulness, honourable motivation and openness infusing respect for others. Hume set great store by *sympathy* and R. M. Hare was in this tradition when he put great store by imagining oneself in the other person's position.[47] There is a proper modern stress on developing *self-awareness*, not unlike the traditional stress on monitoring desires and impulses through temperance and prudence. Elsewhere in this book I will consider *tolerance, forgiveness, loyalty* and *chastity* (see 5.3.3, 8.4, 15.2, 15.3) along with virtues especially prized in the Christian tradition. Prime examples are *faith, hope, love, humility, patience* and *creativity* (see 5.3.4).

The cardinal virtue of prudence helps identify the subtler nuances of the many virtues, while temperance and prudence may also alert us to the pitfalls when a particular virtue overreaches itself and becomes sour. Many 'virtues' can go to seed and show a certain arrogance, becoming disingenuous and priggish. 'Our virtues would be proud if our faults whipped them not and our crimes would despair if they were not cherished by our virtues.'[48] The old doctrine of the 'unity' or 'connectedness' of the virtues can be seen as a warning that this may happen to a particular virtue if left isolated and unchecked. Likewise, the virtue of *innocence*, which unself-consciously refuses to take itself too seriously, helps to guard against this. No virtue is a guarantee of sanctity, but that does not justify a cynicism that sees a virtue as only a mask for subtler and more menacing vices.

3.8.4 Are virtues universal?

Are virtues of universal appeal? Is there a list that has trans-cultural validity, or do they vary from society to society and from one value system to another? A general in wartime may be dictatorial and have self-confidence verging on arrogance. These are hardly 'virtues' we ad-

The Tapestry of Moral Judgement   49

mire in all contexts, but it could be argued that they are virtues in the extremity of battle – provided, of course, they are combined with competence in strategy and logistics! The most sympathetic biographers of Montgomery have conceded that the virtues that made him a brilliant general did not always commend him in civilian life.[49] Some American writers, belonging to a relatively new nation, point to the contrast between the virtues required in a 'frontier' culture and those appropriate for a more settled society. We see this light heartedly in the film *Crocodile Dundee*. Closer to home, the meritocracy of the market economy may need and nurture characters focused on competition, self-reliance and a measure of ruthlessness. All this is fuelled by the promise of dazzling prizes or the threat of failure. Also evident in our contemporary political and business culture is a pronounced unwillingness to acknowledge mistakes; maybe fuelled by a fear of losing face, along with promotion prospects. Both Plato and Nietzsche had a very elitist vision of human life. They stress the virtues of intelligence, nobility and aesthetic enjoyment, but played down a compassion and justice rooted in a belief in a fundamental human equality. Not unlike ancient Sparta, the military culture of Nazism and the Japan of World War II formed a warrior very different from those in the civilian armies of the western allies.[50]

Worrying also is the way in which gender stereotypes have influenced our thinking about virtue. The virtuous woman is a willing subordinate. If she is intelligent she hides it lest she show up her man. She is to be meek, inoffensive and docile. A woman's virtues are those of mothering, nurturing, and generally supporting men released to concentrate on making decisions, making wealth, and exercising power. She nourishes the virtues that make a home rather than make the world. Men may also be imprisoned in an expectation of virtue that betrays gender stereotypes. Men are to be strong, courageous, and adventuresome as they compete in the struggle for existence.

There is debate also about specific virtues. Take, for example, the 'virtue' of courage. In Plato's *Laches* courage is properly so-called and properly esteemed only if serving proper ends.[51] But perhaps it is better to qualify one's admiration for courage than to deny it to the suicide bomber or the SS tank commander invading sovereign territory. A similar difficulty arises over the virtue of loyalty. The loyalty of friends and marriage partners is clearly praiseworthy when it serves their mutual flourishing. But what of the loyalty of Himmler to Hitler? And there may be something more tragic than impressive in the loyalty of a woman to a husband who is persistently abusive and manifestly unworthy of her fidelity. Should her loyalty be balanced against other goods – such as a proper regard for self? Issues such as these are recognized in the traditional idea that a particular virtue has to be monitored through temperance and prudence and expressed in a way that is connected with other virtues.

What general conclusion may we suggest? Some virtues are indeed related to specific social contexts. Aristotle tended to see virtues as enmeshed into a particular form of society. There is sometimes a debate as to what are and what are not laudable character traits. There has to be judgement concerning when a particular virtue has overreached itself and become sour.[52] Each virtue needs to be balanced against others. There is no identikit picture of the perfect moral saint to which everyone is to aspire. We are all different and goodness will manifest itself in different people in different forms. Instructive here is the Christian stress on the distinctiveness of a person's calling. But none of this is to concede to a radical relativism in which 'anything goes'. If the criterion is what nourishes our mutual well-being and what leads to decent relationships then we have a sufficient guide.

3.8.5 Virtues and vices

If there are virtues to admire, tradition also gives us vices to avoid. In the sixth century Gregory identified the 'seven deadly sins'. Virtues were sometimes offered to counter each of these and Chaucer draws on this tradition in the *Parson's Tale*. They are *pride, envy, anger, sloth, gluttony, lust* and *greed*. It is an odd list. It betrays a certain Christian suspicion of bodily passions and enjoyment. It is also odd that things such as cruelty and unkindness are not included. The sins are more self-regarding than other regarding and may betray a worrying preoccupation with saving one's own soul rather than relating well to others. But at least the attempt to identify some cardinal vices gets the discussion going. *Gluttony*, for example, is an obsession with food unmonitored by the virtues of temperance and fortitude. The treatment of the sin of *pride* has a none too respectable history. The weight of western Christian tradition has criticized 'pride' as arrogant self-assertion and self-reliance; a failure to acknowledge our frail humanity, our mutual dependence and our constant need of grace. In the writings of Reinhold Niebuhr we have a brilliant analysis of this.[53] It is valid and salutary as far as it goes. Recent feminist critiques have pointed out, however, that pride such as this tends to be the temptation of able and powerful males. Traditionally, many women have been socialized to have a low sense of self worth. To bully them with accusations of the sin of pride is merely to reinforce their subordination and lack of self-esteem.[54] Sin for such women is the opposite of pride – the failure to appropriate for themselves the dignity and worth that belongs to the daughters of God. The same can be said about oppressed men, since men have sinned against their fellow men as much as against women.

The sin of *anger* also needs careful handling. '*And our playful pastimes let no anger spoil*' utters the sentimental hymn. Surely, however, anger is an appropriate response to exploitation, abuse and injustice? Who cannot be angry at the Holocaust, rape, and children starving or orphaned because of AIDS, bomb or missile? The Hebrew mind was not embarrassed to be angry with God, something our modern sanitized liturgies and 'Praise Services' can forget. But if all this is clear, it is also clear that anger can harden into hatred and resentment. Our anger needs to be watched. This is another example of an impulse that may be wholesome, but which may become unwholesome when not monitored by the cardinal virtues.

It is not surprising that our modern mindset is none too happy with the idea that *lust* is a deadly sin, and Simon Blackburn's monograph attempts to give lust a rehabilitation.[55] It is ridiculous to beat ourselves up because we have sexual desires, enjoy sex, or find another sexually attractive. We might as well beat ourselves up for feeling hungry. Likewise, it is unconvincing to suggest there is something inherently wrong in being carried away by passion as if – following hints of Augustine on a bad day – sexual intercourse should ideally be like a restrained handshake undertaken with procreation in mind. On the contrary, sexual passion may bring intense pleasure and may bless and nourish a relationship of mutual love and delight. Blackburn finds the right note sounded in a somewhat unlikely source – Thomas Hobbes. For Hobbes, lust is a passionate desire for sensual pleasure, the longing for two bodies to be absorbed into each other. But there is also 'a delight of the mind; for it consisteth of two appetites together, to please and to be pleased ... the delight (we) take in delighting.'[56] Thus, A finds pleasure in B, B is pleased at what A is doing, A is pleased at B's pleasure, and so on. Far from being a deadly sin, this brings an intense sensation of shared well-being and nourishes a relationship of love.

We should, therefore, uphold lust's appeal against its conviction. It is not a sin, let alone a deadly one. Of course, lust can be misdirected. There is a danger in an intemperate preoccupation with sex, easily fuelled by the ubiquity of pornography. And there is a danger that the other becomes an object for solo pleasure, or even exploitation, humiliation and abuse. Instead of desiring the other *person*, we can desire their body as a commodity. But lust is not *in itself* a sin – only when it is misdirected, when it is not sanctified by love. We can indeed, following Roger Scruton, render lust a sin *by definition* – by defining lust as sexual desire from which erotic love, tenderness and fidelity have been excluded. We have a right to stipulate how we use words, but the disadvantage of defining lust in this way is that it encourages us to be negative about erotic desire and passion as such.[57]

And *greed*? There is something powerfully counter-cultural in the identification of greed as a deadly sin. An ostentatious greed has become almost a modern virtue for the rich and the celebrity culture. The frantic accumulation of wealth can often be at the expense of much richness in life and character, and can also lead to divisive inequality. There is something hollow, unseemly and unjust in the obsessive consumerism evident in some sectors of our society. This is not to commend asceticism or the disgusted return to the sender of God's good gifts. It is, however, to commend a spirituality that finds fulfilment in the more simple and the more available, and in enjoying without possessing (see 14.4). It follows that Christian faith does not simply moralize about greed. It offers profounder resources for tackling that within the human spirit which feeds greed – the desire for status and trinkets to boost the ego, the thirst for gratification through spiralling consumption, and so forth.

These far too brief reflections do not settle any matters. They merely open a debate. The debate will go on as to what qualities of character we seek to nourish, and how different qualities are to be balanced together; likewise vices. Often so-called virtues and vices are not unqualifiedly good or bad. There needs to be discrimination, self-awareness and judgement. The classic virtue of 'prudence' infuses the art of moral judgement. Prudence takes stock, is realistic, considers the threads and colours in the tapestry and judges how we should behave and what sort of people we seek to be. For this reason, Aquinas described prudence as an intellectual virtue. It is the intelligent application of our moral commitments.

3.8.6 Virtues and moral judgements

'Virtue ethics' not only puts emphasis on what kind of people we are. It may also suggest that persons of virtue have the capacity to judge what is right and good. The good tree produces good fruit. We must not, however, claim too much here, as if the virtues hone in upon the right act like bees to a hive or bears to honey. We cannot link too easily a particular virtue with a particular action or with a particular moral judgement. To use the ugly jargon, virtue ethics must not be allowed to be eliminationist.** In other words, the insights of other approaches may be eliminated because virtue can do all the work for us. However virtuous, we still need guidance or method in making moral judgements. A stress on virtue did not lead the ancient Greeks to see the wrongness of slavery. It did not do the job that a notion of human rights might have done.

A particular form of virtue ethics – the 'situation ethics' of Joseph Fletcher – is guilty of this error.[58] Fletcher rightly objects to an ethic based on inflexible and rigid moral rules. Discarding rules, he urges that all we need is the virtue of love. He treats 'love' as a kind of moral compass, which discerns how to behave, although his illustrations as to what in fact 'love demands' often seem bafflingly intuitive and sometimes contradictory. He confuses a right intention (a loving intention) with a right act. His is an eliminationist approach. Since love is all we need, all other sources of insight can be eliminated. The reality is that however committed we may be to love, we still need resource and method for making moral judgements – such as I have tried to illustrate in this chapter. Love may give us motivation and commitment and nourish our altruism and goodwill. It alone, however, cannot inform a moral judgement. Likewise other virtues can provide rich nuance to our lives, but again we still need other resources besides virtues for making moral judgements. Virtue cannot do all the work in ethics.

Yes – if we cultivate the virtue of love, we will act lovingly. If we cultivate the virtues of humility and generosity, we will act humbly and generously, and so forth. All this is not to be despised. At least it gets us started. But how far it will take us is a moot point. The virtues give us commitment, goodwill and some resource. In addition to the virtues, however, we need other insights to guide us in the art of moral judgement.

3.9 Big words – justice and equality

Ethics is awash with big words, or little words with big meanings. They often carry heavy historical baggage which we need to sort through, but we can hardly do without them. It is a mistake – as some Christians have done – to try to funnel everything through just one word, such as the command to love. An impoverished language means an impoverished vision, leaving us ill equipped to wrestle with the moral dilemmas we face. To revert to our metaphor, each concept can be seen as another strand or colour in the tapestry. In this section we look at just two more, 'justice' and 'equality'.

Justice has many facets of meaning and it would be a mistake to opt for an over-tight definition, which can obscure important aspects. That said, we do need to clarify the concept as best we can. Aristotle's notion of justice refers to basic integrity and fairness in personal relations but, apart from personal relations, the notion of justice is central to social ethics. We thus meet the subtle interplay between an ethic for *personal behaviour* and a *social* ethic for society – an issue to which we will return.

'Justice' is a word used a great deal in the legal context. Legal systems defer to notions of 'natural' justice, which guide laws and legal procedures. Such justice requires equality before the law, impartiality, the presumption of innocence, a right to a fair trial, due process and proper representation. Justice requires that the punishment be just, and that the convicted is not a pawn in some utilitarian strategy for maximizing deterrence or protecting society. There is an issue in contemporary pressure that paedophiles be publicly named. Punishment is about retributive justice, but penal policy is increasingly asking about compensatory justice as well – a just compensation for the victims of crime.

There is also the notion of justice as fairness. In our dealing with one another we should be fair, and society should be fair to its citizens. This sounds great, and, of course, it is an important marker, but the devil is in the detail. What does it mean to be fair? Is it fair that Jane should inherit a million pounds from her parents while John is struggling to get on the property ladder? Is it fair that the receptionist gets only a fraction of the doctor's pay? Aristotle said that justice means treating everyone equally, unless there are morally relevant differences that justify or require different treatment. But what counts as morally relevant? For Aristotle, it was morally relevant that someone was a slave or a woman, just as for western societies it is generally regarded as morally relevant that someone has certain qualifications.

John E. Rawls, writing in the 'social contract'** tradition, invites us to engage in a thought experiment. We envisage ourselves agreeing to enter society, and making a contract together as to the structures and values of the society we agree to. A healthy self-interest is assumed. We make this contract, however, behind a 'veil of ignorance'. This prevents us from opting for an ideology that serves our self-interest.[59] We do not know if we are to be Lord Bertie Wooster, Jeeves or the kitchen maid. We do not know our abilities, social placement or intelligence. We do not know how blessed we will be by luck. Curiously – writing in 1972 – Rawls does not mention gender, but the assumption must be that we do not know that either. We do not in fact know anything that might advantage or disadvantage us. Given all this, we are inclined out of self-interest to agree to a basic justice as fairness. There will be civil liberties, such as freedom of speech and association, freedom of religion and freedom of the press. These freedoms are given equally to all citizens. There will be an even-handed consideration of competing interests. Legal process will be impartial. Regarding the distribution of wealth, the structures will permit the kind of inequality that rewards hard work and initiative. Nevertheless, the distribution serves best the overall well-being of society, and is particularly sensitive to the most disadvantaged. Rawls seems to be proposing that justice as fairness demands a rough compromise as far as the distribution of wealth is concerned. Some inequality is justified to prompt the initiative and enterprise from which society benefits. But the common good and fairness dictates that as far as possible everyone should benefit. Justice also requires a fair distribution of society's burdens alongside its benefits. Such a thought experiment enables us to grasp what justice as fairness involves, since behind the veil of ignorance we are bound ruthlessly to eliminate any considerations of personal privilege.

Rawls takes seriously the claims of a distributive justice consistent with the need to encourage wealth creation, talent and conscientiousness. No doubt hard work and initiative are rightly rewarded. Robert Nozick is more stringent. Ownership is in the hands of individual people. It is people who create wealth through their industry, enterprise and talent. It is immoral for the state to take from people in order to redistribute wealth. This is a form of state theft. If a state taxes to finance welfare, or as part of a redistribution programme, then its action is 'on a par with forced labour'. Tax is permissible only for things such as infrastructure and security. Only a minimal state is a moral state. 'Any state more extensive violates people's rights.' Society's goods are thus acquired and distributed on the basis of legal entitlement and merit. No quarter is given to the vision of the inherent rightfulness of a more equal society.[60] Nozick approves of private charity – but in contrast to redistributive taxation the initiative here comes from the giver.

On this view, justice requires that people keep what they own and demands no more than that they acquire it legally. Nozick is surely right to challenge the Marxist refusal to link a person's contribution to a person's entitlement. Nonetheless, he offers a harsh vision of society. The state is powerless to address mammoth inequalities – including poverty – beyond appealing to the charity of the rich. Furthermore, there is a simplistic naivety in the idea that legal entitlement and acquisition are morally inviolable, since a person's acquisition is possible only because of society's structure together with a large measure of luck. There seems also to be the assumption that the poor are all undeserving. And what about inheritance? Is an entitlement to an inheritance inviolable?

Nozick's social philosophy presupposes an inviolable right to one's own property. By contrast, at least one strand of thinking in the Hebrew Scriptures sees the land as belonging to God and given to humankind on trust. It follows that there is a strong presumption in favour of holding property in common. It is not ours but God's. In pre-modern England the monarch, as God's vicegerent, might give land to those who found favour, often as a reward for valour in battle. This stance may make sense with regard to land and its natural riches, but what about when we create wealth with our own hands and brains? John Locke thus offers the canonical version of the modern theory of a right to property. We have a right to keep the fruits of our labour.[61] This is central to the creed of market capitalism. Of course, 'property' is no longer confined to money and material things. Intellectual property, for example, may bring great wealth and power.

The idea that 'everything should be held in common' is hardly defensible as an ideal, quite apart from practicalities. Our well-being and self-respect require that we each have our own nest with our own straw. One might even appeal to an incarnational theology as resonating with this insight. Even a monk may have his own cell, and his own Bible and rosary beads. This is not so in the *Rule of Saint Benedict,* but even there value is given to communal property.[62] None of this implies, however, that property rights are absolute. The trouble with an inviolable right to property is that it leads to obscene inequalities. Hence the long-standing debate as to the extent to which the state, in the name of a distributive justice, may in a carefully measured way overrule such a right.

There has been much debate in Christian ethics concerning the relationship between justice and love. It seems safe to say that love may predispose the mind in favour of justice. Love never requires less than justice. Again love must respect justice, otherwise 'charity' can be demeaning and paternalistic. There will be situations when love prompts a generosity more than justice requires. Love will challenge structures when they inadequately express justice. Love will certainly find Nozick lacking. On the other hand, in a social context the impartiality of justice may challenge a love that is too partisan, and justice may also challenge a person disinclined to a proper self-love. Justice is for all – including the one who loves. Furthermore, there can be a commitment to justice when the light of love burns dim. That said, for a Christian vision the last word cannot be given to a justice that is calculating and content with fairness and deserts. God's grace gives generously beyond our deserving and for that reason challenges us to build communities that are inclusive, modelled on generosity, and where there is special care for the stranger, the weak and the poor. Writing from a non-theological perspective, Martha Nussbaum also stresses a generous justice extended to the disadvantaged, a generosity not always found in a justice that focuses upon fairness among presumed equals.[63]

Related to all this is another big word – *equality*. Rawls is far more egalitarian than Nozick. Often the term is used in an economic context – concerned with the distribution of wealth. It is difficult to justify total equality. It seems only fair to reward initiative and hard work, and in any case without material incentives it is difficult to see how the world would still go round. If the state were to enact draconian measures to divide the cake equally it would run the danger of reducing it to the size of a bun. The attempt to impose total material equality seems to be a classic example of embracing an unrealistic ideal with the result that the latter state is worse than the first.

None of this, however, justifies complacency over the obscene extremes of wealth (and therefore power) that exist in, say, Britain and America and there is a strong case for revisiting the commitment to a distributive justice of the post-war period – be it one which is realistic politically, consistent with the proper claims of people's entitlement, and consistent with the proper claims of wealth creation; in other words, a better trade off than we currently have. At the same time, an unequal society damages itself through being deprived of the talents of the excluded. Inequality also causes disaffection, social division and unrest. Thus, if measures of redistribution shrink some parts of the cake they may expand other parts. Furthermore, a nation's prime goal should not be that of baking the biggest possible economic cake, a goal subordinating all others.

That said, we hear more today about 'equality of opportunity' than about 'equality of outcome'. For 'equality of outcome' the benefits of society – principally wealth and income – are shared more equally, the debate being about what we mean by 'more'. If there is only 'equality of opportunity' everyone is supposed to begin the race for power and wealth on the same terms, but the prizes still go to the swift and strong. 'Equality of opportunity' is a fine phrase, but the reality is that there can be no equality of opportunity in a society that is seriously unequal economically. The idea of a level playing field meritocracy is a myth. One reason why this is so is obvious. In a meritocratic society social placement depends very largely on education, but access to education is economically dependent. The rich can send their children to private schools or buy expensive houses in catchment areas of 'good' state ones. It is a vicious circle that puts a damper on social mobility. Moreover, 'equality of opportunity' gives no justice to those less well endowed, nor to the sick and disabled. The appeal to 'equality of opportunity' can become a cop out for not facing hard questions of justice. For this reason, some have spoken of an 'equality of possibility' as a concept that is more realistic about reasons for disadvantage and exclusion.[64]

If we are to speak of equality, we need to ask: Between whom, of what and to what degree? The notion has a wider purview than that so far mentioned. There is equality of esteem and rights accorded across the age cohorts and which is blind to ethnic origin. There is equality between the sexes, and equality before the law. None of this, however, can be independent of economic justice. 'Justice is open to all – just like the Ritz hotel', Lord Denning is reputed to have said.

More basically, the notion of equality expresses a conviction about our common humanity. The founders of the American Constitution thought it self-evident that all men are born equal – and we hope the best of them by 'men' meant 'people'. But what does this mean? This is not easy to sort out, either for Christian or for secular thought (see 5.3.1). One thing that it implies, however, is a basic equality with regard to esteem, respect and fundamental rights. Again, the devil is in the detail. What are these rights to which everyone has entitlement? Does everyone have a right to health care? This is a fundamental principle of the British National Health Service – equal entitlement at the point of need – but it is not accepted as such in the American culture.

R. H. Tawney stressed that a greater economic equality is achievable only within a culture where there is a belief in the fundamental equality of human beings, and this is fed by things such education, decent living standards and the right to vote. Such things 'dissolve the servile complex' and give people self-confidence.[65] It means 'one society' that is not class ridden. People are ends and not means. To achieve this requires for many 'intellectual conversion'.[66] It follows that for Tawney greater equality was not to be imposed, or entrusted to grow through inexorable laws of historical development as for classical Marxism. It had to be chosen through the democratic process. He saw as crucial the drip-feed into a culture of Christian values. This raises the question of how much equality, however desirable, is politically achievable. In democracies the achievable depends upon popular consent, or at least acquiescence.

It follows that any attempt on the part of the state and other structures of society to further justice, and even more so equality, will be in tension with a commitment to freedom. The reality is that no society can achieve a perfect combination of justice, equality, social cohesion, freedom and prosperity. New York Harbour has a Statue of Liberty, but not of Justice. The most we can hope for is a tolerable and achievable compromise. And even within a nation – let alone between nations – what is achievable may often be only barely tolerable. The notion of freedom – both personal and social – is discussed elsewhere (Chapters 6, 11 and 12). Justice and equality will be further discussed in Chapters 11 and 12, 13 and 14.

There is a danger that notions of distributive justice and equality can be associated with a paternalistic and even disempowering social engineering. Justice and equality are imposed, say, through welfare programmes and progressive taxation and so can become a largess handed out by the powerful. This leaves unaddressed the causes of injustice through institutional oppression. Justice is not only about everyone being the recipient of their fair share. Justice is about empowering and enabling so that people no longer need the 'powerful' to dispense justice on the less fortunate.

Iris Young objects to notions of distributive justice for this reason. Justice is about extending possibilities for people's lives through, say, an equality of social power, parity of esteem, a proper autonomy, freedom to make choices and enfranchisement. This widening of the notion of justice takes us beyond the distribution of wealth. As examples she points to the injustice of the disenfranchisement of workers in a multi-national company, and the injustice of the way in which certain people are portrayed in the media, as when Muslims are portrayed as potential terrorists.[67] There is injustice in the deprivation of meaningful work, whatever the salary. Gender injustice is another obvious example. In other words, the structures of our society throw up many forms of injustice, which are not properly named when we focus simply on the distribution of wealth. Indeed, in rejecting as inadequate the idea of justice as being concerned primarily with the distribution of material goods, she almost turns full circle in returning to a more classical mode. Justice is about confronting all forms of domination or oppression.

3.10 Fulfilling our nature

Deeply ingrained in western ethical thought is the notion of 'natural law'. An ambiguous concept, different writers may mean different things by it. Can we identify some of the strands?

One strand is the rejection of scepticism and relativism. A distinction is made between laws that express cultural convention, and a moral standard that constrains and guides all human beings – a 'natural law'. The distinction goes back to Plato and his critique of the Sophists. In natural science a 'natural law' is a statement of how physical things *do in fact* behave (or, more accurately, an empirically derived attempt to discern regularities in nature). Likewise, in ethics a 'natural law' is a statement of how human beings – whatever their culture – *ought* to behave. The status and origin of this may be understood in various ways and may sometimes be very obscure; but one thrust of natural law thinking remains this rejection of scepticism. It is not surprising that relations between sovereign states have given impetus to such thinking, as in *On the Law of War and Peace* by Grotius in 1625. Sovereign states can enact laws applying within their boundaries. But are there 'higher' laws governing states themselves?

There is, however, another strand in natural law thinking that is more relevant to our argument. If natural law thinking speaks of what is normative, and not simply conventional, it also finds in what a human person is – their nature – a guide to the right and the good. To pursue the good is to follow and complete one's own nature. The right thing to do is the natural thing to do. This connects with our claim earlier that our exploration of what serves human flourishing is integrated with our vision of what a human person *is*, their 'end'.

3.10.1 Potentials for disaster

A glance at history will show that this approach has sometimes led to disaster. This is because of a tendency towards *social conservatism* on the one hand, and towards *biological reductionism* on the other.

By social conservatism I mean the uncritical acceptance of the *status quo* as 'natural'. It is 'natural' for women to be subordinate to men; it is 'natural' for some to be ruled and others to be rulers; it is 'natural' for women to be primarily child bearers and home makers. Wollstonecraft and Mill were among those who made early challenge to these ideas.[68] It is rarely if ever said of men in a parallel way that their prime natural role is that of fatherhood. There is a terrible tyranny in the insistence that the laws of commerce are the laws of nature and therefore the immutable laws of God: a remark of Edmund Burke.[69] We will encounter later the idea that the 'order of creation' is such as to limit legitimate sexual relationships to the heterosexual (15.4). We are thus prevented from asking awkward questions, taking risks or trying experiments. Our freedom is limited by 'nature'. What has so often been dubbed as 'natural' is now easily seen to be relative to a particular culture or world view. Even worse, the natural law argument has been used to justify the dominance or privilege of one group over others.

Vatican sexual ethics are often criticized for biological reductionism. In sexual intercourse the natural 'given' is the oneness of the 'relational' and the 'procreative'. In other words, sexual intercourse by nature integrates the nourishing of a relationship of love with procreation. The love-making must be open to procreation and the child is a gift arising out of the love-making. It follows that both contraception and *in vitro* fertilization are contrary to natural law. The same is the case with any sexual activity that is not vaginally penetrative, and thereby infertile – masturbation, oral sex and homosexuality.[70] The norm of the 'natural' here is taken from the biological integrity of sex as being about both the uniting of two people and openness to the gift of new life. We must not by deliberate act take what nature has joined together and put it asunder.

There is indeed something wonderful about the way in which a new life arises out of love-making, and Vatican sexual ethics renders a service in reminding us of this. The mistake – in its objection to both contraception and *in vitro* fertilization – is in claiming that what can be said about sexual intercourse in its general biological totality must also be said of every act of sexual intercourse, or that what is generally the case about procreation must be said of every instance.[71] Moreover, *in vitro* fertilization does not prevent a child from being still a gift arising out of a loving relationship. The 'biological reductionism' is found not in respecting the biological realities, nor in seeing such realities as part of nature's gift, but rather in the refusal to allow that the biological realities still permit responsible choices. Natural law arguments here are used to imprison us when we should be free. Reliable contraception is one of the great gifts of the modern world – liberating people to enjoy their sexuality without the fear of serial childbearing. If nature has given us two good things joined together, why cannot we, by responsible decision, judge that sometimes they can be separated? Likewise, why cannot the pain of infertility be overcome through medical science? In a different way, the child still arises out of a couple's love. Thus, the Roman Catholic theologian Josef Fuchs offers a more dynamic approach to natural law: 'The reality we call nature is also matter in our hands to be formed and ... humanized and personalized.'[72]

Biological reductionism is further found in an 'evolutionary ethic', which adopts the 'survival of the fittest' philosophy as a pattern for society, the phrase, incidentally deriving not from Darwin but from Herbert Spencer.[73] A crude 'evolutionary ethic' may thus justify unrestrained capitalism where the strong prosper and the weak are pushed to the walls.[74] Society's development and pattern simply follows that of nature.

This brings us to a further difficulty, and an obvious and crucial one, with taking 'nature' and the 'natural' as a norm for ethics. Why, we might ask, should the 'natural' be, by virtue of being natural, also good? There is an obvious difficulty when straightforward empirical facts about 'nature' are treated as the moral norm. The 'natural' is full of moral ambiguities. Ask any lamb being chased by a lion. We even use nature sometimes as a source of moral warning – as when we speak of the slyness of the fox. Thus the biologist Richard Dawkins is Darwinian in biology but anti-Darwinian in the sphere of human society and human relationships.[75] Adolf Hitler in his *Table Talk* justified his political programmes by an appeal to the pattern of nature. 'The law of selection justifies this incessant struggle by allowing the survival of the fittest. Christianity is a rebellion against nature, a protest against nature.'[76] Such an abuse of evolutionary biology would have appalled Darwin, as it would Dawkins.

It is not therefore surprising that natural law arguments are widely thought to be completely discredited. All too often an appeal to the constraint of 'nature' has violated legitimate human aspiration, and has even been used to justify evil. Existentialism celebrates freedom from such notions with the cry that 'existence precedes essence'**. We are free to pursue our own ends as we judge appropriate, and without fear or favour. There is no common understanding of human good which informs, constrains or lures us. We invent our own good. It follows that for Cupitt the notion of 'human nature' is either empty or a cultural construct.[77]

3.10.2 *Other possibilities*

These are serious concerns, but it is important to remember that some of the profoundest appeals to natural law have been neither conservative nor reactionary. This is so on two accounts. First, they have maintained that in following nature we should follow the 'natural end' or 'true nature' of humanity and this is not necessarily to be identified with biological origins or *status quo*. Sometimes we transcend straightforward empirical nature and in so doing develop nature in a new way, or discern our 'true' nature. Such a vision of our 'true nature' may encourage a rigorous criticism of the *status quo*. It may demand that we transcend the merely biological. It belongs to our nature that we may grow into what we are to become. In theological terms the conception is 'eschatological'**. This was the perspective of Aquinas and, in his own way, Aristotle.[78]

The second reason is a development of this. Humans are rational animals. Thus, for humanity to follow their 'nature' is to follow reason.[79] Reason involves thinking, discernment, working things out. When we use our reason to discern our 'true' nature beyond the *status quo* a 'natural law' approach to ethics can be more revolutionary than reactionary.

Both of these features have implicit within them a response to the obvious criticism of a cruder understanding of natural law which we have just encountered. If morality is about 'following nature' what about those occasions when I have a duty to resist nature? These problems do not arise if we use reason to judge what is our 'true nature'. The question, therefore, is not, '*What is natural?*', if by this we mean that we follow uncritically whatever impulse seems the strongest. The question is rather, '*Are there constraints and guides in our nature which inform our judgement?*' All this is a far cry from the caricature of 'natural law' as a detailed morality read off from biological data and cemented into our consciences.

From this perspective we may critique the approach to sexuality found in the papal encyclicals we have cited on its own strict natural law terms. It is a characteristic of nature that she evolves. As she evolves there develops the novel and surprising. The drama of cosmic evolution provides myriads of examples of this. Thus, sex, beginning as a biological mechanism for perpetuating life, has become that which expresses and nourishes a relationship of love and mutual delight. The latter is as much 'natural' as the former. As argued above, if nature has given us two good things that are conjoined, what is wrong with making a responsible judgement sometimes to separate them? We may use reason to understand this and distinguish between sexual expression that is abusive and exploitive and that which expresses love and gift.

Vatican theology would, of course, affirm this as robustly as any; but why then insist that every act of love making must be open to procreation, simply because 'nature' has bolted them together?

Stimulating as these ideas may be, there is a serious difficulty. If we speak of our 'true end' or our 'real nature' we are no longer reading off natural law from empirical observation. We are introducing an element of evaluation. The more we remain with the empirical, the less useful it is as a guide for moral thinking. The more we depart from the empirical, the more we move into the realm of an evaluation that is neither helped nor hindered by a conception of the 'natural'. Are we arguing in a circle? Our values derive from 'nature' but we define 'true nature' in terms of our values.

The answer is that the argument is more constructively spiral than viciously circular. 'Human nature' is not infinitely malleable clay at the hands of the cultural potter or the potter of existential autonomy. There is a basic givenness. Criticisms of bad natural law thinking merely burn away the dross and allow us to find some guide to our moral thinking in basic facts about our humanity. The errors of the past haunt us, and should do as terrible warnings. Nonetheless, it does seem an enduring fact of human nature that we form companionships, and are nourished by relationships of loyalty and love. It is a fact of human nature that we are creative and gain fulfilment through creativity. It is a fact of human nature that we are embodied and sexual. This involves finding fulfilment in feeling and sensing. Being rational, we find fulfilment through intellectual activity. If these and similar statements are allowed, they do have implications for ethics, as the Roman Catholic moral theologian John Finnis has argued, along with others.[80] Christians may add the insistence that it is a fact of our nature that we are created in the divine image and that our chief end is to glorify God and enjoy God forever. Ethics has to relate to us, to what kind of creatures we are, and to this world. Ethics is not about alien standards imposed upon us by some transcendent realm and unconnected with our nature and our time and place. Despite warnings from past errors, a critical openness (and it needs to be highly critical) to the guidance for moral judgement contained in some conception of what it is to be human must be a strand in the tapestry. If the generalizations of natural law can be oppressive, the totally free particularity of an individual's choice can be shallow, isolated and impoverished. The admittedly imprecise notion of 'true nature' may thus be thought of as an attempt to identify basic and enduring facts about being human such as guide our discovery of what serves our flourishing.

This leads to another aspect of natural law thinking. Precisely because the right and the good resonate with and serve our nature, there is nothing inscrutable or oppressive about ethics. We are not servile subjects of commands and prohibitions that have neither rhyme nor reason. The right and the good follow the 'grain of our nature', and therefore, in Augustine's phrase, we can 'love what is commanded'. This is why the 'Euthyphro Dilemma'[81] is wrongly posed. 'Does God forbid murder because it is wrong, or is it wrong because God forbids it?' It is wrongly posed because it deals with moral standards as abstractions, unrelated to the kind of world we live in and the kind of creatures humans are.

These reflections invite a brief comment on Oliver O'Donovan's work, *Resurrection and Moral Order.* Christian ethics, he maintains, has an objective reference because it is concerned with life in accordance with the 'order of things' as God has made them. The way the universe is determines how we ought to behave.[82] One example is the reality of human nature as social, and this affords a reason for us to pursue, for example, friendship.[83] It is for this reason that a Christian ethic may connect with the wider generic ethical thinking of humankind since all humankind lives within the same created order.

At the same time, we are manifestly confused in our understanding of this created order. Christian perception, however, will clarify our perception of God's created order.[84] 'The Christian sees in Christ and in the order of the world to come the vindication and perfect manifestation of the created order which was always there but never fully expressed.'[85] It is for this reason that he prefers to avoid the phrase 'natural law' speaking instead of 'created order'.[86]

With none of this, offered as a very broad theological framework, I wish to quarrel. Where I am concerned is where O'Donovan is overprescriptive and over-confident in defining in what this created order consists. I do not claim this of his belief that procreation within the marriage covenant of affection and loyalty is resonant with 'created order'. This, he argues, is the way things are with the human condition. It is not just an accident of a particular cultural history.[87] Despite his commendation of 'epistemological guardedness'[88] he is, however, elsewhere over-prescriptive and lacking caution in defining what the created order requires. In sexual relationships, for example, he permits only celibacy and heterosexual marriage. Those who are gay must be within the former category.[89] To this issue we return in 15.4. I wish to follow O'Donovan in finding in 'created order' a guide to ethical judgement but, nonetheless, not to find this guidance always as specific as he does.

To conclude, part of the glory of being human is that we are not imprisoned by nature and instinct in the way other animals are. We have freedom and reason, which enable us to make choices. *What we may become* is as important as *what by nature we are*. Indeed, human nature is about becoming as much as about being. At the same time, we are not made of clay that is infinitely malleable. There are contours in 'human nature' which constrain and guide our ethical thinking. There is a limit to what humans are likely to find leads to their flourishing. We cannot say that *anything* may constitute human good. What is good for us depends on our nature and there is nothing trite in the claim that 'by nature' we find our well-being in freedom, in love, in community with others, in creativity, and such like. We are, nonetheless, a far cry from a tight regimentation imposed by partisan ideas of what 'nature requires'. The broad parameters still leave much room for controversy, but also for freedom and creativity. Some Christians may deplore this. But why? Maybe this is part of what we mean by the glorious liberty of the people of God.

3.11 Conclusion to Part 1

In this first part of the book I have argued that ethics concerns, cautiously, confronting our egoism and ameliorating the human condition, but more ambitiously discovering that which serves our mutual flourishing and expresses decent relationships. Despite differences between us – differences that should be honoured since the freedom to live with our differences is part of what constitutes our mutual well-being – there remains still a common humanity. This enables us to explore together what serves our mutual good. Ethics thus has a proper place in the public realm and on ethical issues we can reasonably expect some meeting of minds.

In this chapter I have drawn on the history of ethical reflection in order to find insight into what considerations might be relevant in making moral judgements. These considerations help to fill out our understanding of what constitutes our mutual well-being. They serve as threads or colours for weaving the tapestry of moral judgement. Having identified these threads and colours, we still need to ask what guidance there is when we actually begin weaving. Before we do that, however, we need to ask what resources can be brought to bear from Christian faith.

The insight of this last chapter makes it clear that so-called secular** ethics is a mature and resourceful area of human thought that should be regarded with respect. So-called 'secular ethics' can serve us well and adequately. Christians are bound, however, to allow their Christian faith to nuance and sometimes significantly reshape their understanding of ethics. In Part 2, I ask how this might be so and thus how theological perspectives might offer further resource to the craft of weaving the tapestry of moral judgement.

Notes

1 This example is Philippa Foot's in 'Moral Beliefs' (1958), reprinted in Philippa Foot, *Virtues and Vices*, Oxford, Blackwell, 1978, p. 111.

2 Dorothy Emmet, *The Moral Prism*, London, Macmillan, 1979. Also Bernard Williams in *Ethics and the Limits of Philosophy*, London, Fontana, Collins, 1985, objects to an expectation of conceptual simplicity in ethics (p. 17).

3 E.g. Carol Gilligan, *In a Different Voice*, Harvard University Press, 1982.

4 Jeremy Bentham, *An Introduction to the Principles of Morals and Legislation*, 1789.

5 John Stuart Mill, *Utilitarianism* (1859), (ed.) A. D. Lindsay, London, Dent, Everyman Edition, 1910, chapter II, p. 9.

6 So-called 'Ideal Utilitarianism' finds expression in Henry Sidgwick, *The Methods of Ethics*, London, Macmillan, 1874 and G. E. Moore, *Principia Ethica*, Cambridge, 1903. A 'theological' version is found in Hastings Rashdall's *Theory of Good and Evil*, Oxford, 1907.

7 D. M. MacKinnon, *A Study in Ethical Theory*, London, A. & C. Black, 1957, p. 46.

8 John Stuart Mill, *On Liberty* (1861), Everyman Edition, 1910, pp. 67–8.

9 Mill, *Utilitarianism*, chapter 5, p. 42.

10 John Austin, *The Province of Jurisprudence Determined*, London, John Murray, second edition, 1861, p. 101.

11 R. M. Hare, *Freedom and Reason*, Oxford, Oxford University Press, 1963, p. 223.

12 As argued by J. L. Mackie, *Ethics Inventing Right and Wrong*, Harmondsworth, Pelican, pp. 89–90.

13 Thus, R. M. Hare, *Freedom and Reason*, pp. 15–18.

14 Immanuel Kant, *Groundwork of the Metaphysics of Morals*, (ed.) H. J. Paton, *The Moral Law*, Hutchinson, 1948, p. 84.

15 E.g. John Locke, *An Essay Concerning the True Original Extent and End of Civil Government*, 1690, especially chapter 5.

16 Mary Warnock, *An Intelligent Person's Guide to Ethics*, London, Duckworth, 1998, p. 66.

17 Kieran Cronin, *Rights and Christian Ethics*, Cambridge, Cambridge University Press, 1992, pp. 252, 259.

18 Article Five.

19 Thomas Nagel, *The View from Nowhere*, Oxford, Oxford University Press, 1986, p. 176.

20 C. Fried, *Right and Wrong*, Cambridge, Massachusetts, Harvard, 1978, p. 9.

21 Nagel, *The View from Nowhere*, p. 177.

22 Fried, *Right and Wrong*, p. 13.

23 F. H. Bradley, *Ethical Studies*, Oxford, 1876, second edition, 1927, pp. 160ff.

24 W. David Ross, *The Foundations of Ethics*, Oxford, 1939, pp. 84–6.

25 Plato, *Republic*, I.331.

26 John Betjeman, poem on 'Christmas'.

27 Michael Ignatieff in Kenneth Roth and Minky Worden (eds), *Torture: Does it make us safer?*, London, New Press, 2005.

28 Thomas Aquinas, *Summa Theologiae*, II-II 66.7.

29 Paul Ramsey, 'The Case of the Curious Exception' in Gene H. Outka

and Paul Ramsey (eds), *Norm and Context in Christian Ethics*, London, SCM Press, 1968, pp. 67ff.

30 Jean Porter, *Moral Action and Christian Ethics*, Cambridge, Cambridge University Press, 1995, p. 96.

31 John Paul II, *Veritatis Splendor*, Vatican, 1993, paragraph 75.

32 *Veritatis Splendor*, paragraph 67.

33 John Finnis, *Natural Law and Natural Rights*, Oxford, Clarendon, 1980, pp. 86ff.

34 *Veritatis Splendor*, paragraph 90.

35 As suggested by Charles E. Curran, *The Moral Theology of John Paul II*, London, Continuum, 2005, p. 138.

36 *Veritatis Splendor*, paragraph 80.

37 Kant, *Groundwork of the Metaphysics of Morals*, p. 84.

38 See Dorothy Emmet, *Rules, Roles and Relations*, London, Macmillan, 1966.

39 Susan Wolf, 'Moral Saints' in R. Crisp and M. Slote (eds), *Virtue Ethics*, Oxford, 1997, pp. 79ff.

40 Kant, *Groundwork of the Metaphysics of Morals*, pp. 59–65.

41 H. J. Paton, *The Categorical Imperative*, London, Hutchinson, 1947, p. 48.

42 Elizabeth Anscombe's 1958 paper was an early influential attempt to revive interest in 'virtue ethics'. This is 'Modern Moral Philosophy' reprinted in many symposia, for example W. D. Hudson, *The Is/Ought Question*, London, Macmillan, 1969. Also R. Crisp and M. Slote (eds), *Virtue Ethics*, Oxford 1997.

43 John Stott, *New Issues Facing Christians Today*, London, Marshall Pickering, second edition, 1990; N. Gumbel, *Searching Issues*, Eastbourne, Kingsway, revised edition, 1998.

44 Karl Rahner, *Theological Investigations*, Vol. II, London, DLT, 1975, pp. 271ff.

45 E.g. Proverbs 4.23; Micah 6.8; Matthew 5.3ff.; Galatians 5.22–3; Colossians 3.12–14.

46 E.g. Reinhold Niebuhr, *An Interpretation of Christian Ethics*, New York, Harper, 1935; *Moral Man and Immoral Society*, New York, Scribner, 1932.

47 E.g. David Hume, *Treatise of Human Nature*, Part II, Book II, Section VII, (ed.) L. A. Selby-Bigg, Oxford, 1888, pp. 369ff.; Hare, *Freedom and Reason*, pp. 122, 171.

48 Shakespeare, *All's Well that Ends Well*, Act 4, Scene III.

49 E.g. Nigel Hamilton, *Monty. The Battles of Field Marshall Bernard Montgomery*, London, Hodder & Stoughton, 1981, pp. 225–7.

50 Max Hastings, *Armageddon*, London, Macmillan, 2004, p. 105.

51 Plato, *Laches*, 192.D ff.

52 Charles Causley's poem 'Twelve Types of Hospital Visitor' is a good satirical exposure of this danger.

53 E.g. Reinhold Niebuhr, *The Nature and Destiny of Man*, London, Nisbet, 1941, Volume I, chapter 7.

54 E.g. Mary Grey, *Redeeming the Dream*, London, SPCK, 1989, pp. 17–19.

55 Simon Blackburn, *Lust*, Oxford, Oxford University Press, 2004.

56 Thomas Hobbes, *The Elements of Law Natural and Politic*, (ed.) J. C. A. Gaskin, Oxford, Oxford University Press, 1994, Pt. I, Chapter IX, Section 15, p. 555, quoted by Blackburn, *Lust*, p. 86.

57 Roger Scruton, *Sexual Desire*, London, Weidenfeld & Nicolson, 1986, p. 344.

58 Joseph Fletcher, *Situation Ethics*, London, SCM Press, 1966.

59 John Rawls, *A Theory of Justice*, Oxford, Oxford University Press, 1972, pp. 136–7.

60 Robert Nozick, *Anarchy State and Utopia*, Oxford, Blackwell, 1974, pp. 167ff.

61 E.g. John Locke, *An Essay Concerning the True and Original Extent and End of Civil Government*, (1690), chapter 5 'Of Property', (ed.) W. S. Carpenter, London, Dent, Everyman, 1924, pp. 129ff.

62 As seeen in the duties of the cellarer in Chapters 31 and 32 of the *Benedictine Rule*.

63 Martha C. Nussbaum, *The Frontiers of Justice*, Cambridge, Massachusetts, Harvard University Press, 2006, especially chapters 1–3.

64 Anthony Giddens, *The Third Way*, Cambridge Polity Press, 1998, pp. 101ff.

65 Richard H. Tawney, *Equality*, London, Allen & Unwin, fourth edition, 1952, p. 120.

66 Richard H. Tawney, *The Acquisitive Society*, London, Fontana, Collins, 1921 and 1961, p. 176.

67 Iris Young, *Justice and the Politics of Difference*, Princeton, 1990, pp. 16ff.

68 Mary Wollstonecraft, *A Vindication of the Rights of Woman* (1792), John Stuart Mill, *On the Subjection of Women* (1869).

69 Edmund Burke, *Thoughts and Details On Scarcity*, (1795), W.V.157.

70 E.g. Sacred Congregation for the Doctrine of the Faith, *Persona Humana*, Vatican, 1975, Section IX.

71 English Catholic Bishops, *In Vitro Fertilization: Morality and Public Policy*, 1983, paragraph 24. See also John Paul II, *Evangelium Vitae*, Vatican, 1995, Chapter 1, Paragraph 14; and *Catechism of the Catholic Church*, Geoffrey Chapman, 1994, pp. 2377–79.

72 Josef Fuchs, *Human Values and Christian Morality*, Dublin, Gill & Macmillan, 1970, p. 116.

73 See Mary Midgley, *Evolution as a Religion*, London, Methuen, 1985, pp. 6, 118.

74 A. G. N. Flew, *Evolutionary Ethics*, London, Macmillan, 1967.

75 Richard Dawkins, *The Selfish Gene*, second edition, Oxford, Oxford University Press, 1989, pp. 200–1. Likewise in *The Devil's Chaplain*, Weidenfeld & Nicolson, 2003, pp. 10–11.

76 Quoted by Mary Midgley, *Evolution as a Religion*, p. 119.

77 Don Cupitt, *The New Christian Ethics*, London, SCM Press, 1988, pp. 12, 114.

78 Aquinas, *Summa Theologiae*, I.5.5.

79 Aquinas, *Summa Theologiae*, I-II q.93–4.

80 Finnis, *Natural Law and Natural Rights*, pp. 86ff. We recall also the earlier reference to Nussbaum.

81 Plato, *Euthryphro*, 10A.

82 Oliver O'Donovan, *Resurrection and Moral Order*, Leicester, Apollos, second edition, 1994, p. 17.

83 O'Donovan, *Resurrection and Moral Order*, p. xi.

84 O'Donovan, *Resurrection and Moral Order*, p. 19.

85 O'Donovan, *Resurrection and Moral Order*, p. 53.

86 O'Donovan, *Resurrection and Moral Order*, p. 85.
87 O'Donovan, *Resurrection and Moral Order*, p. 69.
88 O'Donovan, *Resurrection and Moral Order*, p. 19.
89 O'Donovan, *Resurrection and Moral Order*, p. 70.

Part 2

Christian Perspectives

4

Placing Christian Ethics

4.1 Introduction

My neighbour and I are both keen gardeners. Often we chat about matters horticultural over the fence – Have you tried this new variety of petunia? How can we rid the aubergines of white fly? – and so forth.

My neighbour is an atheist and I am a Christian, but our theological disagreement does not impinge upon our horticultural deliberations. I may indeed claim that the whole earth, and, of course, my garden in particular, is charged with the grandeur of God, but such high themes do not affect how we look after our patch. The right pH rating for azaleas is the right pH rating whether or not there is a God. In theological terms, God has given horticulture 'autonomy'. It is part of creation, and as part of creation it has separate being. Horticulturalists may attend to their craft free from the fear of being harassed by theologians.

But suppose our conversation moves away from petunias and aubergines. My neighbour's ageing mother is in her nineties, in residential care, and fed up with life which she feels has no quality. She prays every night that the 'Lord will take her'. 'We would not let a rabbit suffer like that,' he says, protesting against a law that criminalizes the medical assistance of dying. Or suppose we find ourselves discussing military intervention to effect 'regime change', or suppose we discuss the claim of a single woman in her forties that she has a 'right' to a child.

We have now moved from gardening to ethics. Can atheists and Christians debate ethical issues together? Can there be a meeting of minds? Is ethics 'autonomous' like horticulture – or for that matter chemistry or Greek grammar? Is there an 'autonomous' area of ethical thought which serves as common ground for Christians and atheists? Or are there 'secular'** ethics and 'Christian' ethics and never the twain shall meet? When we discuss ethical issues, to what extent, if at all, do we appeal to considerations that make sense to us and to others *simply as human beings*? Or to what extent do we appeal to considerations that weigh only for Christians? Both Christians and non-Christians care passionately about ethical issues. But how is their passionate concern related? How are we to understand the relationship between so-called 'Christian' ethics and the wider 'secular' ethical thinking of humankind?

In Part 1 I argued that it is primarily as human beings, and not as Christians, that we make moral judgements. So-called 'secular' ethics is a mature and resourceful tradition of human thought and we can get on perfectly well without religion. We can approach ethical issues with competence and sophistication without any appeal to theology. It is for this reason that ethics can find its place within the public realm. In the last chapter I illustrated the rich insight to be gained from secular moral philosophy – so-called.

Ethics can manage well without religion. At the same time I wish to argue that Christian faith introduces a rich further dimension. It is to this that I now turn in Part 2. Tertullian posed the question 'What has Athens to do with Jerusalem?' 'Jerusalem' is a metaphor for the community of faith. 'Athens' is a metaphor for the wider human community and its thought and culture. In doing ethics, do we begin in Athens or in Jerusalem? And wherever we begin, when do we visit the other place, for how long, and what is the purpose of our stay? Do we try somehow to bring Athens and Jerusalem together? Or do we spend all our time in Jerusalem and completely ignore Athens? In our multi-faith society we need to ask, of course, not only about Jerusalem and Athens but also about Mecca, Calcutta, Amritsa, Lhasa and others. We will consider this question in Chapter 8. For the present we confine ourselves simply to Jerusalem and Athens.

In responding to Tertullian's question many fall into one or other of two polarized camps. In the one camp there is the slogan: *Keep religion out of ethics!* Religion is at best irrelevant to, at worst an enemy of, the good life. In building a society that is free, just and sustainable, religion is part of the problem, not part of the solution. In the other camp are Christians who insist that Christian ethics are so distinctive in style, basis and content, that there is limited common ground with those outside the community of faith. So-called 'secular' and so-called 'Christian' ethics are alternatives – even opposed. Christians stage their own ethics party, to which Christians only are invited and where the fare is anyway only to Christian taste. *Christian ethics is special!*

The position of this book is different from either stance. Standing somewhere in the middle, I wish to defend a position more complicated and nuanced. In Part 1, I argued that it is primarily as human beings that we explore ethical matters. We appeal to reasons, considerations and visions that may be common to us all. This is not to suggest that agreement is always easily gained. Neither is it to deny that the whole enterprise is complicated and contentious. But it is simply a fact that there is public debate about ethics, which does not work within any theological perspective. Whether we are atheist or Christian we do ethics as human beings and not exclusively as atheist or Christian. It follows that we can seek with a measure of confidence a meeting of minds and common ground. We saw in Part 1 that the resources of so-called 'secular' moral philosophy bring rich resources to the making of moral judgements, resources that give depth and focus to our notion of well-being and flourishing. Athens is to be respected and its insights valued and cherished.

At the same time, however, I wish to argue that religious belief properly nuances our approach to ethics in all kinds of ways – providing a wider context, a deeper rationale and motivation, and sometimes a radical reshaping.

4.2 Keep religion out of ethics!

Some in the churches assume that by right they occupy the high moral ground. Ethics is their trade. From this vantage point they survey with dismay 'declining moral standards' and the 'moral confusion' of society. The Church is a beacon of moral rectitude in a wayward land.

Many, however, dispute this. Religion is an enemy of the good life. Christian ethics is subject to a stringent moral critique. People reject religion on grounds that are in part moral. We put our heads in the sand if we do not listen to this case, wrestle with it, respond to it and learn from it. This is serious. People outside the Church (or even within it!) are hardly interested in debates about an 'essential' or 'economic' understanding of the Trinity, 'orders' of ministry, or how the Council of Chalcedon of 451 may speak to us about the person of Christ. But they do look at the Church's stance on ethical issues, and in the eyes of many 'Christian ethics' it has lost its credibility. Some in the nineteenth century rejected Christian doctrine, but retained the Christian ethic. Many today, however, reject what they perceive to be Christian ethics as well.

4.2.1 The style of Christian ethics

First, Anthony Grayling and Simon Blackburn represent many who object that religious morality is based on unthinking obedience to divine commands. These commands may have neither rhyme nor reason as far as we can see. They need not serve human well-being. We just obey. Obedience is what is central, even blind obedience.[1]

Not surprisingly, Grayling cites the story of Abraham and Isaac.[2] Although he does not make the connection, he follows Kierkegaard's classic interpretation.[3] God's command overrules Abraham's clear sense of his duty as a father. There is a 'teleological suspension of ethics'. In other words, Abraham's sense of duty towards his son is overruled by something higher. This something higher is a divine command that brutally violates his profoundest conviction as to how a parent should behave.

Such religious morality, based on blind obedience, is anti-humanistic for two reasons. First, because what is commanded may not serve, indeed it may even diminish, human well-being. Second, it is anti-humanistic because even if what is commanded does serve human good, the call to unquestioning obedience violates our dignity and proper autonomy. We should do the right and live the good life because we discern ourselves how we should live. The truly moral person does not do what is right in blind obedience to some inscrutable authority.[4] The truly moral person is appropriately autonomous, owning their vision of the right and the good. A humanist morality treats us as adults capable of discerning and judging. This recalls the critique of 'religious morality' by Patrick Nowell Smith. Religious people are infantile in their approach to morality because they simply obey the given of inscrutable rules.[5] They do not behave as mature adults who think through their own moral judgements, for which they can give reasons and which they can themselves own.

If, however, we discern for ourselves, we do not need the crutch of religious authority. At most, the authority can nourish and deepen our insight. Once, however, that insight has been gained, the authority may be discarded. Our flourishing and dignity are found in part in the freedom to rely on our own moral vision. This connects with a theme dominant in an earlier generation of critics, the idea that no *moral* conclusions can follow from *factual* claims about the will or commands of God. We need, it is urged, some broader basis on which to appreciate the commands of God as being good, since 'logically there is no reason why an almighty and omnipotent being might not be a perfect stinker'.[6]

Again, the appeal to authority connects uncomfortably with an authoritarian religion which keeps company far too readily with intolerance and bigotry. This is the classic charge of Gibbon, Hume and Russell.[7] If the truth is located in one place, that is God, and if I have privileged access to that truth, then why should I be tolerant and understanding towards those who have the temerity to differ? For this reason Hume preferred polytheism to monotheism because it is more tolerant and easy going.[8] So-called 'postmodernism'** is kind of demythologized** polytheism.**

Moreover, the appeal to authority and obedience is naive. The appeal is often a front to further the power of Church, priesthood or pastorate. My obedience diminishes me as a free human being. At the same time it preens the plumage and massages the egos of popes priests or pastors who love to poke into and control the lives of others. In particular, they try to control people where they are most vulnerable – when they are in bed.

4.2.2 *The content of Christian morality*

There is a second strand to the attack. This is the critique of the *content* of Christian morality, along with its *style* as involving blind obedience. R. A. Sharpe mocks the idea of a God who frets about whether we use the sheath or the rhythm method. How can we love and worship such a small-minded and petty deity?[9]

An example focused upon by Sharpe is the idea that sexual intercourse must always be open to procreation.[10] For those who wish to have a baby, conception within love making will be a wonderful and beautiful thing. To say, however, that every act of love making must be open to procreation is to impose intolerable strains. Either love making must be restricted in a way that is unreasonable, or there may be a baby which cannot be provided for. At worst, a woman is condemned to serial child bearing which takes over her life and which may even shorten it. Contraception is one of the great liberating agents in the modern world because it allows people to enjoy sex without the fear of an unplanned pregnancy. Yet Vatican theology condemns as intrinsically evil the use of contraceptives, not by an appeal to what serves human well-being, but by an appeal to a 'natural law', which requires every act of sexual intercourse to be open to procreation.[11] The status, rationale and basis of this 'natural law' remains obscure. At this point, Christian ethics diminishes human well-being and adds to the sum total of human misery.

Of course, many Christians – including many Roman Catholics – will strongly critique this Vatican theology. But such a theology remains profoundly influential and it is not surprising that many react angrily to the *content* and not simply the *style* of what they judge to be Christian ethics. Other examples, including those from Protestant traditions, may be given (see 7.1, 15.4).

There is, moreover, an even sharper sting in the tail. Even when religion is at the service of bad morals we cannot critique such stances because they are based on inscrutable authority. The issue is not only or even primarily the content of religious ethics, so much as the refusal to be self-critical and the obeisance before an authority that cannot be questioned. That this is the kind of authority to which we are subject is explicitly stated in John Paul II's *Veritatis Splendor*.[12]

Sometimes a stance based on *authority* is supplemented by supporting *argument* – for example, an argument that what is received on authority does in fact serve our well-being and commend itself to reason. There is no objection in principle to this approach. Nonetheless, the arguments are often in danger of becoming disingenuous because counter arguments are not allowed the full force of a challenge. For example it might be claimed that contraceptives encourage irresponsible sex and expose women too much to unwanted sexual predators.[13] Maybe there is some truth in this, but this argument alone hardly justifies total prohibition. It does nothing more than illustrate the ambiguities that are woven into many situations. The insistence that contraceptives offer overwhelmingly a great blessing need not require the denial that there may be occasions when they encourage irresponsible sex. There is little in this world that is devoid of ambiguity.

Critics of Christian ethics have a right to demand that apologists come clean. Either they stand by their inscrutable authority, like it or lump it, or they commend an ethic based on arguments we can all scrutinize. We cannot have it both ways, appealing to arguments when we can find them, but then resorting to this kind of authority when the going gets tough. If we are not prepared to follow the argument where it leads and in the end question the authority, then we should stick to our guns and appeal to authority and to authority alone. It is disingenuous to appeal to supporting arguments only when it suits. Allow reason to support the deliverances of authority and it will soon rise up to torment it.

4.2.3 Motivation in Christian ethics

There is a third critique of Christian ethics – a critique of the motivation behind Christian behaviour. The claim here is that a truly worthy motivation is one that does the right for the sake of the other person.[14] A moral motivation is focused on the other and we are committed to their dignity, rights and well-being *for their sake*. Although Kant is at times difficult to interpret, and even sometimes obscure, this has a certain connection with Kant's claim that the other person is to be seen as an end, and never merely as a means.[15] Humanist motivation is genuinely moral. Humanists honour rights, obligations and justice – for the sake of the other.

Religious motivation, by contrast, takes the focus away from the other person. Religious motivation is anti-humanistic. We do what is right, not for the sake of the other person, but rather because God commands it. Nowell Smith enjoyed bullying Thomas Brown's *Religio Medici*: 'I draw not my purse for his sake that demands it, but for his that enjoins it.'[16]

At worst, the religious motivation is deeply self-centred. We do what is right for fear of punishment, or to cultivate or save our soul.[17] Such a motivation, however, is not moral but prudential. Self-preservation is a corrupting reason to accept a moral injunction. I should renounce violence towards my wife because I grieve to see her hurt. If I renounce violence because God will punish me my motivation is prudential and self-centred. I am no longer interested in my wife's welfare. I am wanting to save my own skin. If God is an invisible and ubiquitous police officer, then this subverts genuine morality. I should do what is right for the sake of the other, not because God is watching me.

Suppose, however, I love because God loves. This seems a purer motive, but the religious dimension is still corrupting of the moral motivation, since I act out of love for God rather than love for the other person. 'Do not oppress the poor, the widow, the stranger and the fatherless.' That is an admirable sentiment. The motivation is moral. To add 'Thus saith the Lord' is to add a religious motivation that is not only superfluous but corrupting of moral motivation.[18]

Ethics, then, must remain an autonomous and wholly 'secular' matter. Religion is at best an irrelevant, at worse a damaging influence. *Keep religion out of ethics!* It is tempting to dismiss a little too easily Grayling and others as attacking a crude caricature of Christian ethics, which no theologian would be prepared to defend. That, however, would be going too far. Some of the mud sticks and we need to learn from the critique. The whole of this book may be seen as an attempt to explore a style of Christian ethics that escapes these criticisms, while also learning from them. Although neither makes the connection, Grayling and Blackburn reject the approach to Christian ethics *very broadly* associated with medieval thinkers such as Duns Scotus and William of Ockham. For the most extreme strand of the Ockhamist tradition, ethics is indeed derived from the arbitrary will and command of God. Such commands can have no inherent rationale, since any rationale would constitute a constraint upon God and thus compromise God's omnipotence. It follows that God could choose to command adultery, and if God were to do this, then adultery would become a meritorious act. For this approach Grayling and Blackburn are quite right to see unthinking obedience as the prime virtue. I will describe this approach as 'Ockhamist'** even if William of Ockham's actual position may have been more nuanced.[19]

Rather surprisingly, they do not properly acknowledge the existence of a radically different style of Christian ethics, the one associated *very broadly* with Thomas Aquinas. In outline such a style locates the right and the good in that which serves the flourishing of human life as women and men, embodied and social, pursue their 'natural' end. For Aquinas, God could not command adultery or make adultery commendable *without also changing human nature* – without our ceasing to be the kind of creatures for whom relationships of reciprocal tenderness and loyalty answer deep needs and serve our well-being.

For Aquinas, there is no question of servile obedience to 'inscrutable oughts' since the right and the good are about our nourishment. Sin is offensive to God only because sin is damaging to God's creatures, whose flourishing is the divine will.[20] Furthermore, we can *all* engage in rational enquiry into what serves our mutual well-being, irrespective of religious belief, even though Christian faith will offer to this public debate its own insights. It is this alternative perspective that I will explore in this book.

4.3 Christian ethics is special!

If then there are those who regard religion as the enemy of morality, insisting we should keep religion out of ethics, at the other end of the spectrum are those who regard Christian ethics as independent and all-sufficient. *Christian ethics is special!* In consequence – to recall Tertullian's image – Christian ethicists remain in Jerusalem and do not engage as attentively as I believe they should with the wider ethical quest of humankind. I consider a number of examples. They are different but they bear family resemblance. Very broadly speaking they lie in the Ockhamist tradition.

In *The Moral Vision of the New Testament*, the American writer Richard Hays argues that we may identify in the New Testament a thrust of ethical instruction that is clear, coherent and very specific. It is normative for us today because the Bible has a privileged access into the things of God.[21] What we discover to be the teaching of the New Testament has trumps over all other considerations. 'Reason and experience come into play in enabling us to interpret Scripture; they cannot be used simply to overrule or dismiss the witness of scripture.'[22] Hays offers a sophisticated biblicism. The cash value of this, to give one example, is the imperative that we be pacifists. Engaging with and challenging the 'just war' tradition is either unnecessary or the dice is loaded since we are bound by the teaching of the text. He does offer arguments in favour of a counter cultural 'non-violent resistance' and not unreasonably expresses disquiet at how violence easily begets further violence. He does not need, however, to argue that force never offers protection of the weak or that force is never effective in confronting tyranny. 'The reasons for choosing Jesus' way of peace making are not prudential ... No, if our reasons for choosing non-violence are shaped by the New Testament witness, we act in simple obedience to ... God.'[23] Likewise, his rejection of non-celibate homosexual relationships is based entirely on his reading of the authoritative text.[24]

A similar approach is found in Stanley Hauerwas. Hauerwas maintains that every person is part of a community and tradition and that their moral stance will be formed within that tradition. The Christian is shaped by a community that remembers the story of Jesus and the narrative of God's saving work. It follows that an ethic always requires an adjective. It has to be Christian, Jewish, Islamic, Buddhist, Humanist – or for that matter Nazi or Stalinist.[25] No ethic is free from a historical and cultural location.

All this is undoubtedly true, and Hauerwas says valid things about the Church as a community of moral formation and about its counter-cultural witness. But it need not follow that we cannot aspire to a universal discourse in ethics, as opposed to talk of the ethics of this or that tradition. It does not follow that there can be no debate between traditions, and a learning and correction through debate. Furthermore, our lives are informed by a number of interconnecting 'narratives'. He does not appear to deny this. Nonetheless, his dominant emphasis is on the discontinuity rather than the continuity between Christian ethics and the wider ethical reflection of humankind. He has drunk deeply from the well of the thinking of Alasdair MacIntyre, and his retreat into a distinctive Christian ethic is encouraged by MacIntyre's pessimistic estimate of any scope for contemporary consensus on ethical matters.

Non-violence is central for Hauerwas. Christ renounced any form of coercion and relied on the evocative power of self-sacrificial love and a willingness to be 'handed over' to his enemies. Since Christ is the 'image of the invisible God' non-violence 'is at the very heart of our understanding of God'.[26] It follows that 'peaceableness' is the hallmark of Christian life. This peace is not to be achieved by our power. 'Rather it relies on the close, hard, and seemingly unrewarding work of witness, a witness which it trusts to prevail in a fragmented and violent world.'[27]

When Hauerwas speaks of violence, he is not speaking simply of the resort to war. By violence he appears to mean any form of coercion. I support violence when I call the police after a burglary, or generally when I rely on the law to protect my property. Welfare programmes are based on violence – the coercive power of the state demanding taxes which pay for them. While not drawing these conclusions as explicitly as I have just done, it is clear that this is the drift of his thought. He remarks that violence is the 'warp on which the fabric of our existence is threaded. The order of our lives is built on our potential for violence'.[28] One recalls Hobbes' belief that without fear of the coercive sanctions of the state life would be a 'war of all against all'.[29]

Hauerwas does not pretend that the winsome and compelling example of peaceable lives is guaranteed to melt every heart. The hope of Romans 12.20 remains only a hope. He acknowledges the tragedy and dangers of his position. The peace to which Christians bear witness may well make the world more dangerous.[30] Peaceableness not only leaves the witnessing Christian unprotected, it leaves other victims un-protected also. The consequence is that commitment to peaceableness may involve less and not more justice. We seek justice – but not a jus-tice that requires violence. Where the values of non-violence and justice are in conflict, it is non-violence that always has trumps.

He thus parts company, as does Hays, with an earlier American Christian ethicist, Reinhold Niebuhr. For Niebuhr, in a 'fallen' world there needs to be realism about what can be achieved and the vocation of Christians in the rough and tumble of the world is to help to mould social structures in such a way as to make our political, economic and social institutions work as well as possible for justice. Resort to coer-cive power is unavoidable. Power and conflicting powers are facts of life. The gospel, understood as calling us to sacrificial love, presents in its fullness an impossible ideal – and we make matters worse if reliance on the evocative power of self-sacrificial love becomes the norm for society. It remains, however, an ideal towards which we can move and which always troubles our complacency.[31]

Hauerwas is uneasy, however, about Christians co-operating with others in building tolerable structures of uneasy peace and achievable justice. This is because it involves acquiescing in structures of coercion and violence. Instead, the Church should be set more over and against society as a witness to non-violence. 'The first social task of the church is to be the church.'[32] The Church is the Church when it witnesses to non-violence. Within it people are shaped into the demeanour of non-violence and peace. In all this, Hauerwas acknowledges the influence of the Mennonite tradition and the writings of John Yoder.

The upshot of Hauerwas's position is that while, in principle, there may be dialogue between Christian and non-Christian on ethical mat-ters, in fact among the Babel of contemporary ethical traditions there is limited scope for agreement. Furthermore, the widespread acceptance of coercion as a basis for an uneasy peace and proximate justice sets a limit to co-operation. Moreover, since this peaceableness is based on Scripture and his doctrine of God he does not engage as closely as he might with a reasoned ethical critique of his position. Indeed James Gustafson goes as far as to accuse Hauerwas – probably a bit unfairly – of having a 'tribal God' with an ethic that forfeits any ground for engagement with the wider society.[33]

We can draw out a number of interconnected and crucial things from the presentations of Hays and Hauerwas. Because Christian ethics are based on an authoritative text or theology, there is limited ground for engagement with the wider ethical reflection of human-kind. At the *level of basis and rationale* Christian ethics is special. The crucial thing to notice is that if Christian ethics is simply a matter of obedience to the ethical teaching of the New Testament, no other considerations being allowed any voice other than a subservient one, then 'Christian ethics' is so special in its foundation that there can be no significant contact or conversation with the wider ethical reflection of humankind. Hauerwas is less biblicist than Hays, but the basis of his ethic remains explicitly and centrally theological. If the basis for ethics is so all pervadingly theological there is limited scope for dialogue with those who do not accept the theology.

Moreover, because Christian ethics is so special, there is limited scope for Christian action in co-operating with others in building a society of imperfect but achievable justice and peace. Hauerwas in particular is cautious about this because it means acquiescing in structures of violence. At the level of *style of life and action* Christian ethics is special. The Church witnesses to a counter-cultural way of life, on peace-ableness, on the character of marriage, and on abortion, all having a definitive theological underpinning.[34] But how are people expected to respond to that witness if they cannot share the faith? On Monday morning church members belong to other communities as well – especially those of work. How do they 'make common cause in a variety of ways with others who do not share their religious convictions'?[35] His is more an ethic of the Sunday pulpit than one that resources our living during the week.

In consequence, the emphasis is upon *the church as a distinct society* bearing counter-cultural witness to its own values.[36] The distinctiveness of the church sub-culture receives more emphasis than working with others for the common good. No doubt there is an element of this in any understanding of church, and in any understanding of Christian ethics. Hauerwas, in particular, does us service in drawing our attention to the Church as a community of moral formation, at least often counter-cultural. The point about Hays and Hauerwas is that this focus becomes central and lacking sufficient nuance. Hauerwas contrasts rather than connects an ethic based on narrative and tradition and one based on nature and reason.[37] For example, he departs from the Lutheran insistence that marriage is a gift of God to all humankind, and sees Christian marriage as having a distinctive character.[38]

These characteristics are evident also in the English writer John Stott. Stott's method for resolving ethical issues is simply that of asking what Scripture teaches. Christians are committed *a priori* in advance to whatever Scripture may be shown to teach.[39] We do not engage ourselves in ethical enquiry on the basis of arguments that may be subject to public scrutiny. We instead defer to the teaching of the text. It may indeed be argued that what Scripture teaches is confirmed in reason and experience but if in some instance it is not, then our reason needs tutoring and our experience is distorted.

We take as an example Stott's treatment of grounds for divorce. There are only two permissible grounds – sexual infidelity and the desertion of an unbelieving partner. This conclusion is not arrived at by ethical reasoning; it is simply derived from the biblical text, since these are the only grounds cited in the New Testament.[40] While Stott would, of course, be outraged by persistent cruelty and abuse within a marriage, he is hesitant to regard this as a proper ground for divorce without New Testament permission. He is sympathetic to the expansion of the Greek word 'porneia' in Matthew 19.9 (usually translated 'sexual infidelity') to include cruelty but he is not wholly convinced. He is therefore inclined to allow only separation in such cases.[41] Even the permission to remarry seems to be dependent upon Deuteronomy 24.1ff.[42] Stott does not believe Christians should seek to impose their standards on others and so he is sympathetic to irretrievable breakdown of marriage as the ground for divorce in a pluralistic society, but within the Church and for Christians it is different.[43] Stott is writing within the Ockhamist tradition. Christian ethics is special because derived directly from the revealed will of God, in Stott's case located within the text of Scripture. Ethical arguments concerning persistent cruelty and abuse as an appropriate ground for divorce count for naught. What has trumps is how a Greek word in Matthew 19.9 is to be translated.

One final example may be given. This is the encyclical *Veritatis Splendor* by John Paul II. John Paul attacks the understanding of freedom which exalts above all else a person's liberty to make unfettered individual choices.[44] On the contrary, our true freedom is found in loyalty to the truth. This is because God's truth is trustworthy, life-enhancing and expresses love.[45] John Paul's stress is not on freedom by itself, but rather freedom in truth. A freedom, not nourished by truth, or in defiance of truth, withers and dies. It becomes a self-inflicted starvation.

This argument is powerfully developed and there is much in it most Christian readers will warmly welcome. The problems come later. First, it belongs to the papal office to identify and teach this truth. Speaking of moral truth John Paul says: 'The task of interpreting these prescriptions was entrusted by Jesus to his Apostles and to their successors with the special assistance of the Spirit of Truth.'[46] It follows that a properly tutored conscience and mind will conform to the teaching of the papal office.

But second, part of the substance of this truth concerns our bodies. 'A doctrine which disassociates the moral act from the bodily dimensions of its exercise is contrary to the teaching of scripture and tradition.'[47] It follows that homosexual relationships and the use of contraception belong to the category of 'intrinsically evil' acts. In consequence, we have

– on these issues – an ethic which is based on the authority of the papal office. Despite the commitment to reason and to natural law in the Vatican's tradition, we are not given persuasive arguments for regarding the things mentioned as 'intrinsically evil'. The task of interpreting moral prescriptions belongs to the papal office, whose prescriptions must be faithfully kept.[48]

If, in the broadest sense, William of Ockham is a medieval forebear for this approach, Karl Barth, in some of his writings at least, is a twentieth-century forebear. At one stage in his thinking, he claims that ethics, merely as ethics, are a manifestation of sin. 'Man wants to know of himself (as God does) what is good and evil. He therefore wants to give this answer himself and of himself. As a result, and in prolongation of the fall, we have "ethics" … Revelation and the work of God's grace are just as opposed to these attempts as they are to sin … The grace of God protests against all man-made ethics as such … It does so by completing its own answer to the ethical problem in active refutation, conquest and destruction of all human answers to it.'[49]

A few pages later he speaks of Christian ethics acting with regard to a 'general conception' of ethics as did the Israelites when conquering Canaan. 'Christian ethics cannot possibly be its continuation, development and enrichment. It is not one disputant in debate with others. It is the final word.'[50] The presupposition here seems to be that the consequences of the 'fall' are such as to take from humanity any possibility of 'true being' apart from grace.[51] He thus rejects the 'Roman Catholic co-ordination of moral philosophy and moral theology' because it fails to acknowledge the radical implications of the 'fall'.

At their face value these seem astounding claims, even taking into account Barth's experience of struggle with Nazism. It is possible, of course, to interpret Barth as offering nothing more than hyperbole to jolt our complacency. In our ethics – as also in our theology – we should have humility and openness. We must not assume we have it all 'sussed'. We are indeed guilty of sin if we make pretentious claims about our understanding and vision. If this is what Barth is saying, then we may agree, and it applies as much to theologian as to ethicist.

What are we to make of his claim that there can be no ethics apart from divine revelation? If by this he means that goodness, virtue and authentic moral discernment, wherever they be found, owe their being ultimately to the divine grace infusing all things, then this is a legitimate Christian interpretation of human experience. That, however, is very different from saying that what we call 'Christian Ethics' is privileged over and against so-called 'secular' ethics. A more conciliatory – but still imperialistic – comment might indeed suggest such an interpretation: 'Thanks to the wisdom and patience of God … Christian insights and deductions may actually exist where their Christian presuppositions are wholly concealed.'[52] Elsewhere, Barth does indeed say that the reception of God's Word is not dependent upon the Church's witness. That said, monologue delivered to others, rather than dialogue with them, seems to rule the day, save that beneficiaries of the monologue may know some of the lesson already.

Again, if Barth is claiming that theological perspectives properly critique so-called 'secular' ethics, then I have no difficulty. But he does not seem to be open to a similar critique from these secular ethics themselves. To imply the careful ethical enquiry of our secular contemporaries is guilty of sin in a way that the careful work of their opposite numbers working in theological ethics is not seems preposterous. The default position of Barth is to remain satisfied in the Christian ghetto since within it there is all that is needful.

These issues are deadly serious. If Christians do their ethics in a Christian ghetto they deprive themselves of the rich wisdom to be gained from a wider ethical debate. Wisdom is found in Athens as well as in Jerusalem. There is much to be learned from, for example, J. S. Mill, Karl Popper and Isaiah Berlin, just as early Christian thinkers learned from the Greeks. Atheists such as Simon Blackburn write excellent books on ethics, much better than many by Christians.[53] Contemporary moral philosophers are often committed to exploring specific ethical issues in a way in which their forebears, more interested in the genre and logic of ethical language and general 'meta-ethical' questions, were not. They often bring to the analysis of ethical issues an incisiveness and sophistication not always equalled by Christian contributions.[54] It is deplorable when a Christian superiority complex blinds us to this and the result is the impoverishment of Christian thought.

The converse, however, is also true. A Christian ghetto mentality encourages others to ignore Christian contributions. For instance, a recent seminal survey of the literature of ethics gives only scant reference to Christian thought. Only one volume from the impressive Cambridge University Press *New Studies in Christian Ethics* library is mentioned in the bibliographies.[55] This is to their cost since there is rich insight in Christian thought, much that can be illuminating for those who do not share its theological underpinning. For example, Christian thought has long pondered the nature of freedom and autonomy, and the relationship between individual and community, in a way that may give depth to the all too shallow treatments of such themes in some secular writings. The Bible is dismissed as a 'barbaric bronze age text' and as a 'loony book' by Richard Dawkins,[56] and Grayling's caricature of so-called Christian ethics fails to find in the Christian tradition anything of value for the enlightened.[57] Jerusalem remains Jerusalem and Athens remains Athens to their mutual impoverishment.

The Ockhamist tradition casts a long shadow. All this is the almost inevitable consequence of a style of Christian ethics that sees ethics as settled finally by a religious authority. To those who accept this religious authority, nothing more is needful. To those who do not accept it, nothing is compelling.

4.4 Taking 'secular' ethics seriously

The above examples indicate a certain style of writing in Christian ethics. There is an assumption that Christians have a privileged insight into the right and the good. Christians are the experts while others are only amateurs. A 'theological' ethic has a secure foundation. All else is built on sand. So-called 'secular' ethics may therefore be ignored or dismissed, or at most treated as a learner at the feet of theologians. Christian ethics may be done in a Christian ghetto because the ghetto has everything we need.

The paragraph I have just written is strongly worded. I do not accuse all the writers I have mentioned of all these things. Nonetheless the paragraph does describe an attitude which is all too common.

In contrast, I wish to appeal for a greater humility in the Church. Christians do not have a monopoly of, or privileged access to, moral wisdom. So-called 'secular' ethical thinking has to be respected and engaged with attentively. Often the Church has to learn from stringent criticism of some styles of Christian ethics. The appropriate response is sometimes penitence and rethinking rather than the expulsion of the Canaanites from the land.

I make this appeal for a number of reasons; and these reasons build on our explorations of the first part of this book.

First, there is the simple observation that many of our contemporaries take moral issues very seriously. They have a deep commitment to the world's poor, to social justice, to the environment and the welfare of animals. In personal relations they are committed to integrity and decency. There will indeed be many who ignore moral questions. It is not that they have a bad conscience, but rather that they have no conscience at all. Their lives are 'a-moral'. That some belong to this category is clear; but it is also clear that many are people of high moral seriousness. This is evident from television programmes such as *Question Time*, or from reading the columns in newspapers, to say nothing of our day-to-day encounters.

Christians sometimes bemoan a 'decline in morality'. It is sometimes argued that the religious revivals of the past built up within our culture 'moral capital' that is now rapidly running out, heralding a dark age unless another revival tops up the account. This type of argument, however, should be offered with extreme caution. Certainly there have been changes in moral perception – especially with regard to sexuality – but these changes are not necessarily all bad and many have been embraced responsibly and with due consideration. A change is not necessarily the same as a decline. In some areas, such as awareness of gender issues, rights of minorities, and our responsibilities towards animals, we may have a moral sensitivity to which some of our more religious forebears were blind. There are indeed serious and difficult questions about the extent to which the ethical commitment of our secular contemporaries may owe more than some are willing to acknowledge to a culture and mindset formed by a religious tradition. This issue will be tackled later in the book (especially 5.3 and 5.6). It is not adequately tackled, however, by simplistic talk of declining moral capital. The integrity of the commitment found among our secular contemporaries to living a good life must be honoured.

The second reason derives from this. Not only do many of our secular contemporaries have a carefully thought through moral position. Sometimes they do not like what they see in 'Christian ethics' and subject it to a stringent *moral* critique. This has already been illustrated. The apologetic task of responding to these criticism cannot be ignored. Moreover, Christians will not only answer their critics. Sometimes there will be learning from the critics and a consequent reshaping of Christian thought.

The third reason concerns participation in the public realm with a view to serving the common good. If Christians have a style and basis for ethics that has no continuity with 'secular' ethics, then there is little scope and little common ground for participating in public debate – as Daniel Dennett points out.[58] There are two incompatible paradigms – secular and Christian ethics. Christian ethics are dependent upon an explicit theological foundation not elsewhere acknowledged. While I can discuss with my atheist neighbours the best time to prune roses or the effect of diet upon cholesterol, I cannot discuss ethics, since my ethics depends wholly upon a religion which they do not share. We have already seen that writers such as Richard Hays and Stanley Hauerwas largely retreat into the culture of the Church, playing down the imperative to share in the struggle for a wider justice.[59] Likewise, as we have seen, John Stott has a distinctively Christian understanding of the ground for divorce which he concedes will not be acceptable to the wider society because based on the authority of Scripture. By basing his ethics entirely on the authority of Scripture, Stott handicaps himself in contributing to the wider ethical debate in society. His is an ethic persuasive only to those who accept this approach to scriptural authority and interpretation. The issue is all the starker because it was following the recommendation of the Church of England Report,

Putting Asunder[60] that the Divorce Law Reform Act of 1969 replaced the notion of matrimonial offence with that of 'irretrievable breakdown of marriage' as a basis for divorce. This report, however, did not base its stance wholly on Scripture. In mainstream Anglican tradition it appealed to what may reasonably be judged to serve human well-being and the public good. Such an appeal allowed it to contribute to the wider debate in society. Stott is thus departing from the dominant Anglican tradition, deeply influenced by Hooker, for which moral reasoning has an integrity of its own, enjoying broader country than an ethic based simply on biblical texts. 'The natural measure whereby to judge our doing, is the sentence of Reason, determining and settling down what is good to be done' is a typical statement.[61]

There are, of course, other examples. Many more conservative Christians insist that sex must be confined to legal marriage, or that all gay people must remain celibate, simply out of deference to Scripture's teaching, as it is perceived to be. There is no appeal to a moral reasoning we can share. The mental paradigms do not connect. An appeal to Scripture will cut no ice with my atheist neighbour, and so there can be no debate.

Some Christians are content that this be the case. They even glory in the isolation of Jerusalem from Athens. Why should there be a meeting of minds between Christian and non-Christian on ethical issues? They are content to keep apart, separate, distinctive and exclusive. The price of such a position is, however, considerable. Christians can no longer engage in the political and ethical debate of the wider society because there is no connection between an ethic that is based directly and exclusively on theological premises and one that is not. Moreover, and crucially, it also disables the Church in attending to its responsibility for the wider good.

And here is a worrying twist to the tale. Some Christians are attracted to the idea that there are certain moral stances that mark them off as being distinctive. Often a distinctive sexual ethic is cited. Gumbel, for example, counsels converts on becoming Christians to stop having sex unless they are legally married, and those who are gay or lesbian to become celibate.[62] There is, after all, a long tradition of religious groups marking themselves off as being different on account of some moral stance. Distinctiveness and identity is something highlighted in a culture influenced by a so-called 'postmodern' strand where the quest for truth or appropriateness is replaced by the focus upon identity and a particular style. Is it, however, a healthy attitude to prefer that which is 'distinctive' to Christians rather than that which commends itself to wider humanity and enriches the wider community?

There is a further point; and one suggested by reflecting on Hume who in the eighteenth century robustly offered an approach to ethics not tied to the theologian's apron strings. Christians – like all people of goodwill – have a deep commitment to the health of society and the well-being of others. It follows that they should have a deep commitment to encouraging and honouring ethical seriousness even when there is no belief in God. A strident insistence that ethics depends directly and explicitly upon religion only undermines this. Hume mocked the idea that ethics depends on religion, since it would mean those with no religion would have no morality.[63] Yes, there will be weaknesses in secular ethics, which the theological critic needs to probe, just as theologians should be open to their secular critics. But the strengths need also to be recognized and the insights cherished. It is outrageous when Christians try to undermine the genuineness of secular ethics in a disingenuous evangelistic ploy to manifest the 'need for the gospel'. Here, as in so many areas, as Bonhoeffer reminded us, the gospel speaks to us in our glory and strength and not only in our weakness and need.[64] *Wherever* goodness and truth are found they are to be acknowledged and honoured.

Christians may protest at this point that I am giving our secular contemporaries too clean a bill of health. Yes, it might be responded, there is much goodness to be admired outside the community of faith. But secular morality is precarious. Its light shines falteringly and precariously and is easily snuffed out. For every secular person who seeks to live a responsible and compassionate life there are two or three who recognize no moral constraints and who live only for themselves. What about those for whom life is a struggle against others to make as much money as possible, no matter at whose expense and with no concern for social justice? And what of the horrors of the explicitly atheistic regimes of Hitler, Stalin and Pol Pot? Later in this book we do indeed need to ask how secure is a solely 'secular' morality and whether it finds firmer focus within a wider theological context. For the moment, we need to recognize ungrudgingly the nobility of the quest for the good in many who have no religious faith. Wherever goodness is to found it is to be affirmed and celebrated.

Furthermore, if secular morality is precarious *so also is religious.* Christians are as adept as others at avoiding moral challenges when the moral challenge is inconvenient. Christians are perhaps more skilled than most at peddling moral stances which are anti-humanistic. Abuse of power and the manipulation and undermining of others can be as common in church structures as in any others. In some areas – such as how women and those of minority sexual orientations are treated – the Church struggles to catch up with the moral commitments of the wider society. Furthermore, the war crimes of the people of God make some chapters of history grim reading. The reality is that for many the churches have lost moral credibility on account, for example, of attitudes towards homosexuality, and because of attitudes towards women in leadership. This is true even if it is also true that the churches have set a good example on how to debate issues in depth, and on how a community might handle radical disagreement. At the same time, ecclesiastical politics can be as dirty as any other kind.[65] The current climate is not one that invites Christian triumphalism. It rather invites a good measure of penitence and humility. It requires also a corporate Christian vigilance lest religion through distortion becomes an arrogant and controlling zeal, lacking gentleness. One of the dangers of the retreat into the Church as a counter-cultural community for the formation of character, such as commended by Hauerwas, is that the Church listens less to, and thus profits less from, the stringent critique of those outside it. A Church exposing itself to public debate is a Church chastened, and sometimes the Church needs chastening.

Moreover, the issue is not simply that Christians are sinners like the rest of people. The issue is also that religion is vulnerable to distortions that make it especially susceptible to moral critique. Since 11 September 2001 the association between religion and intolerance – noted in Hume, Gibbon and Russell – has resurfaced as a concern widely commented upon. Related to this is the fear that religion can breed a zeal that sometimes undermines relationships of decency and respect for the integrity of those who do not share that zeal. It follows that religion can engender bigotry and exclusivenesses. These concerns are serious and need careful discussion (see 5.3.3). While arrogance and bigotry are critiqued as strongly within religious traditions as outside, such concerns can nonetheless be missed if we remain in Jerusalem and do not engage with protagonists in Athens. If we allow a fixation on the speck in our neighbour's eye, we may miss the great lump in our own.

In the above paragraphs I have spoken of 'secular' and 'Christian' ethics and such talk can give the impression that people are in one or other of alternative camps. The reality, however, is more complicated. The reasons and visions that persuade our secular contemporaries in ethics may also persuade Christians. It follows, as was argued in Part 1, that it is first and foremost as human beings, rather than as Christians, that we undertake the ethical task. Ethics is a *human* concern and not an exclusively *religious or theological* one. May I invite Christian readers to engage in an imaginative exercise? Let them try to 'think away' their Christian faith and belief. Would this involve the immediate evaporation of their commitment to social justice, human rights and to treating others with respect and regard? Would they suddenly throw away all integrity? We need not deny that this 'thinking away' of Christian belief would remove significant reinforcement to our commitment to justice and the dignity of the other person. We need not deny that an important source of motivation and confidence would be removed. Our ethical perspective may become differently nuanced, and some changes may be quite radical, but we would still remain committed to living good lives. I recognize that the idea of 'thinking away' is problematical and some may argue they are so radically formed as Christians that nothing of themselves would be left. Nonetheless, there does seem to be a valid distinction – however fuzzy – between a basic humanness and our being formed as Christians. It is this that makes public discourse about ethics possible. The important point is that our moral thinking and moral commitments have a strong measure of independence from any religious stance we might have.

All this connects with a rich theology of all humanity made in the divine image, and of God's grace embracing all. This should mean an end to religious tribalism. God's image may be tarnished (in Christians no less so than in others), but the image is still there. The reality of the divine image within us means that within *human* and not only within *specifically Christian* thought and experience we may be given a vision of the right and the good. In consequence, it is not a matter only of recognizing the moral commitment and moral vision of our secular contemporaries. It is also a matter of recognizing that *Christians* do ethics as *human beings* and not simply as Christians. It may be true that it is in God that 'we live and move and have our being'. But the God in whom 'we live and move and have our being' gives a measure of autonomy to creation and therefore there is a dignity in the 'secular' and a worth and value in thought that is not at every point explicitly theologically grounded.[66] If the 'earth is the Lord's and the fullness thereof', it is not necessary to give everything a colour wash of religiosity. If 'the earth is the Lord's and the fullness thereof', if we all bear – however tarnished – the divine image, and if our focus is on a 'realm of God' wider than the Church, then there should be a stringent *theological* critique of the focus on separateness and set-apart-ness I have illustrated. The position I am indicating here resonates with a theology that gives a proper autonomy to the 'secular'. It resonates with the dictum that God's 'grace' does not nullify but rather perfects 'nature'. There is a danger that we become more interested in identifying standards of behaviour that mark off Christians as being distinctive than in identifying that which commends itself to a wider reason and conscience. And that I believe is tragic.

Notes

1 A. C. Grayling, *What is Good?*, London, Weidenfeld & Nicolson, 2003, e.g. pp. 59, 83–5, 218–9; Simon Blackburn, *Being Good*, Oxford, Oxford University Press, 2001, p. 10.

2 Grayling, *What is Good?*, p. 84.

3 Søren Kierkegaard, *Fear and Trembling*, (1843), Princeton, 1941, pp. 64ff.

4 Grayling, *What is Good?*, p. 70.

5 P. H. Nowell-Smith, 'Morality Religious and Secular' in I. T. Ramsey (ed.), *Christian Ethics and Contemporary Philosophy*, London, SCM Press, 1966, pp. 95ff.

6 The phrase is that of H. D. Aiken. Quoted by John Hick (ed.), *The Existence of God*, New York, Macmillan, 1964, p. 15.

7 Edward Gibbon, *Decline and Fall of the Roman Empire*, 1776–1788, chapter 15, (ed.) J. B. Bury, Volume II, London, Methuen, 1896, pp. 2ff.; Bertrand Russell, *Why I am not a Christian*, London, Allen Unwin, 1957, p. 27; David Hume, *The Natural History of Religion* (1757), especially Section 9, ed. Richard Wollheim; *Hume on Religion*, London, Collins, Fontana, 1963, pp. 64ff.

8 Hume, *The Natural History of Religion*, Section 9.

9 R. A. Sharpe, *The Moral Case Against Religious Belief*, London, SCM Press, 1997, p. 56.

10 Sharpe, *The Moral Case*, pp. 67, 71 and 73.

11 E.g. Paul VI, *Humanae Vitae*, Vatican, 1968, especially paragraphs 11–14.

12 John Paul II, *Veritatis Splendor*, Vatican, 1993, paragraphs 25, 27, 64, 116.

13 E.g. C. E. M.Anscombe, *Contraception and Chastity*, Catholic Truth Society, 1980.

14 Grayling, *What is Good?*, p. 72; Sharpe, *The Moral Case*, p. 6; Julian Baggini likewise objects to a 'divine command' approach to ethics and also attacks religious motivation as being selfishly prudential: Julian Baggini, *Atheism: A Very Short Introduction*, Oxford, Oxford University Press, 2003, pp. 37–41.

15 Immanuel Kant, *Groundwork of the Metaphysic of Morals*, ed. H. J. Paton, *The Moral Law*, London, Hutchinson, 1948, p. 90.

16 Nowell-Smith, 'Morality', p. 104.

17 Thus, Don Cupitt, *The New Christian Ethic*, London, SCM Press, 1988, p. 16.

18 Sharpe, *The Moral Case*, pp. 56–7.

19 G. Leff, *William of Ockham*, Manchester University Press, 1975, pp. 455f. Ockham's argument concerning the unfettered sovereign will of God is found in his *Commentary on the Sentences of Peter Lombard*, 2.15.353.

20 Thomas Aquinas, *Summa Theologiae*, I.103.1. Also *Summa Contra Gentiles*, Book III, Chapter 122.

21 Richard B. Hays, *The Moral Vision of the New Testament*, Edinburgh, T&T Clark, 1996, p. 269.

22 Hays, *Moral Vision*, p. 341.

23 Hays, *Moral Vision*, p. 343.

24 Hays, *Moral Vision*, p. 379ff.

25 Stanley Hauerwas, *The Peaceable Kingdom*, London, SCM Press, 1993, p. 1.

26 Hauerwas, *Peaceable Kingdom*, p. xvii.

27 Hauerwas, *Peaceable Kingdom*, p. 15.

28 Hauerwas, *Peaceable Kingdom*, p. 144.

29 Thomas Hobbes, *Leviathan*, Part I, Chapter 13, p. 82 in edition ed. Michael Oakeshott, Oxford, 1946.

30 Hauerwas, *Peaceable Kingdom*, p. 145.

31 The argument has its early presentation in Reinhold Niebuhr, *An Interpretation of Christian Ethics*, New York, Harper, 1935.

32 Hauerwas, *Peaceable Kingdom*, p. xviii.

33 Quoted by Jean Porter, *The Recovery of Virtue*, London, SPCK, 1994, p. 30.

34 Stanley Hauerwas, *A Community of Character*, Indiana, Notre Dame, 1981, pp. 155–229.

35 David Fergusson, *Community, Liberalism and Christian Ethics*, Cambridge, Cambridge University Press, 1998, p. 76.

36 Hauerwas, *Community*, p. xi.

37 Hauerwas, *Community*, p. 54.

38 Hauerwas, *Community*, pp. 70, 176.

39 John Stott and David L. Edwards, *A Liberal Evangelical Dialogue*, London, Hodder & Stoughton, 1988, p. 104.

40 The 'Matthean exception' and the 'Pauline privilege' (Matthew 19.9 and 1 Corinthians 7.10–16) John Stott, *New Issues Facing Christians Today*, London, Marshall Pickering, 1990, pp. 291ff.

41 Stott, *New Issues*, p. 296.

42 Stott, *New Issues*, p. 206.

43 Stott, *New Issues*, pp. 50ff., 305.

44 John Paul II, *Veritatis Splendor*, paragraph 32.

45 *Veritatis Splendor*, paragraph 10 and 35,

46 *Veritatis Splendor*, paragraph 25. See also paragraphs 4 and 26–7.

47 *Veritatis Splendor*, paragraph 49.

48 *Veritatis Splendor*, paragraph 25.

49 Karl Barth, *Church Dogmatics*, Edinburgh, T&T Clark, Volume 2, Part 2, 1957, p. 517.

50 Barth, *Church Dogmatics*, Volume 2, Part 2, p. 519.

51 Barth, *Church Dogmatics*, Volume 2, Part 2, p. 530.

52 Barth, *Church Dogmatics*, Volume 2, Part 2, p. 542.

53 Simon Blackburn, *Being Good*, Oxford, Oxford University Press, 2001.

54 E.g the essays in Hugh LaFollette (ed.), *Ethics in Practice*, Oxford, Blackwell, 1997. Also Helga Kuhse and Peter Singer (eds), *Bioethics*, Oxford, Blackwell, 1999. Also Ronald Dworkin, *Life's Dominion*, London, HarperCollins, 1993.

55 Hugh LaFollette (ed.), *The Oxford Handbook of Practical Ethics*, Oxford, Oxford University Press, 2003.

56 Richard Dawkins, *The Devil's Chaplain*, London, Weidenfeld & Nicolson, 2003, pp. 118 and 157.

57 E.g. A. C. Grayling, *The Meaning of Things*, London, Weidenfeld & Nicolson, 2001, pp. 99f.

58 Daniel Dennett, *Breaking the Spell*, London, Allen Lane, 2006, p. 296.

59 Hauerwas, *Community*, p. 92.

60 The 'Mortimer' Report, *Putting Asunder*, London, SPCK, 1966.

61 Richard Hooker, *Laws of Ecclesiastical Polity*, I. viii.8.

62 N. Gumbel, *Searching Issues*, Eastbourne, Kingsway, 2003, pp. 47, 71ff.

63 David Hume, principally in his *Enquiry Concerning the Principles of Morals* (1751), ed. L. A. Selby-Bigge, Oxford, 1902.

64 Dietrich Bonhoeffer, *Letters and Papers from Prison*, English translation, London, SCM Press, third edition, 1967, pp. 326–7.

65 See Stephen Bates, *A Church at War*, London, Hodder & Stoughton, 2004.

66 See Vatican II, *Gaudium et Spes*, 1965, paragraph 34.

5

An Ethic of Grace: A Christian Colouring of Ethics

5.1 Facts and values

There is a difference between a statement of 'fact' and a statement of 'value'. It is one thing to say that something 'is' the case. It is another to say that it 'ought to be' the case, or that a particular state of affairs is 'good' or 'evil'. If I say of a nation that nobody has more than five times the income of the poorest, then I am stating a fact about the distribution of wealth. If, however, I then say this is a *morally equitable* distribution I am going beyond the language of 'fact'. I am using the language of 'value'.

For some, this difference is absolute. Between 'facts' and 'values' there is an unbridgeable gulf. Whatever the 'facts' about universe and humanity happen to be, such facts have no purchase upon our understanding of morality. Of course, we take facts into account when making a moral judgement, but the facts remain a neutral canvas upon which we paint *our* picture of morality.[1]

This seems to be going too far. The languages of description and of evaluation may be different. There may be no logically tight deduction from the former to the latter, but that does not mean there is no legitimate movement of a less formal kind. Our morality has to relate to this world and to the human condition. Furthermore, some 'facts' may be experienced as being 'value laden' – like the fact that my mother has been a loyal, loving, generous and wise parent.[2] This fact may be, indeed should be, experienced as eliciting my response of gratitude, respect, and a sense of obligation.

We test this idea through two thought experiments.** First, we imagine human beings as significantly different from what they are. They are totally incapable of feeling any strong physical sensation, apart from an intense and regular pang of hunger and the enjoyment of eating food. Their mental life is purely 'rational', focused on seeking food. They have no emotional life, being incapable of what we experience as hurt, longing, grief, pain, delight and love. It follows that human beings are like some other animals – their natural state is one of alone-ness. They do not naturally bond with others in communities.

I am envisaging a world in which the facts about humanity are radic-ally different. It seems absurd to say that this would have no effect upon ethics. Ethics have to relate to the human condition as we find it. Ethics does not exist in some transcendent world unconnected with the world we live in. The recognition of this is one of the abiding merits in the 'natural law' tradition. Our moral vision is deeply woven into the fabric of what sort of creatures human beings are. By the same token what is good for an owl, rabbit, deer or honey bee will be different because they are all different creatures.[3]

The second thought experiment is nearer home. For Darwinian biol-ogy, human beings are the products of a long process of evolution. Over millions of years chance mutations occurred as animal organ-isms reproduced themselves, giving resultantly modified organisms an advantage or a disadvantage in the search for an ecological niche. The process is repeated millions of times and as a result through natural selection we have the present flora and fauna, including Homo Sapiens. It may be that if a series of cosmic disasters had not wiped out the dinosaurs, our ancestors would not have found their evolutionary op-portunity. Humankind is thus the product of a mindless evolutionary process – the non-random natural selection of random mutations. The watchmaker is blind.[4]

The above paragraph is a mixture of biology and background meta-physical mood music. The biology of evolution through natural sel-ection is securely grounded and it seems inconceivable that further research will lead to the abandonment of this paradigm. The 'facts' of evolution are not always seen, however, as being morally neutral. People hammer out their morality in the light of their understanding of the human situation. Some have argued that our evolutionary origins give us no encouragement to honour the dignity and worth of the other person.[5] 'Social Darwinism' has tolerated harsh competition in society with no safety net. The fittest are the best.[6] Others, by contrast, argue that precisely because of our precarious evolutionary origin there is all the more reason to honour and look after one another.[7] We are alone in the universe and if we do not look after one another no one else will. Again, co-operation and mutual dependence are just as much biological realities as is competition, and such co-operation is good for survival. Darwin himself emphasized this.[8] It was rather Herbert Spencer who emphasized the struggle. Furthermore, the perspective has certainly encouraged us to be more sensitive to animals.[9] There is thus a consid-erable literature about the ethical nuances of evolutionary biology.

The purpose of this last paragraph is not to make cheap jibes about how belief in evolution may undermine respect for human worth and dignity. It simply points out that many have pondered the ethical implications of this fundamental paradigm, therein illustrating the claim that fundamental 'facts' are not always experienced as morally neutral.

5.2 Truth claims about God

What about truths concerning God, as Christians may believe them to be? The ultimate is not the physical cosmos but rather the supreme personhood of God. Upon God the universe ultimately depends. Can we say that these truths have purchase upon our ethics? I have argued that our ethics do not exist in a hermetically sealed compartment unconnected with our beliefs. Facts concerning the human condition, as they are believed to be, are bound to connect with our values. Belief in God is belief in the one 'in whom we live and move and have our being'. Given that the 'fact/value' divide is bridged at a number of points, it seems absurd to deny Christians the right to allow their theistic belief significantly to nuance their understanding of ethics.

My position differs, therefore, from that of Hywel D. Lewis, writing in the middle of the last century. Although a devout Christian, Lewis embraced a universal ethic, based on common ethical intuitions, unnuanced by Christian belief. This was in part a reaction against the perceived theological imperialism of Karl Barth and Emil Brunner which dismissed all 'secular' ethics. For Lewis, by contrast, ethics is as independent of religion as chemistry.[10] A similar position is found in Richard Holloway.[11] The argument of this book, as will be clear by now, is that it is primarily as human beings that we do ethics, and to that extent agreeing with Lewis, but that Christian faith offers an additional perspective. This is true of the threefold but overlapping dimensions of content, reason and motivation.

Those who have denied the relevance to ethics of belief in God have often appealed to an unbridgeable 'fact/value' divide. It is a point of logic that no moral conclusions follow from what is factually true – even factually true about a god. As suggested above, a total fact/value divide is difficult to sustain and is less likely anyway to be defended today. The denial of relevance has, however, often been reinforced by a stark, cold and chilly conception of God. God is essentially an 'omnipotent will' who issues inscrutable commands. We fawn obsequiously before this heavenly sergeant major and follow the commands in blind obedience. If the commands have neither rhyme nor reason, but rather lead to our impoverishment, then our louder protest still has no avail. Thus the fact/value divide is reinforced by the construction of a conception of God completely devoid of value.

This approach to theological ethics is the object of protest by a long line of critics – Anthony Flew, Kai Nielsen, Richard Robinson, P. H. Nowell-Smith, Anthony Grayling, and Simon Blackburn.[12] Morality, it is insisted by contrast, is about apprehending for ourselves the right and the good. It is not about following blindly the mandates of another – even the divine other. Things are valued 'in themselves' independently of their being the subject of a divine command. Furthermore, why should the commands of omnipotence be good? Unless we adhere to a theological version of the idea that 'might is right' it could even be our moral duty to resist the monster, even though on grounds of prudence we would be foolish to try. Those who 'dare'st defy omnipotence to arms' know they will be crushed, but they might still be content to be ultimate martyrs in the cause of morality.

We encountered this criticism in an earlier chapter (4.2.1). It is directed at the approach to Christian ethics traditionally associated with William of Ockham, and we noted that many current styles of Christian ethics are essentially Ockhamist.** Fair or unfair to William of Ockham himself, this tradition has a highly personalized conception of the moral law, being derived from the inscrutable will of omnipotence.

Some Christian philosophers have argued, as a point of logic, that God, ultimate in rationality and being, must also be ultimate in goodness.[13] That said, it is more fruitful to widen the whole context of the debate. Let us accept the fundamental thrust of the critique of a theological ethic based simply on the cold and chilly idea of God as brute omnipotence issuing inscrutable commands delivered on the plate of absolute authority.

There is, by contrast, a fuller and warmer conception of God. After all, as Richard Price remarked in 1758, 'What can be more preposterous, than to make the deity nothing but will; and to exalt this on the ruin of all other attributes?'[14] For this conception, God is not Supreme Commander of Combined Earth Operations. God is rather the one who gives out of love, wisdom, generosity and grace. God is like the ideal parent. After all, the image of God as 'Father' is central to the teaching of Jesus – the maleness of the image is not the point. Furthermore, we are made in the divine image. It is best to see this as a fertile and provocative metaphor rather than as something to be defined with closed precision. It speaks of our capacities to reason, to love, to be creative, to enter relationships, to delight in and to grieve over the world. These are feint echoes of the nature of God.

If something like this is our vision of God, then emphasis will be placed not upon divine power, will or command, seen in isolation, but rather upon God's love, wisdom, mercy and grace. God is thus apprehended not as 'brute fact', but as the one who is supreme value and before whom we are lost in wonder, love and praise. This is not to deny that there is a proper religious response to the infinite power of God upon whom we ultimately and absolutely depend. But this is not a response to brute force. It is rather a response to one who is also infinitely wise and good. Power alone may evoke a response of fear, prudence and even admiration; but hardly of devotion and worship. In the response of 'awe', fear is transformed through praise and adoration. Indeed, the evocative character of God's love depends to a large degree upon the perception that it is the love of the one whose love infuses all things. Moreover, such love relinquishes a large measure of control, since it is of the essence of love to allow the other to be, and to work with the other rather than to overrule it. Quite apart from anything else, such a relinquishing of control seems essential if the 'problem of evil' is not to be ultimately fatal to faith. It is implausible to see this world with its suffering as in the iron grip of an omnipotent God. It may, however, be plausible to see this world as owing its being to a God who patiently relies on the persuasive lure of goodness, wisdom and love – working with the process rather than controlling it through omnipotent might. The believer's response to God is to God in the divine fullness, or rather to as much of that fullness that we dare to claim we grasp, not to the meagre abstractions or shallow caricature cited above.

Does this mean that at the behest of the critics referred to in section 4.2 we cease to speak of God's 'will' or God's 'commands'? Are such notions examples of bad language in theology? Not exactly. The notion of the divine command (inevitably understood analogically) conveys a sense of the urgency of the moral imperative. Likewise there can be no objection to speaking of moral imperatives expressing the divine will. Such language, however, is to be understood against the background of the richer framework outlined in this chapter. It is not to be understood as speaking of terrorizing and arbitrary fiats, issued by some tyrant in the sky, and supported by menacing threats of imposed punishment if we disobey. This kind of emotive language, beloved of religion's critics, is a mammoth caricature.

What all this adds up to is the claim that God is a God of grace and our living is a response to that grace. If there are central claims that Christians wish to make about God, claims that nuance everything else we say, then this is such a claim. God's grace embraces the whole of creation. Every human being has value because upheld by the love of God. No sparrow falls without our heavenly father knowing. The Christian vision is that the dimension of reality the sciences investigate has the further dimension of being expressive of God's wisdom and the bearer of grace. Built into the structure of our experience is the promise that there will always be resources of grace. It follows that our fitting response is that we allow our whole nature to be transformed 'so that we may discern the will of God – what is good and acceptable and perfect'.[15]

5.3 A colouring in of ethics

If this begins to sketch an understanding of what belief in God involves, how might it nuance our ethical belief? The answer is that it will nuance it in countless ways, sometimes indeed radically reshaping. It will affect the overlapping dimensions of motivation, justification and content. We leave behind the idea of blind obedience to the inscrutable will of menacing omnipotence. The approach instead is to ask what might be a fitting, reasonable and lured response to a God of wisdom, love and grace. This is very different from obeying commands, still less blind obedience to seemingly arbitrary dictates. This is an odd idea anyway since Christian thought has never wavered in its belief that God's will *is for our good*.[16]

Here the point is illustrated in a few indicative areas. For the rest there is a continual exploration.

5.3.1 *The dignity and sacredness of every human life*

Convictions about the love and grace of God are rightly experienced, not as bare facts but rather as facts that take on a depth and evoke a response. Beliefs about God are not morally neutral. Truths about God are not truths about a morally neutral 'bare fact'. God is rather the one who is supreme value. If I believe that we all owe our being to the love of God, and furthermore that this love embraces all, then it is a fitting response to recognize in my neighbour sacredness and dignity. The other person has been given life by God and is made in the divine image. The sense that we are all loved of God as a common divine parent nourishes a regard for one another and a commitment to one another's well-being. We are not involved here in a tight process of formal reasoning. Nonetheless, the movement from belief to response – involving both heart and mind – is no less real for that. I noted above that the fact that someone is my mother or father, daughter or son, husband or wife, is not experienced as a bare fact but rather as a value-laden fact that evokes a response. The manner of our response to God is not dissimilar to the manner of our response to one another, and these responses resonate with one another.[17]

None of this for a moment implies a refusal to acknowledge the deep commitment of secular humanists to values such as these. It is merely claimed that for the theist these values receive an additional context, rationale and motivation. At the same time, it is possible to speak too casually and complacently about the sacredness of the individual and of our mutual obligations towards one another, as if all this is securely grounded. I emphatically do not claim that it is *only* in theistic belief that such value claims find a rationale. Nevertheless, belief in the dignity and rights of each individual and in our obligations towards one another receives powerful reinforcement from the belief that we all share in the all-embracing love of God. We can thus begin to sketch the way in which human rights and elementary duties are, for the theist, strengthened because they are seen as appropriate responses to the conviction that God is our creator, and in whose 'undistinguishing regard'[18] we all share. Our value commitment receives a rationale from our beliefs concerning what a human person *is*. As Rashdall remarked, the love of God is a stimulant and complement to the love of others.[19] To abuse a fellow person is to dishonour God[20] as their creator. Helen Oppenheimer and Basil Mitchell both quote Thomas Traherne: We love a fellow creature:

> for sparkling eyes and curled hair ... which they should love moreover for being God's image, a mine and fountain of all virtue, a treasury of graces and a child of God.[21]

An ethic that centres on response to this kind of God is a far cry from the caricature of those who object to obeisance before naked divine power. When Malachi asked his hearers: 'Have we not all one father? Has not one God created us? Why then are we faithless to one another?' he was not appealing to the inscrutable decrees of some monarchical deity.[22] He was rather inviting us to acknowledge that we are all alike embraced by the love of God, and that it is a fitting response to be faithful to one another.

We encountered earlier the objection that religion poisons the purity of moral motivation. We should respect the other person *for their sake*, and not because God loves them (4.2.3). This, however, assumes a false polarization. There is no false polarization in the quotation from Traherne above. A Christian's motive is as much focused on the other person as is the atheist's. A wider understanding as to what a person is, as made in the image of God, does not detract from that, even if it may reinforce it. Furthermore, if we speak of the love of God as being an additional motive, this is additional to and supportive of respecting the other person for their sake. It is not an alternative. It is difficult to see how there can be any moral objection to seeing things in this way.

It is odd that so many critics should characterize Christian ethics as blind obedience to God's forbidding commands since Karl Barth, the twentieth century's foremost theologian, also strongly resisted such an idea:

> Man (sic) as man is still free in the face of power ... He can sink under it; he can be annihilated by it. But he does not owe it obedience, and even the most preponderant power cannot as such compel him to obey ... By deciding for God he has definitely decided not to be obedient to power as power.

The divine claim resides rather in God's graciousness towards us:

> God has given us himself. He is not only mighty over us. He is not only the essential good. He is not only our complete satisfaction ... He has graciously turned to us ... He has made himself ours.[23]

Far from 'blind obedience', this moral vision persuades the mind and engages the will. This is implicit in the biblical notion of covenant. In a covenant relationship God does not demand unthinking obedience. There is a partnership in which our part in the great adventure of creation is one of freedom, dignity and value, as we respond to grace. Of course, the covenant partnership is unequal. But can we seriously complain that our relationship with God is not one between equals?

Human beings may be endowed with rich gifts and graces. That said the sanctity of each individual life is not based ultimately on the worth of these particular gifts and graces but rather on a value conferred by the fact that we are each a child of God. This is a good basis for discussing Peter Singer's critique of 'the traditional western ethic', which he believes has collapsed.[24] The essence of this is belief in 'the sanctity of every human life'.[25] Singer attacks this as in part a Christian stance. Although not mentioned by name, Singer seems to be in John Paul II's sights in *Evangelium Vitae*.[26]

Singer considers the 'sanctity of every human life' to be based on a belief in equal worth. He rejects the 'old commandment' which states *'Treat all human life as of equal worth.'* This is absurd when we think of a 'severely malformed baby ... an elderly man with advanced Alzheimer's disease ... or a patient in a persistent vegetative state'. *'Recognize that the worth of human life varies'* is his 'new commandment'.[27]

We need to ask, for whom is this worth? Singer predominantly argues that it is worth for the person whose life it is. A person has a right to life – but not all that is physiologically human has personhood. It is consciousness over time that is crucial, and thus the capacity for subjective experience with conscious interests, hopes and desires. Where there is no consciousness or the prospect of it, there is no sense in speaking of such life as having the same worth. There is no awareness of interests to which the worth may attach. This permits us to make 'quality of life' choices in hard medical cases.

Singer's fundamental claim, then, is that the sanctity of life, and all the rights we attach to it, depends upon consciousness and awareness of interests over time. It does not apply to a living human physiology without consciousness. This is a valuable, although not uncontroversial, contribution to our thinking about hard medical cases (see 16.2 and 16.4). It is, however, more a question of when we have, and when we do not have, a human person. This need not imply that the 'worth of human life varies' if by 'human life' we mean *conscious* human life.

Would Singer claim that the worth of *conscious* human life varies? It seems that he might, and this impression is reinforced by his insistence that, although we should not discriminate on the basis of species, not all animals (including human animals) have equal worth because of different capacities and relationships. Singer concerns himself with the more distressing medical conditions, generally those where there is no consciousness. The argument could, however, be broadened. The fully conscious are not of equal capacities or of equally worthy character. The richness of their interpersonal relationships varies. It is not clear how an ethic based on the worth of a human life, combined with a recognition that 'the worth of human life varies', would fare in the hands of those less humane than Singer. The less able and the boringly ordinary, with poor indicators of worth, deemed to be 'ethically relevant characteristics' and thus reason for a lower regard, could easily become frighteningly vulnerable. Does this imply an acceptance of a disturbing feature of modern culture whereby we easily rank people according to ability, success, looks, wealth, and such like?

Christian insistence upon the 'sanctity of human life' does not depend upon people's worth, measured in terms of abilities, quality of relationships, richness of experience, and so forth. Something does seem to have gone wrong if we say of a prejudiced Alf Garnett that he has the same worth as a Beethoven, Mother Teresa or Desmond Tutu. At the same time, something has also gone wrong if we suggest God loves Alf Garnett any less. Apart from varying worthiness, we are all embraced by God's love. In this respect, we all stand equal before God. The love of God unconditionally embraces everyone. For the Christian this is the ultimate foundation of the dignity and sacredness of every person.

At the same time, the undistinguishing love of God is also a love that nourishes and ennobles us, and this connects with Singer's valuing of worth. God does not insult us by loving us in a way that cares nothing for what we are. Perhaps the love of human parents for their children gives us a clue. This love is given simply because they are their children;

and yet this love nurtures qualities and gifts and graces, drawing out what is within them. We are loved for what we are, as God's people, but also for what we may become. We are loved 'while we are yet sinners'; and yet the mind has not yet conceived what God 'has prepared' for us.[28]

This is not to beg the question against abortion or medically assisted dying, or against difficult 'quality of life' judgements in medical care (see 16.4). Singer has done a service in clarifying some of these. It is not clear, however, that in order to make judgements in these areas we have to abandon a belief in the fundamental sanctity of life in favour of an exclusive focus on varying worth. There are some slippery slopes we cannot avoid, but this one we can.

5.3.2 Body and spirit

Human beings are 'embodied'. We are not ghosts squatting in machines made of flesh. Science helps us care for our bodies. On the whole, we love our embodiment – the enjoyment of good food, warm beds, the stunning panorama of nature, the arts, exercise, hot showers and sex. We can hardly separate 'body' and 'spirit', and if we try to envisage disembodied existence, we find ourselves inventing a new type of body to connect us with the world. It seems that the best explanation of the mystery of consciousness is that it is 'emergent' within nature as living organisms evolve. It is a corollary of this that we can experience the 'physical' as nourishing the 'spiritual' and 'personal', as, for example, through our sexuality and in music and all forms of art. This sacramental** dimension to experience is seen paradigmatically for Christian spirituality when the water of baptism and the bread and' wine of the Eucharist 'become for us' that which speaks powerfully of the heart of Christian faith.

It has not always been so. The Christian Church took root in a culture which was deeply suspicious of the physical. We should not be too hard on people then. They were subject often to pain and poverty unknown to many in the West today. No wonder many dreamt of being delivered from their physicality. The Church, however, never wholly surrendered to this. Because the world owes its being to the goodness and wisdom of God, it is basically good, worth while, and the proper object of our investigation and enjoyment. Our concern here is not with the meaning or justification of the belief that everything ultimately owes its being to the creatorship of God, nor with how this claim is to be related to scientific cosmologies. If, for the sake of argument, we may accept the basic intelligibility of the idea, we are left to explore the kind of evaluative response it encourages. The onus of proof is on those who adopt a world renouncing asceticism which rejects interest in or fulfilment derived from material things. Delight in the beauty and interest of the earth is an appropriate response to belief that it is God's good gift to us. Delight in one's own creativity, and in the creativity of others – artist, sculptor, scientist, architect, musician, gardener, technologist, writer, engineer, etc. – is appropriate since we are here mirroring the creativity of God in whose image we are made. It implies a positive delight in our sexuality, one of the many 'sacramental' dimensions of our being, connecting the 'physical' and the 'personal'.[29] While some Christian thought is influenced by dualistic and ascetic ideas this kind of conviction has never been completely lost. Calvin delightfully remarked that God created food not only for our sustenance but also for our enjoyment![30] None of this sanctions extravagant acquisitiveness, since our physicality needs also to express gentleness, simplicity and justice.

A theology of God as creator, and a theology of incarnation for which the Word has become flesh, thus has enormous implications for ethics. If the earth is God's creation and God's gift, we are prompted to ask what this implies for our attitude towards it and our use of it. Christian ethics must take seriously this world, and our 'physical' needs. It follows that we cannot take refuge in a false spirituality that ignores the imperative of justice or the hard questions of politics and economics in our common life together (see Chapters 11, 12 and 13 especially). None of this is exclusive to a Christian vision, but it is nonetheless a vision that is characteristically Christian, and underpinned by its theology.

5.3.3 Tolerance and humility

If we follow much contemporary wisdom, the typical Christian is an arrogant 'know all', intolerant towards those who presume to differ. Care must be taken lest Christians are given political power since they will use it to regulate people's lives and at worst to persecute the heretic.[31] '9/11' is interpreted as an act of religious fanaticism.[32] There is an alarming resurgence of many sinister brands of religious extremism in all of the world's monotheistic religions. Grayling speaks of the legacy of religion as including the 'familiar horrors of intolerance, bigotry and persecution'.[33] Religious certainties are impervious to reason.

This indictment has a long history. Gibbon, Hume and Russell in their different ways all claimed that monotheism encourages harshness, cruelty and bigotry.[34] The logic of this charge can easily be grasped. If I believe in God, it follows that I believe in one truth and one way. God has revealed all this to my religion. Therefore, those who oppose me oppose God. Why should I be tolerant towards such temerity? Error has no rights![35] The typical monotheist is clench-fisted and intolerant.

Some have claimed this is the case with any belief in truth. 'To possess the truth is to have the right to act in its name ... Truth has licensed torture, exploitation and mass murder ... The history of truth is the history of our subjection'.[36] In the case of religious truth this is especially so. No wonder Hume favoured polytheism as more gentle and easy going.[37]

No Christian can be complacent at this point. Both present and past give many examples of an association between religion and intolerance. A mere *correlation* between religion and intolerance, however, should not beg the question over the direction of causality. Sweeping generalizations about religion being the cause of intolerance, conflict and such like, easily betray a shallow grasp of the psychological and cultural factors at work. Does religion cause the intolerance, or is it that those of intolerant disposition fix upon religion as a form of expression? It is extraordinarily difficult to generalize with any confidence but it does seem that it is often the latter. A theology biased towards intolerance may reinforce an authoritarian personality, but such a theology may be adopted in the first place because it appeals to such a personality. Politics and 'single issue' pressure groups may suffer the same fate.

It is important to ask what we mean by intolerance and why it is so abhorrent. Tolerance does not imply indifference to matters of truth or even lack of conviction. It does, however, imply humility over how much one may have grasped, and gentleness towards those who see things differently. It implies openness to new and correcting insight. Intolerance involves a refusal to allow people the right to freedom of thought, expression and lifestyle, even when no harm is done to others. The enjoyment of that freedom is part of what our flourishing involves. All this is consistent with intolerance towards, say, political oppression, domestic abuse, cruelty to children, inhumane treatment of animals, and so forth. Freedom is restricted here, however, only for the sake of freedom.

Authoritarian intolerance is abhorrent because it infringes people's rights and proper autonomy, and because it is in danger of saying to others: 'Because you are different, we do not share a common humanity.' But suppose this response cuts no ice. How do we address the mental paradigm of those who believe their religion, in giving privileged access to the truth of God, confers the right to rule, often menacingly, over those who are different? And, anyway, since they have access to the truth and will of God they are imposing it upon others *for their own good*. This is the essence of the problem.

This position, however, is theologically as well as ethically flawed. There are powerful forces within theistic belief which challenge bigotry and intolerance. There is, first, the insistence, strongly rooted in Christianity, that faith and worship cannot be forced, but must be freely given. Religious convictions spread through commendation and persuasion, not by force. The 'rule' of God is a gentle one, which waits upon our free response.

But second, the assumption of the critic is that belief in God tempts us to validate human wisdom and power with divine reinforcement. This, however, is not inevitable. On the contrary, belief in God at both intellectual and emotional levels more readily counsels self-criticism, openness and humility. God's thoughts are higher than our thoughts[38] and this should humble our thinking:

> ... The glories of thy mind
> Leave all our souring thoughts behind.
> God is in heaven, we dwell below;
> Be short our tunes, our words be few;
> A sacred reverence checks our songs,
> And praise sits silent on our tongues.[39]

The transcendence of God renders relative all that is human.[40] No human doctrine or image can capture completely the whole truth of God. To be a human being is to be limited. Our limitations apply not only to our knowledge, but to every aspect of our lives. This is suggested by a doctrine of sin. A doctrine of sin is too superficial if we think of it as doing nothing more than accuse us of specific misdemeanors. Sin speaks also of our condition, not necessary always blameworthy, as both limited and flawed. This doctrine alone challenges the arrogant 'know all' attitude of some Christians. It challenges complacent assumptions regarding the purity of our motivation. Is my zeal for God corrupted by my pride and thirst for power – my desire to be on the side of the right and the true, and to see that right and truth perfectly? The doctrine of our solidarity in sin challenges also the moral absolutizing of any group over others – black or women or left or right, or those of a particular religion. It challenges the over-confidence of the ethicist who too easily demonizes the industrialist, the farmer, or the research scientist. Before the transcendence of God we are made acutely aware of the finiteness of our understanding and the limits of our powers. Before the otherness of God there is appropriate humility and openness.

In the *Areopagitica*, John Milton presents the image of truth being shattered and the millions of pieces scattered to the four corners of the earth. We need patience, humility and openness as together we gather up the pieces. More to the point, we need humble openness to others in the quest for truth, and in that humble receptivity we learn through our shared quest.[41] Milton's vision is that only in a society of freedom of expression and tolerant openness can we make progress in our search for truth. This quest for truth requires an open and not a closed society. Toleration implies no lack of commitment to truth. On the contrary, we better apprehend the truth through this respectful engagement with one another. Milton wrote this over two centuries before Mill's *On Liberty!* We thus have a richer understanding of toleration than that which sees it as nothing more than an indifferent or even cynical willingness to 'live and let live'. This deeper understanding expresses respect and openness as together we discover a richer life and vision.

There are, of course, theologies that resist this approach. Through a definitive revelation God has given us an insight into truth – even infallible truth – that enables us to rise above the relativities of history and our sinfulness in believing, leaving behind the necessity to glean wisdom through patiently attending to one another. That such theologies sometimes encourage or reinforce intolerance there can be no doubt. My claim is the more modest one that there is no inevitability that theism adopts this paradigm. The claim to a 'revelation' that takes us above the relativities of being human is difficult to sustain and can be guilty of idolatry. It can express human pride more than it speaks of God. It fails to recognize that we 'see through a glass only darkly' and that God 'is above, we are below, wherefore it behoveth our words to be wary and few'.[42] Furthermore, secular ideologies can also become the idols of our fantasies. If the transcendence of God relativizes our religion, so also does it relativize our secular idols. None has a claim to absolute loyalty and so our freedom is safeguarded.

It is understandable that a certain frame of mind longs for certainty, and some styles of religion pander to that longing. Certainty can easily, although not inevitably, breed zeal and intolerance. It is a mistake, however, to see religion as giving us certainty. In making that mistake religion can easily massage the ego into thinking itself free from error, and into thinking that we know and understand more than we do. A more authentic faith recognizes that life is much more about risky adventure and exploration than about certainty; and that the adventure of discovery is stimulating and humbling. While Christians have a 'reason for the faith that is in them',[43] the heart of religion is not certainty but faith, hope, love and a trust that enables us not only to live with uncertainty, but even to embrace it as belonging to the heart of the human condition.

Theism has historically given us confidence in our quest for understanding since the universe, being God's creation, is worth while, intelligible and accessible. As such, theism has contributed to the intellectual climate that has made science possible. At the same time, as Richard Niebuhr argued,[44] the transcendence of God relativizes all that is human. It thus acts as a check on pretensions to a knowledge that constructs reality for our benefit or which offers an ideology of self-glorification. Belief that God's thoughts are higher than our thoughts encourages a constant self-criticism – hence the twin emphases upon the prophetic and upon repentance – and a patient and loving enquiry that is willing to be surprised, upset and humbled. All this is at the heart of theistic faith and is light years away from a mindset that allows theism to amplify and validate our prejudices. Those who live within the churches know how evident sometimes is the bullying and arrogance of the self-appointed moral and doctrinal vigilante. But for everyone who answers this description there are a few score whose faith bears fruit in gentleness, openness and grace.

Belief in the transcendence of God, therefore, together with the dialogue partners of Scripture and tradition give religion inherent resources for self-criticism and self-correction. We see this in how churches have confronted the patriarchal assumptions of the past, how the world church criticized the Dutch Reformed Church's support of Apartheid, and how the Muslim majority is contesting misrepresentations of the notion of *jihad*. Such resources for self-criticism and self- correction are not found in totalitarian ideologies such as Nazism, and when religion takes on a totalitarian form the power of this self-correcting voice is not silenced for long.

5.3.4 Christian virtues?

I have just argued that theistic belief nurtures humility, openness and gentleness more readily than intolerance and bigotry. This suggests that theistic belief encourages certain dispositions of character, and so we are taken back to our earlier discussion of virtues. If some virtues may have a universal appeal, and if some are appropriate to a specific cultural context, certainly some resonate specially with theistic belief, and receive through it a certain colouring. Of course, they may also flourish without it.

We have already looked at the 'cardinal' virtues, and to these Aquinas added the so-called 'theological' virtues of faith, hope and love.

The virtue of *hope* expresses an essentially positive and confident attitude based on the *faith* and trust that 'in all things God works for good with those who love God' and that God's grace will never be withdrawn. Indeed, Hans Küng finds in such a confidence, so deeply ingrained in humanity, evidence of the promoting of the Divine Spirit working within us.[45] In extremity, this can be shaken, and in the face of suffering it may sometimes feel insensitive to express it. That said, it is difficult for Christians always to silence what Peter Baelz called 'the defiant nevertheless of faith'.[46] 'In spite of all overwhelming victory is ours through him who loved us.' 'All shall be well and all manner of things shall be well.'[47] Psalms such as numbers 8, 147 and 148 express such a vision, enabling us to embrace life with a confidence infused by love and praise.

The theological virtues of faith and hope thus express what is a fundamental implication of belief in God, something that is manifest in all theistic religions, for example Judaism, Islam and Sikhism, as well as Christianity. Because the ultimate reality is God, life may be embraced with confidence as fundamentally good. Such a faith and hope inspires the good life, since enthusiasm and confidence are nourished as we align ourselves with the wholesome purposes of God which we see in the life God has given us. This is one of the foundation reasons why theistic religion issues in righteousness of life. By contrast, an atheistic view can – although not, of course, inevitably – lead to a despair or even cynicism, betraying an underling sense of hopelessness, and issuing in complacency and indifference and even callousness.

And so we come to *love*. It is tempting to think that with love we have now reached the easy bit. After all, Christians are into love in a big way! In fact, the notion of love is complicated. Only some brief indication here can be given as to some of the issues. The matter is complicated not least by the fact that the English word 'love' can translate at least seven Greek words,[48] each with different shades of meaning, thus reminding us that concepts in historic debate do not easily correspond to our usage.

It is quite common in Christian thought to conceive of 'love' as a kind of 'general benevolence'. Thus, Anders Nygren[49] encouraged the idea that Christian love is to be understood in terms of 'agape' – a Greek word which, for Nygren, speaks of a love that is wholly self-giving, interested solely in the well-being of the other, and asking for nothing in return. We love in this sense by an act of will, uncomplicated by our feelings. There is strength in this analysis in two respects. First, it reminds us that *sometimes* we may give to someone for their sake alone, neither seeking nor gaining any return. Second, we are reminded that *sometimes* there is demanded of us a stolid commitment to the well-being of somebody, even if we cannot muster liking or affection. More generally, Nygren rightly reminds us that love involves commitment to the well-being of the other for their sake.

There are problems, however, if we see this as anything like the full picture. First, there are all the familiar difficulties with any notion of 'general benevolence' (see 3.2). Second – and more to the point – why confuse 'love' with 'general benevolence'? To define love in this sparse 'agape' sense is to detach it from much ordinary usage, and many rich dimensions of human experience usually described in terms of love. Agape love, *as agape*, is devoid of liking and affection. Agape love, *as agape*, is not enriched or delighted by the other, because agape, *as agape*, does not recognize any winsomeness in the recipient of this love. Agape, being wholly giving, is in danger of becoming cold and chilly. Kierkegaard said we 'blindly love everyone'.[50] Let's call this agape '*Giving*' love.

These reflections invite a bold insistence that love is about liking, affection, warmth and delight.[51] To love someone is to find pleasure in them and to be enriched by them. After all, we can hardly love God with an agape love. God is infinitely worthy of love as the fulfilment of longing. For Augustine our love of God is rooted in desire and longing.[52] Generally, we want to be loved with this kind of love. We want to feel there is something about us that can enrich another's life. We want to be loved for what we are. Nygren's characterization of agape misses all this, together with the reciprocity of love. A love that is determined to be giving but never receiving can become paternalistic and priggish. It can even feed our pride in being the one who gives, but never needing to receive. Furthermore, we cannot all be all the time into agape love and agape love alone. If I am to *give* my love someone must be willing to *receive* it! Suppose a lover tells his girlfriend that there is nothing about her that delights him, but that he loves her with a wholly dispassionate giving love, receiving nothing in return? In all probability he will be due for the boot. Let's call this '*Valuing/Enjoying love*'. Nygren was keen on agape '*Giving love*' because he believed the love of God is pure agape. In order to affirm, however, the unstinting generosity of God's giving love we need not deny a divine love which also delights in and joyously contemplates creation. Such a love also involves grieving over it and with it.[53]

Valuing/Enjoying love need not be a love that is egocentric, simply using the other person as a source of pleasure. This is a danger, but where such love is reciprocal people find pleasure and fulfilment in one another. A love that delights in and finds pleasure in another person is one of the richest experiences of being human. Such a love also makes us vulnerable to the other. Can we expect, however, to love *everyone* we know in this way? We can predispose the mind and heart and look with expectancy upon others, confident about finding in them, as made in the divine image, much that is precious. Helen Oppenheimer has written of an attitude of openness to finding in our fellow creatures that which we may cherish.[54] It nonetheless remains a tall order to expect to love everyone we know in this manner. Are we then left with a universal Giving love, with a Valuing/Enjoying love added wherever possible? Love thus has both an 'agape' element, which is essentially disinterested and generous good will, and an 'eros' and 'philia' element, which enjoys and is enriched by the other. No doubt 'romantic' love involves both, with a heavy dose of the second, a passion alive with sexual chemistry.

Is this all that is involved? It is right to react against an exclusive emphasis on 'agape' love by insisting upon the wholesomeness of simply finding pleasure in someone. There is, however, a danger that such an emphasis excludes people. Aristotle reasonably points out that we tend to befriend those in whom we find pleasure.[55] Such love is bound to be selective. What of those who do not score high in the Valuing/Enjoying stakes? Are they simply to be left demeaned and patronized as the recipients of pure agape? It seems we need to explore other dimensions to love as well.

One such dimension is an *Enhancing love* that helps to create worth. To be loved is an ennobling experience. The love of another draws the best out of us and helps us realize our potential. Christian thought has commonly said this of the love of God. God's love is indeed generous giving, but God gives love in order to reconcile and sanctify. Parental love will, in human terms, have this dimension. The more we are loved, the more we become lovable. This does not imply someone has no worth until we love it into being! Such a suggestion would be preposterous. What our love contributes to another person is only part of the picture.

Can we say there is a fourth dimension not quite covered by any of these three? Perhaps we can call it something like *Recognition love*. This is a love that simply arrests our awareness and makes us respond to the utter givenness of the other person as a fellow human being in their uniqueness and dignity, and who, for the Christian, is in that givenness a fellow child of God. This is a love that does not depend on any qualities they have and yet it warms to the other person in their uniqueness and dignity in a way not open to the cold dispensations of agape. This is a love that loves a person for their unique individuality, 'for themselves alone' and not, say, for 'their yellow hair'.[56] It can, however, unleash a recognition of qualities.

Of course, in our actual experience of loving, these and other elements are all jumbled up, and that is a mercy. An analysis, however, is valuable because it alerts us to the importance of each of these and other dimensions.

We are to love our neighbour *as we love ourselves*.[57] Although maybe not intended in the original text, the saying reminds us that there is a proper self-love. Such a self-love, self-respect and an appropriate attention to our own needs, is not only taking seriously God's love for us, alongside the love of others. It also equips us to love others and give to their lives as they give to ours. We cannot give unless we have also been willing to receive. There is a difference between the *selfish* and the *appropriately self-regarding*. Indeed, the determination to be always the one who gives can express a subtle pride and an unhealthy kind of self-reliance. A willingness to receive is as much part of Christian living as a willingness to give. Sometimes receiving forgiveness is more difficult than giving it – especially if in giving it we enjoy the buzz of occupying the high moral ground. It is simply not true that in *every* context it is better to give than to receive.

Likewise, there is a difference between self-sacrifice devoted to some specific worthy end, and a denigration or disregard of self. Self-affirmation and a nurturing of self is a proper response to the belief that we all share a common dignity as children of God. We cannot exclude ourselves from this. Women in particular – but not only women – have sometimes been ill served by a Christian insinuation that their needs are not to be heeded; that their life is one of sacrifice for others pure and simple. When the Church's call for self-sacrifice and self-giving has lacked balance and nuance it has been guilty of a subtle form of abuse. Self-love and a proper attention to self takes us back to the notion of *Valuing/Enjoying love.* The heart of love is enjoyment and being nourished through enjoyment. We enjoy one another, and God and God's creation. That is the essence of love and of salvation. We should not be embarrassed to affirm this robustly on account of a false moralizing accusing us of self-seeking.

(On love and justice see 3.9. On love for animals and creation see Chapter 14.)

4 A cultivation of love is a proper response to the love that holds all things in being. Closely allied to love is *compassion*. It is a 'feeling to-gether' – an empathy with another's needs and vulnerability – in which we seek to ally ourselves, however inadequately, with the all-embracing compassion of God. This allows a *generosity*, in time, goodwill and material things, not least because we are released from the things that hold back our generosity; our clinging to things that are the principal sources of security. We need them so much that we cannot give. Of course, generosity can become unwisely profligate. That means, however, that we have to exercise judgement, not that we are to become niggardly. Vigilant self-criticism is also necessary to watch, lest generosity become a velvet glove to cover a fist intent on control and power.

So much for what Aquinas called the three prime theological virtues – although I do not claim here to have followed his own analysis. As remarked elsewhere, however, there is no value in a linguistic impoverishment, which can give us only an impoverished vision. In other words, there is no wisdom in offering a closed, let alone a short list of Christian virtues. We look at a few more possible examples – some suggested by the classic passage in the Epistle to the Galatians – but the selection is only indicative.

Gentleness is a fundamental 'fruit of the spirit' mentioned by Paul and also mentioned in the third beatitude.[58] In some quarters gentleness has a bad press, perhaps because of the insipid picture of 'Gentle Jesus, meek and mild'. It has a bad press also because gentleness keeps too close company with weakness, self-effacing meekness and timidity. It is better to understand gentleness primarily as about how we relate to others. There is indeed a proper gentleness with regard to oneself, but such gentleness is consistent with inner strength, and a fitting self-respect and self-regard. Gentleness is about relating to others in a manner that is courteous and sensitive, rejecting the temptation to control and wield power. In order to be gentle, Williams argues, 'I must deprive myself of a great deal of what I am, the me clamouring to be harsh and violent.' He proceeds: 'Much apparent insistence on moral principles is disguised violence. That is why it disturbs the world while failing to convert and heal it.'[59] Benevolence without gentleness can be aggressive and manipulating. Gentleness involves the refusal to manipulate and control, and to use others for our own aggrandizement. Gentleness arises out of an ability to accept ourselves with quiet minds, and for the Christian that ability comes principally from the knowledge that God accepts us. Because the grace of God allows us to be gentle to ourselves we can be gentle towards others. A close cousin of gentleness is the willingness to forgive. The subject of *forgiveness* will be treated later in the book (8.4).

'My dear Watson,' said Holmes, 'I cannot agree with those who rank modesty among the virtues. To the logician all things should be seen exactly as they are, and to underestimate oneself is as much a departure from the truth as to exaggerate one's own powers.'[60] Conan Doyle may have here a salutary first word, but not the last word on modesty and humility. *Humility* is not to be confused with self-denigration, and certainly not self-hatred. Humility is consistent with recognizing our goodness and strength. Humility is rather a recognition that much of what we have and are has been received, combined with the knowledge that we are human and therefore limited. Humility thus combines with self-awareness and self-criticism. The heart of humility is realism about the human condition. Humility is about being 'earthed' in the truth – the word may have the same root as 'humus' meaning 'earth'. [61] Humility is not self-denying or self-depreciating, while at the same time humility eschews all pretentiousness and arrogance. Humility is about being *real* about oneself. Our humanity is made of crooked timbers, and even when sometimes the timber is straight and the grain pleasing, we remain limited and fallible. But humility implies an acceptance of this limitation, a refusal to take ourselves too seriously, a willingness to acknowledge failure or error without embarrassment, and indeed to laugh at ourselves. All this becomes possible when we allow ourselves to be upheld by grace. It is tragic that some Christians have protested when Christianity is mocked. Laughter can, of course, express cruelty and gloating ridicule. Nonetheless, satire and mockery – even when unfair or aimed at a caricature – remind us of our folly, foolishness and pomposity, and of the importance of being able to laugh at ourselves. When it is God who is mocked, rather than our religion, does God need our zealous protection? Perhaps the pretentious belief that God does is a greater blasphemy than is the mockery.

It is perhaps unusual to speak of *creativity* as a Christian virtue. Nonetheless, it is important to name and celebrate the reality – namely that if we are made in the image of the creator God we manifest that image through our creativity. The staggering achievements of humanity in art, science and technology receive here a theological rationale. As made in the image of God, we share in and celebrate God's creative work. But what of those who build not cathedrals in stone but 'cathedrals of the mind'? Christians have been more ambivalent about creativity here. It is rather their role to preserve the 'faith once delivered to the saints'. At worst, the Christian mindset is reactionary and conservative, suspicious of new ideas. The reality is, however, that the Christian tradition displays deep relativity and flaws alongside its riches. There needs to be continued creativity as we test our tradition, and seek through conferring with the insights and experience of others, to tune our ears further as best we can to a least a few bars of the great symphony that is God. The history of the Church is blighted by the dead heaviness of ecclesiastical control and the bullying of religious zealots, but the dominant note is still one of astonishing intellectual creativity, 'as if religion were intended for nothing else but to be mended'.[62]

Patience must be cited as a further characteristically Christian virtue – indeed, a central one. It is born out of a realism which recognizes that things are not readily perfectible, that 'wheat and tares' grow together, and that our obligations, although real and urgent, do not embrace the whole cosmos. The prayer of Reinhold Niebuhr is often cited – that we be given courage to change the things that can be changed, serenity to endure the things that cannot, and wisdom to discern the difference. We live in the tension between the 'now' and the 'not yet'. This world with all its ambiguities and tragedies cannot become a utopia and so there has to be patience arising out of a realism concerning what is achievable. Without patience we can become sometimes frantic and fanatical or at other times despairing. That said, patience combines with a hope based on the conviction that each day may, nonetheless, be an occasion of grace.

Talk of Christian virtues recalls the idea of the Christian life as 'the imitation of Christ'. Does this mean imitating the character of the historical Jesus? There are at least two difficulties here, erecting a 'caution' although not necessarily a 'halt' sign. First, the historical portrait is ambiguous and incomplete, making it easy for us uncritically to project on to it our own image. It is not obvious that we are guilty of this, however, when we discern in the Gospels, say, a love, compassion, generosity, grace, and steadfast loyalty to others, such as to be our example. Second, Christ's vocation was special and in a vastly different context. The notion of 'disciple', partly for this reason, keeps a proper distance from the notion of 'imitation'. Maybe at least as much emphasis should be placed on the notion of 'Christ' as being an icon of the restored image of God in humanity, the 'true' Adam. This prompts theological reflection on what manner of people we are to be as the children of God, informed and stimulated by the portraits of Jesus in the New Testament, but not treating him as a model for unimaginative copying.

The above is only illustrative of how Christians may see their belief in God as 'colouring' the whole area of ethics. In no way does it claim to be exhaustive. Other allusions are explored elsewhere in the book. Moreover, the motifs of incarnation, cross and resurrection are important. Christian thought has from its beginnings found profound ethical insight in incarnation, cross and resurrection, seen as motifs that have a significance beyond their setting in witness to Jesus. Incarnation speaks of the abolition of a damaging dualism between body and spirit, religion and life. It speaks of God being with us, in this world, in grace. The cross speaks of our 'fallen' nature, as well as of the self-sacrifice involved in confronting it. It speaks of the evocative power of love and of a reorientation of our lives as we 'crucify our lower nature' and 'die to sin'.[63] If the cross keeps alive a proper Christian realism in a 'fallen world' and a rejection of over-optimistic utopianism, the motif of resurrection speaks of hope and renewal and the resource of grace. All three speak of a God of redemption, and a God whose grace never abandons us. These themes are only noted here because they pervade the whole of a Christian approach to ethics.

Loyalty will be discussed in 15.2.

5.4 God in our own image?

The above paragraphs may, however, read too complacently. A tray of watercolours, say, may have 50 or so different colours. To pursue the metaphor, I have simply drawn attention to a dozen or so, leaving on one side the exploration of the others. But the metaphor implies everything is clear and easily harmonized. What about when discordant visions of the good life are read off from differing beliefs in God? With regard to virtue, for example, the ideal of Christian character commended by the strong tradition of muscular Christianity deriving from Charles Kingsley and others has been somewhat eclipsed, partly through the influence of feminist theology. We should not be too ready to follow modern convention and see the conflicting when in fact we should see the complementary. The fact remains, different visions of God and differing personalities will throw up differing theological ethics. Is then everything relative?

The argument so far may therefore have been developed too swiftly. There is a fundamental difficulty to face. I have argued that certain beliefs in God prompt a value response. But maybe I have done nothing more than make God in my own image? I have taken a humanistic understanding of ethics, centred on the dignity, well-being and worth of persons, and then I have projected these values on to God. It may feel satisfying, but this congenial God is a human invention. What about other conceptions of God, more menacing? Suppose theological belief, far from encouraging the compassionate, humanistic ethic defended in this book in fact encourages and reinforces all kinds of harshness and authoritarianism that holds people in chains.

5.4.1 A savage God

This charge can easily be illustrated. For much of history, Christians have believed God is essentially cruel. After all, he consigns to the torments of everlasting hell either those predestined to it, or those given punishments far beyond their deserts. How can *everlasting* retributivist punishment ever be just? Has the mammoth cruelty evidenced on every page of western history been encouraged by the belief that God is essentially cruel? God's cruelty encourages and justifies ours.[64] If we delve deeper, we find that we all inherit the guilt of Adam and Eve. Because this inherited guilt is so great, we all deserve hell, although God in grace might save some. This belief encourages us to see our fellows as corrupted by guilt and sin. There is no encouragement to treat them with either sympathy or appreciation. Furthermore, our own self-respect is sapped because of our sin. At worst, this theology has produced guilt-obsessed neurotics, sapped of self-respect and confidence as they cower nervously before their angry god, beholding with disgust and suspicion their fellows, likewise riddled with sin. After all the Prayer Book enjoins us to confess that we are 'miserable offenders' and that there is 'no health in us'.[65]

It is arguable that contemporary western culture is worse, terrorizing us with impossible ideals and expectations over bodily beauty, earning power, lifestyle, parenting, sexual athleticism, knowledge, skills and such like. Furthermore, in contrast to Christian tradition there is nothing by way of the offer of forgiveness and grace. But this does not excuse the distortions of which Christianity has sometimes been guilty.

Doctrines of election can correlate with an ugly exclusivism. If we are 'God's people' or 'God's country', then others are dehumanized. Humanity is divided into the elect and the rest, and our duties are limited to the elect. At worst, all kinds of cruelty and deprivation may be meted out on those who are not within the holy citadel. It is significant that the only church that had a measure of sympathy with apartheid had a Calvinistic theology.

> We are a garden walled around
> Chosen and made peculiar ground
> A little spot enclosed by grace.[66]

Alongside this, monarchical understandings of God have connected with monarchical systems of government. If God is sovereign over the universe, the 'King of kings, Lord of lords, and only ruler of princes' then it is a short argument to maintain that this God has delegated authority to king, bishop, pope or pastor. They exercise authority by 'divine right'. James I, in *The Trew Law of Free Monarchies*, in 1598 claimed that kings are appointed by God and answerable only to God. Subjects must treat kings as God's representatives and to rebel against a king is to rebel against God.[67] A theocratic government is thus inconsistent with some of the fundamental principles of democracy, namely the answerability of a government to the governed, participation of the citizens in government, and checks and balances that minimize the abuse of power.

If God is to inspire our moral vision, then God had better mind the divine behaviour and set a good example. Alas, again and again God has let us down, despite repeated warnings from liberal theologians and secular critics. It seems best to give God the sack.

5.4.2 *God as Trinity*

A contemporary example is more innocuous but illustrates well the dilemma. A certain style of Trinitarian theology speculates concerning the inner life of God. In God there are three 'persons' – three 'divine individuals'.[68] This inner life of God is an exchange of love, non-hierarchical and non-competitive. It follows for writers such as Moltmann that human communities, inspired by the vision of the Trinity, should be similarly non-hierarchical and non-competitive. A Trinitarian theology encourages human collaboration and equality. Furthermore, this is not so with 'undifferentiated monotheism', which is monarchical, validating hierarchical structures and authoritarian relationships.[69]

Alarm bells easily ring at this point. Do we have here an authentic vision of God, arrived at independently of our moral judgement, and then to find that our moral vision is by it informed and clarified? Or is this democratic vision of God a projection of our own image? It all seems to gel a little too easily with modern ideas of mutuality, collaboration and democracy. The suspicion arises that this conception of the Trinitarian God is too easily made in our modern western image.

Furthermore, Moltmann has not established his case that 'undifferentiated monotheism' has an inherent tendency to validate hierarchical structures of power. Sometimes it has, but monotheism need not express itself in this way, as I argued above (5.3.3). In the Hebrew Scriptures monotheism serves as a check and control on all earthly power. Furthermore, process theology has no difficulty, without the aid of Trinitarian distinctions, in conceiving of God as one who works patiently with the process, relying on the lure of love and respecting the autonomy and freedom of creation.[70] It is important to defend monotheism against Moltmann's charge, not least because theistic faiths such as Judaism and Islam are not Trinitarian in Moltmann's sense. But that does not make their theism inherently hierarchical and authoritarian.

5.4.3 Caution and confidence

The problem then remains. When a conception of God informs our ethics, is this God merely our invention, echoing back and validating our own partisan and all too human ideas?

It was Feuerbach who chastised believers for making God in their own image.[71] As Pailin has argued, however, there are two charges here that need to be distinguished.[72] The first charge is that of *anthropomorphism*. This simply maintains that we think of God in terms of our own experience and categories of thought. This, however, we cannot help doing. There is no alternative. Furthermore, if we are made in the divine image we may have some confidence that we have within us that which can grasp something of God.

The further charge is more damaging, and that is the charge of *invention*. We cannot help but *think* of God in our own image. But do we *invent* God in our own image? Up to a point we clearly do. However robust our theism our vision is bound to be distorted. Is theism, however, a complete invention, or is there a measure of 'seeing through the glass darkly'? Although God is 'more than' our 'little systems', may they still serve as 'broken lights'?[73]

To deal with this adequately needs far more space. The best I can do here is to offer the following as the essence of a response. If there is a rational basis for believing in God, it must be because belief in God is implied by reflection upon human experience, the human condition, and the 'nature of things' as we see it. There may also be, of course, the further claim that God is experienced more directly in and through all this. At least from the time of the Book of Job and the writings of the Hebrew prophets religious believers have returned again and again to the question: What understanding of God is consistent with the rest of our knowledge and experience? *Within this our value commitment and vision will play an important part.* The argument of this book is that an ethic that resonates with theistic belief *also has its own inherent rational.* This encourages us to believe that in the interplay between the two we are involved in more than invention. It is too simple, therefore, to say that we begin with a conception of God and then 'read off' appropriate values. At the same time, it is too simple to say that we do nothing more than make God in the complacent image of ourselves. Our discernment of value and our struggle to gain some authentic vision of God have varied and interrelated sources. The two go together. The argument is constructively spiral rather than viciously circular. This is why there is a proper moral critique of theology. 'Shall not the judge of all the earth do right?'[74]

5.5 Our chief end

I have argued in this book that ethics is about discovering what serves our mutual well-being, and that this quest is bound to be informed by our understanding as to the 'end' of human life.

In struggling with the latter, can we bring together some of the hints contained in our discussion so far? We can make excessive heavy weather of this question, as if the 'end' of human life is about obscure metaphysics, and even worse a metaphysical purpose which we cannot own but which is imposed upon us. It is better to say that the 'end' of human life is to be found within our mutual flourishing. Our 'end' is to flourish together in just and decent relationships! Indeed, for Christian theology our 'end' is to enjoy salvation, and this means essentially well-being and wholeness. 'I came that they might have life and have it abundantly.'[75] As we have seen, critically evaluated conceptions of 'human nature' and 'human need' will help to give content to this. We flourish through relationships of love and mutual respect, through creativity, through intellectual enquiry and scientific investigation, through community, through delighting in the beauty and wonder of the earth, through enjoying the beautiful and the true, through the quiet minds of the cultivation of virtue, and so forth. At the same time, as I have insisted, there is a personal colouring as well as a commonality about our well-being. Part of our well-being involves having the freedom to find this. As Brunner remarked, to affirm creation is to affirm the individuality of each person and thing.[76]

'*Our chief end is to glorify God and enjoy God for ever*', or so says the Westminster Confession. In this way the above suggestions receive a new focus and dimension. Many will understand the phrase 'enjoying God' as in part cultivating a sense of the presence of God and a relationship with God through prayer and meditation. This gives their life a 'hidden source of calm repose'.[77] Others, more impoverished in their spirituality, or perhaps only different, are diffident about some of these claims. But few Christians would deny that 'glorifying and enjoying God' is also something we do *through* and not *apart from* our living in the world and relating to others. The God of nature and the God of grace are one. We glorify and enjoy God through living and not contracting out of the life given to us. But our living is informed by the conviction that it is God in whom we live and move and have our being. A good portion of what this might mean is that we are delivered from petty anxieties over our prides, weaknesses and failures, and released also from the need to exaggerate or trumpet our gifts and strengths. We are released from the mug's game of trying constantly to prove ourselves, and to pretend that we are superior to others. It is God who accepts and so we can accept ourselves. It is God who justifies. Who then condemns? We are thus released to seek to live lives of simplicity, gentleness and responsibility. We are released to enjoy the world without frantically accumulating more and more of what we possess – trinkets and baubles to symbolize our status or prop up our egos. We are released to see our fellows as companions, rather than as competitors in the struggle for status and esteem. It follows that the whole of our life and attitudes – our priorities, choices, ways of relating, and above all our values and respect for virtue – are nuanced and sometimes radically reshaped by our vision of God. It is through all this and not apart from these things that we glorify and enjoy God and thus find 'our chief end'.

In spite of the world's suffering, the confidence that God is with us in generous and gentle grace, working in all things 'for good for those who love God',[78] can still be maintained. This issues in thanksgiving and praise. Joy is seen by Paul as a fruit of the Spirit, and this springs from the praise of God, who is good. Christian spirituality is adept at finding reason to throw parties in the most unlikely of places, finding cause for rejoicing while at the same time grieving with the sad. This is a mindset that confronts the cruel secular Calvinism of much contemporary culture, which insinuates that joy is available only to the extravagantly rich and successful, normally still young and beautiful, the rest being losers. God's grace is not so parsimonious. While poverty is disempowering and dehumanizing, there is also a Christian virtue of simplicity and of delight in the ordinary and available. A 'secular' understanding of flourishing is thus deepened and critiqued by our vision of our chief end as being to glorify God and enjoy God for ever.

It is extraordinary that the idea is around that the God of the Hebrew Scriptures is obsessive and narcissistic, intent on perpetual self-preening through enjoying the infinite congratulations of human creatures. The divine vanity, it is urged, is not a good role model.[79] Such a thought probably never crossed the Hebrew mind, nor for that matter the minds of Vivaldi and Mozart when they wrote their Glorias. It is *we* who are nourished by offering praise and thanksgiving, in a way not dissimilar to the way in which we are nourished and inspired by love, by great art, music or the wonder of the physical world – all of which anyway are 'charged with the grandeur of God' – thus giving impetus to our praise.

All this brings us full circle. Ethics, I have argued, concerns discovering our mutual flourishing. At the same time our understanding of what constitutes our flourishing must be informed by the kind of creatures human beings are. A central fact about humanity is that we exist in relationship and so ethics must concern our relationships with one another – and also our relationship with the earth and other creatures (see Chapter 14). In this chapter we have moved from the emphasis of the first part of the book to a greater emphasis upon our relationships, since our response to God is understood analogously as a kind of personal relationship. It is not about unquestioning obedience to commands. It is a response to grace, and a response centred on wonder, love and praise. In this relationship we flourish and find our well-being. It is this central relationship that nuances all others. It is worth recalling the claim of H. H. Farmer that theism is the response to the ultimate as personal.[80] We are drawn into a response of wonder, love and praise because the grace of God lures our response and in that we find well-being. 'It is our joy and salvation always and everywhere to give thanks and praise.'[81]

5.6 Conclusion

As with our earlier exploration of the colours, threads and stitches, making the 'tapestry' of moral judgement, so in our exploration of how belief in God might nuance our ethics, the above is only indicative and illustrative. It would be folly to presume to offer anything approaching a complete analysis. For example, we saw earlier how Hauerwas draws implications for our living and relating from the vision of God's manner of relating to the world – a manner that is gentle and peaceful. Undoubtedly, this is a crucial dimension even if not everyone will agree with the radical implications Hauerwas draws (see 4.3 and 13.3). Later in the book we will consider a proper emphasis on *freedom* as receiving a powerful theological rationale (Chapters 6, 11 and 12). Furthermore, again and again we are seeing that a Christian emphasis on the 'fallen' nature of the world guards against unrealistic expectations and utopian dreams that easily become nightmares. There is a proper optimism about grace, but also a proper realism that guards against false expectations. The fact is, pondering how belief in God nuances our living is a task never completed.

I have used the metaphor of a Christian 'colouring' of our moral convictions. Sometimes, however, that metaphor may seem too bland and time serving. Does Christian faith do nothing more than take 'human' morality and give it a colour wash of a deeper rationale and motivation? Surely it is more radical? 'Do not be conformed to the pattern of this changing world, but let your whole nature be transformed.'[82] Should we speak not of continuity but rather of radical discontinuity?

The answer seems to be that it is both – and much will depend on the context. The proper response of Christian faith to Apartheid, racism and sexism, say, will be defiant and sometimes costly confrontation. Bonhoeffer and the German Confessing Church found this when confronting Nazism, and especially its persecution of the Jews. We live in a 'fallen' world. None of this, however, entitles Christians, as a matter of course on ethical matters, to act as did the Israelites in the land of Canaan – to repeat Barth's metaphor. [83] If there is a critical engagement with so-called 'secular ethics', there is also an appreciative one and sometimes a humbled one when the Church has to repent of its errors and learn. 'Grace perfects nature. It does not nullify it.' That basic perspective allows a judgement in each context as to how far nature may have fallen from grace. And, of course, Christians are very good at falling from grace themselves.

The world is full of decent and humane people who have no belief in God. Any attempt to explore how belief in God may reinforce, deepen and motivate a compassionate and humanistic ethic must recognize and honour that. No Christian should fail to value attempts to discover a 'secular' rationale for such an ethic.[84] In particular, it is not appropriate when we do this in order to beef up the 'need for the gospel'. This is to dishonour God and the value and autonomy God has given to the secular world and its life.

Christians need to be humbled by the deep pathology to which religion is subject, to say nothing of lost credibility occasioned by stances on, say, contraception, homosexuality, and attitudes towards women. The crimes of the people of God have been horrendous and they continue to be so. Suspect theologies have encouraged harshness, intolerance and cruelty. Monotheism inherently prompts a universal vision with universal sympathies, but we so often kidnap it to serve our tribalisms.

That said, humanity without the critical challenge and vision of theistic belief is often even worse. Secular critics rightly protest against the monstrous and varied crimes of the religious. But rarely, if ever, have the religious descended to the utterly vile contempt for humane values manifest in the regimes of Nazism, Stalinism and Pol Pot. The religious persecutions of Christian history, utterly outrageous as they were, were never totally closed to a moral constraint and self-criticism that is at the heart of religion.[85] Thus, the collect claims that only the vision of God can 'order the unruly wills and affections of sinful' humanity.[86] Humanity *with* theistic belief can be pretty awful, but without it can be even worse. It is a moot question whether a wholly secular understanding of what humanity is will be sufficient in the long run to sustain a commitment to the sacredness and dignity of persons; and to that extent the death of humanity may follow the death of God.

This is not to make the outrageous claim that each individual believer in God is a better person than the atheist. We are all different, have different life experiences and begin from different places and with different resources. The fundamental issue is not comparing this individual with that. The issue more concerns values that are deeply influential in our cultures and mindsets and that help to form us. The task of the Christian tradition – in partnership with other theistic traditions – is to struggle to present to each generation and to each culture a belief in God that is both intellectually and morally compelling, while appealing also to the heart. The future of humankind as we journey through the increasingly perilous twenty-first century may depend upon this as much as upon anything else.

Notes

1 This was the view urged by R. M. Hare in *The Language of Morals*, Oxford, 1952, e.g. p. 46; and *Freedom and Reason*, Oxford, 1963, pp. 214–17.

2 As Helen Oppenheimer argues in *The Character of Christian Morality*, The Faith Press, Leighton Buzzard, 1974, pp. 42–3.

3 As Philippa Foot argues in *Natural Goodness*, Oxford, Oxford University Press, 2001, especially chapter 2.

4 The metaphor is that of Richard Dawkins in *The Blind Watchmaker*, London, Longmans, 1986, following William Paley's *Natural Theology* (1803).

5 See J. Rachels, *Created from Animals: The Moral Implications of Darwinism*, Oxford, Oxford University Press, 1990. Rachels sees belief in 'human dignity' – by which is meant belief that 'human beings are in a special moral category; from a moral point of view human life has a special unique value' – as inconsistent with Darwinism (p. 4). He replaces this with a 'moral individualism' which accords to each a consideration appropriate to their characteristics (pp. 176ff.).

6 Anthony G. N. Flew, *Evolutionary Ethics*, Macmillan, 1967, p. 5. Also Mary Midgley, *Evolution as a Religion*, London, Methuen, 1985, pp. 6–8, 32–35, 119–20.

7 E.g. Richard Robinson, *An Atheist's Values*, Oxford, Oxford University Press, 1964, p. 157.

8 E.g. especially the third chapter of Charles Darwin, *The Origin of Species* (1859).

9 E.g. Peter Singer, *Practical Ethics*, Cambridge, Cambridge University Press, 1993, second edition, pp. 72ff.; and Richard Dawkins, *The Devil's Chaplain*, Weidenfeld & Nicolson, 2003, pp. 20ff.

10 Hywel D. Lewis, *Morals and Revelation*, London, Allen Unwin, 1949, pp. 6, 15–17.

11 Richard Holloway, *Godless Morality: Keeping Religion out of Ethics*, Edinburgh, Canongate, 1999.

12 E.g. Kai Nielsen, *Ethics without God*, London, Pemberton, 1973; Richard Robinson, *An Atheist's Values*, Oxford, Oxford University Press, 1964.

13 E.g. Richard Swinburn, *The Coherence of Theism*, Oxford, Oxford University Press, 1977, pp. 179ff.

14 Richard Price, *A Review of the Principal Questions in Morals*, chapter 5, in L. A. Selby-Bigge (ed.), *British Moralists*, Oxford, 1897, Volume 2, p. 151.

15 Romans 12.2.

16 Thomas Aquinas, *Summa Contra Gentiles*, Book III, chapter 22.

17 As Helen Oppenheimer argues in *The Character of Christian Morality*, Leighton Buzzard, Faith Press, second edition, 1974, pp. 42ff, especially p. 50.

18 The phrase is from Charles Wesley's hymn 'Thou hidden source of calm repose'.

19 Hastings Rashdall, *Theory of Good and Evil*, Oxford, 1907, Volume II, p. 260.

20 Note Genesis 9.6.

21 Quoted by Basil Mitchell, *Morality, Religious and Secular*, Oxford, Oxford University Press, 1980, p. 127. Also Helen Oppenheimer, *The Hope of Happiness*, London, SCM Press, 1983, pp. 138–9.

22 Malachi 2.10.

23 Karl Barth, *Church Dogmatics*, Vol II, Part 2, Edinburgh, T&T Clark, 1957, pp. 553–7. One is reminded of T. W. Manson's claim that the ethics of the Bible are 'the ethics of gratitude': T. W. Manson, *Ethics and the Gospel*, London, SCM, 1960, p. 20.

24 Peter Singer, *Rethinking Life and Death: The Collapse of our Traditional Ethics*, Oxford, Oxford University Press, 1994, p. 1.

25 Singer, *Rethinking Life and Death*, p. 165.

26 John Paul II, *Evangelium Vitae*, Vatican, 1995, e.g. Paragraph 2.

27 Singer, *Rethinking Life and Death*, p. 190.

28 Romans 5.6; 1 Corinthians 2.9. These two themes have been explored in Christian theology under the headings of justification and sanctification.

29 1 Timothy 4.1ff.

30 John Calvin, *Institutes*, III.x.ii.

31 E.g. A. C. Grayling, *What is Good?*, London, Weidenfeld & Nicolson, 2003, pp. 207–8.

32 A recent study by a Chicago professor argues that religion is rarely the root cause of terrorism, but may more often be used as a tool by terrorists. Robert Pape, *Dying to Win: Why Suicide Terrorists Do It*, London, Gibson Square, 2006.

33 A. C. Grayling, *The Meaning of Things*, London, Weidenfeld & Nicolson, 2001, p. 119.

34 See Chapter 4, note 7.

35 Gregory XVI, *Mirari Vos*, Vatican, 1832.

36 C. Belsey in J. Natoli and I. Hutcheson (eds), *A Post Modern Reader*, New York, University Press, 1993, p. 555.

37 David Hume, *The Natural History of Religion* (1757), Section IX, ed. Richard Wollheim, London, Collins, Fontana, 1963, pp. 64ff.

38 Isaiah 40.

39 Hymn of Isaac Watts, 'Eternal power, whose high above'.

40 H. Richard Niebuhr, *Radical Monotheism and Western Culture*, London, Faber, 1943, pp. 31–7.

41 John Milton, *Areopagitica* (1644), Everyman Edition, ed. Kathleen Burton, London, Dent, 1927, p. 30.

42 1 Corinthians 13.12; Ecclesiastes 5.2.

43 1 Peter 3.15.

44 H. Richard Niebuhr, *Radical Monotheism and Western Culture*, London, Faber, 1943, pp. 31–7.

45 Hans Küng, *Does God Exist?*, London, Collins, 1978, pp. 422ff.

46 Peter Baelz, *Prayer and Providence*, London, SCM Press, 1968, p. 112.

47 Romans 8. 28ff., Julian of Norwich, *Revelations of Divine Love*.

48 Transliterated – Agape, Ludus, Eros, Pragma, Storge, Mania, Philia.

49 Anders Nygren, *Agape and Eros*, London, SCM Press, pp. 75–80, 732.

50 Søren Kierkegaard, *Works of Love*, Harper Torch edition, 1962, 2.C, p. 80.

51 So, C. S. Lewis, *The Four Loves*, London, Geoffrey Bles, Fontana, 1960, pp. 25ff.

52 Augustine, *Confessions* 1.1.

53 Psalm 46 speaks of God 'delighting' in us. See also Charles Hartshorne, *A Natural Theology for our Time*, La Salle, Open Court, 1967.

54 Helen Oppenheimer, *The Hope of Happiness*, London, SCM Press, 1983.

55 Aristotle, *Nicomachean Ethics*, 1156b ff.

56, W. B. Yates, poem 'For Anne Gregory'.

57 E.g. Levitcus 19.18.

58 Galatians 5.23 and Matthew 5.5.

59 Harry Williams, 'Gentleness' in Alec Vidler (ed.), *Traditional Virtues Reassessed*, London, SPCK, 1964, pp. 8ff.

60 Arthur Conan Doyle, *The Memoirs of Sherlock Holmes*, 'The Greek Interpreter', *Strand Magazine*, 1893.

61 Esther de Waal, *A Life Giving Way: A Commentary on the Rule of St Benedict*, London, Geoffrey Chapman, 1995, p. 51.

62 The phrase is from Owen Chadwick, quoting Hudibras in *The Reformation*, Harmondsworth, Pelican, 1964, p. 445.

63 Romans 6.6ff; Galatians 5.24.

64 As Bertrand Russell argued.

65 *Book of Common Prayer*, Prayer of General Confession.

66 Isaac Watts, *Hymns and Spiritual Songs*, 1707–1709.

67 David Starkey, *Monarchy*, London, HarperCollins, 2006, p. 92.

68 The phrase is in Richard Swinburne, *The Christian God*, Oxford, Oxford University Press, 1994, pp. 170ff.

69 Moltmann, Jürgen, *The Trinity and the Kingdom of God*, London, SCM Press, 1981, chapters 5 and 6.

70 E.g. Charles Hartshorne, *Omnipotence and other Theological Mistakes*, Albany, State University of New York, 1984.

71 Ludwig Feuerbach, *The Essence of Christianity* (1841), translated by George Eliot, New York, Harper, 1957, early chapters especially.

72 David A. Pailin, *The Anthropological Character of Theology*, Cambridge, Cambridge University Press, 1990, pp. 31ff.

73 Alfred Lord Tennyson, *In Memoriam*, Prologue.

74 Genesis 18.25.

75 John 10.10.

76 Emil Brunner, *The Divine Imperative*, translated by Olive Wyon, London, Lutterworth, 1937, p. 172.

77 The phrase is that of Charles Wesley in a hymn with this as first line.

78 Romans 8.28.

79 E.g. Daniel Dennett, *Breaking the Spell*, London, Allen Lane, 2006, p. 265. Also R. A. Sharpe, *The Moral Case Against Religious Belief*, London, SCM Press, 1997, pp. 29–30. Richard Dawkins, *The God Delusion*, London, Bantam Books, 2006, p. 31.

80 H. H. Farmer, *The World and God*, London, Nisbet, revised edition, 1936, p. 6 and chapters 1 and 2.

81 A typical phrase from modern liturgies.

82 Romans 12.1.

83 Karl Barth, *Church Dogmatics*, Volume 2, Part 2, p. 522.

84 E.g. as in Simon Blackburn, *Being Good*, Oxford, Oxford University Press, 2001 and, apart from its unfocused anti-religious polemic, A. C. Grayling, *What is Good?*, London, Weidenfeld & Nicolson, 2003.

85 Henry Kamen, *The Spanish Inquisition*, London, Folio Society, 1997.

86 Collect for the Fourth Sunday after Easter.

6

Autonomy, Authority, Community

6.1 Autonomy

Enormous emphasis is placed by many today upon our 'autonomy' when making moral judgements. This may not be everywhere as evident as in university philosophy departments, but the issue is still important. We have already seen that Patrick Nowell-Smith and Anthony Grayling object that what they call 'Christian ethics' fails to give proper place to our autonomy.[1]

The notion of 'autonomy' speaks of our freedom and self-determination. But what more specifically does it mean to exercise 'autonomy' in making moral judgements? It might mean that morality is about choice. All that matters in any instance is that I follow my choice, free from external constraint. But there is a difficulty here. We do not excuse the torturer or the child abuser when they appeal to autonomous choice. To say that 'morality is about choice' sounds a wonderful affirmation of freedom. But when it is interpreted to mean 'I choose my morality', alarm bells sound. For an extreme stand on 'autonomy', it does not matter what I choose. What matters is simply that it is me who does the choosing. An autonomous choice, however, is not necessarily a moral one. My choice may be mistaken. The evil of the Holocaust is not constituted by my autonomous decision to denounce it as evil, any more than the Holocaust becomes meritorious when Hitler autonomously chooses otherwise. Morality is about recognizing and discerning the good, not about choosing as I might choose wallpaper, or rhubarb crumble instead of chocolate brownie. Nothing is *required* of us. If the essence of morality is unfettered autonomous choice, then the Marquis de Sade becomes a romantic hero of autonomy.[2]

What then becomes of 'autonomy' if we are constrained after all? The notion of autonomy is valuable for two reasons. First, although ethics is about discerning and recognizing rather than subjectively choosing, what we discern commends itself to us. We can own it. It as 'as if' we had chosen ourselves. We are not aware of an external constraint that fails to commend itself. Traditional language about 'conscience' expresses this sense of 'autonomy'. For conscience, the moral imperative and the moral commitment become internalized. Augustine spoke of loving what is commanded and desiring what is promised. Kant spoke of the moral imperative as shining like a 'precious jewel'.[3] How can this be so? It is so, I suggest, because what is discerned is that which serves our common flourishing. We are recognizing values which nourish us. If ethics is about discerning our mutual good, it is not surprising that we can 'own' our moral judgements.

Second, the idea of autonomy is alert to a 'hermeneutic of suspicion'** that is vigilant lest traditions of morality imposed upon us express the power and prejudice of those intent on controlling us, and whose credentials are shoddy. If 'authorities' are tainted by human prejudice and thirst for power, then confidence in our own autonomous judgement can expose this. Even when there is no thirst for power, authorities may still speak falsely. It is precisely because so many authorities have been discredited that people take refuge in their own autonomous judgement. An obvious example is when those who are gay reject the insistence of married heterosexuals that they must remain celibate; and including instances when they accept an ethic of decency in relationships at least as stringent as those who fashion the prohibitions. The notion of autonomy speaks of our freedom and confidence to challenge authorities when their dictates fail to persuade or when they are life diminishing.

6.2 Authority

In many people's minds there is a head-on collision between these ideas of autonomy and Christian ideas of 'authority' and 'obedience'. I noted earlier the angry complaints of Grayling and Blackburn in this respect[4] (see 4.2). Do these notions mean that Christians have to submit to and be obedient to the 'authority' of the moral teaching of Church or Bible, even if it fails to commend itself to conscience and reason? Obedience is not allowed to question, and in being thus forbidden our humanity is diminished. It is best here for Christians to take avoiding action to prevent collision. A 'hermeneutic of suspicion' reminds us that the Church's teaching is always historically relative. It may express the misguided or historically relative thinking of influential formers of thought or, even worse, a thirst for power in a church's hierarchy. Human reason may err. But it is likely to err less than a servile obedience to unquestioned authority. At least reason by its nature is continually self-critical.

Christian thought should not, however, be too defensive. It is true that ecclesiastical traditions have sometimes been, and still are, controlling and authoritarian. There is a deeply alarming resurgence of authoritarian Christian mutations at the present time. But at the same

time, loudly resonating through all Christian history, is the insistence upon freedom. 'For freedom Christ has set us free!'[5] The western
emphases upon liberty and autonomy, and the right to follow conscience, were developed in large part through Protestantism, even if
some Protestants were deplorably more interested in demanding their
own freedom than in granting it to others. The theological rationale
behind all this is that we are called to the maturity of the people of
God, in which we love God 'with all our mind',[6] thus leaving behind
unquestioning servility. This means that 'obedience' (if that concept
is still used) is best seen as a loyalty and a commitment to a vision.
It is not unquestioning servility. Indeed, there is in much traditional
Christian thinking the quaint idea that God has, through 'revelation',
given us what we might have worked out for ourselves if only we had
not been so cussed, so inept in our thinking and so susceptible to self-
deception. As such, it gives 'reason' a lift! The essential point is that
for a Christian understanding, the 'authority' of God is not an abusive
and controlling one. It is the authority of a vision that persuades and
wins us over.

What then becomes of the 'authority' of Bible or tradition? It is best
to understand such language as expressing gratitude that although
small we may see far because we stand on the shoulders of giants.
Left to ourselves, we see no further than our own back yards. Along
with much that is toxic, there is much that is astonishingly rich in our
heritage. It has 'authority' in the sense that we recognize its worth, we
have openness to being nourished by its wisdom, and we allow ourselves to be formed by it when we can make it our own. At the same
time, we nurture both capacity and confidence to discern and judge
for ourselves what is wholesome. We are not to be bullied into accepting what does not commend itself to reason and conscience. That is
what the insistence upon a proper autonomy means. And such a proper
autonomy is a birthright of those who enjoy the glorious liberty of the
people of God.

I do not believe Beethoven's symphonies are great music because Sir
Simon Rattle says so. I recognize their genius myself. I can still do this
even if I cannot pitch a note. It is something similar when Christians
recognize the authority of Christ, the Scriptures and the riches of the
Christian tradition. There is a worth and a depth carrying its own
credentials, feeding and inspiring us. The Word has become flesh, and
dwells among us full of grace and truth. We grow through being open
to this nourishment, not by neutralizing all external influence and allowing wisdom to well up from within, out of our pristine autonomy.
Instead of being fed by love, gift and grace, we are starved within our
own feeble resources. Indeed, there is a danger that we give exaggerated regard to autonomy over and against being nourished and find-

ing sources of rich belonging. Basil Mitchell calls preposterous Kant's claim that 'even the holy one of the gospels must first be compared with our ideal of moral perfection before we can recognize him as such'.[7] It is as if we could, of course, have written the Sermon on the Mount ourselves if only we had given half a mind to it. This is very far from the kind of authority that beats us into submission. It connects with the idea of 'obedience' as being captivated by a vision rather than as unthinking servile submission.

Back to Beethoven. Suppose Sir Simon Rattle warmly commends music I cannot connect with? Do I hastily discount his authority? Not exactly – given his authority I try to broaden my sympathies and appreciation. In the same way, some claim in Scripture or tradition may violently cut across my moral vision. Do I immediately suspend reason and conscience to obey the 'inscrutable command'? The proper response seems to be to remain open and critical, including, of course, critical of myself. Maybe my reason and conscience need tutoring to take on board the new insight. Maybe my moral perceptions have been too shallow. Nevertheless, if it continues to fail to commend, if it remains inscrutable for too long, the odds are that reason and conscience are a better guide than some appeal to extraneous authority. Or at least judgement should be suspended. Forsyth allowed that we may believe 'ahead of our experience' but that, nonetheless, we believe 'in terms of it'.[8] 'Blind unbelief is sure to err'[9] claims William Cowper; but not as much or as dangerously as blind belief.

There is a type of freedom that is born from lack of confidence and trust. I am suspicious of anything beyond myself and I find nothing compelling or inviting. With suspicion or even despair I take refuge in a freedom, which is freedom from all outside myself. I have freedom to live with my own impoverished autonomy. Christian freedom, by contrast, is a freedom to be what by God's gift one is – a child of God enjoying the blessings of God. It is the freedom to respond to love, and in that response to love and cherish all that God has made. This is the rich Christian consummation of what Iris Murdoch saw in her protest against setting the self over and against an alien world, seeing in love, goodness and beauty – such as the beauty of the kestrel – that which draws us out of ourselves and beyond ourselves.[10]

All this reminds us that Christianity is not a religion of controlling authority. It is a religion of grace. This is forgotten when in the tradition of Malebranche, Feuerbach, Cupitt and Grayling we see God and humanity as competitors for power and dignity. John Chrysostom speaks a more authentic Christian note: 'In honouring God we do honour to ourselves. Those who open their eyes to gaze on the sun receive delight ... Much more is this true with respect to God. Those who admire and honour God do so for their salvation.'[11]

6.3 Belonging, community and tradition

Maybe the argument needs to be more robust, and indeed more realistic sociologically. The rhetoric of 'autonomy' can sometimes blind us
to what is unavoidable, namely that we belong to communities, cultures and traditions. The 'autonomous self' beloved by the rhetoric of
liberalism is a myth. We are all of us part of and deeply formed by the
communities and traditions to which we belong. Christians belong to
a community of faith in which they are formed. The same is true of
humanists and atheists who have their parallel sacred tradition.[12] To
cut ourselves off from our traditions is to render ourselves starved and
impoverished. A pristine autonomy is exposed to this danger. Yes, there
needs to be a 'hermeneutic of suspicion', but alongside it there needs to
be a 'hermeneutic of receptivity' in which we gratefully receive from
the tradition in which we stand. To stand in the Christian tradition is
not to be deafened by the megaphone of an ecclesial totalitarianism –
although that is a danger. It is to stand in a living tradition that invites
us to engage with it critically and creatively. Even – indeed especially
– the biblical tradition is a living one in which latter biblical writers
and editors engage critically and creatively with their predecessors.

Writers such as Hauerwas have stressed that Christians belong to
the 'narrative' of the Christian community.[13] Moral judgements and
the formation of character will be within this context. He has done
a service in reminding us of this, challenging the myth of the autonomous self, discerning alone through the exercise of pure reason. Likewise, he says valuable things about the Church as a community of
moral formation.

That said, the Church's influence can be toxic as well as wholesome.
The right and the good cannot be defined simply as that of a particular tradition. Furthermore, traditions are diverse and the boundaries
porous. We are all part of different and interpenetrating traditions.
Alongside working within a tradition and being nourished by it, there
has to be the capacity for critical judgement. Traditions need their
prophets and rebels. I don't think Hauerwas would deny any of this,
but his focus is much more centred on the Church than is the position defended in this book. Furthermore, Hauerwas is commending
a vision of the Church as he thinks it should be. He is not describing
the Church as it is. Moreover, if we withdraw too much into Church
culture we not only deprive ourselves of the resources of the world beyond. We may also fail to expose ourselves to its salutary and stringent
critiques.

What, however, of those who have neither time, ability nor inclin-
ation to think and discern for themselves? They are quite content to
accept on authority what they are told the Bible or Church says, or

what pope, priest or pastor say. Are they to be 'forced to be free'? They believe their tradition is trustworthy, and are content to follow it. It is not experienced as being *imposed*. Maybe it is for others in the Church, more philosophically minded, to worry about 'hermeneutics of suspicion' and exercising judgement. The Church, in contrast to a university philosophy department, is not confined to those of a certain caste of mind. Is it really for everyone 'odious subjection' and a 'sin against one's own soul', to use Cupitt's phrases, to adopt the former position?[14] We are 'a heretic in the truth if we believe things only because ... pastor says so' declares Milton.[15] That is well said, but is it true for everyone? What actually is wrong with making a judgement that one may trust another person's moral discernment, or that of a moral tradition, as being clearer than one's own? It is possible that Kierkegaard was defending something like this in his meditation on Abraham's willingness to sacrifice his son Isaac in obedience to the divine command. Abraham trusted God's moral vision as having greater clarity and depth than his own! The trouble here, however, is that we must ask how Abraham knew that this was the divine command. If our own moral judgement is the clearest way of discerning the divine will, is there another route more reliable – and, in particular, when that route conflicts so radically with our own moral vision?

Paradoxically, do we do violence to people's freedom if we deny them the right, if they so wish, to adopt a more subordinate and unquestioning approach? This is a difficult question and a general answer cannot be given for each specific individual. Somehow the Church in its pastoral ministry has to support and nourish people in a way that is sensitive to who they are and where they are. Some within the community of faith may be content to rely on the authority of their tradition. But the Church, in its culture and ethos, should hold out the ideal of the Christian as properly autonomous, enjoying the liberty of the people of God. This gives to every Christian the right to make judgements their own, and to enjoy their own vision, rather than rely on the authority of others. And their vision may sometimes have a freshness not enjoyed by those with academic and ecclesial prejudices.

The Church must care pastorally for those who cannot stand or who resist the strong winds of autonomy. This, though, is the lesser problem. The far greater problem concerns those who long to ask questions and to explore, but who feel they do not have 'permission'. Moreover, are the numbers of those in the first category exaggerated by those who are in authority, and who do not wish their authority to be questioned? Paternalism may be attractive to those who show it, but it is less so to those on the receiving end; and paternalism, especially when combined with religious zeal, can easily become the tyranny of domination and control.

We cannot escape responsibility for the moral judgements we make, nor for our manner of life. But at the same time we belong to communities of moral formation. Nurseries, schools and homes may form people in basic sensitivities, fairness, courtesy, co-operation, the peaceful resolution of conflict, and so forth. The Church is a 'school for character' in that people are inspired and stimulated by the example of its saints. The Scriptures are read and the tradition pondered. At least in the past people were formed by 'common prayer'. Baptism and Eucharist are, in part, ritual enactments of commitments to a certain kind of living and to certain values. Esther Reed comments about the Eucharist: 'Its egalitarianism exposes and condemns prideful claims to power and is efficacious for the building of just and peaceful communities. Its materiality affirms the significance and value of oneself and one's own material or physical existence, and teaches that care of oneself and one's body is integral to the respect and dignity due to someone created in the image of God.'[16] None of this is guaranteed to be benign and wholesome. People can be formed into narrowness and bigotry. At the same time, the liberal ideal of the wholly autonomous person is a myth. While the word 'formation' must not imply manipulation, it remains true that it is through engaging with one another in our communities with their memories and treasures, be it critically and creatively, that we are nourished.

Enlightened critics repeatedly charge Bible and Church for holding people in chains through imposing harsh and life-diminishing restrictions. The gospel of secularism grants liberation and the salvation of autonomy. And, of course, in contrast to the toxic prejudices of religion, secularism is free of constraining and life-diminishing dogmas.[17] It is a serious indictment of the Church and of how Christians sometimes abuse Bible and tradition that this charge often sticks. So often what is peddled in the name of God is in fact peddled in the name of power. There is, however, another side to the coin. Theological niceties aside, it is a historical fact that the Church has designated a canon of Scripture over against itself as norm and judge. More generally, the Church has never totally forgotten that it lives under the judgement of God. Scripture's call to justice, humility, compassion, love, mercy and grace can never be silenced and in the Church it has again and again saved people from their worst folly. There are moving stories of slaves being given Bibles and told to read the text: 'Slaves obey your masters.' They had the temerity to read other texts, which spoke of justice and liberty for the captives. It is not clear that secularism has anything as powerful to offer.

Notes

1 A. C. Grayling, *What is Good?*, London, Weidenfeld & Nicolson, 2003, p. 118.

2 Basil Mitchell, *Morality, Religious and Secular*, Oxford, Oxford University Press, 1980, p. 39. The de Sade of history does not conform totally to his caricature. See John Phillips, *The Marquis de Sade*, Oxford, Oxford University Press, 2005.

3 Immanuel Kant, *Groundwork of the Metaphysic of Morals* (1785), ed. H. J. Paton, *The Moral Law*, London, Hutchinson, 1948, p. 60.

4 Grayling, *What is Good?*, pp. 59–60. S. Blackburn, *Being Good*, Oxford, Oxford University Press, 2001, p. 10.

5 Galatians 5.1.

6 E.g. Matthew 22.37.

7 Mitchell, *Morality, Religious and Secular*, p. 152.

8 P. T. Forsyth, *The Principle of Authority*, London, Independent Press, 1913, second edition, 1952, p. 211.

9 William Cowper in the hymn 'God moves in a mysterious way'.

10 Iris Murdoch, *The Sovereignty of Good*, London, Routledge & Kegan Paul, 1970, p. 84.

11 John Chrysostom, *Fourth Homily on Timothy*, Nicene and Post Nicene Fathers, Volume 13, Edinburgh, T&T Clark, 1994, p. 421.

12 E.g. Ludovick Kennedy, *All in the Mind: A Farewell to God*, London, Hodder & Stoughton, 1999, chapters 7–10.

13 E.g. especially *A Community of Character*, Indiana, Notre Dame, 1981.

14 Don Cupitt, *Taking Leave of God*, London, SCM Press, 1980, pp. 3–4.

15 John Milton, *Areopagitica*, London, Dent, 1927, ed. K. M. Burton, p. 27.

16 Esther D. Reed, *The Genesis of Ethics*, London, Darton, Longman & Todd, 2000, p. 251.

17 Atheism has its own Holy Scripture which is given a fundamentalist reading. An example is the Bertrand Russell 'Tea Pot' text with its ridiculous comparison between belief in God and belief in a teapot orbiting the sun. This fails to grasp the difference between belief in God and a straightforward empirical claim – and consequently the differences in the kind of justification that might be given for such a belief. Yet it continues to be quoted as a proof text. Another example is the way in which the notorious exchange between Wilberforce and Huxley at the British Association in 1860 is repeated in its classical myth form with no account given of historical research into its original setting. See Richard Dawkins, *The Devil's Chaplain*, London, Weidenfeld & Nicolson, 2003, pp. 80, 117, 149. Also Richard Dawkins, *The God Delusion*, London, Bantam Books, 2006, pp. 51–5. For an entry into the historical context of the reception of Darwin see Stephen R. L. Clark, *Biology and Christian Ethics*, Cambridge, Cambridge University Press, 2000, chapter 1; and Mary Midgley, *Evolution as a Religion*, London, Methuen, 1985, pp. 10ff.

7

The Use of the Bible in Christian Ethics

It is a mistake to see Christian ethics as a matter of obeying specific moral injunctions delivered authoritatively in the text of the Bible. This is a mistake for at least four main reasons. These four reasons overlap, but it helps understanding to separate them out. First, the Bible simply fails to deliver the goods in terms of clarity. On a vast range of ethical issues the Bible is either silent or little more than suggestive and, in any case the various biblical traditions may not speak with one voice. Even where the Bible appears to be specific, there are often great problems of interpretation and application. It is thus worth stating the obvious. The Bible is not a dictionary of ethics with a definitive article on all the main topics.

The second reason follows from this. The Bible comes from cultures and expresses mindsets often profoundly different from our own. Biblical ethics in all its diversity belongs to its own time and not to ours. We must not assume the biblical writers answer our questions, or that they would readily understand the terms in which we pose them. This is not to deny there is insight to be appropriated – but the process of appropriation involves our own engagement with the issues and we cannot escape taking responsibility for how we handle this engagement.

The third reason likewise follows. The ethical teaching of the Bible is a mixed bag. Many ethical insights rooted in Scripture remain, of course, compelling. Other biblical teaching, however, is subject to moral criticism. For example, while not misogynist, the culture of the Bible is deeply patriarchal. In the Hebrew Bible a man's inappropriate sexual behaviour is generally seen as wrong, not because a woman has been abused or betrayed, but because another man's prerogative has been violated.[1] Slavery within the Bible is never challenged as an institution, although there are laws about the humane treatment of slaves. Magnificently impressive as they were, the Hebrew prophets were blind to gender injustice. At his best Paul is likewise magnificent, but he disappoints us in Romans 1.18ff. where our estrangement from God is evidenced primarily by misguided sexual passion, while the injustices, brutalities and oppressions of the ancient world are only alluded to in various catch-all notions, for instance, 'wickedness' and suchlike.

The final reason is that if at times the Bible appears to lay down the law, at other times it instead invites and resources our own moral judgement. It invites us to see with our own eyes rather than simply follow its directives. We owe in part to the Hebrew prophets just mentioned the courage to adopt a prophetic stance as we engage with the biblical material critically and constructively as well as appreciatively.[2] The basic stance of this book may thus be claimed to be, as much as any other, essentially *biblical*. Ethics is not about obeying injunctions delivered by some ancient text or indeed by any similar authority. Ethics is rather about nurturing our own moral vision and adopting a moral stance for which we give reasons. Many times we do indeed find that we can align ourselves with some specific biblical injunction. Good examples seem to me to be 'You shall not bear false witness against your neighbour' and 'If it is possible, so far as it depends on you, live peaceably with all.'[3] In such cases, however, we will align ourselves because the injunctions commend themselves in their own right, not simply because they are in the Bible. This remains true even when the Bible has helped to mould and feed our moral insight. This argument may be expressed theologically. God is not the kind of God who demands obedience to authoritative commands. God is rather the kind of God who invites us to nourish our own vision.

In this chapter I develop these themes further. I also offer a suggestion as to how the Bible might in a very different, more modest but still highly significant way resource our thinking in ethics.

7.1 Detailed moral instructions

One approach then to the use of the Bible in Christian ethics treats the Bible as a source for specific and highly focused moral judgements. The authoritative text yields moral prescriptions, and the Christian's duty is to follow. It is not for us to question Scripture, and the moral instruction of the text is clear. This approach seems increasingly common. One style of evangelicalism is characterized, at least in part, by taking a specific line on ethical issues, a line deemed to be 'biblical'. This was much less so a generation ago. Thus, Dennis Nineham writing in 1976 on the use and abuse of the Bible found no reason to give particular attention to the Bible's use and misuse in the field of ethics.[4]

Examples of this approach are legion. John Job maintains that those who are gay and lesbian are bound to celibacy because this is the requirement of six or so biblical texts he analyses.[5] For John Stott, as we have seen, divorce is permissible on two grounds only. The one ground is adultery, and the other is the desertion of a non-believing partner. This is because these are the only two grounds given explicit warrant

in the New Testament.[6] Again as we have seen, Richard Hayes argues
for a pacifist stance. What is of interest is not so much his *conclusion*
in terms of a particular ethic, but rather his *method* in arriving at it.
His pacifism is based upon New Testament texts. He does not focus on
the debate between pacifist and just war traditions, since his method
is to follow Scripture as the norm[7] (see 4.3). We will note later that
Gumbel claims that Scripture teaches that sex before marriage is morally wrong, and that this constitutes 'our maker's instructions' for us
(see 15.3).

Some appeal to biblical authority for the use of corporal punishment in the upbringing of children – supported by a whole pantheon
of texts. 'God's word instructs us to use this kind of discipline', we
are told. The quotation is from a book with the unembarrassed title:
Spanking. God's Way of Discipline.[8] The appeal is not to develop-
mental considerations, but rather the authority of Scripture. It is not
surprising that Simon Blackburn objects that the Bible sanctions child
abuse.[9] There are even some who commend a 'domestic discipline' for
wives, including corporal punishment, administered by their husbands
as heads of households. This, we are assured, is not domestic abuse
since it nurtures an appropriate demeanor of submissiveness. This is
based on a somewhat dubious reading of texts such as Proverbs 3.11–
12, 10.13, 13.24, 2 Timothy 2.24, Hebrews 12.11, 1 Peter 3.1ff. and
Revelation 19.7 in the light of Ephesians 5.22. Domestic discipline is
not for children only.[10]

Christian history yields many other examples, now largely abandoned. It was not uncommon for slave owners to appeal to biblical
authority, even neglecting the fact that Hebrew slavery was a more
humane institution than Caribbean, with Deuteronomic laws regulating it. The *Rule of Saint Benedict* is adamant that a monk may not
have private property, *Acts* 4.32 being cited in support.[10] The medieval
rejection of lending money at interest was not based solely on scriptural authority – appeal being made also to the Aristotelian notion of
the barrenness of money and the consequent injustice of seeking gain
from money alone – but an appeal to texts including Exodus 22.25,
Deuteronomy 23.19–20 and Psalm 15.5 was certainly made. Scriptural
warrant was sought for a theory of the divine right of kings, and still is
widely in the Unites States for capital punishment. Acts 19.19–20 has
been used to justify censorship, the denial of liberty of conscience and
the burning of books deemed erroneous.[11]

There are a number of serious difficulties with this approach.

7.2 The problem of consistency

First, if we appeal to the authority of Scripture for specific moral prescriptions we are bound to be consistent. We cannot pick and choose.
Scripture is the authority and we must follow everything that Scripture
says. We do not use Scripture as a source of stimulus and insight, but
involving our own judgement as to what remains compelling and persuasive, and why. If we engage *our own judgement*, the text of Scripture is no longer an unquestioned authority.

Few are in fact willing to accept the totality of Scripture's ethical
injunctions. Most approach Scripture selectively and influenced by a
tradition of interpretation. As has been remarked, texts sanctioning
slavery or condemning lending money at interest have been largely
forgotten. The condemnation of homosexuality in Leviticus 20.13 is
treated as authoritative, but why not the insistence that homosexuals
be put to death? And why has the parallel text in Leviticus 18.19 concerning sexual intercourse during a woman's menstruation been quiet-
ly overlooked?[12] Why do we ignore Deuteronomy 24, which condemns
marrying a second time one's divorced wife – also described as an
abomination? One of the most direct ethical injunctions of Jesus is in
Matthew 19.21. Very few Christians take it at face value. It may be objected a 'face value' reading lacks sophistication. Or is a 'sophisticated'
reading simply one constructed to evade the challenge?

Conservative evangelicals within British Methodism tend to follow
mainstream contemporary evangelicalism in giving authority to Scripture's perceived condemnation of gay and lesbian partnerships, and
yet the great majority show impressive loyalty to Methodism's commitment to the mutual partnership of women and men at every level
of the church's life. They thus part company, sometimes to their cost,
with evangelicals of other traditions who insist, on the basis of biblical
authority, upon a differentiation of role, at least in church and home,
where males have a certain 'headship'.

The problem, therefore, is that few are prepared to follow through
consistently the use of Scripture as an inscrutable authority. But if
Scripture is the final authority, on what basis do we follow Scripture
at some point (e.g. over homosexuality) but not at others (e.g. capital
punishment, male headship over women or lending money at interest)? Complete consistency is hard to stomach, but if we are inconsistent, how do we justify our selection from the text if the text is final
authority?

7.3 Guiding principles?

A possible response to this difficulty is to argue that *Scripture itself gives us a basis for selection or interpretation*. Scripture gives us identifiable 'thrusts', an 'emerging consensus' or 'guiding principles'. A 'thrust' may overrule specific texts, or at least determine their interpretation. If the focus is here, rather than upon specific texts, the clarity of Scripture's teaching and its final authority is maintained.

For example, specific ethical injunctions in Scripture may be but culturally specific applications of an underlying principle, and it is the principle that has authority. The detail of the instructions of Leviticus 25 are hardly practical for us – but we grasp the underlying principles they express, those of fairness, justice and communal solidarity. Likewise, the condemnation of usury may be generalized as a condemnation of exploitation.

Over some questions this is no doubt an admirable approach. It does seem we can discern some clear and all pervading biblical themes. A commitment to justice for the oppressed is an example. This remains clear, however unclear the 'small print' of refining our concept of justice and its application (see 3.9 and 12.4). Even a straightforward biblicism could powerfully argue that the specific texts tolerating slavery are overruled by this central thrust.

It is one thing, however, to say that *sometimes* we can do this. It is quite another to say we can do it on every issue that concerns us. The reality is we sometimes do not find, simply on the basis of examining the text, a clearly evident thrust. After all, Scripture is a collection of diverse writings coming from diverse epochs and communities. It should not be surprising if on some matters, instead of finding a single thrust, we find only a tangled web and a lot of loose ends.

I give here two examples where *on the basis of studying the text alone* we find no clearly identifiable thrust of ethical teaching, but rather ambiguity.

The first example is the woman/man relationship. Suppose we argue in the following way. The Bible comes from a patriarchal milieu in which women are often invisible, subordinated to men, defined in terms of their relationships with men, and denied equal social power and dignity. Nonetheless, there is a hint of equality in the claim of Genesis that God created male and female, and in Paul's affirmation that in 'Christ there is neither male nor female'. The thrust of the Bible is towards mutual partnership and equal social power, without hierarchy or imposed stereotypes of complementarity.

Now it is one thing to argue on *ethical and theological grounds* that it is these hints of Scripture that are the most compelling. If we so argue we are no longer seeing the text as the final authority. Instead, our discerning arises out of a dialogue between our own vision and that of the text. The text itself can remain the deciding authority only if the thrust is determined *on exegetical grounds* – that is by analysing the text itself and allowing the text to yield its own thrust.

It is difficult, however, to claim that a simple analysis of the text yields unambiguously such a thrust. Some have tried it, and it is a defensible position, but it is not coercive. The reality seems to be that there is no overall thrust. To illustrate, I focus on Ephesians 5.23, which claims the 'husband is the head of the wife as Christ is head of the church' and a similar text in Colossians 3.18ff. We could argue that in these passages there is beginning a process of re-evaluating the man–woman relationship in the light of the Christian vision. What is impressive is how far they manage to escape from and challenge the brutality of patriarchy. Man is the head of woman, but *as Christ is the head of the Church*. The point is that Christ loved the Church and gave himself for it. Husbands are to love their wives as Christ loved the Church. We are most faithful to the spirit and intention of these texts if we follow through the trajectory of re-evaluation which they begin. Supported by other texts we find ourselves leaving patriarchy behind, ending up affirming full reciprocity and parity of esteem and social power.

This is an attractive line of interpretation. The problem is that it is an interpretation that engages in *theological dialogue* with the text. It is not an interpretation that is delivered *simply on the basis of exegesis*. We see this when we consider works such as *Evangelical Feminism and Biblical Truth* by Wayne Grudem.[13] Grudem insists that we have no right to appeal to the 'trajectory argument'. The scriptural text is as it is. What has authority is the text, not a trajectory we derive from it. The trajectory argument in effect assumes the text needs correction. The writers did not quite grasp the implication of their vision, but we do! We simply have no right, claims Grudem, to sit in judgement upon the text in this way.

The second example claims that the thrust of biblical teaching is that built into creation is the normative character of the man–woman relationship such as to require those who are gay or lesbian to remain celibate. It is this thrust that compensates for any ambiguity in specific texts where homosexuality is mentioned. My argument is that there is much more of a 'reading into' Scripture here than a 'reading out' of it. Furthermore, other thrusts, with a different conclusion, can also be identified. I will return to this later (see 15.4).

The problem, therefore, is that attempts to find some guiding principle of interpretation *within Scripture itself* and *solely on the basis of exegesis* are on many issues enormously contentious. This is, in fact, a version of the old exegetical principle that we use the Bible to interpret

the Bible. Sometimes this may work, but often it does not work because of the diversity and lack of clarity within the biblical writings.

7.4 Further issues

We are thus led to a further clutch of difficulties with seeing the Bible
as a source of authoritative and specific moral injunctions. Given the
diversity of biblical writings there can be no presumption of uniformity in ethical perspective. Furthermore, the world of the Bible is vastly
different from our own. The differences in culture, mindset and frame
of reference, are immense. Each biblical passage or book has its own
specific context and perspective. Any attempt to appropriate ethical
teaching for today will involve digging up an ethical injunction from
its original habitat and planting it into one very different. Are we so
sure it will root? Sometimes the cultural differences are obscured by
familiar language. For the Hebrew Scriptures, adultery appears to be
an offence of a man 'against the woman's husband'.[14] This contrasts
with the modern emphasis on adultery as being primarily a betrayal
of the trust of one's own spouse. Likewise, 'most often in the Old
Testament "peace" comes as a result of the total defeat or even an-
nihilations of Israel's enemies'. Modern notions of reconciliation are
not part of it.[15]

In using Scripture, we cannot avoid the fact that we are involved
in a process of selection, interpretation, appropriation and application. However authoritative the Bible may be at source, application
and interpretation involves all the ambiguities and uncertainties that
attend to human affairs. As has often been remarked, an infallible
Bible is useless unless it is infallibly understood, infallibly interpreted
and infallibly applied. To claim this of our reading is bold indeed.
How can we be sure that a text coming from a different culture and
mindset unambiguously addresses and answers our questions in our
context?

An example is how some base a pacifist ethic upon the New Testament. The context of the New Testament Church was that of a tiny
community living under Roman occupation. A 'just rebellion' would
have been suicidal. Christians as yet had no responsibility for sharing
in political decision making and so a notion of a 'just war' would not
have been part of their thinking. There are indeed profound ethical
visions in the New Testament about 'turning the other cheek', 'loving
one's enemy', and the redemptive power of love and sacrifice. But to
claim in a totally different context that the New Testament requires
pacifism of sovereign states in circumstances not envisaged by the
New Testament writers is to ignore the profound differences between

its context and ours. The ethic simply cannot be transferred without much further ado. This is not to suggest that pacifism is without a serious defence. But it must be defended by argument and not simply by appeal to the authority of the New Testament. Furthermore, there is no specific biblical teaching on a host of pressing contemporary issues. For hundreds of years the nature and role of the state has been top of the agenda for ethical debate; and yet biblical guidance – especially in the New Testament – on this crucial question is rudimentary.

If these concerns are ignored, there is the danger that we read uncritically our own perspective back into the text, so it can then be echoed back to us amplified and validated. Moreover, very often the demand that we submit to the 'authority of Scripture' is in reality no such thing. It is rather the demand that we submit to *another person's interpretation* of Scripture. We are blind if we do not see how much the game of power politics is played out in the Church on this particular pitch.

7.5 A more cautious approach

We are left with conclusions that will be to some liberating, and to others disturbing. Many specific texts, read in a straightforward way, are relative and culture bound in what they appear to teach. Sometimes we can with cogency identify underlying principles but not always. At worst, principles of hermeneutics (that is principles of interpretation) can be in danger of becoming disingenuous attempts to preserve the authority of the text by massaging its 'meanings' in order to make it palatable.

There seems no way out of these difficulties provided we adhere to the fundamental presupposition on which they are based. That presupposition is that the text of Scripture is the final authority, and our role is to listen to its teaching and obey. We are back with the approach to ethics against which Grayling, and others protest. Christian ethics is a matter of obedience to inscrutable commands (see 4.2). But as far as Scripture is concerned, inscrutable or not, what is actually commanded is often far from clear. Scripture speaks to its own time and not always directly to ours, and one biblical writer or editor may not cohere with another.

What I describe as a more cautious approach involves two things.

First, it involves doing away with the idea that Christian ethics is about following the injunctions of authoritative texts. As Daphne Hampson remarked, it is a deep violation of the dignity of women to suggest their position in the modern Church is dependent upon how ancient texts are read. Even if the ancient texts are interpreted in their favour, the violation of dignity still remains.[16] The affirmation of the mutual partnership and equal social power of woman and men is securely grounded ethically and theologically and infused throughout by our experience of being human. This affirmation does not need the permission of ancient texts.

The final 'authority' is not the biblical text, but God. The Bible is both glorious and flawed. It is flawed because it is the work of human beings, and inevitably relative to particular cultures, mindsets and contexts. To give to the biblical text final authority is to be guilty of idolatry – giving a finality and ultimacy that belongs only to God. We may sometimes feel disappointed by a particular text, but we will also be staggeringly inspired by another. That is why it is glorious as well as flawed. It is glorious because of its continued capacity to point power- fully to that which is *beyond* itself, a vision of God. This is why talk of *interpreting* the Bible can be a red herring. The issue is not how the *text* is interpreted, but rather what vision of God *beyond the text* the text might for us facilitate.

Talk of the 'authority' of the Bible can be misleading. Because of some mystique attached to the Bible's authority, we can easily find our- selves approaching the text with the heavy expectation that it will al- ways speak a definitive word; on every question we must first ask 'what the Bible says'; we need carefully worked-out methods for yielding the text's meaning for today, sophisticated 'hermeneutical principles', and so forth. Released from this burden, we can approach the text in a more relaxed and less tidy way. Using critical scholarship as well as we are able, we labour to allow the text to speak from and to its own time and in its own context. Scholarly analysis of the text allows the text to speak for itself, often in its strangeness, rather than be simply a dummy for our thoughts. We then reflect on its impact upon us, engaging our minds, our knowledge and experience, and that of others. There can be no assumption that every passage or text will speak to us. There can be no assumption that the Bible will offer significant insight on every issue. The impact will be at different times, offensive,[17] minimal, pedestrian, stimulating, mind blowing and life changing. The Bible will stimulate, jolt, nourish, resource, challenge and judge. Often it will do this precisely on account of its foreignness, thus challenging our own cultural myopia. But it will not always yield the definitive or authoritative word.

All this presupposes that there is a stubborn 'givenness' about the text over and against our interpretation. It can hardly be denied that we read the text through our own lenses of understanding. We bring to the text our questions, our perspectives and categories of thought. If we are not aware of this, we can easily end up reading into the text what we want to find, or what we expect to find. It seems to me, however, preposterous to suggest, and yet this seems to be the drift of some thinking, that 'reader perspective' is everything, and text nothing. It is as if the text is like some abstract work of art or a piece of bland music – nothing more than the vehicle or stimulus for our own thoughts and feelings. A text is *a medium of communication*, not just something on which to hang our thoughts. That is why the craft of the biblical scholar is so important. It enables us – to some degree – to go beyond our perspective and feel our way a little into the thought world and setting of the text itself. It is not clear why some people trouble to write books explaining that 'reader perspective' is everything and text nothing. If so, why do they labour so hard crafting their own texts, which apparently communicate nothing?

Talk of a 'thrust' in Scripture, some 'emerging consensus', some 'spirit' behind the 'letter', may sometimes be justified, but we should be vigilant lest we adopt such expedients when not justified in order to protect the text's authority. Any authority the Bible has is a *derived authority*. It is derived from its continued capacity to bear witness to God who is always larger than the text. Little is gained from trying to interpret the whole of the Bible's ethics from the perspective of some guiding principle, or from trying to find in all biblical ethics a focus on one common theme – 'love' or 'justice' being among the most commonly chosen candidates. Of course, love and justice – variously understood – are central biblical themes, but we suffer from linguistic impoverishment if we funnel everything through them, neglecting the complementary and integrating biblical themes of, say, covenant, mercy, gratitude, and much else. We impose upon these diverse writings a simplicity and uniformity that is not there.

The second thing is implicit in the above. It is *we* – as individuals, churches and traditions – who use Scripture. It is *we* who judge how its insights are to be appropriated, and it is *we* who must take responsibility for this. This remains true even when we speak also (as we must) of allowing Scripture's vision to mould us because we recognize its depth and worth (see 6.2). Biblical teaching on ethics is diverse, belonging to its own time, sometimes remote, sometimes puzzling or even objectionable. There is no way in which an impartial exegesis or the application of some principle of interpretation can render it all consistent and palatable. A process of selection, interpretation and appropriation is inevitable and we must take responsibility for this. We are human beings and there is no escaping human foolishness and folly. An appeal to 'the Bible' cannot release us from the uncertainty and ambiguity that belongs to the human condition. Still less should we be too ready to claim the authority of Scripture for what may be only *our judgement* as to that to which it points.

7.6 Two basic claims

In the light of the above I wish to make two basic claims.

First, despite all these cautions there are family resemblances evident in biblical ethics. In particular, *biblical ethics is about hammering out what kind of being and what kind of living is a fitting response to our vision of God*. Amid the diversity in biblical writing this is a recognizably dominant theme. I thus claim that the fundamental standpoint of this book – as outlined in earlier chapters – is essentially biblical. The biblical writers may not always see eye to eye over their understanding of God, or on how we should live as the people of God, but their quest is recognizably the same. It is our privilege to continue the quest and to be immensely resourced, but not controlled, by their labours and by the vision they were granted. The Bible, therefore, is not a text that stands over and against us as some kind of coercive authority. It is a living tradition of exploration of which we are part and in which we are invited to share. The God who speaks to us through our own experience and vision is the same God who speaks to us through the Bible. Between the Bible and ourselves there is a resonance because the same God is with us.

Second, the biblical writers and editors rarely 'lay down the law' in an authoritarian fashion. 'Biblicism' is not 'biblical'. What we often find in the Bible is an attempt to address ethical issues in a specific context with the implicit expectation that others will do the same in theirs. The 'wisdom' literature of the Hebrew Bible, in particular, reads not as final injunctions for all time but as guidance and resource for our own judgements in our own setting. The expectation is that we follow the basic method of Scripture, rather than the detailed moral prescriptions of a particular text. The method is essentially that of asking in our context what it means to live as the people of God, given God's call to a radical 'turn around', to justice and liberation, and given that God's will is for our good. It is remarkable how creative the biblical writers are themselves in developing the tradition handed on to them. The biblical tradition is a tradition in dialogue with itself. In other words, we reject the assumption of the Ockhamist tradition that an authoritarian God lays down the law on authority. This is the Heavenly Headmaster or Sergeant Major beloved of Christianity's critics.[18] It is rather that God more gently invites us to nourish our own vision and our own capacity to discern.

In this way, the Bible becomes a wise conversation partner in our own discerning of the things of God. It is too simplistic, however, to say that we sometimes allow our 'reason and experience' to overrule the 'authority of Scripture'. God's revelation does not come to the biblical writers in any manner different in kind from how it comes to us. Our own reflection, reasoning, experience and discernment, feeble thought it may be, is of the same kind as the reflection, reasoning, experience and discernment richly evident in the Bible. As the cliché has it, we see far because we are on the shoulders of giants – but we see with similar eyes. It is not an authority over and against us but a living source of nourishment. But, precisely because of this, we are invited to engage with the biblical material critically and creatively. If we dissent from some strand of biblical thinking, it will be almost inevitably be because we judge some other aspect speaks more authentically. And it is to be *biblical* to exercise that right and responsibility.

Relevant here is the notion of the 'meaning' of a text. The primary craft of the biblical scholar is to explore the meaning of the text as intended and understood by the original editors or writers, and all this within its original context. But once this text becomes part of the bloodstream of the Christian tradition, it may yield new meanings and implications of which the original writers were unaware. It may illuminate totally new situations. Scholarly investigation as to original intention and context informs and stimulates our present thinking, and puts a check on idiosyncratic meanings, which do violence to the text. But such scholarly investigation should not inhibit fresh visions arising out of the text in a radically different setting. Moreover, the criteria for assessing these fresh visions is primarily ethical and theological rather than merely exegetical. By the same token, there is no imperative that when listening to Beethoven's Pastoral Symphony we should fix in our imagination an early nineteenth-century breed of Austrian cow.

The approach I am suggesting gives us no guaranteed certainty over the specifics in our complex world. But we have sufficient for the journey. There is a story of a king who was granted his wish that everything he touched would turn to gold. He regretted it when he touched his daughter. It is a mistake to long for a Bible made of the gold (or dross) of having always the final authoritative word. The Bible is a living tradition of exploration into God and we are invited to join in that exploration. Maybe authoritative interpretations of the biblical text respond to a yearning for certainty that is not available to us. Is this related to the old Gnostic heresy of seeking salvation through the certainty of knowledge? We are called to live, not in the certainty of our wisdom, but in humility and openness and grace.

In no way is this to escape the way in which the Bible uncomfortably interrogates us. We are interrogated over our preoccupations with accumulating wealth, over our attitudes to strangers, over our pretentious prides, over our collusion with injustice, over our indifference to those beyond our most intimate circle, over our lack of grace and gratitude, over the 'hidden depth of inbred sin'. We may also be challenged by the Bible's lack of emphasis on, and charity towards, sexual sins as opposed to the sins of injustice, hypocrisy and the misuse of wealth.

Moreover, despite immense differences and scholarly argument over the detail, we should not allow sophistication to blind us to some grand biblical themes. God is a God of righteousness and grace. This calls for and inspires our response in penitence, love, compassion, generosity, gentleness, humility, gratitude, joy and hope. One of the great advantages of having the canon of Scripture as a point of reference is that we are not allowed for long to neglect this offer and challenge.

7.7 The 'ethical' teaching of Jesus?

This is a complicated subject! Space permits nothing more than a few tentative observations in an attempt to get our bearings.

Constructing the ethical teaching of Jesus is a bit like envisaging the picture of a jigsaw with only a few pieces to go on. Even worse, the pieces we do have are jumbled up with pieces from other puzzles, and we are not sure which is which. The four Gospels in the New Testament do not belong to the genre of modern academic history. Granted that all historians will select and interpret their material, that genre still expresses a commitment to finding as accurate a portrait of the past as possible. The Gospel writers, by contrast, while not blind to the demands of what we might call 'historical accuracy', allowed the Jesus material to engage with their own contexts. The result is that Matthew, Mark and Luke, as much as John, impress their own imprint upon their portraits of Jesus. The results are literary and theological masterpieces but, while they contain history, they also manifest the continued reflections of the earliest churches. Discerning the 'Jesus of history' behind these portraits is a perilously difficult task. For example, two of Britain's most distinguished New Testament scholars – E. P. Sanders and James Dunn – differ on the extent to which Jesus adhered to the Jewish law.[19]

The very title of this section may be challenged. It is by no means obvious that Jesus saw himself as offering ethical teaching as we might understand it. That said, it remains true that his message had implications for how we live. Some things can be claimed with reasonable confidence. The ethic of Jesus does not stand alone. It arises out of his vision of God, and this vision was focused upon the 'kingdom' of God. The kingdom is where God 'reigns' and where that reign is recognized and honoured. In the kingdom there is a radical critique of hierarchy and status. God has put down the mighty from their seat and exalted those of low degree. Greatness is to be found in serving. People's worth does not depend on social status or wealth. In the kingdom, there is the offer of forgiveness to sinners and the acceptance of sinners. Although the demands of God are stringent, there is gentleness and mercy shown to those who fail. Repentance allows a new beginning. In the kingdom, injustice and hypocrisy are confronted, but at the same time the kingdom is about mercy and grace. The kingdom is therefore good news for the poor, the ostracized and marginalized. In the kingdom, relationships express love and generosity, mirroring the love and generosity of God. Our place is not earned. It is a gift. Living is about joy and gladness rather than burdensome duties because life is infused by the praise of God. And so we could go on.

The above paragraph paints only a broad brush picture, and like any sketch will betray a certain slant. A painstaking analysis of the text will fill out the detail and point to other dimensions – with various degrees of certainty. Biblical scholars constantly readjust their kaleidoscopes – but the colours they see are generally from the same spectrum. There is an identifiable perspective. However much debate over the detail and nuances, the thrust is decidedly different from the ethical teaching of, say, Genghis Khan or the Nazi SS.

An enormous amount has been written about the likelihood that Jesus expected the imminent coming of the kingdom. This appears to mean that God would soon 'break into history' and establish the kingdom in some dramatic way, radically discontinuous with life as people knew it. This appears to have been a not uncommon expectation at the time; and tragically understandable for those oppressed and in poverty and for whom history offered no hope. But here we meet a problem. It used to be envisaged that the kingdom would grow gradually in human society as people responded more and more to the gracious invitation of God and the powerful vision of the gospel. That, however, does not seem to have been the expectation of Jesus. The kingdom would instead come dramatically through a decisive divine act. Most scholars add the crucial rider that the kingdom, although an immanent expectation, was nonetheless believed by Jesus to be already anticipated or inaugurated. Other scholars are even bolder, being uncertain that the language is to be understood literally, rather than metaphorically as a way of speaking of the radical nature of God's call to a complete 'turn around'. And can we be sure that Jesus was sure, that he thought in our categories, or did not change or develop his thinking?

What implications has this for the ethical teaching of Jesus? Did his teaching apply only to a future kingdom, but not to this world? Was it an 'interim ethic' – an ethic binding Christians only in the short run up to the kingdom? The kingdom did not come. What validity then has an ethic that presupposed it?

The significance of the failure of the kingdom to arrive can, however, be exaggerated. The 'kingdom' stands – speaking loosely – for human life and society ordered according to God's gracious and wise will, where God's 'reign' is recognized. The expectation that it would arrive in its fullness may have been disappointed, but we can still look for partial realizations and at least be challenged by 'kingdom values' in the here and now. This has led to a long debate about how and in what way the values of the kingdom may be realizable in a 'fallen world'.

New Testament scholars, such as Jack Sanders,[20] go too far when they dismiss the ethic of the New Testament as being of little import because it presupposed the immanence of the kingdom. For us it matters not that the kingdom did not arrive in its fullness. It matters not whether or not the ethic of Jesus was initially an 'interim' ethic for those awaiting the kingdom. The contemporary Christian can still take the vision of the teaching of Jesus – an ethic arising out of his vision of God – and allow it to resource and challenge ethical judgement now. Furthermore, the idea that the kingdom is both 'now' and 'not yet' can readily speak to our condition. Our present existence is full of provisionality, ambiguity and imperfection; and yet it is still gifted by God, and that gives us hope. There has, however, to be a judgement as to how this ethic may have purchase now. One example of a profound engagement with the issues is the thinking of Reinhold Niebuhr. To this I will refer at greater length later (10.2).

One conclusion seems clear. The teaching of Jesus cannot be seen as a new law for the very different context of today. Christians may or may not be socialists or pacifists, but if they are they must take responsibility for their position and argue for it. There can be no direct appeal to the authority of Jesus. By the same token, a saying attributed to Jesus should not be given trumps in a critique of modern divorce law. The Jesus of Mark was probably enunciating God's intention for marriage, and the ideal towards which we aspire. The text in Matthew is not legislating for all time about grounds for divorce when marriages fail. Jesus worked with small groups of oppressed people in a backward province under Roman occupation. He was not legislating for states and for how economies should be structured in the twenty-first century. The Jesus tradition is challenging and mind blowing, but we are the ones who appropriate what is compelling and we must take responsibility for what we appropriate.

We encountered earlier the suggestion that we might discern some 'thrust' in Scripture on an ethical issue, and the principle that we 'use the Bible to interpret the Bible'. What about using Christ as the criterion for interpreting the Bible? Few Christians would argue with the spirit of this, but it is not as straightforward as it may sound. By 'Christ' do we mean the historical Jesus only, or do we mean Christ as further mediated through the experience of the Church through the Spirit? If the latter, how do we identify the specifics? If the former, do we know enough to take us beyond the broad perspective outlined above? We need to be aware further of the danger of making Christ a reflection of our own face at the bottom of a murky well – the metaphor of George Tyrrell.[21] Is this being done when we claim the support of Christ over rules and regulations regarding sex? I do not doubt there is substance in the appeal to Christ as a principle of interpretation, but there is not so much as to take away the need sometimes to make our own judgement; and that is always fallible.

It may be disconcerting to some that there is so much ambiguity. But is it too fanciful to speculate that in this ambiguity we may discern the wise providence of God? The ambiguity releases us to make our own judgement, to nourish our own vision, and in that to exercise the glorious liberty of the people of God. Moreover, it is not I hope succumbing to the peril of modernizing Jesus[22] to see Jesus himself as seeking to nurture within his disciples their own vision rather than an obedience in following the letter of his law. Indeed some of the saying of Jesus read less like prescriptions and more like an attempt to prod people into thinking. Richard Hays allows the Gospel writers to reflect on the Jesus tradition and transpose it into the key of a new context. For this reason he shows limited interest in the teaching of the historical Jesus. What has authority for us is not the Jesus of history only, but the text of the New Testament as it is.[23] There is a lot going for this approach theologically. God is with us through the totality of the Bible's witness and not in Jesus alone. Certainly, in so far as biblical writers were aware of their predecessors, they betray no inhibitions about engaging with them critically and creatively. Yet Hays appears reluctant to allow the continuing Church a similar liberty of reflection and appropriation under the gentle guidance of the Spirit. With the closing of the canon, this permission ceases and we are bound by the letter of the text. But why should this be so?

7.8 An illustration – the Sabbath

I now look at a specific theme in biblical ethics and reflect on how on it the Bible might possibly speak to us today. The theme is that of the Sabbath. I do not follow a formal or structured 'principle of interpretation'. I simply look at the text as its stands and try to understand it in its original setting. The text is allowed to speak for itself – in so far as it can, given all the lenses of understanding through which we read it. I also ask how it might speak in our contexts.

How can we get a feel for the many and varied references to the Sabbath in Scripture? Without I hope imposing an alien scheme, there seem to be a number of interconnected themes. What is important is to put out of our minds any stereotype of a traditional British Sunday. That is not what the Bible is describing when it speaks of the Sabbath!

First, the Sabbath is about being released from the burdens of work and having time for rest, but also time for reflection and nourishment. God's will is that life should not be filled with burdensome toil. There must be space for renewal, celebration and party. This is God's gift. This need not imply a negative attitude to work. But life is about a rhythm of work and other things.

Second, the Sabbath is certainly about religious observance (Isaiah 1.13; Luke 4.16) but the two aspects are connected. The rest and re-newal that the Sabbath affords is God's gift. It follows that the rest and renewal of the Sabbath should be infused with praise and thanksgiving to God for the gifts we enjoy.

But, third, injustice can prevent some people from enjoying the Sab-bath. If I am oppressed and the victim of injustice, then life may be so hard and raw that there is no opportunity to enjoy the Sabbath. At the bleakest, I cannot take time off since I have to work every waking hour simply to keep alive. It follows that biblical thinking about the Sabbath is connected with justice. If God gives not only work but also rest and refreshment, then justice demands everyone should be able to share in it. Thus, Leviticus 25 has some interesting structural arrangements for rectifying the inequalities and injustice that inevitably arise in society. A dominant biblical theme is that the earth is God's gift and so there must be justice in sharing it.

There is scholarly debate over the detail regarding the attitude of Jesus to the Sabbath, but it does seem clear that he regarded the Sabbath as a gift for our good, and any legalistic approach to the Sab-bath that undermines human good must be challenged. 'The Sabbath is made for us and not we for the Sabbath.' Incidentally, the extent to which Jesus was innovative here may have been exaggerated. Evidence suggests Jesus is often repeating the wisdom of many of his Jewish contemporaries. He is not initiating a debate. He is rather participating in an ongoing debate within the Judaism of the time. There is even the suggestion that healing is not merely permitted on the Sabbath. On the contrary, it is especially appropriate on the Sabbath since the Sabbath is about the gift of health and wholeness (John 7.23). Furthermore, Matthew 11.18–19 may be suggesting that what is almost ritualized in the regular Sabbath points to the generosity and gentleness of God, which embraces the whole of life.

Then, fourth, there is the quaint idea that the land and our animals also share in the Sabbath. Every seventh year the land shall have a Sab-bath (Leviticus 25.1–8). This, at least in part, connects with the theme of justice. While on Sabbath what the land yields is available for the poor to reap. Such a generosity and commitment to justice is appropriate given that the land is God's gift (Deuteronomy 8.17–18). Thus, both Sabbath and Jubilee express a commitment to rectifying injustice (Deuteronomy 15.12–18). It is not clear if this quaint notion expresses a sense of respect for the earth and a check against a mindless exploitation. But even if not, we do no violence to the text in our ecologically aware age to allow it to point to that insight. At least one day in seven we are reminded that our grip over nature is limited.

There seems to be a lot here we can connect with. The Sabbath is a gift. It is not about tiresome restrictions but about rest and enjoyment. The sweat of labour is not to fill the whole week. No one should be so burdened, either by society's or by their own expectation that they are denied rest, refreshment, and time for play (Hosea 2.11). This is essential to health and well-being. The wisdom of this insight is clear, and it has nothing to do with a strict 'sabbatarianism' with its 'killjoy' Sunday. Those who make time to listen to Beethoven on Wednesday evening or go to the gym before work on Monday are enjoying God's gift of the Sabbath! John Knox and John Calvin played bowls together *on Sunday*! We should not take ourselves so seriously that we think the world goes round only because of constant contact between grindstone and our nose. That said, Christians have tended to privatize their 'oases of serenity'.[24] We have lost what our Jewish neighbours have preserved, the communal Sabbath.

The Hebrew Bible's commitment to justice demands that everyone should enjoy the Sabbath. No one's leisure is to be at the expense of another's overwork. There are lessons here for many a household at least! As for wider society, economic injustice can deprive people of their right to refreshment when low wages mean long hours of work or when the rich out price opportunities for leisure. In this area as in others our society is judged by the Hebrew Scripture's commitment to justice.

Some writers contrast an Aristotelian view that we rest in order to equip us for work,[25] with a more Hebraic view that we work in order to enjoy rest. It is not clear this kind of ranking or contrast is helpful, and may betray a typical religious suspicion of economic activity. Perhaps it is best to value equally both work and rest and in any case the two categories can hardly be separated. Our 'leisure' may be very creative and our 'work' can be fulfilling and have worth in itself. Nonetheless, the notion of Sabbath may point to the vision that life is not about endless toil and frantic acquisitiveness. There is the invitation to 'let go', to find contentment in the simple and more ordinary and not be swept along by a mindset that runs faster and faster in order to gain more and more of the extravagant and expensive. The gift of the Sabbath grants us freedom from chasing the idols of riches and to find freshness in what by God's grace is not only simpler but also more available. The notion of 'Sabbath' warns us that accumulation can become an end in itself. Instead of liberating us we are enslaved by it.

Even this, of course, can sound like sentimentalism to the ears of the poor. But that again takes us back to justice. And for those who are not poor there are hard questions as to how these ideals can have purchase, given the constraints and pressures of our lives. Nonetheless, the notion of Sabbath invites us to look behind the hustle and bustle and dream a few dreams. They may not all be totally unrealistic.

Notes

1 Esther Fuchs, *Sexual Politics and Biblical Narrative*, Sheffield, Sheffield Academic Press, 2000, pp. 116ff.

2 Rosemary Radford Ruether, *Sexism and God-Talk*, London, SCM Press, 1983, pp. 22ff.

3 Exodus 20.16 and Romans 12.18.

4 Dennis Nineham, *The Use and Abuse of the Bible*, London, SPCK, 1976, pp. 211–12.

5 John Job, *Headline*, article on website.

6 John Stott, *New Issues Facing Christians Today*, London, Marshall Pickering, second edition, 1990, pp. 291ff.

7 Richard B. Hays, *The Moral Vision of the New Testament*, Edinburgh, T&T Clark, 1996, pp. 339ff.

8 Roy Lessin, *Spanking: God's Way of Discipline*, Minneapolis, Bethany, 2001.

9 Simon Blackburn, *Being Good*, Oxford, Oxford University Press, 2001, p. 11.

10 There are various websites on 'Christian Domestic Discipline'.

11 Gregory XVI, *Mirari Vos*, Vatican, 1832, Paragraphs 14–16.

12 According to John T. Noonan in *Contraception*, Harvard University Press, 1989, p. 532; this has been widely held to be a mortal sin in the Catholic tradition. I owe this reference to Charles Curran.

13 Wayne Grudem, *Evangelical Feminism and Biblical Truth*, Sisters, Oregon Multnomah, 2004, pp. 345–55.

14 Cyril S. Rodd, *Glimpses of a Strange Land*, Edinburgh, T&T Clark, 2001, p. 28.

15 Rodd, *Glimpses*, p. 327.

16 Daphne Hampson, *Theology and Feminism*, Oxford, Blackwell, 1990, p. 32.

17 Thus Phyllis Trible has spoken of 'texts of terror': Phyllis Trible, *Texts of Terror*, Philadelphia, Fortress Press, 1984.

18 E.g. P. H. Nowell-Smith, 'Morality: Religious and Secular' in I. T. Ramsey (ed.), *Christian Ethics and Contemporary Philosophy*, London, SCM Press, 1966, pp. 95ff.

19 E. P. Sanders, *The Historical Figure of Jesus*, London, Allen Press, 1993, pp. 218ff.; and J. D. G Dunn, *The Living Word*, London, SCM Press, 1987, pp. 44ff.; and *Jesus Remembered*, Cambridge, Eerdmans, 2003, pp. 563ff.

20 Jack T. Sanders, *Ethics and the New Testament*, London, SCM Press, 1975.

21 George Tyrrell, *Christianity at the Cross Roads*, (1909), p. 49 in edition published by George Allen & Unwin, London, 1963.

22 The phrase is that of H. J. Cadbury from *The Peril of Modernizing Jesus*, London, SPCK, 1962.

23 Hays, *The Moral Vision*, p. 160.

24 The phrase is in Chief Rabbi Jonathan Sacks, *Faith in the Future*, London, Darton, Longman & Todd, 1995, p. 134.

25 Aristotle, *Nicomachean Ethics*, 1177a12–1177b25.

8

Athens, Jerusalem … Mecca, Amritsar, Lhasa

Throughout this book I have argued that Christians should respect the seriousness with which many of our secular** contemporaries approach ethical matters, and engage as partners with so-called secular ethical thought. To use Tertullian's metaphor, Christians live in both Jerusalem and Athens. But what about Mecca? What about Amritsar and Lhasa?

We live in a multi-faith society. The Church, of course, always has. Medieval Christendom encountered at many levels a highly sophisticated Muslim culture and, despite the scandal of the Crusades, the relationships sometimes expressed nobility, openness and tolerance on both sides. There were impressive multi-faith societies in eighth-century Baghdad and in the Convivencia in Spain. Nonetheless, for obvious reasons, the multi-faith context of the modern world is deeply impressed upon our consciousness.

8.1 The 'internal' dialogue

All this has implications for relationships, at both personal and institutional levels. Christians are committed to 'justice, courtesy and love'.[1] In addition, however, there is a theological question. We need a theology adequate to the fact that Christianity is not the only faith. Other faiths inspire the allegiance and nourish the lives of millions. This search for an adequate theology may be called the 'internal dialogue' among Christians as they seek a self-understanding that takes this plurality fully into account. Just as our understanding of being human, and doctrines of creation and providence, have to be cognizant of developments in the sciences, so our theology has to take into account the reality of other faith traditions.

My suggestion is that we begin with the wrong question if we ask about 'Christianity', whether or not Christianity is a 'superior' or the 'final' religion, the 'fulfilment' of humankind's religious quest, whether or not it is God's will that all should eventually become Christians, and such like. These are wrong questions. At worst, they give us a Christian superiority complex, which rightly irritates neighbours of other faiths.[2] They may also encourage Christians to take themselves too seriously, leading to the mental and emotional strain of a cognitive dissonance that tries to press Christianity to carry a burden it cannot bear.

They are wrong questions because the focus is on *Christianity*. The true focus should be on *God*. It is a tragedy when our prime allegiance is to something called 'Christianity' rather than to God.[3] God is greater than and beyond Christianity. God stands over and against Christianity as judge as much as validator. Christianity is both glorious and flawed. It is glorious when it points beyond itself to God's truth, goodness and grace, and when Christians manifest in their lives the 'fruits of the spirit'. It is flawed because of its historical and cultural relativity, its self-serving ideologies, idolatrous pretensions and acquiescence in injustice. The question, therefore, is not how other faiths relate to Christianity, but how all of us (whatever our faith tradition) relate to God. This gives no religious tradition an overall privileged position. This is a good model with which to consider our relationship with explicitly theistic faiths. I recognize the matter is more complicated with, for example, non-theistic Buddhists. The same attitude of humility and openness, however, applies. People of other faiths have a right to be self-defining. That said, it is not unreasonable for Christians from their perspective to interpret Buddhist wisdom and goodness of life as manifesting the gentle inspiration of God's spirit.

The insight that a particular faith tradition should be relativized by the otherness of God is deeply rooted in Jewish and Christian thinking. Isaiah confronted an idolatry that worshipped that which is not God. Idols may be made of theology and religious tradition as much as of wood and stone.[4] This illustrates a deeply seated biblical vision that God is always beyond and greater than our understanding.[5]

My suggestion, then, is that faith should be God-centred, not Christianity-centred. Christian belief is that the 'earth is the Lord's and the fullness thereof', and that God has never been left 'without a witness'.[6] God is greater and wider than, and cannot be owned by, any one religious tradition. This enables us to honour with gratitude how God has blessed other faiths alongside how God has blessed our own. It is worth noting that some early Christian theology employed the notion of the 'Logos Spermaticos' – the 'Word' of God is universally present in creation. For Justin Martyr this 'Word' is the one of whom 'every race were partakers'.[7] Thus, the 'Word' Christians experience may be the same 'Word' that may be present in other faith traditions. In Sikhism the notion of *Shabad* is a direct parallel to this notion of logos. A possible interpretation of the prologue to John's Gospel is that the Word made flesh in Jesus is the same Light that 'enlightens everyone'.[8]

A 'God-centred' faith will allow Christians to bear witness to what they believe God has given them and which they offer to share. But a God-centred faith will also allow Christians to feel unthreatened if other faith traditions have in some respects a more creditable record or a fresh insight. This may not give glory to Christianity. But that does not matter. It gives glory to God. For example, Judaism has arguably often succeeded better than Christianity in finding a proper balance between right living and right believing. Both are important, but Christianity arguably has more often fallen into the error of exalting doctrinal rectitude over righteousness of life and this has encouraged exclusivism, intolerance and even persecution. It has often not heeded the warning that 'heresy' is more about 'manner' than 'matter'. In consequence, Judaism has a better record of maintaining within the community a 'loyal opposition' and those with 'doubts'. To take another example, although the issue is debated among scholars, it is arguable that eastern religions on the whole have a better record on what we now call 'environmental issues' than has the Christian tradition. Of course, given the immense diversity within all religious traditions and their long and complex histories, generalizations are extraordinarily difficult to justify. In the respects mentioned, Christianity at its best has succeeded gloriously but, at its worst, it has failed abysmally. This tension between the glory and the failure is found in all faith traditions.

The point is that a God-centred faith takes us beyond the temptation to show Christianity in the best possible light, or as always having trumps in a comparison. People of other faiths are not competitors or those longing for 'fulfilment' in Christianity. A good Muslim, Sikh or Jew is to be honoured as a good Muslim, Sikh or Jew, and has a right to be self-defining. They are not 'anonymous Christians'.** They are those with whom we share a common humanity and in whose lives God's grace is manifest. The conversion we seek is not that everyone convert to Christianity, but that we *all* convert, and convert again and again, to God. Instead of being threatened by the richness in other faiths we should rather give thanks that God's magnanimity in self-disclosure has been so liberal. We must therefore resist a Christian mindset that delights in finding fault with other faith traditions, scratching all the time for evidence to demonstrate Christianity's superiority. A mindset that believes in the ubiquity of God's spirit with God's people should rather look with confidence for what speaks of God, thus delighting in what we may hold in common and in a greater richness we may enjoy through sharing.

The rather cold word 'dialogue' has become almost standard jargon to describe this kind of approach. What it stands for, however, is far from cold. Christians relate to people of other faiths as neighbours and friends, and with a commitment to 'justice, courtesy and love'. There will be a penitence for the mammoth sins of the churches and Christians. At the same time, there will be a desire humbly to offer and share what we believe God has given to us, be it always with 'gentleness and reverence'.[9] All that, of course, may be served on the salver of an uninterrupted monologue. Dialogue, by contrast, involves listening, understanding, empathy, openness, receptivity. If we are to use the language of 'mission', then Christian mission is about listening and receiving, as well as about telling and giving, as together we seek a fuller alignment with the '*missio dei*', God's mission to the world.

Helpful here is the Muslim scholar Omid Safi's distinction between tolerance and a richness gained through diversity. 'Tolerance' can easily become simply allowing the other to exist, but the other must not affect my life. He protests: 'I don't want to "tolerate" my fellow human beings, but rather to engage them at the deepest level of what makes us human, through both our phenomenal commonality and our dazzling cultural differences.'[10]

Dialogues do not always go smoothly. Inter-faith dialogue is not like a happy family opening presents on Christmas morning. Thomas Ogletree has spoken of a 'hospitality of ideas'.[11] At the same time, if Christians are entitled to claim that an authentic vision of God must be consistent with what they see in Christ, there will sometimes be puzzlement, misunderstanding, disagreement and also hurt. We are human and that is life. Senses of hurt as to how one's faith tradition has been misrepresented or treated cut deep. Hindus and Buddhists often need to be convinced that Christians no longer believe about them what some earlier missionaries once wrote. The fact remains, however, Christians always have allowed a belief in our common humanity and in the ubiquity of God's grace to enable them to learn from those outside or before the Christian tradition – the Greek philosophers, Maimonides, Ibn Rushd, Martin Buber, Mahatma Gandhi and others. What is exciting about the modern world is that we have only just begun.

How does all this square with special beliefs Christians may have about Jesus Christ? To explore this, I focus on a classic text, John 14.6: '*I am the way, and the truth, and the life. No one comes to the Father except through me.*' I will not attempt here a rigorous analysis of what this might have meant to John, although it is worth commenting that John's Gospel was not written within the corridors of power, but rather out of a small persecuted community struggling for a hearing for its fresh vision. Furthermore, the context of the verse is a conversation between Jesus and Thomas about issues within a small early Christian community. The context is not that of a conversation about people of other faiths. Here I will attempt to ask rather how the verse might be interpreted by us, or speak to us, in our different context.

The emphasis should be upon our understanding of God, and of the manner of our approach to God – that is the 'way' by which we 'come to the Father'. In Christian experience the name of Jesus may be crucial since he is the one through whom, above all, Christians are given this vision of God. A like vision, however, may be given to people of other faiths in other ways. What is central is the one to whom Jesus points. 'Through me' can thus be understood as 'by my way' – that is through a life of openness, love, vulnerability, self-giving and all those qualities that open us up to the generous grace of God. Thus interpreted, John 14.6 should 'never become a triumphalist slogan though which just a few of God's children may minister to their own self-esteem, coming to believe that they alone are the specially favoured'.[12] Jesus may be central to Christian devotion because in Christian experience he is for them the pivotal one who points to God. He will not, however, be so pivotal for others of other faith traditions. Other texts in John's Gospel might be read as being consistent with such a position.[13] In particular, for the prologue of John's Gospel the Word of God, seen signally in Jesus, is the same Word which is present everywhere. We 'come to the Father', not exclusively through Jesus, but through the 'Word'. The 'Word' is God's gracious invitation and luring love, manifest signally in Jesus certainly, but manifest also throughout the infinite strands of creation and human experience. The 'Word' may be made flesh in Jesus, but between Jesus and the 'Word' there is not a numerical identity. As we saw above, this vision is expressed later in Justin Martyr's *Second Apology*.

A Christian is thus a person who belongs to a tradition that looks to Jesus as the 'image of the invisible God' and the 'author and finisher' of their faith. Part of what it means to be a Christian is to belong to a tradition that sees Jesus as its principal icon of God. Moreover, at the level of spirituality a Christian may have intense personal devotion to Jesus. All this can be said within the Christian community about what Jesus may mean for Christians. This is all fully consistent, however, with the belief that what God gives to *us* signally through Jesus, God may give to other faith traditions *in other ways*. To affirm that God has richly blessed us through Jesus does not involve a denial that God has richly blessed those of other faiths as well. Such an idea may indeed connect with the suggestion of Chief Rabbi Jonathan Sacks that God blesses us through our historical and cultural differences.[14] Christians are fully entitled to claim that what is authentic elsewhere must be consistent with what they see in Jesus. After all, we need some feel for how we might 'discern the spirits, whether they be of God'.[15] Nevertheless, there is a wrong kind of stress on Jesus, which has the effect of preventing God from being God. God's blessings are generously and widely given. There is a kind of Christian exclusivism, which implicitly denies that 'the earth is the Lord's and the fullness thereof' and that God's Spirit blows where God's Spirit wills. Jesus may point to that which is universal, and in so doing points beyond himself.

Both Scripture and the classical Christian tradition have balanced a special focus on Christ with a wider focus on God's all-embracing engagement with the world. The inclusion of the Hebrew Scriptures within the canon is crucial here, affirming the authenticity of its faith. 'Inclusive' texts are found alongside 'exclusive' ones.[16] Furthermore, the doctrine of the Trinity can be seen as, among other things, offering a model for combining a focus on *Christ* with a recognition that what we receive through Christ is received from *God who is creator*, who is everywhere present *through the Spirit*. Thus, what Christians receive through Christ may be given to other faith traditions in other ways 'through the Spirit'.[17] Indeed, Wilfred Cantwell Smith has argued that if we say there is 'no other name' by which we may be saved we are implicitly denying the reality of the work of God's Spirit. In his words we are in danger of a 'Unitarianism of the Son'.[18] Again, theologies of incarnation and atonement may speak not only of what we see in Jesus, but also of deep truths about the human condition and of God's wider engagement with humankind.[19] Israel Selvanayagam is among many who point out that in the biblical tradition God makes a covenant with Noah, who represents 'every living creature that is found upon earth'.[20]

John 14.6 may thus be interpreted as affirming what Jesus means to Christians, and as an expression of gratitude for what God gives us through him. None of this implies a judgement on other faith traditions, nor a denial of how God has blessed them. If the jargon is helpful, the text is in this way interpreted *doxologically*, that is as an expression of praise, rather than *theologically* as marking boundaries beyond which faith in God is intrinsically lacking. When a loving daughter exclaims: 'You are the best mum in the world!' she is speaking of what her mum means to her. She is not saying her school friends' mums are all rubbish.[21]

Suppose, however, this approach does not persuade. Instead, it is insisted that there is something crucial about the person and work of Jesus to which Christianity alone bears witness.[22] It does not follow that Christians who hold this need be out of sympathy with the tone of this chapter. It is merely that they bring to the dialogue something extra to share and contest.

None of this compromises a commitment to the fitting and the true. But we express and honour rather than compromise such commitments when we engage in an unending quest into the unfathomable riches of God, a quest that combines both loyalty to what Christians have been given and grateful openness to the riches God gives us through other faith traditions.

8.2 The 'external dialogue'

By the external dialogue I mean engaging with people of other faiths with a view (in so far as the focus is on ethics) to exploring together a vision of the good for life and society. In the above section I have suggested a theological rationale for this, and the manner in which we might engage in it.

People of other faiths are different from Christians. We should not expect to find an easy and premature agreement, still less some bland common denominators. Even when there is similarity in ethical teaching, there will be difference in theological and cultural underpinning. Mental paradigms may be different, and boundaries between what Christians might define as the 'ethical' and the 'religious' drawn differently. This diversity is in many ways to be welcomed because in dialogue across differences, while sometimes different perspectives may remain irreconcilable, there are often insights and nuances that can enrich the Christian tradition, as Christian insight can enrich the vision of people of other faiths. A good example of this mutual enrichment through dialogue is found in *Christian Ethics: A Jewish Perspective* by Roland Green.[23]

The temptation to find premature and superficial agreement is to be avoided, but so also is the opposite danger of exaggerating differences. We share a common humanity and experience a common human condition. For example, the UN charter has been critiqued for its 'western' emphasis on 'rights' as distinct from 'duties' and 'obligations', which some perceive as having a greater emphasis in Hindu traditions. But are the two emphases irreconcilable? Earlier in the book I suggested that the language of 'rights' serves as an important strand in the tapestry of moral judgement, but few would argue this language does all the work of ethics (see 3.4). Western thought likewise struggles with finding a proper balance between 'rights' and other loci of value such as obligations and duties. This is not to suggest that the Hindu and other traditions simply mirror the western debate. These have their own cultural and religious colouring. It is to say, however, that there is a forum in which dialogue can take place. If one faith tradition finds echoes in another (and, of course, there will be many echoes) the echoes gain a deeper resonance and tone because of the distinctive cultural and religious context. There is strong reason for rejoicing at our diversity and difference because in dialogue there is promise of finding a richness far beyond settling for a common denominator. But, of course, discrimination and critical judgement must always be there. Cheap jibes about 'pick and mix' are unfair.

I now point to four indicative areas where this might be fruitful.

8.3 Democracy and theocracy

In the wake of '9/11' Samuel Huntingdon published a book on the 'clash of civilizations'.[24] He sees the future as being dominated by a clash between the culture and ideology of liberal democracy and a more theocratic Islam, each with their own oppositional self-definition. In a theocracy the state rules on behalf of God and is accountable only to God. Unfortunately, God calls people to account all too gently. It is therefore a short step to oppressive totalitarianism. Evidence of this is seen in the Taliban and in the 'Muslim Brotherhood' movement. The Islamic State is a state that rules according to Islamic law and this alone gives it legitimacy. The notion of *jihad* is radicalized and politicized and becomes a struggle against anything deemed not Islamic, including a struggle against more progressive fellow Muslims. Sayyid Qutb is among those who contrast pure Islam with *jahiliyya*, the ignorance evident in modern apostasy. Related to this is Wahhabism, a radicalized Islam confining itself to Qur'an and Sunna, ignoring the later Islamic intellectual tradition. From this perspective it is the role of the state to impose uniformity. Various forms of 'Islamic states' have been tried, say in Pakistan under Zia ul-Haq, in Iran under Ayatollah Khomeini and in Afghanistan under the Taliban.

The reality, however, is more complicated and more reassuring. These movements are not representative of Islam as a whole any more than the American right is representative of Christianity. It is a grotesque caricature to suggest that Islam is monolithic and inevitably committed to a theocracy that is *de facto* totalitarian or despotic. That there are totalitarian states in the Muslim world is beyond doubt, but here the political ideology and abuse of power is at variance with much that is dominant in the Muslim tradition. We bear false witness against our neighbour if this is denied, as Christianity is misrepresented if its less reputable expressions are seen as being the norm. Furthermore, the governments of predominantly Muslim countries are not necessarily expressive of or validated by Islam. In 1924 the Grand National Assembly of Turkey abolished the Caliphate, which by then was hardly any more a political power, and many states have insisted on a separation between political power and religion, a political and theological stance expressed, for example, in the work of Abd al-Raziq.[25] An oppressive state such as that of Iraq under Saddam may have used the rhetoric of Islam in its propaganda but it was not an Islamic state.

Ahmad Moussalli finds the notions of democracy and pluralism to have deep roots in Islamic thought, and points out that the protection of individual rights and the legitimization of intellectual and religious differences finds deep recognition in Islamic history. He also claims a deeply Islamic notion is that of the 'people' as the source of ultimate political sovereignty. Such ideas 'provide the Muslim world with common ground with the west'. He continues: 'While the history of the highest Islamic political institution, the caliphate, is mostly a history of authoritarian governments, the economic, social, political, and intellectual history of Islam abounds with liberal doctrines and institutions'. He instances the notions of equality, justice, freedom, consultation, consensus, difference and minorities.[26] The 'fundamental law of the first Islamic state distinguished between religious authority and political authority'.[27] This is seen especially when history is written 'from the edge' instead of through the eyes of those with political power. Often in Islamic societies these principles led to toleration and a full acceptance of non-Muslims in the political structure. Given that no one can claim to be God's sole representative, resort had to be made to human judgement. Islam, like Christianity, has sometimes tasted the idolatry of equating the human with the divine, and those in power have sometimes found the taste sweet, but the religious protest has never been silenced. Thus, the basic notions of the *Shari'ah* protect people and societies from state tyranny. Mutual consultation is a key commitment.[28] Indeed, medieval Islamic thought was offering an analysis of human rights and the mutual relationships between rulers and ruled at a time when western regimes were far more authoritarian, and often based on the notion of the divine right of the ruler. While the history of Islam is chequered, historically, Muslim societies have often been more tolerant than Christian ones. Examples are to be found in Cordoba in Muslim Spain, Baghdad in the eighth and ninth centuries and the Mughal Empire. Moussalli argues that movement towards democracy in Islam is reinforced by the perception of a correlation between miserable economic and social conditions and lack of democracy.[29] The key doctrines of *Shura* (consultation) and *Ijma* (consensus) point to a government's legitimacy in a people's consent. Likewise, the doctrine of *ikhtilaf* opens the way for the acceptance of freedom of thought and speech.[30] Justice is a central theme in the Qur'an as in the Bible.[31]

Moreover, and of central importance for mutual understanding between Muslims and Christians, all this has a theological ground in expressing the worth, dignity and rights of everyone as a child of God.[32] 'The essential value of human life is God given.'[33]

It is this vision that is allowing an increasingly strong Muslim voice to challenge traditional patriarchy in a way similar to what is happening in Christianity. Just as biblical texts such as Colossians 3.18ff. and 1 Peter 3.1ff. have received a massage through contextualization, and a neutering through an appeal to a more authentic theology of equality, some Muslim scholars have similarly interpreted texts in the Qur'an, such as Sura 4, verse 11 and Sura 2, verse 282.[34]

It is true, of course, that Ahmad Moussalli's view[35] would not be universally shared. Opposing it is the insistence that democracy defers to the will of the people, while Islam, by contrast, is obedient to the will of God. Democracy is a human fabrication based on human and not divine understanding. Theocracy and democracy are thus in opposition and the Muslim must embrace the former. In consequence there is no separation between religion and state.[36] There is only a short step from this to totalitarian control. The trouble with theocracy is that it tends to validate human structures of power.

It is important to remember that a parallel debate has taken place within Christianity. Pope Gregory XVI's encyclical *Mirari Vos* in 1832 likewise rejected democracy in favour of theocracy.[37] Later in the book (see 11.1–11.4) I give reasons why I believe Christians have been right to embrace, and to help develop, the values and commitments of free and democratic societies. There is not space here – neither have I the competence – to explore further how these issues may present themselves within Islam. Sufficient has been said, however, to encourage a fruitful dialogue, and this will include an appreciation of Islam's deep commitment to communal well-being, to hospitality and to a compassion that challenges the individualism, alienations, and deep inequalities of western society.

This conclusion is encouraged also by the work of Tariq Ramadan, who takes up these themes in a way that is similar to Ahmad Moussalli. Faith for the Muslim, as for the Christian, does indeed express itself in the whole of life and not just the so-called private dimension. The Qur'an, like the Bible, has a vigorous and demanding social message – but that does not mean we 'merge the categories of the religious and the political'. Judgement has to be exercised in making political decisions. In particular, Ramadan speaks of honesty, service, fairness and justice.[38] He speaks of a commitment to the common good (*al-maslaha*) and robustly of human rights.[39]

The concept of *tawhid* – the oneness and supremacy of God embracing the whole of life – is, of course, affirmed. There is, however, a distinction between 'Islamic principles related to religious ritual and those that concern the affairs of the world and society'. He adds: 'In the history of Christianity, arriving at this "distinction of orders" led to the necessary establishment of a clear separation between ... church and state. This structuring, and the use of the space that it assumes, is very accessible to Muslims because it is close to their way of conceiving of the nature of their relationship with God and the modalities of their acting in the world.'[40] For this reason, Ramadan rejects as 'restrictive and out of context' those Muslims who decline to participate in the political processes of western democracies.[41] He adds: 'The role of Muslim communities in the West is to defend principles, not interests, and if it transpires that it is in their interests to have their universal principles respected, it should be clear that their fight for these principles serves society as a whole.'[42]

We are speaking here, not about western political institutions, still less the often deeply disingenuous foreign policies of western democracies, and certainly not the hegemonies of their militarism and pseudo-colonialisms. What is important is rather the commitment to the freedoms and rights of the individual along with enfranchisement, transparency and accountability in the political process. There are also the checks and balances that minimize the abuse of power. All this implies an open society that is rich because of free cultural and intellectual exchange. While Ahmad Moussalli finds much common ground between Islam and the values of western democracy, it must not be thought Islamic tradition is uncritical of 'western liberalism'. The vision of society as a collection of individuals, each pursuing their own ends guarded by toleration and 'rights' has limited attractiveness. Thus, Muslim thinkers (like Christian) have struggled, for example, to mitigate the human costs of a market economy. 'Muslim banking' is an example of such an attempt (see Chapter 12). Likewise, as has been noted, there is an emphasis on community, solidarity and justice – an emphasis lacking, or at least down played, in western liberalism. I return to these themes in Chapter 11. Enough has been said, however, to show there is scope for continued dialogue.

At least two important conclusions follow. First, Christians should add their weight to the exploration of these richer and more authentic traditions in Islam, instead of indulging in the simplistic negative rhetoric of some western propaganda. The characterization of Islam, for example, as inherently violent is bearing false witness against our neighbour. It is part of the wider prejudice that theism is inherently violent and all theists stand or fall together at this point (see 5.3.3). It is sufficient here to maintain that, historically, Islam has been an immense humanizing and civilizing force, through its insistence amid the tribalism of the middle east that there is in fact only one tribe, the human race under God, a belief encouraging the qualities of *abad* – compassion, kindness, civility, and respect for others.[43]

Second, the economic and political context cannot be ignored. The tragedy is that the Islamic world, after its magnificent cultural achievements within and on the perimeter of medieval Europe, is in many places now struggling politically and economically and there is a perception of western hegemony and hypocrisy, a perception often justified, and all this combined with post-colonial resentment. The causes and the cures of radicalism are complex, but we can do worse than begin with this basic recognition (see 13.6).

8.4 Forgiveness and the Holocaust

In this section I attempt to do two things. First, I explore the notion of forgiveness from within the western Christian tradition. Having done that I ask if this might be a subject for fruitful conversation with those of the Jewish faith.

'*Forgive us our sins as we forgive those who sin against us.*' The centrality of forgiveness in the Lord's Prayer signifies its centrality in Christianity. But how is forgiveness to be understood? Suppose I am hurt through someone's callousness or indifference? The hurt may be trivial, or it may be life shattering. My son is murdered, my wife raped, I am tortured or I lose both legs in a terrorist bomb.

If the offence and hurt are grave the emotional fall-out will cut deep. I may feel overwhelming anger and resentment. There will be outrage that my life has been violated. I may feel the offender should suffer punishment for their offence. These reactions are not only understandable, they are also not necessarily unworthy or inappropriate, although one would not say this of other possible reactions, such as spite and malice. Christianity is wrong if and when it seeks swiftly to leapfrog over all these responses and expect a premature forgiveness. I say '*in so far*'. Within the diversity of and subtleties of Christian thought this is not always the Christian response, *but it is sometimes*, and it is certainly sometimes the perception.

It is helpful at this point to make two distinctions. The first is the distinction between *interpersonal forgiveness* and *communal forgiveness*. For the moment, we consider only the former. The second distinction is between '*forgiveness*' and '*reconciliation*'. By forgiveness I refer to the attitudes and disposition of the one offended. By reconciliation I mean a restored relationship. The former does not necessarily issue in the latter. A woman beaten and abused by her estranged husband might muster attitudes of forgiveness, but that is consistent with her never wanting to see him again. Moreover, even if she wants reconciliation, the blockage may be on his part, in his attitudes and in a failure to repent. For true reconciliation, both parties play their part.

I return to my main argument. In the experience of being hurt, forgiveness is not the only and rarely the foremost response and neither should it be. It is proper to express outrage and anger and this may signify a proper self-respect. Furthermore, there has been a serious disregard of moral standards and outrage rightly expresses this. A premature forgiveness can imply a lack of self worth – or a lack of respect for the moral values that have been defiled. 'I do not matter. Standards of decency and respect do not matter either. Let's forget it. I forgive you.' There is something hollow in this response, recalling S. J. Perelman's jibe 'To err is human, to forgive is supine.'[44] The value of forgiveness is ranked over and above the self-respect of the person harmed and the values that uphold that respect. The reality of judgement cannot be lightly passed over. As Jeffrie Murphy remarks, we 'risk supporting a morally flabby worldview wherein wrongdoing is not taken seriously and in which wrongdoers are given insufficient incentive to repent, atone and repair'.[45]

A response to offence may also include a desire for 'revenge'. This is a difficult concept to handle. 'Revenge' can describe a hateful vindictiveness that demands repayment tenfold. Different, however, from this type of vindictiveness is the belief that there is something inherently appropriate in an offender suffering for their offence. In the case of criminal acts, the state takes over and imposes punishment and, as Kant argued, punishment is immoral if it has only a utilitarian rationale. There must be a retributive dimension that is just and appropriate to the crime, and that honours the criminal's personal responsibility.[46] For the victim to think this appropriate, and even to desire it, is understandable and not obviously wrong. That said, Romans 12.19 and John 8.7 properly counsel caution. Our knowledge of the other person is fallible. Are we so sure we know what they deserve? Furthermore, knowledge of our own failings should counsel magnanimity. The limitations of our understanding of others, and awareness of our own failings, commend humility in judging our fellows.

The sense that it is right that the offender should suffer for their wrongdoing need not necessarily, however, issue in the demand for punishment inflicted by some authority, despite the widely offered argument in the past that this is inherently appropriate in all circumstances, because punishment signifies and declares our respect for the moral law. Such a social philosophy was the presupposition of some forms of penal substitution approaches to atonement theology.[47] In the absence of punishment, the offender may still suffer, but in the different sense of suffering the internal anguish of repentance. One of the fascinating developments of atonement theology derives from the realization that if there is genuine repentance, punishment, at least in personal relationships and the family, becomes inappropriate and irrelevant.[48] And in any case, repentance leads to renewal in a way that punishment may not.

There are other emotional responses that are understandable, and yet more difficult to justify. I may allow hatred of the offender to dominate my mind. Resentments can similarly take over. The offender's final and most lasting offence is to poison my inner life. Anger, resentment, hatred and similar emotions need to be 'worked through' and if they remain be given only limited lodging space. There is wisdom in the injunction 'Be angry but do not let the sun set on your anger.'[49] This text is, in fact, quoted by Bishop Butler who argues there is a proper place for resentment, but warns against it dominating and consuming our thoughts.[50] Is, however, a person who has never resented injury to be thought of as saintly or rather as servile? There was a place in Athens for the Furies.

Despite its currency in the Church, the notion of 'forgiveness' is difficult to define. I have described it as an attitude or disposition of the person hurt. Forgiveness involves dealing with one's emotions of anger, hurt, outrage and resentment. But it also includes cultivating goodwill and magnanimity towards the offender. There is a refusal to dehumanize, and this may be encouraged by the fact that we are all sinners and all in need of grace. Perhaps more centrally, forgiveness is a willingness to put a bracket around the offence, to draw off the sting of its power to continue to hurt and poison in the future. The offence may not be forgotten. But it is not remembered in the sense of being 're membered' – its reality (its 'member') being remade in the present. Thus, Bishop Butler spoke of forgiveness as primarily a matter of inner disposition. I overcome the intensive negative feelings I have towards someone on account of their behaviour. It is essentially a change of heart.[51]

Christian faith gives us a humbling perceptive. We are not to take ourselves too seriously and, above all, we are not to see ourselves as obviously morally upright and the other as the epitome of evil. If my neighbour is made of warped timbers, then so am I. If my grain is a little straighter, is this really a cause for pride or more for humble gratitude for what I have received? There is also the dogged Christian hope, not only that everyone is a child of God but also that no one is beyond the reach of divine grace. And if the unrequited offence has wounded my self-respect – can my self-respect really be damaged by this one person, since I find it sufficiently in the knowledge that I am a child of God? A Christian perspective will be the first to challenge an easy assumption that the hurt is all on one side and the blame, itself a problematical notion, all on the other. But that is very far from saying it is always or even usually 'fifty fifty'. In our relation-ship with God, giving some estimate of the extent of our guilt is of limited importance since the divine grace nourishes us in all the com-plicated mishmash that makes us what we are. But in relationships with one another, some estimate of our blame and culpability is often unavoidable.

The magnanimity of forgiveness can lead to reconciliation. It is at this point that we meet most urgently the often repeated moral objection to forgiveness. Does a willingness to forgive treat too lightly the horror of the offence forgiven? Occasionally, the victims of horrific terrorism have been quick to assure the media that they 'forgive' the criminals who have destroyed their lives. Sometimes they are Christians who feel it their Christian duty. It is difficult not to be moved and impressed, and yet there is kind of forgiveness which is given too lightly or prematurely. Christian theology has responded to this difficulty by insisting that forgiveness must, at least normally, correlate with repentance. If we speak only of forgiveness, we leave the offender unconfronted, unchanged, and ready to offend again. There might even be a moral outrage at the kind of forgiveness that appears to ignore or belittle the horror of our inhumanity towards one another. Repentance is a harrowing facing up to who we are and what we have done. The dark and sombre 'penal substitution' theories of atonement are perhaps best seen as metaphorical models, which point (although not very well) to this insight. They speak of the gravity of evil and of the costliness of both repentance and forgiving grace. Neither is cheap. When, however, the magnanimity of forgiveness and the reality of repentance (each to an extent evoking the other) come together, there are opened up possibilities for reconciliation and renewal which are unequalled. The generosity of the offer of forgiveness – risky as it is – can empower, although it cannot guarantee, the response. The story of Jesus and Zacchaeus is an instance of this.[52]

Sometimes certainly. Often? We may hope so. But can we say 'always'? Much of the above seems a bit heavy if we are thinking of offering and accepting apologies over trivial matters. Such everyday exchanges keep relationships sweet. But can we really expect a parent to forgive their son's murderer, or the young woman whose legs were blown off by a terrorist, now struggling with two prostheses, to forgive that terrorist? What about the horrific example posed by Dostoevsky? Can we expect a peasant woman to forgive the landlord who sadistically makes her watch her child being torn apart by vicious dogs?[53]

Every Christian must hear the call to forgive. The call to forgive is a response to the magnanimity of God which we seek to imitate.[54] What is a proper general expectation, however, may not be reasonable in every instance. Christian compassion and gentleness should caution against making too great a demand on the victims of humanity's worst crimes. In particular, it is often unreasonable to expect reconciliation. Sometimes it may happen and it is a miracle of grace. But to expect it always is unreasonable, even callous.

Churches are sometimes guilty of bullying victims with a demand for premature forgiveness. Suppose a woman is suffering violence or emotional abuse? The violence and abuse is recognized, but then there is embarrassment. Such things do not happen in Christian circles. We are too nice. There should be no conflict. The matter is swept under the carpet with a demand that the victim forgives. Such a premature demand for easy forgiveness only compounds the abuse. Furthermore, if the victim is not ready to forgive, or feels forgiveness is inappropriate in the absence of repentance, the victim becomes the offender by failing to oblige the demand of such misguided pastoral zeal. In particular, church culture is at its worst when those in positions of power abuse their power and then demand forgiveness as a right, despite the absence of repentance. The abuse is thus compounded. On the other hand, in other contexts the ready offer of forgiveness can itself become a means of wielding power. There is the enjoyment of the high moral ground and the gift of forgiveness becomes a subtle means of controlling people and putting them in our debt. We are generous in our forgiveness with an eye to our own ends. Vigilant self-awareness and grace are necessary if we are to avoid these perils.

To return to the distinctions made earlier, *reconciliation* in every instance seems an unreasonable expectation. In some instances, hurt may cut too deep. But can we expect a *forgiving attitude* in every instance? Here there needs to be gentleness in supporting people as they deal with their hurt and sense of outrage. There is indeed the danger that if the anger overwhelms, the damage to the soul becomes more grievous than the damage, say, to the body. On the other hand, people should not be bullied, as they often are in the Church, with appeals for premature and full 'forgiveness'. In any case, 'forgiveness' is not a single thing that people either have or do not have. There are degrees in the forgiving spirit. There are plenty of resting places between violent hatred and passionate love.

So far I have spoken of human–human relationships, but what of the divine–human? It is a precious truth of Christian faith that God forgives those 'who truly repent', also granting them time for 'amendment of life'. Having received ourselves the forgiveness of God, we are enabled and inspired to forgive others. This, however, is consistent with the frank acknowledgement that there are some relationships where a reconciliation cannot reasonably be expected, even if sometimes it does happen. But what about the offenders' reconciliation with *themselves*? Can we *always* forgive ourselves? Suppose I rape, torture and then murder a teenage girl? I then experience a change of heart and go through the agony of full repentance. Can I reasonably expect her parents ever to be reconciled? More stringently can I ever forgive myself and be reconciled to myself? Does the glorious truth that 'God forgives and so I can forgive myself' apply in all conceivable circumstances? To deny this seems to limit the grace of God. To affirm it seems unbelievable. Can we resolve this dilemma or is this an instance of the dark tragedy that casts its shadow on the human condition?

What is the fundamental mistake of Christians who demand that in every instance of hurt, forgiveness should be expected, or even be the immediate and the dominant response? The mistake is essentially failing to recognize that values conflict. There is a conflict between the *prima facie* value of forgiveness and other *prima facie* values – self-respect, anger and outrage at a violation of moral order, the crucial importance of repentance if reconciliation is to have any integrity, and the victim's proper right to express hurt.

I have spoken of the *personal* forgiveness of the *individual victim*. But what about the dynamics of *corporate* guilt and *corporate* forgiveness? This language is different and fraught with difficulties. What does it mean to say the current residents of Liverpool and Bristol share guilt for their forebears' part in the slave trade over a century before they were born? To what extent am I, whose family suffered no death in World War II, the victim of what the Nazis did to Britain in the early 1940s before I was born?

Contemporary Jews have a stronger claim to be suffering still from the Holocaust, and not least because of a strong sense of it being a corporate attack on the people of the covenant, but the fact remains the notions of corporate guilt and corporate forgiveness have different dynamics, especially a generation or two removed. Writers such as H. D. Lewis argued that the concepts of blame, praise, guilt, responsibility and forgiveness, apply to individuals only and not to groups. We may repeat the sins of our forebears, but that is not the same as saying we are responsible for theirs.[55]

Within their own terms, Lewis's arguments are persuasive. That said, we cannot escape the fact that we belong to nations, faith traditions and communities, and the language of 'corporate guilt' and 'corporate forgiveness', fraught with difficulties as it is, does attach even though the meaning is smudged. The language of corporate repentance and corporate forgiveness is not necessarily incoherent, even though it has a different logic. We cannot but be moved by expressions of regret issued by the Vatican over the failings of previous generations, nor by the gestures of reconciliation between the citizens of Coventry and Dresden. Such expressions enable nation to speak peace unto nation and allow ancient enmities to be left behind. At the same time, there is no easy answer to the question of *who* is doing the forgiving, and who has a *right* to forgive save the prime victim.

In the above paragraphs I have sketched how theological reflection may critique Christian thinking and spirituality regarding forgiveness. Such a critique will find much that is wholesome, but such a critique will also raise questions. What has all this to do with inter-faith dialogue? The subject remains deeply painful, and understandably so, to many Jews, and a Christian has a proper reticence about tackling the subject, given the mammoth suffering inflicted upon the Jewish people. That said, Chief Rabbi Jonathan Sacks himself addresses the subject.

Hans Küng offers a Christian perspective to the Jewish tradition.[56] At the same time, Jewish experience and insight surely have things to teach Christians.

It is, of course, far too simplistic to speak of contrasting 'Christian' and 'Jewish' understandings of forgiveness. Both faith traditions are diverse and every conceivable option will in each have been explored. Nonetheless, there are some broad differences, and differences connected with differing historical experience. Jonathan Sacks has written powerfully about forgiveness. There is nothing he has written that a Christian cannot read without warm appreciation. It would be ungrateful and disingenuous, however, to suggest it could have been written as easily by a Christian. If Jew and Christian speak the same language, they do so 'with a different accent'. The Jewish historical experience deeply accents Sacks's treatment of forgiveness. Jews, far more than western Christians, know what it is like to be the victims of communal hatred and persecution. He consequently puts great emphasis on how communities may from generation to generation remember past victimhood, and thus continue to try to settle old scores. Forgiveness powerfully allows the vicious circle to be broken. 'Not only individuals, but a people, can be forgiven.'[57] He notes that Israel and Palestine both have long memories, both having experience of displacement, loss, impotence and exploitation. Penitence and forgiveness on both sides may break this cycle of violence and recrimination.[58]

No Jew can speak lightly of the inhumanities that may call for the forgiveness, and so Sacks stresses as strongly as any the importance of repentance, although he allows that in some relationships the offer of forgiveness and reconciliation may be appropriate without repentance.[59] He also feels the force of the objection that by forgiving the suffering of the community we fail to keep faith with the dead. In tension with this, however, is the stronger imperative of forgiveness. I must forgive, he says: 'for the sake of my children and theirs, not yet born. Hating the German people will not bring back to life one victim of the Holocaust. Hating Palestinians will not bring Israel one step nearer to peace ... I forgive because I have a duty to the future no less than to the past ... The duty I owe my ancestors who died because of their faith is to build a world in which people no longer die because of their faith ... That is why we must answer hatred with love, violence with peace, resentment with generosity of spirit and conflict with reconciliation.'[60]

Because of the tragedy of Jewish experience, the Jewish tradition may speak of these themes with a special power, credibility and integrity and, in particular, with an emphasis upon repentance and the communal nature of both victimhood and forgiveness.

8.5 'Widening the circle of love'

His Holiness the Dalai Lama speaks of 'widening the circle of love' – in other words widening the circle of those to whom we feel love and compassion beyond our immediate circle. Indeed, the goal is that our love and compassion should extend to all.[61] Although he does not address the issue, I don't think he would be unsympathetic to the contrasting insight that we have particular obligations to those to whom we are specially bound (e.g. our families), nor would he be hard on those who find the challenge difficult (see 3.2). Even if our love and compassion cannot be all embracing, we can all 'widen the circle of love' and that in itself is a stringent challenge. He offers practical advice as to how this can be done, meditations that connect with the spiritualities of the western tradition. There is plenty of ground here for fruitful conversation between Buddhist and Christian approaches.

It is important to recognize, however, that this ethic is intimately integrated with his Buddhist philosophy, and in two key respects.

First, there is the stringent Buddhist critique of egocentric craving and greed. While there is an internal conversation in Buddhism as to what kinds of desire might be appropriate, the fundamental thrust remains. Inordinate cravings and greed are bound to be frustrated since this world does not deliver the goods. If we seek to satisfy them, let alone stimulate them, we will be disappointed. Best to purge the soul of such yearnings and thus to make ourselves less and less vulnerable to the frustration, disappointment and suffering that attend those who expect life to satisfy all their longings.[62]

There does seem to be a difference between the Christian and the Buddhist (and for that matter Jaina) perspective here. Christian thought – like Jewish and Islamic – tends to be more positive about human longing. If the 'chief end of humanity is to glorify God and to enjoy God for ever', then the end of human life is about satisfying a properly directed longing through delighting in God. This God, however, is creator and delight in God is infused with delight in God's gifts. There is, therefore, a proper Christian sensuousness in which we enjoy our physicality and the good things life offers. A Christian doctrine of the earth as God's good creation yields a positive and confident attitude, which sometimes contrasts with non-theistic religions.

At the same time Christian thought has challenged extravagant acquisitiveness and greed, commended a delight in the ordinary and available together with a demeanour of moderation, contentment and simplicity. At this point, there is a convergence with Buddhist understanding. The hyper-stimulation of wants endemic in market capitalism receives a robust Buddhist critique, which may resonate also with the Christian. Furthermore, both Buddhist and Christian are likely to see frantic acquisitiveness as rooted in insecurity. For the Christian, this insecurity is to be met primarily through faith in God. For the Buddhist it is met by pointing to the inevitable disappointment that awaits those who see life as about satisfying our cravings. The latter insight may be incorporated into the former, although for the non-theistic Buddhist the former will not be incorporated into the latter.

What has all this to do with 'widening the circle of love'? For the Dalai Lama frantic acquisitiveness and the longing for the satisfaction of our cravings inhibit the widening of love since acquisitiveness leads to greed and injustice. Released from this mug's game we are liberated to widen the circle of love. Again, at this point Christian and Buddhist perspectives converge.

The Dalai Lama secondly finds positive reinforcement for 'widening the circle of love' in a belief in reincarnation. He points to what we owe to our mothers. The gratitude we have elicits and empowers our compassion. But suppose the stranger was, in a previous incarnation, my mother? Given the possibility of infinite reincarnations, everyone was at one time my mother.[63] For most westerners this idea raises difficulties. What credibility does the notion of repeated reincarnation have? Indeed, what *coherence* does it have since there is no continuity of selfhood and memory? A genetic inheritance hardly amounts to reincarnation. Or is the idea to be seen as a metaphor of our solidarity as a human race? That said, the Dalai Lama finds the imperative of love and compassion as being reinforced by a belief concerning *what a human person is*; and this converges with Christian perspectives for which it is likewise reinforced, save that this reinforcement comes from the belief that we are all children of God rather than from reincarnation (see 5.1–5.3.1).

The Buddhist, Jaina and Christian perspectives here are radically different, and the differences will remain. Nonetheless, the Dalai Lama insists that our common humanity precedes our being Buddhist or Christian.[64] These reflections suggest there can be fruitful conversation and not inconsiderable convergence through a sharing of insights.

8.6 A global ethic?

Religion, in some contexts kept under wraps by the Cold War superpower conflict, is increasingly a factor in the modern world in a way that has surprised, and sometimes disappointed, the prophets of secularism. Huntingdon's idea of a 'clash of civilizations' expresses the fear that religion may be a source of conflict rather than peace and co-operation. The danger is real and so there is urgency about the question: On the subject of this book – ethics – do the world faiths essentially conflict or is there a basic consensus on how we should live and behave?

The answer must be both yes and no. The world religions are different. Within them the language of ethics, even if recognizably the same language, will be spoken with different accents. Similar ethical stances will relate to different social context and different underlying philosophies, as we have seen in the above section. Sometimes there are radical differences and even the language is sometimes different. For example, Hinduism's caste system, based on *Karma*, is in some conflict with ideas about justice central to Judaism, Christianity and Islam.

There can be no easy harmonization. At the same time, amid the diversity there are connecting and overlapping visions and commitments. This should not surprise us if we share a common humanity. To carry the argument forward, I refer briefly to the work of two highly significant figures.

First Hans Küng has issued the challenge: 'No survival without a world ethic. No world peace without peace between religions. No peace between religions without dialogue between religions.'[65] Küng has stimulated inter-faith dialogue in part with a view to identifying a 'global ethic' based on a sufficient working consensus. He claims many common themes may be identified across faith traditions. Fundamentally, there is a belief in our common humanity issuing in respect for the other person. This is expressed in a culture of equal rights, mutual obligations towards one another, non-violence, tolerance, truthfulness and justice. This focus on humanity and our common well-being confronts the subordination of humans to natural fate, human oppression or market and technological fundamentalisms. It also issues in an 'obligation to stand on the side of the poor and the oppressed'. The environmental crisis has promoted a revisiting of the virtues of simplicity and moderation, and living in harmony with nature. We have responsibility both for one another and for the environment. There is a widespread 'belief that love, compassion, unselfishness and the force of inner truthfulness ... have greater power than hate, enmity and self interest.'[66] There is an emphasis on 'trust in life, generosity, tolerance, solidarity, creativity and social commitment'.[67] Furthermore, all religions generate 'virtues' and so there are here common themes in the teachings of world religions.[68] The 'Golden Rule' in various forms is found in most faith traditions. Küng was a key figure in the 1993 'Parliament of the World's Religions' in Chicago, which affirmed a common commitment to ideals such as non-violence and respect for life, a culture of justice, tolerance, truthfulness, equal rights and partnership between women and men.[69] This impetus encouraged things such as the 1998 'Universal Declaration of Human Responsibility' and the UN Year of Dialogue Among Civilizations in 2001.

We can claim too much for all this. Those who attended the 1993 parliament were not necessarily representative. Some of what is affirmed is only 'widely' rather than universally held. 'Core values' are coloured in differently depending on social and belief context. Many religious people, Christians no less than others, fail seriously to live up to their profession. The claim to equal partnership of women and men describes an ideal and not a reality. Religions can be the pitch on which we play out our power games and religion can be hijacked for self-interest. To secular critics the rise of fundamentalism and extremism mocks this consensus.

On the other hand, we can claim too little. Many passionately believe such extremism ignores the core commitments of their faith traditions. Küng does point to an essential consensus, even if abstracted from historical and metaphysical contexts, and even if in need of much scholarly qualification. Scholars of different religions are more and more claiming that notions of 'rights' are deeply rooted in many religious traditions and are not the imposition of modernity. Yes, 'rights' need to be correlated with obligations and other values, but that is par for the course in any serious ethical reflection. It may also be objected that what Küng is offering is all rather general and that there is much argument over the detail. This is, of course, true, but the general is not the same as the bland or the trivial. The least that Küng has shown is that people of different faiths may find much common ground on which to dialogue. This will lead to an enrichment through sharing almost certainly more often than it will lead to irreconcilable difference. Moreover, even when there is such a difference, we continue to respect and honour our common humanity.

The second figure is Chief Rabbi Jonathan Sacks. The Chief Rabbi objects to the tendency in western thought to value the 'universal' over the 'particular'. He finds much in common among religions, for example, 'reverence, restraint, humility, a sense of limits, the ability to listen and respond to human distress'.[70] At the same time, Sacks wishes to value diversity – the 'dignity of difference'. Universalism must be balanced with respect for the local and particular. In the Hebrew Scriptures there is a covenant with both Noah (representing humankind) and Abraham (representing Israel). The Jewish people are a particular people, and one of the insights of Judaism is the valuing of this rich diversity. Judaism does not rush from the particular to the universal, a mindset which he sees as one of the legacies of Plato. 'God, the creator of humanity, having made a covenant with all humanity, then turns to one people and commands it to be different in order to teach humanity the dignity of difference.'[71] An overstress on the universal leads to a 'diminution of the rich textures of our shared life, a potentially disastrous narrowing of the horizons of possibility'.[72] Communities and faith traditions are different; just as each individual human person is unique, special and irreplaceable. It is through conversation with those who are different that we find our own lives are enlarged.

I do not see any conflict between Küng and Sacks. If Küng points to what we hold in common, Sacks points also to the rich colouring of different traditions and faith experience. We should not be content with a common denominator of abstract nouns. Rather, through respect, attending and listening, we should seek a mutual enlargement through sharing both the common and the different. If this is not possible, the future is bleak indeed.

Notes

1 Kenneth Cracknell, *Justice, Courtesy and Love*, Peterborough, Epworth, 1995. The phrase is that of Thomas Ebenezer Slater.

2 E.g. S. Radhakrishnan, *Eastern Religions and Western Thought*, Oxford, 1939, p. 345.

3 Thus, Wilfred Cantwell Smith, *Towards a World Theology*, London, Macmillan, 1981, p. 82; and *The Meaning and End of Religion*, New York, Macmillan, 1963, p. 126.

4 E.g. Isaiah 40.18.

5 E.g. Job 28.20ff.; Ecclesiastes 5.2.

6 Psalms 24.1; Acts 14.17.

7 Justin Martyr, *The First Apology*, chapter 46, p. 178 in *Ante-Nicene Fathers*, Volume 1, Edinburgh, T&T Clark, 1996.

8 John 1.9.

9 1 Peter 3.16.

10 Omid Safi (ed.), *Progressive Muslims*, Oxford, One World, 2003, p. 24.

11 T. Ogletree, *Hospitality to the Stranger*, Philadelphia, Fortress Press, 1985.

12 Kenneth Cracknell, *In Good and Generous Faith*, Peterborough, Epworth, 2005, p. 60.

13 E.g. John 1.9.

14 Jonathan Sacks, *The Dignity of Difference*, London, Continuum, 2002, p. 53. See later pp. 177–8.

15 Thus, Israel Selvanayagam, *Relating to People of other Faiths*, Tiruvalla Christava, Sahitya Samithy, 2004, p. 239.

16 E.g. Genesis 9.16; Isaiah 45.1–5; Malachi 1.11; Acts 2.21.

17 It is best to use the language of the 'Spirit' to express this insight. Such 'theocentric' language is not guilty of Christian imperialism. By contrast 'Christocentric' language which speaks of the 'Christ' as in some way active incognito in other faiths may be so received. For example, R. Pannikar, *The Unknown Christ of Hinduism*, London, Darton, Longman & Todd, 1964, p. 54. Also *Redemptor Hominis*, Vatican, 1979, especially Section 12. Notions of 'baptism by desire' and Rahner's notion of 'anonymous Christianity', while more generous than unmitigating exclusivism, are open to the same criticism, as is language about the 'eternal son' being present in other faiths.

18 Wilfred Cantwell Smith, *Questions of Religious Truth*, London, Gollancz, 1967, p. 24.

19 Examples of this approach are to be found in S. M. Ogden, *The Point*

of Christology, London, SCM Press, 1982; John Hick, *The Metaphor of God Incarnate*, London, SCM Press, 1993; J. Hick and F. Knitter, *The Myth of Christian Uniqueness*, London, SCM Press, 1987. Also David A. Pailin, *God and the Processes of Reality*, London, Routledge, 1989, p. 185.

20 *Genesis* 9.17; Israel Selvanayagam, *Relating to People of other Faiths*, pp. 160–7.

21 Doxological interpretations are offered in Schubert M. Ogden, 'What does it mean to affirm "Jesus Christ is Lord"' in *The Reality of God and other Essays*, London, SCM Press, 1967, p. 203; also Wesley Ariarajah, *The Bible and People of other Faiths*, Geneva, WCC, 1985.

22 E.g. Brian Hebblethwaite, *The Incarnation*, Cambridge, Cambridge University Press, 1987, e.g. pp. 5, 21ff., 27ff.

23 Ronald M. Green, 'Christian Ethics: A Jewish Perspective' in R. Gill (ed.), *The Cambridge Companion to Christian Ethics*, Cambridge, Cambridge University Press, 2001, pp. 138ff.

24 S. P. Huntingdon, *The Clash of Civilisations and the Remaking of World Order*, New York, Simon & Schuster, 1997.

25 Abd al Raziq, *Islam and the Principles of Government*, 1925.

26 Ahmad S. Moussalli, 'Islamic Democracy and Pluralism' in Omid Safi (ed.), *Progressive Muslims*, p. 287.

27 Moussalli, 'Islamic Democracy', p. 292.

28 *Qur'an* Sura 3.159.

29 Moussalli, 'Islamic Democracy', p. 291.

30 Moussalli, 'Islamic Democracy', p. 295.

31 *Qur'an* Sura 16.90.

32 *Qur'an* Sura 15.29 Sura 38.72.

33 Omid Safi, 'Introduction' to Omid Safi (ed.), *Progressive Muslims*, p. 3.

34 See, for example, Zaym Kassam, 'Islamic Ethics and Gender Issues' in J. Runzo and N. M. Martin, *Ethics in the World Religions*, pp. 115ff.

35 Another Muslim writer in fundamental agreement with Ahmad Moussalli is Reza Aslan, *No God but God*, New York, Random House, 2005.

36 B. Lewis, *The Crisis of Islam*, London, Weidenfeld & Nicolson, 2003, p. 36.

37 Gregory XVI, *Mirari Vos*, Vatican, 1832, especially Paragraphs 14–20.

38 Tariq Ramadan, *Western Muslims and the Future of Islam*, Oxford, Oxford University Press, 2004, pp. 86–8.

39 Ramadan, *Western Muslims*, pp. 161–2, 144.

40 Ramadan, *Western Muslims*, p. 145.

41 Ramadan, *Western Muslims*, p. 159.

42 Ramadan, *Western Muslims*, p. 169.

43 *Qur'an* Sura 36.60 17.70 and especially a number of references in sura 7.

44 Quoted by J. G. Murphy, *Getting Even*, Oxford, Oxford University Press, 2003, p. 19.

45 Murphy, *Getting Even*, p. 115.

46 Immanuel Kant, *Lectures on Ethics*, translated by Louis Infield, London, Methuen, 1930, pp. 52ff.

47 E.g. R. W. Dale, *The Atonement*, London, Congregational Union, 1892, pp. 390ff. Also John Scott Lidgett, *The Spiritual Principle of the Atonement*, London, Epworth, fourth edition, 1907, pp. 269–70.

48 E.g. Horace Bushnell, *The Vicarious Sacrifice*, London, Strahan, 1871, pp. 383ff., 412.

49 Ephesians 4.26. R. C. Moberly, *Atonement and Personality*, London, John

Murray, 1911, pp. 26ff.; John McLeod Campbell, *The Nature of the Atonement* (1856), London, James Clarke, fourth edition, 1959, pp. 144ff., 371ff.

50 Joseph Butler, *Sermon*, 'Upon Resentment', 1726.

51 Joseph Butler, *Sermon*, 'Upon Forgiveness of Injuries', 1726.

52 Luke 19.1–10.

53 Fyodor Dostoevsky, *The Brothers Karamazov*, London, Random House, Everyman Edition, 1992, Part II, Book 5, chapter 4.

54 Matthew 18.23ff.

55 H. D. Lewis, 'Collective Responsibility', *Philosophy*, 1948.

56 Hans Küng, *Judaism*, London, SCM Press, 1992, pp. 391ff.

57 Jonathan Sacks, *The Dignity of Difference*, London, Continuum, 2002, p. 184.

58 Sacks, *Dignity*, p. 189.

59 The importance of repentance in the Jewish tradition is stressed in A. Cohen, *Everyman's Talmud*, London, Dent, Section VI; and in D. and L. Cohn-Sherbok, *An Encyclopaedia of Judaism and Christianity*, London, Darton, Longman & Todd, 2004.

60 Sacks, *Dignity*, p. 190.

61 Dalai Lama, *Widening the Circle of Love*, London, Rider, 2005, pp. 41–3.

62 Dalai Lama, *Widening the Circle of Love*, pp. 101–2.

63 Dalai Lama, *Widening the Circle of Love*, p. 48.

64 Dalai Lama, *Widening the Circle of Love*, p. 1.

65 Hans Küng, *Global Responsibility: In Search of a New World Ethic*, London, SCM Press, 1991, p. xv.

66 Küng, *Global Responsibility*, pp. 53–63.

67 Küng, *Global Responsibility*, p.46.

68 Küng, *Global Responsibility*, p. 58.

69 Hans Küng and Karl-Joseph Kuschel, *A Global Ethic*, London, SCM Press, 1993.

70 Sacks, *Dignity*, p. 13.

71 Sacks, *Dignity*, p. 53.

72 Sacks, *Dignity*, p. 22.

9

Why then Be Good?

In the first chapter the question was posed: '*Why should I act morally when it is not in my own interest?*' There are really two questions here, the one of rational justification and the other of motivation. What can be said to the person who will not be put out for the sake of others? And what can we say to *ourselves* when *we* are that person? This is a difficult question to answer; and it is no wonder that some have looked to propaganda, threats and sanctions to keep people moral. There is the nervousness that if we press the radical question '*Why?*' we let the cat out of the bag, for there is no answer. The fact is there is no fully adequate answer, and indeed it is not clear what would constitute a fully adequate answer. Nonetheless, we can perhaps make some progress.

The whole area is very complicated and just when we think things are getting clearer the mist reappears. First, the question of *motivation* is inordinately complicated. So-called 'psychological egoism' claims that all motivation is self-regarding. This claim, however, is either false or trivial, depending on how it is understood. It is false to deny that people sometimes do genuinely put themselves out and make great sacrifice for others. Of course, one can perceive their motives as being 'really selfish', and sometimes they are, but to say that motivation is always selfish is to misconstrue the evidence in order to fit the theory. Yes, people may sometimes appear to be altruistic when in fact they seek to wield power or court praise. But people may also make great sacrifices out of a genuine concern for others or out of a genuine sense that this is their obligation.

Suppose, however, we say that our acts (unless externally compelled, as when we are dragged out of the room) always derive from our choices, impulses, motives, etc.? This may be true but it is trivially true. It does not prove psychological egoism in the strong sense. We must not beg the question and assume that all motivation is self-centred. The choice or impulse may be deeply and even sacrificially altruistic.

Second, we might ask what is a *worthy* motive? Kant praised the motivation of 'doing duty for duty's sake' and the implication is that this unique moral motivation is distinct from all other human dispositions. As argued earlier, however, this does not ring true (3.8). If I act out of compassion, sympathy or gratitude, this seems laudable, but is it, in Kant's understanding, acting 'for duty's sake'? And if not, does it matter? Suppose I help someone for their sake, genuinely desiring their well-being? This seems wholesome as a motive, no matter whether or not I am acting 'for duty's sake'. The best course is to be critically appreciative of a whole complex of dispositions that nourish the good life and not try to isolate some distinct 'moral' motivation, which is to be prized above all else. It was this perception that allowed Bishop Butler to claim that self-love and service to others need not be mutually exclusive because of common dispositions of benevolence and sympathy.[1] Many do have dispositions of sympathy and benevolence. They genuinely want the well-being of others.

Third, it is important to distinguish between the self-regarding and the selfish. I am selfish when I allow my own wants and interests to violate the proper claims of others. But there is nothing wrong in a self-regard that does not conflict with my duties. There is a proper attention given to self, and indeed we can give to others only if we ourselves are fed and nourished. We love our neighbour *as* ourselves, not *instead* of ourselves. Moreover, we should honour the desire of others for *our* flourishing.

Sometimes love of self and love of others easily coincide. Suppose my daughter or son needs a kidney transplant to save their life. Without hesitation I donate one of my kidneys. My act, however, is hardly praiseworthy or even self-sacrificial since I have no personal interest stronger than the well-being of my son or daughter. If, however, I do not deserve praise, what I have done is surely a right and virtuous act.

Happily, our own interests and those of others often coincide, and so we can be fairly confident about tackling the question of altruism within our own immediate circle. We are bound together and I cannot benefit from the networks to which I belong unless I am committed to decency, honesty and fair play. If I lie, cheat and commit fraud among my nearest and dearest I am myself the loser as much as they. People need the goodwill of others and they cannot get it unless they also give it. This connects with Kant's insight that I must be able to will that the maxim of my action becomes a universal law. I cannot, however, reasonably will this in the case, say, of lying or promise breaking. If I break a promise or utter a lie, I, in so doing, claim a privilege I do not allow to others. This is because the benefit from the lie or broken promise depends on the social expectation of truth telling and promise keeping. ('What if everyone were to do it?') Aquinas made a similar point.[2] Furthermore, I genuinely care about those I love. My own well-being is enmeshed with theirs.

The closer I am to people, the more obvious this is – but as I move away from my intimate circle, the argument becomes less compelling, even if to counter that my obligations become more diffuse. Television brings the world's need into our living rooms with a force much stronger than our altruism or motivation. Rhetoric about the 'global village' and our being 'bound together' will not dislodge an inherent selfishness that is often at odds with justice, let alone charity. I may acknowledge that for our own corporate well-being we do indeed need to pull together, but if I cheat, it will surely not make much difference, especially if I play it shrewdly so that people do not notice. The expedient of the cunning fox is as old as Plato.[3]

The purist may be unhappy even with the argument thus far. It is true that in my immediate circle I am a loser if I do not behave decently. This, however, is nothing more than the old policy of 'honesty pays'. My motivation is prudential and self-serving. It is not moral.

This objection, however, is both too high-minded and misses the point. Admittedly it sounds suspicious to say we are honest (we take honesty as our example) because 'honesty pays'. It is suspicious because it sounds as if attending to our duties is rather like buying shares in Honesty Incorporated PLC so as to benefit from the high dividends. This, however, is misleading. To pursue the metaphor, the 'dividends' of morality are not 'paid' *extraneous* to the morality. We are not honest for the sake of some benefit *other than and beyond* the honesty. On the contrary, the 'dividend' of living the good life is *intrinsic* and not *extrinsic*. Once this is recognized, it will be seen that we are not being disingenuous or prudential if we so attend to the demands of morality. Morality is about that which leads to our mutual flourishing. Yes, I suffer if I am not moral and I benefit if I am, but the rewards are intrinsic to the demand of morality – the rewards found in seeking to live a life of generosity, responsibility, integrity, and goodwill in human relationships. I must find these ideals genuinely attractive. Maybe we should understand in this way the dominant theme of rewards in the teaching of Jesus. The rewards are not external to living the good life – the adult equivalent of having a sweet for being good. The vision of morality is to see that our highest well-being is to cultivate a life of virtue and to live a life of compassion and integrity. It means 'dying to a self', which resists this and rising to a new self with this commitment. Whosoever will seek their life will lose it, but whosoever will lose it will gain it. This is not selfish prudence, since only a heart set genuinely on virtue and right doing will be able to appreciate the reward.

This is essentially in line with the answer both Plato and Aristotle give to the question; and there is a striking resonance with their answer and that of the first Psalm. In the *Republic* there is no answer to the question of Thrasymachus: 'Why be good?' if we seek a reason for being good extraneous to the intrinsic attractiveness of a good life. There may sometimes, for some people, be extraneous reasons, but they do not apply always to all people. We need to grasp that the disposition set on the good life is the one everyone should rationally choose because those with such a disposition are, as the Psalmist said, 'like trees planted by the waters'. It is not that we construct an understanding of what our well-being involves and then discover that by good fortune the ethically responsible life fits it. It is rather that ethics is the invitation to form our dispositions in accordance with its vision and thereby to discover our deepest well-being. This is not to deny that horrible and selfish people may enjoy happiness. But it is to claim they miss the profounder depths of human flourishing. The blessings promised by the beatitudes of Jesus are rich indeed; but they have attraction only to those with the right disposition of heart.[4]

The essential insight is that well-being and well-doing are bound together. This should not surprise us if ethics is about attending to our deepest needs and our mutual flourishing. It may, however, require a change around in attitude to see that the end of life and the fruition of life is to pursue the good. To ask, therefore, Why should I be good? and Why should I put myself out for the sake of another? is a bit like asking: Why should I listen to that symphony? Why should I have that walk in the woods? Why should I have that meal? It is even like the question: Why should I cultivate that friendship? or What is the point of falling in love? The good life is about blessing others and being blessed ourselves. This is the insight contained in the misleading saying – often dismissed rather unfairly as being too high minded by half – that virtue is its own reward. Bishop Butler remarked: 'Let it not be taken for granted that the temper of envy, rage, resentment, yields greater delight than meekness, forgiveness, compassion and goodwill ... Conscience and self-love, if we understand our true happiness, always lead us the same way.'[5]

For Christians, all this may be reinforced by the vision of God as evoking gratitude and praise; and so our common life is seen within the context of the love and worship of God. We thus meet the claim that the grace of God enables us to do and be what might otherwise not be within our power. There need be nothing mysterious about this claim. 'Grace' is the name given to God's favour shown in 'creation and redemption'. To be the object of love, understanding, mercy and care, is an enabling and ennobling experience in ordinary human relationships. There should be nothing surprising or mysterious in the claim that this is the case also, but very much more so, with our relationship with God. Christian faith offers primarily not a moral demand but salvation – and this includes an enabling grace that inspires and nourishes the best within us. If we rid ourselves of the idea that we must do the right simply 'because it is right' and duty 'for duty's sake' and allow a legitimate place for the motivations of gratitude and love we can see a legitimate place for grace in the moral life – since it is grace that elicits our response of gratitude and love. It warms the heart and strengthens the will. To see our lives as a fitting and enabled response to the grace of God is, as we have seen, a far cry from living in self-centred and prudential fear of 'God the Policeman', a metaphor rightly mocked by Dennett as undermining a healthy moral maturity.[6]

When Austin Farrer remarked that good fortune is more fertile of goodness – including moral goodness – than extremity,[7] he was not denying how impressive it is when those worn down by life's cruelties still manage great qualities of character. When poverty and social exclusion, however, cause resentment and a sense of injustice, it is not surprising that there is a higher incidence of crime. If Christians believe in enabling grace, the imperative of justice follows, since injustice is a human check against the free flow of the grace of God.

The theme of this chapter recalls a classic theological battle between Augustine and Pelagius in the fifth century. There is not the space here to detail this in its original setting, but some comment as to how the broad themes may connect with contemporary contexts may be helpful. Augustine and Pelagius were arguing to some extent at cross purposes. Polemics and exaggeration aside, they both offer important insight. Pelagius was right in saying that our actions are genuinely our own. Admittedly, the phrase 'genuinely our own' is problematical, but we need some such concept if we are to affirm personal freedom and responsibility. Pelagius was also right in saying we are capable of doing and being good. At the same time, Augustine was right in insisting our capacity is wounded, and in saying our actions and lives tend to be evil unless assisted by grace. But in speaking of assisting grace we should not think of grace as being a kind of impersonal power, available to us only if we are properly plugged in. Still less should we think of grace as something experienced separate from and extraneous to the rest of our experience. On the contrary, it is the grace of God in 'creation and redemption', which is constitutive of our being, and which inspires the will, warms the heart and excites the mind. Worship, prayer and reflection comprise among other things opening our minds and hearts to the reality of the grace which infuses our whole being. It follows that our wills are both our own and yet also the work of God, since it is to the work of God and God's grace that we owe our very being.

If only Hitler had read these paragraphs! How history would have been different! I satirize myself in order to deflect the satire of others. Even Jesus failed with Judas. I am under no illusion as to how feeble these considerations may appear, given the stubbornness and wickedness of the human heart and I speak of my own wickedness and stubbornness as much as presuming to speak of that of others. Nonetheless, the 'still small voice' of these considerations continues to beckon us in another direction, and with a compelling power.

Notes

1 Joseph Butler, *Fifteen Sermons*, Number 1, 'Upon the Social Nature of Man'.

2 Thomas Aquinas, *Summa Theologiae*, II-II.110.1.

3 Plato, *Republic*, II.365.

4 Matthew 5.3ff.

5 Joseph Butler, the same sermon quoted above.

6 Daniel Dennett, *Breaking the Spell*, London, Allen Lane, 2006, p. 283.

7 Austin Farrer, *Love Almighty and Ills Unlimited*, London, Fontana, 1966, pp. 167–8.

Taking Stock: Weaving a Tapestry or Muddling Through?

10.1 Summary of the argument so far

In conclusion, the quest of ethics is the quest to discover what manner of living, what choices and judgements, what actions, what dispositions of character, and what ways of relating to one another, serve our mutual flourishing. Alongside speaking of our mutual flourishing, I have suggested it is helpful to speak explicitly of ethics as concerned also with discovering appropriate relationships, both personal and more structural. This is partly because to be human is to be in relationship, and so our mutual well-being is found very largely in our relationships with one another. It is so also because notions such as responsibility, rights, obligations, justice and so forth focus on our relationships. It is so further because ethics cannot ignore our relationship with the earth and with other living things (see Chapter 14). Furthermore, some basic conception of common human aspiration and need (what a human person *is*) gives a rationale to this whole enquiry and helps to locate it in the public forum.

All this makes powerful sense as a 'human' and 'secular' enquiry. For a number of reasons, I have argued that Christians should strongly resist the temptation to attempt a theological *coup d'état* of ethics. Nevertheless, for the theist the conviction that our fundamental relationship is with God 'in whom we live and move and have our being' provides a deeper rationale and resonance for all this. Our relationship with God radically nuances our relationship with one another, with other living things and the earth.

We have thus traced some of the insights that may guide our ethics, some from more general ethical reflection, and some from Christian faith. They serve as threads, colours and stitches, for 'weaving the tapestry of moral judgement'. These reflections help to clarify questions, alert us to dimensions easily overlooked, identify important insight, as well as revealing the fallacies of some ethical thinking and some of the pitfalls. There is a difference between a tapestry which is rich and one that is bland. There is a difference between one that is well woven and one that is shoddy.

This leads to a conclusion that some may find disturbing, although my suggestion is that no other conclusion is possible and we have to live with it. We may even find it liberating. In weaving the tapestry of moral judgement we often find there is no one tapestry that is the one and only correct one. Different pictures may sometimes be offered, each or all in their own way compelling. In other words, there is not always a single 'right answer' to a moral question.

This is true at a more theoretical level. For example, in giving a moral assessment of the constituents of our complex motivations, we can hardly aspire to anything like geometrical precision. Suppose, for instance, in an act my motivation manifests elements of gratitude, altruism, pity, affection, competitiveness, self-love, a sense of duty, and a measure of interest in my reputation? To take another example, it is not clear how we rank the *moral saint*, who is free from temptation, with the *moral hero* who struggles against temptation. And often there may be bits of both moral saint and moral hero within us at the same time.

It is true also over more practical matters. It is not always clear what we should do or how we should behave. I say 'not always'. Sometimes a moral judgement is clear and obvious. There is no uncertainty about the condemnation of sexual abuse, rape, mugging an elderly lady to steal her pension, and a host of other things. There is no difficulty in honouring the husband who cares devotedly for his wife through sickness over the cad who deserts his wife for someone else. But on many an issue there is genuine ambiguity. Indeed, the word 'dilemma' is used to speak of a moral question that does not admit of an unambiguously correct solution. No response is without its difficulty. We are entitled to take some comfort from this. Sometimes the best we can do is make the most responsible and informed judgement we can. But we should not beat ourselves up because we cannot find the one right answer that is free of ambiguity. In the third part of this book this will be amply illustrated.

There is an avenue of trees in a park, let's say a type of maple, and the trees have a natural life expectancy of about 130 years. One dies and then another. They will all die within the next 20 years or so. When should we fell and replant? After the first death? After 50 per cent have died, or when 70 per cent have died? Or should we wait until the last death? There is no one right answer. A reasonable judgement has to be made bearing in mind economic, environmental and aesthetic considerations, but there is no single correct time to fell. Questions in ethics are often similar. They do not always admit of a single unequivocally correct solution.

10.2 Three reasons

Why is this so? It is so for at least three principal reasons.

First, while there is often, although not always, confidence over 'basic values' and 'general moral principles', there is often uncertainty over how these are expressed in the rough and tumble of life. Sometimes values and obligations conflict and we struggle to find a proper balance. The ends that we seek are often in tension and we have to negotiate a trade off. More radically, we may sometimes be unclear which values and obligations in fact apply. How is retributivist justice to be balanced against mercy? How is justice for the criminal balanced against punishment seen as deterrence and as protection for the public? How do I balance my obligation to provide my children with the best possible education with my obligation to support a system which offers a good education to all? What limitation on my freedom is justified in order to give you a greater social justice? When does care and concern become patronizing and intrusive? How do I relate my specific obligation to my family with a wider commitment? The list of possible examples is almost endless. In such cases, we may be confident about underlying values but there is great uncertainty as to how they are applied and balanced. We have no option but to make the most responsible judgement we can. But we cannot be sure we get it right – indeed that there is one and only one right solution.

This point may be given a sharper focus. Some approaches to ethics seek clarity and certainly through adopting a single stranded approach. This clarity and certainty is sought, however, at the expense of embracing a bogus simplicity. The most obvious example is classical utilitarianism, according to which we determine what is right by asking what leads to the greatest possible happiness of the greatest possible number. A more broadly based consequentialism will simply judge an action by its consequences. Other single-stranded approaches will focus on specific duties, or ask 'what love demands', or how we honour 'rights'. Others will focus on some other principle, such as the impartial consideration of interests. Peter Singer's distinguished contribution to ethics seeks clarity through adopting a single-stranded consequentialist programme. My argument is that even if we do focus on a single strand, so as to travel the road to certainty, we soon end up in the ditch. Single-stranded approaches are not as simple as might at first sight appear. For example, even the simplest form of consequentialism, utilitarianism, soon runs into difficulty over the impossibility of a 'hedonistic calculus', that is the calculation of the effects of alternative actions in terms of the maximum pleasure they will produce. More generally consequentialism is too simplistic, not only because the ends we seek are often incommensurable, but because it easily fails to address the tension between individual rights and the wider good, and the tension between our general commitment to benevolence and our specific duties to those to whom we are bound in special ways. These issues have already been discussed (see 3.2) .

The argument of this book is that we should resist the temptation to embrace a bogus simplicity by focusing on one strand of ethical insight and one strand alone. This approach is counter-intuitive simply because our ethical insight is multi-faceted. Ethical judgement is like weaving a tapestry in which we seek to benefit from the many strands of ethical insight, such as we have illustrated. Single-stranded approaches instead aspire to (and here I return to the metaphor) a plain-coloured cloth rather than a tapestry. On many issues, however, certainty eludes us precisely because there is no clear and obvious way in which we balance the various insights. At the same time, the overarching commitment to our common well-being gives us a framework within which to work responsibly and reasonably. This does not give us certainty, but it does give us sufficient for the journey.

The second reason is one of considerable magnitude, implicit in our discussion so far. Prophetic zeal and moral vision are useless – even harmful – when we lack knowledge of the context we address. There is a difference between a 'fact' and a 'value'. Nevertheless, when making a moral judgement we take into account relevant facts. Here, however, there is often greater uncertainty than over our moral commitment. If we give people a right to die, will elderly people then be put under pressure to think it is their duty to die? Our moral judgement depends here in part upon our capacity for sociological prediction. What lifestyle has the most responsible 'carbon footprint'? Does corporal or capital punishment act as a serious deterrent? To what extent does my consumption affect Third World poverty? If a war is judged to be a 'just war', this will be based in part upon an estimate of the outcome of military action, but events are rarely obedient to the predictions of politicians and generals. Botany must inform our moral assessment of genetically modified crops. A study of economics will inform our understanding of the ethics of wealth creation. Sometimes the factual and the ethical are intertwined, as when we debate the moral status of human embryos. The very language we use when speaking of the unborn (human person? unborn child?) can be value laden and to that extent load the dice. Attempts to enlist science in the quest to find a 'cause' and 'cure' for a particular sexual orientation are value laden. The armchair ethicist is always in danger of warped or naive judgement because of an inadequate understanding of the facts. Ethics is thus given a bad name. It is dismissed as a county next to Kent.

It follows that the ethicist needs to draw on the insight of the sciences. Many ethical stances in the past have been rendered obsolete because based on obsolete science. It is embarrassing to record that barely 100 years ago it was regarded as fact that women were less intelligent (or more stupid) than men. In the past, some have followed Descartes in believing animals do not feel pain. An ethic of a just war will have to learn from history. An ethic of sexuality will try to keep abreast of our understanding of the nature of human sexuality. Our modern knowledge of how human life develops in the womb again informs our ethical judgement as to the moral status of the unborn.

In particular, the social sciences can help us understand the structural context in which people live, and which shape their mindsets and perspectives, together with the structural and institutional expression of injustice, racism and sexism – as when employment opportunity and property laws disadvantage women. The social sciences can also plot the relativity of our mental paradigms, thus making us more self-aware and self-critical.

Somewhat surprisingly, it is often the science that lets us down, since science like any human enterprise is limited in its grasp. In particular, attempts to predict the effect of our choices, or to predict what issues will face us in ten years' time, are highly fallible. In the 1960s it was widely believed technology would herald the 'age of leisure'.[1] It has not turned out like that. The *Club of Rome* report of 1972 made predictions on the basis of the then available technology, and did not take sufficiently into account technological innovation.[2]

Just as in the past people were threatened with eternal hell as punishment for their sins, so we are now threatened with earthly hell because our way of life is releasing more and more carbon dioxide into the atmosphere, causing spiralling global warming. The science however is unclear and the causal connection between carbon dioxide released through industrialization and global warming remains a matter of scientific contention. It is not impossible it will prove as fanciful as the Victoria idea that cholera was spread through smells. On the other hand it may not be fanciful. And yet an enormous amount depends on this, including justice for developing nations needing more and more energy. Gigantically important policy judgements have to be made on the basis of uncertain understanding. It is not a good place to be in.

Crucially, 'marshalling the facts' is not always a value-free activity. It is so easy to see only what we want to see. We twist the facts to support our pet ethical theory. We can do this without being aware of what we are doing. Again, the effort to awaken self-scrutiny is vital. All kinds of single-issue lobbies are tempted to follow their own holy tradition of 'facts', immune from proper scrutiny. After all, facts have a tiresome tendency to explode ideologies. Life is not simple. The life of our nations – and even more so the life of our global village – is mind-blowing in its complexity. Any moral judgement will be based on some attempt to get a handle on what is going on and how the future is going to pan out. It is impossible but we have no option but to try to do our best.

The third reason is that ethics is not simply about personal individual behaviour. In addition to a personal ethic there is also social ethics – our vision for a just society and our struggle to build it. For a limited deontologism** this may not be so (see 3.6). What is important is not what happens, but what I do. I must keep my hands clean and do my duty within a narrow area. This, however, is surely far too limited. We must also have a social ethic. I do not suggest that issues concerning the ethics of personal behaviour are simple. Far from it. Social ethics, nonetheless, is more complicated and riddled with more intractable ambiguities. To a certain extent I have control over my own life. But how do we express ethical values in the structures of society where there are conflicts, competing interests, radical differences and where human altruism and integrity seem often to be heavily diluted by evils of all kinds? Societies are increasingly complex and sometimes we feel there is not sufficient understanding of what is going on – and still less what will be going on in the future – to make a judgement. Furthermore, there will be inevitable trade offs between conflicting values and competing interests.

Very broadly speaking, Christians have divided into three camps over this. First, there are those who soft-pedalled their responsibility for the wider society. Instead they retreat into the counter culture of the Church. Second, there are those who have high hopes for expressing fully 'kingdom values' even in a 'fallen' world. Some forms of socialism and pacifism are examples of this. Earlier generations even spoke of building the kingdom of God on earth. Third, there are Christians who embrace what might be called a 'two realms' model. For this model we accept that the values and hopes of the 'realm of God' cannot be realized in their fullness in this 'fallen' world. Many high hopes are unrealistic. The reality and ambiguity of the human condition, with conflict and competing interests, alongside limited altruism, will not allow it. At the same time, while the 'kingdoms of this world' cannot be expected to become 'the kingdoms of our God and of his Christ', nevertheless we can labour to build a proximate and achievable justice and fairness. In broad outline this is in continuity with the stance of Augustine and Luther.[3] I say 'in broad outline', because the detail of Augustine's and Luther's exposition in their time need not detain us, nor the way in which Lutheran thought has revisited the issues since the experience of Nazism. If this be our stance, however, there is bound to be struggle, ambiguity and compromise. It is not though the kind of compromise that sacrifices integrity, but rather the kind of compromise that is realistic about working for the slightly better because the best is not within our grasp.

The reality is that most Christians will have at least a toe in each camp. The important question is 'Where, predominantly, are the feet?' People will differ on where they draw the line between confidence and caution, and no doubt the line will be drawn differently at different times and on different issues.

As we have seen, Stanley Hauerwas is predominantly in the first camp (see 4.3) and strands of pacifism and socialism are in the second (see 12.5 and 13.3). A 'two realms' ethic has a classic expression in the thought of Reinhold Niebuhr. For Niebuhr, in a 'fallen' world we need realism about what is achievable, and the vocation of Christians in the rough and tumble of the world is to help to mould social structures in such a way as to make our political, economic and social institutions work as well as possible for justice. Resort to coercive power is sometimes unavoidable. Power and conflicting powers are facts of life. The gospel presents in its fullness an impossible ideal – and we make matters worse if we try to realize this ideal in its fullness. An example of doing this is when Christians dream of relying upon love and goodwill in social or even international relations, thus neglecting the structures that deliver a tolerable justice and peace. Gospel ideals remain, however, those to which we can move and which always trouble our complacency. For Niebuhr it is unrealistic to believe that religious and moral ideals will serve as anything more than a leaven in society. The structures of society cannot be based on the leavening influence of the few.[4] Human self-interest and conflicts of interests and power belong to the reality of social life. We must be realistic about the conflict between the 'real' and the 'ideal', as well as the conflict of power and interest in society.[5] This, however, is not a counsel of despair. We can work for the 'establishment of tolerable harmonies of life, tolerable forms of justice'.[6] It is thus vital to see that Christians are offering more than the 'leavening in the lump' of lives of responsibility and integrity. They are offering also a commitment to building institutional structures, which manage conflict of interest and deliver as much justice as possible. They also avoid embracing impossible ideals that can easily leave the vulnerable unprotected and may even be at the expense of a proper recognition of liberty.

All this resonates with the notion of the 'politics of imperfection' explored by Anthony Quinton.[7] Politics in a democratic society is not about embracing 'perfect' solutions to society's questions. We must take seriously the reality of conflicting interests, and competing values not easily reconcilable and never perfectly so. Realism recognizes that many problems in human life and society are not ideally soluble. Karl Popper warned against 'utopian engineering' in which we dismantle the institutions of society and try to start all over again. The communist revolution was obviously within his sights when he made this attack. Human life depends on the intimate fabric of our culture and its institutions. Yes there can be change – but we need to proceed patiently and cautiously, not least because our capacity to predict the outcome of our actions is severely limited. Popper even thought the utilitarian vision was too unrealistic, as well as being paternalistic and even in danger of slipping into tyranny. Instead, he preferred to speak more cautiously of focusing on alleviating the graver forms of suffering.[8]

10.3 Beginning weaving

Suppose I have succeeded in identifying some of the threads, stitches and colours available for weaving the tapestry of moral judgement. There remains the crucial question: 'How, in fact, do we go about weaving?'

This is not an easy question to wrestle with in the abstract. We can, however, find some guidance to help us get going. We identify the relevant factual data, as far as we can. In doing this we maintain a critical eye on account of the issues alluded to above. We then ask about the boundaries of the situation and all the constraints on action and aspiration. We scan in our minds the various value commitments that might be relevant, and the resources offered for making moral judgements, such as we have illustrated. We need then to exercise 'judgement' or 'wisdom' – the cardinal virtue of 'prudence'. We do this in consultation with others, and inevitably as part of a moral tradition, but the element of judgement and our responsibility for the judgement we make cannot be shirked. The making of a moral judgement is an art, not an exact science. Weaving the tapestry is not the textile equivalent of painting by numbers. The whole area is riddled with ambiguity and constraints. But that does not mean any response is as good as another, or that there is no difference between a good and a bad argument. This is why prudence or wisdom is a cardinal virtue. To use Porter's metaphor, the good life is more like writing a book than baking a cake where there is a strict recipe to follow to the letter.[9]

It follows that we must reject as inadequate two common positions in Christian ethics – positions that can sometimes even be closet attempts to shield us from this messiness and uncertainty.

The first is the claim that 'all we need is love'. In its most extreme form 'love' is treated as a built-in moral compass that points to the right thing to do or the right line of action to follow. This is a delusion. While in some contexts it might be fruitful to ask what is the response of love, love does not bring with it the capacity to make moral judgements. Even in personal relationships we need a richer resource of insight, and certainly much more so in social ethics. Love may give us motivation and inspiration. It may sustain us through difficulty and despondency. It may generate goodwill. Love, however, by itself is an insufficient guide to action. We need insight and resource in the craft of moral judgement. Love alone does not give us that. Another way of expressing the same point is to say that for a rich vision we need a rich language. Throughout this book we have encountered examples of the rich language we use in ethics – rights, duties, justice, flourishing, virtues, and suchlike. We impoverish our language if all these are eliminated because 'all we need is love'.

The second is the appeal to 'middle axioms'. J. H. Oldham coined the phrase as a programme for the Christian contribution to social ethics.[10] A 'middle axiom' is an ethical stance taken between two extremes. At the one extreme, Christians confine themselves to platitudinous and vacuous generalities. At the other extreme, they commit themselves to the detail of a specific social or economic policy. Those who opt for middle axioms reject both extremes. Platitudinous generalities are of little use. They also, however, reject the option at the other end of the spectrum. For a start, the Church as a collective and Christians as individuals may not have the expertise required for formulating detailed judgements in social or political policy. Furthermore, there is a distinction between a basic ethical ideal and a policy commitment aimed at bringing it about. We must not confuse commitment to the former with commitment to the latter. For example, economic sanctions as a means to an end must not be given the same moral status as the end sought – the holding to account of an oppressive regime with an appalling human rights record. Likewise, there is a difference between progressive taxation as a means to securing greater economic equality, and the greater economic equality itself embraced as an ideal.

The imperative to confront an oppressive regime might be a 'middle axiom', while the commitment to do this through economic sanctions is simply one policy commitment as a way of achieving this. The imperative to spread wealth more equally might be a middle axiom, but the commitment to doing this through progressive taxation is merely one possible means to an end. A 'middle axiom' sought a middle way between vague generality and detailed social or political policy.

The notion of middle axiom is not without value. It reminds us of a distinction between a value commitment and a means to achieve it. The latter should not be given the same moral status as the former. The notion has value in reminding us how complicated is the making of moral judgements, and especially in social ethics where highly complicated social and economic variables are involved, where our understanding is limited, and our capacity to predict the effects of our actions even more so.

All that said, we cannot enjoy the luxury of standing on the dry and firm rock of middle axioms, leaving it to others to get their feet muddy. We have to struggle with issues more detailed and more specific. The Anglican report, *The Church and the Bomb*,[11] for example, did not confine itself to a middle axiom, such as the imperative to do all we can to rid the world of nuclear weapons. It offered as a contribution to debate a reasoned policy as to how we might move towards achieving this (see 13.4). It is in the complexity of the real world that we have to make judgements. The insight of the Christian tradition – and increasingly of the world Church – should not be muted through being restricted unnecessarily to middle axioms. Christians and church bodies can 'consult the experts' as readily as anyone else. The churches with their local and international networks are well equipped for this. The contribution of church bodies – including the World Council of Churches – to ethical debate is at its best of a high order.[12] Of course, we will not always get it right, but probably no less so than others, and anyway Christians have no right to enjoy the luxury of avoiding being wrong by declining to speak. That said, we must speak with openness and humility.

The proof of the pudding is in the eating. In Part 3 I look at a selection of moral issues and ask how they might be addressed. I try to put to work the insights and perspectives explored in the first two parts of the book. As we wrestle with difficult moral issue in the real world we will find that things are messy, untidy, uncertain and mind-bogglingly complicated. But that is the world we live in and we cannot avoid making judgements – however cautious and ambiguous – as to how to behave, what ends to pursue, and what manner of people we seek to be. At the same time, however, we are not completely at sea. To that extent, the more confident metaphor of 'weaving the tapestry' is appropriate. We can do more than just muddle through.

Notes

1 Dennis Garber, *Inventing the Future*, Harmondsworth, Penguin, 1962, pp. 9, 89ff.

2 The 'Club of Rome', *The Limits to Growth*, 1972.

3 E.g. Augustine, *City of God*, Books 14–16, especially 14.28.

4 Reinhold Niebuhr, *Moral Man and Immoral Society*, 1932 (London edition, SCM Press, 1963), p. 73.

5 Niebuhr, *Moral Man*, p. 62.

6 Reinhold Niebuhr, *An Interpretation of Christian Ethics*, 1932 (New York, Meridian edition, 1956), p. 10.

7 Anthony Quinton, *The Politics of Imperfection*, 1978, London, Faber.

8 Karl Popper, *The Poverty of Historicism*, London, Routledge, second edition, 1972. Also *The Open Society and its Enemies*, London, Routledge, fourth edition, 1962, especially Volume 2.

9 Jean Porter, *The Recovery of Virtue*, London, SPCK, 1994, p. 102.

10 W. A. Visser 't Hooft and J. H. Oldham, *The Church and its Function in Society*, Chicago, Willett, Clark, 1937, p. 6.

11 *The Church and the Bomb*, London, CIO Publishing, 1982.

12 E.g. Ronald H. Preston (ed.), *Technology and Social Justice*, on the Social and Economic Teaching of the World Council of Churches from Geneva 1966 to Uppsala 1968, London, SCM Press, 1971.

Part 3

Some Specific Issues

The Body Politic and the Body of Christ

11.1 The body politic

The year is 2050. Since the turn of the millennium events in Britain have unfolded in a quite unexpected way. In 2015 a group of right-wing Christians formed a new political party – the *Christian Britain Party*. A remarkable revival of conservative Christianity occurred, staging a *coup d'état* of the historic denominations and leading also to the growth of large independent churches in every community. 'Vote for Christian Britain' was the line of the churches and by 2050 the *Christian Britain Party* was in government.

A radical programme to Christianize Britain is set in motion. Anti-discrimination legislation against gays is rolled back. Sex outside marriage incurs a fine, and contraceptives become available only on prescription. It is illegal for doctors to prescribe to anyone unmarried. Children born to a single parent have to be forfeit to an adoption agency. They will be better cared for by a good Christian family. Abortion is made illegal, although adoption is available, as in the case of rape. The divorce law becomes much stricter, and it is generally difficult for a woman to initiate a divorce, since the husband is head of the household. Equal opportunities in the work place are soft peddled so as to encourage women to be homemakers and mothers. After all, the birth rate has dropped alarmingly and there are now stricter immigration controls. Capital punishment is reintroduced, as is corporal punishment in schools. After all, both have biblical sanction. People of other faiths are tolerated but they must not proselytize or criticize Christianity, and they are forbidden to wear distinctive dress or religious symbols in public. Sunday trading is abolished, along with sport and entertainment on Sunday, in order to encourage the proper observance of the Lord's Day. Welfare benefits are skeletonized. They are inappropriate since the Lord will reward hard work with prosperity. Books, press articles, films and plays criticizing, let alone mocking or satirizing Christianity are banned. Such material might lead people astray and disturb the peace and harmony of the community. In the next King's Speech legislation will be proposed requiring science

academics in government-funded universities to sign a declaration dis-
avowing Darwinian evolution.

This is an unlikely prospect for secular Britain, with its culture of
tolerance. It would also be strongly disowned by many 'conservative'
Christians.[1] That said, the fear that something like this is the hidden
agenda of far too many Christians prompts writers such as Grayling
to see religion as a 'serious threat' to the well-being of society and
to demand that it has no place in the 'public domain'. The Taliban
represent religion in its unadulterated and true form. 'It is only where
religion is on the back foot, reduced to a minority practice, with an
insecure tenure in society, that it presents itself as essentially peaceful
and charitable.'[2] Although in a free society people may 'believe as they
wish', Grayling insists religion must, for these reasons, be confined to
the 'private sphere, as a matter of private observance only'[3] – presumably like membership of the Putney Cacti Club. This represents an interesting reversal. In the seventeenth and eighteenth centuries atheists
were regarded as dangerous.[4] Now, for Grayling, it is theists. Richard
Dawkins, likewise, expresses alarm at the totalitarian programme of
'Dominion Theology' and hints it is increasingly representative of the
religiously minded.[5] The worry is thus widely felt that religion brings
in its train divisiveness and a desire to control. It should therefore be
quarantined out of harm's way within the realm of the private. The
default position of religious believers is the yearning for totalitarian
control, while apparently the default position of atheists is the embrace
of freedom and tolerance.

Is it possible to offer a more creative and more positive approach
to the Church's participation in the body politic? If the policy of the
Christian Britain Party outrages humanists, my argument is that it
should equally outrage Christians. I say this for three reasons, and
in these three reasons Christians and liberal humanists may perhaps
make common cause.

First, it belongs to the dignity and right of every human being to
enjoy maximal freedom and autonomy over their own lives. How adult
lovers conduct a consensual relationship is not the business of the state.
We must enjoy freedom of thought and expression following the truth
as we perceive it. On Sunday we are free to worship God or, in H. G.
Wells's phrase, free to 'spit in his empty face'. Religious faith and
worship is a sham unless freely given. What is fundamentally wrong
with the programme of the *Christian Britain Party* is that it violates
the dignity of the person by making them subject. The partisan state
decides what is good for people. Well-being is conformity to the model
of life determined by the state. This is at worst totalitarianism and at
best ugly paternalism. Instead of protecting liberty, the state abuses
its power by imposing totalitarian control arising out of a vision that

many will not share. As John Locke classically observed, people cannot opt out of the state, since the state encompasses everyone. Thus, states have a special obligation to honour freedoms.[6] The enjoyment of freedom is intrinsic to the well-being of humanity. We are diminished as persons if we are subject.

Freedom then has intrinsic worth. There are also, however, utilitarian arguments in favour of freedom. It is through such maximum freedom that the community flourishes as well as the individual. A 'closed' society where there is censorship – political or through social sanctions – inhibits the free exchange of ideas and their testing in public debate. Societies stagnate. Relevant here is John Milton's image, referred to earlier, of truth as shattered and scattered[7] (see 5.3.3). Relevant also is Popper's insistence that a rich and prosperous society is the *result* and not the *precondition* of free democracy.[8] It is only when society is open and receptive to the initiative and creativity of its members, uninhibited by state control and censorship, that society can prosper. This is because society's prosperity – economic, cultural and intellectual – depends on the creativity of its citizens.

The third reason is that everyone is fallible and everyone has the capacity to be selfish, greedy and dishonest. Power is easily abused. Democracy comprises checks and balances against the abuse of power. The principal one is that political leaders are subject to periodic election. There might also be a constitution, separation of powers, and independent judiciary. There will also be the scrutiny of opposition parties, the free press, and so forth. Without these checks and balances and without answerability to the electorate, those in power might find that their power tends to corrupt and that absolute power corrupts absolutely.

Against all this, it is sometimes argued that society's cohesiveness depends on a high degree of consensus, and hence there may be an 'enforcement of morals' for the sake of the common good. Mandell Creighton argued that this was the prime motive behind the intolerances of the past. Fear of anarchy demanded strong state control.[9] James Fitzjames Stephen and Patrick Devlin have voiced sympathy for moderate forms of such arguments over the past century or so.[10] It is one thing, however, to say that *some* fundamental moral consensus is necessary for society to exist. It is quite another to argue that any substantial lack of consensus threatens society. It may even enrich it. It is certainly true that there is a robustness in modern Britain which allows maximum freedom without fear of anarchy such as may not be enjoyed in all cultures. Where Afghanistan is now Britain was a millennium or so ago. But this sober reflection does not undermine the fundamental thrust of the argument so far.

Despite the fact that the Church properly has a narrower boundary than the state, these insights apply also to the Church. The Church needs to give maximum freedom to its members, to be a community of free intellectual enquiry, and to have checks and balances within its structures to widen enfranchisement and prevent the abuse of power. It is sometimes said that the Church is not a democracy but a theocracy. To this it may be countered that we best discern the will of God through the whole body of the Church 'conferring together'. This is the thrust of Milton's *Areopagitica*. Furthermore, it is a Christian insight that God 'rules' through a truth that persuades, and above all through a love and grace that elicits our free response.

Our starting point in this chapter, however, is not the Church but the state. Our hard-won freedoms are precious but precarious. The way in which Nazism took root in one of the most sophisticated of Christian cultures is an awful warning. Our freedoms need to be cherished and protected. It should be clear by now that the stance of this book is that the three considerations just outlined resonate with a Christian vision. The first is an implication of a commitment to the dignity of the human person as a child of God. The second receives a classic defence in Milton as referred to elsewhere (see 5.3.3). As for the third it resonates with a Christian realism regarding human nature which is neither depraved not easily perfected. As Reinhold Niebuhr put it, our capacity for justice makes democracy possible. Our capacity for injustice makes democracy necessary.[11]

For some, this vision of society is based on scepticism regarding the possibility of consensus over common values. Without consensus we must accept pluralism and diversity, with the state acting as referee to give everyone a fair allocation of space. There is no common morality apart from a commitment to tolerance. For the most extreme version of this stance, freedom must be asserted because truth is denied. It is crucial to insist, however, that a libertarian vision of society need not depend on such scepticism. Christians may not share this scepticism but are just as committed to the open society for the three reasons I have indicated. For Milton, toleration and freedom were necessary preconditions for the search for truth. Toleration and freedom were not simply left over after the quest for truth had ended up in disillusionment.

So far we have a fairly simple political philosophy. The focus is on individuals, living as they choose, enjoying unmolested the fruits of their labour, and enjoying also freedom of association and expression. In the maximal exercise of freedom – the freedom nurturing people of self-respect and initiative – both economy and culture are enriched. The focus thus is not on the overarching state. We have a minimal state in order to allow space for each individual to enjoy autonomy and live as they see fit. Of course, they will build communities, but communities that are pluralistic and entered into freely. Freedom is restricted only to prevent its abuse when others are enslaved. Liberty is restricted in the name of liberty.

It is important to note that this is a philosophy of the *state*. It is not a philosophy of *life*. It is therefore beside the point to argue, as some theological commentators have done, that this vision leaves individuals isolated, unresourced and in constant competition. This may indeed happen, but only if a philosophy of the state becomes also a philosophy of life. On the contrary, the purview of the state is restricted so as to allow this wider life to flourish.

We arrive therefore at the famous principle of John Stuart Mill: 'The only purpose for which power can rightly be exercised over any member of a civilized community against their will is to prevent harm to others. Their own good either physical or moral is not a sufficient warrant.'[12] This sounds a good principle, *and it is a good principle*. The state has a fundamental duty to protect the liberty of its citizens. On many of the programmes of the *Christian Britain Party* the state should be neutral. It is not, however, as straightforward as it sounds. There are fuzzy edges.

Even as a principle of criminal law, although basically sound, it may need a massage here and there. For example, the law upholding the institutions of monogamous marriage, and even in some instances protecting private property, seem to express a moral commitment not easily covered by Mill's principle. The American Supreme Court has upheld laws against polygamy, implying a moral bias favouring monogamy not justified simply on the basis of Mill's criterion.[13] Why should the state not allow an openly polygamous contract of marriage as an alternative to monogamy? Furthermore, any abortion law, and any law concerning embryo research, will be based on a judgement as to the moral status of the unborn. The second sentence of Mill's principle is more controversial. It seems to rule out any kind of state paternalism – protecting people from themselves. Human dignity and freedom require a massive onus against this, but maybe it is sometimes justified, especially with regard to minors.

All that this shows, however, is that life is messy. Reality will always press upon the boundaries of slick principles. Mill's principle rightly indicates where the burden of proof lies. There is a massive onus against interfering with individual liberty. It is normally justified only for the sake of the wider liberty of others. It is particularly important here to emphasize the difference between a moral judgement and a political judgement as to what should be covered by the criminal law. It does not follow that because we judge something to be morally wrong 'there should be a law against it'. For example, Archbishop Geoffrey Fisher believed homosexual behaviour was a sin, but he also believed there is a difference between sin and crime, and so supported its decriminalization.[14] Archbishop Ramsey, likewise, supported the decriminalization of homosexuality on the grounds that what consenting adults do in private is none of the law's business. His concern was that the law should be humane and just, despite his own personal traditional approach to the ethics of homosexual relationships.[15] Indeed, the Wolfenden Commission, which recommended the decriminalization of homosexual relationships, was set up in part in response to an Anglican report on *The Problem of Homosexuality*.[16] The purpose of law is not to uphold in a heavy sense a detailed moral code. It is rather to protect liberty and to guard against exploitation. Thus, the legal regulation of, say prostitution, is a matter different from its moral assessment.

So much for the narrower purview of the law. Suppose we move to the wider remit of the state and ask how Mill's principle fares? What does it mean to say that the state should protect people's freedom? First, there is the concept of *'freedom from'*. My liberty needs to be protected 'from' attack by murderer, thief, terrorist, mugger and foreign aggressor. We have thus a minimal state as 'night watchman',[17] protecting life and property.

If I am lucky and resourceful, enjoying health and wealth, I may be content with this. But what of those less fortunate? The value of freedom is limited if I cannot make use of it. It follows there must also be a *'freedom to'* enjoy all the benefits of society and to participate fully in society.

Immediately, we face a flood of questions that any democracy will have to face. How do we manage the economy so as to achieve a tolerable balance between wealth creation, free enterprise and an appropriate distributive justice and environmental concern? How is healthcare provision to be structured and financed, and how is the tension between infinite demand and limited resource to be managed? What divorce law achieves a proper balance between compassion for those in failed marriages, upholding the institution of marriage, justice for each party and concern for any children? Is there a case for censorship *in extremis* – for example, the unrestricted access on the internet to sado-masochistic material encouraging violence against women? Should there be state subsidy for the arts? How is choice in education to be related to the state's responsibility to ensure just access to education for all? How is distributive justice to be related to a justice that speaks of a strong *prima facie* right of a person to their legally acquired income or property? What commitment does society have to equality? And what is the nature of the equality to which society is committed? What is to be society's penal policy? Is punishment about protecting society, deterrence, reforming and rehabilitating the criminal, or signifying society's outrage at crime? And if it is about all of these how are they to be balanced? What individual 'rights' does society recognize? What social philosophy guides the state's welfare provision? What is society's responsibility for those who cannot swim in the rough seas of meritocracy and competition? What is the nation's responsibility for the wider world, through aid programmes, fair or free trade, immigration policy and hospitality for asylum seekers? What is a society's stance on a whole range of issues in 'medical ethics'? The state cannot be simply a night-watchman; although that does not mean it should be a nanny, still less a nanny in jack boots.

All of these questions are subject to keen public debate. This is par for the course in an open society and for the political process. Questions of value cannot be avoided. The 'Body Politic' cannot be a value-free 'administration of things' in Marx's phrase. It is difficult to see how society as a whole could acceptably be organized on the basis of value neutrality, apart from a commitment to maximum liberty and toleration. Mill's criterion is about individual liberty and the scope of criminal law. But this leaves untouched most of the responsibilities of the modern state.

It is worth trying to bring all this together with some sketch as to how we understand the role of the state in a pluralistic and democratic society. The 1662 *Book of Common Prayer* speaks of the state as being concerned with the 'punishment of wickedness and vice' and the 'maintenance of true religion and virtue'.[18] It is salutary to reflect how dated, indeed how objectionable, this conception of the state now feels. It is at once too wide and too narrow.

It is too narrow because the mindset of the Prayer Book does not see the state as a major provider, or even as having a role in the economy. It is also, however, too wide. It is too wide because it links 'wickedness' with 'vice', thus failing to grasp the distinction we have seen Fisher and Ramsey acknowledged between crime and sin, along with the broad distinction Mill drew between 'other regarding' and 'self-regarding' actions.[19] There is no clearly defined dividing line here, but a state must honour the insistence that the realms of crime and of proper regulation over codes of practice in disputed areas (as over abortion and medically assisted dying – see Chapter 16) are not coterminous with the realm of ethics or of private behaviour and private morality. There are realms of private behaviour and individual judgement (including the liberty to engage in 'vice') that are none of the state's business.

This conception of the state is too wide in a further and crucial respect. It is not the business of the state to preserve 'true religion'. There must be a separation between church and state. Again, this is not quite as simple as it sounds. A separation need not exclude forms of partnership, but the main thrust of this separation is clear enough. The state does not privilege any religious position, still less disadvantage

another. The state is religiously neutral, and as such is released to protect the liberties of differing religious traditions, including the liberty
of those who belong to none. Moreover, unencumbered by the hollow crown of Erastian** privilege, but also Erastian control, religious
groups are free to be different from the state and thus contribute freely
and creatively to society (see also 8.3).

11.2 The Body of Christ

What is the relationship between the Church as the 'Body of Christ' to
this 'body politic'?

The opening paragraph of this chapter employs the shock tactic of
offering a terrible warning. It presents a picture of a totalitarian Britain. The Church uses what political muscle it has to impose authoritarian control. Calvin's Geneva is uncomfortably close to this model,
and Gregory XVI in 1832 denounced in *Mirari Vos* the freedom of
conscience and press, together with the separation of Church and state.
The state, at the Church's bidding, thus embraces a vision of what
human life should be and imposes it through taking away individual
liberty. There is enough in the programme of some right-wing Christian groups, as well as the practice in some countries where the Church
has political power, to counsel vigilance.[20] Christians need to confront
the temptation to control and regiment people and to lay that ghost.
Religion can breed a confidence and a zeal, the knee-jerk reaction of
which is to ban, to censor and to control. The stance of Gregory XVI
was, of course, dramatically reversed by Vatican II with its declaration
on religious freedom, *Dignitatis Humanae*, in 1965.

What is the alternative? One is for the Church to retreat into its
own sub-culture. This is the 'sectarian' option. Christians cultivate an
alternative lifestyle in community with other Christians, but the wider
world is left to its own devices, unless of course it hears and responds
to Christian 'witnesses', although what the wider world is to do with
the witness is not always clear. We have seen that Stanley Hauerwas
tends towards this view in his vision of the Church as an alternative
community committed to peaceableness. This involves giving modern
culture and politics the long spoon treatment since it all depends upon
a measure of coercion. In a very different way this was the tendency
of Catholicism arising out of the first Vatican Council, and especially in England where the establishment was Protestant. There was to
be a Catholic sub-culture as self-sufficient as possible, with Catholic
schools and even Catholic universities, businesses and trade unions.
The massive citadel of Up Holland near Liverpool is an architectural
expression of this. The strength of this approach is that it recognizes

the importance of 'belonging' and of the Church as a community of formation. It resonates with the idea that the role of the Church is to change individual lives, and through these lives there is influence for the wider good.

This approach can, however, lead to religion becoming privatized and ghettoed. This would appear to be the position favoured by Anthony Grayling. As we have seen, he argues the default position of religion, by its nature, is that of totalitarian control and persecution. It is thus dangerous to allow religions quarter in the 'public domain'. Religion should be 'a matter of private observance only'. Grayling rightly raises questions about, say, the appropriateness of establishment, but there is a lack of clarity about what it means to preclude the Churches from the 'public domain'. Does he mean that the President of the BMA may be allowed to comment on some issue in medical ethics, or the Director General of the CBI on levels of income, but not the Archbishop of Canterbury?[21] Is he objecting to the Church's massive involvement in charitable and community programmes? Or is he simply challenging inappropriate power and privilege enjoyed by religious institutions? If only the latter there need be no quarrel. The Church should not court power or seek special privilege. Again, I urged earlier the rightness of the separation between Church and state. A separation, however, need not imply the privatization and individualization of religion. On the contrary, through the separation the Church is released *to be itself* and to contribute in its own characteristic way to the body politic. But how? The model I offer here may also be persuasive to other faith communities as well.

11.3 A 'mid position'

I wish to argue that there is a 'mid' position between seeking totalitarian control on the one hand and a retreat into a Christian sub-culture on the other. This is the option of participating in public debate, in charitable and community programmes and in civil society, *but out of a commitment to what might be called the 'common good'.*

I consider two test case studies. The first is somewhat dated, and of only marginal importance, but it illustrates well the point. This is the *'Keep Sunday Special'* campaign of the early 1980s. The campaign was confused because two bandwagons became hitched together. In the one 'sabbatarians' maintained that Sunday is a day for religious observance and that Christians should use their muscle to seek state support for clearing the pitch on Sunday, so as to encourage people to worship. The whole community should be beholden to the desire of a minority to worship. In the other the mainstream churches argued that the community's health is served by having one day a week that is different. They commended an essentially biblical understanding of the Sabbath as the gift of rest within the rhythm of personal and communal life. Allied to this was a concern for the exploitation of workers – especially women working in the service sector.

My point is that the first type of argument (like 'prohibition' in American in the 1920s) expressed an inappropriate attempt by Christians to impose a partisan position on the rest of society. The second type of argument, at least as presented, was motivated by concern for the health of the community and justice for its members. This argument is controversial and may or may not persuade, but at least the motivation was that of seeking the public good, notwithstanding the repost of those seeking to call the Church's bluff by asking why this different day of the week had to be Sunday! Because it was focused on the common good, it was a position that could be argued in the public realm without any theological presuppositions.

The second case study concerns the contemporary debate over faith schools and I confine my discussion to those of the churches. The debate is often based on the assumption that church schools are about disingenuous proselytism and propaganda. Sometimes they are, and where they are this should be challenged. Some of the more recently founded faith schools add cause for this concern. My suggestion is that the purpose of a church school is not to proselytize but rather to provide good education, and one based on Christian principles. The phrase 'Christian principles', however, is not to be understood in any partisan way. By education based on Christian principles I mean things such as – speaking indicatively – an education that respects, values, and seeks to nurture as appropriate each individual. It is not an education that privileges university entrants, dismissing others as failures. I mean an education that is committed to developing a capacity for free and critical enquiry, and independent and mature judgement. I mean an education that is concerned with the 'whole person' and not simply providing fodder for the economy. I mean education that does not discriminate on the basis of race, religion, gender or sexual orientation. There is nothing platitudinous in all this. On what grounds do secular humanists believe such values are safer in the hands of a state monopoly than, in the case of church schools, a partnership between state and Church? They are, of course, never so secure that we may relax vigilance.

Christian education will certainly give serious place to the study of religion on the curriculum, but again the purpose of this is not proselytism but rather to engage critically and creatively with an important strand of human culture, thought and quest. As I remarked, education must be about nurturing the capacity to make critical judgements, and in *all* areas of life. If the result of this engagement is that pupils confirm their atheism, so be it. The education will render the atheism better informed and more considered. Admittedly this is a far cry from the 'religious instruction' envisaged by Butler's 1944 Act, but that belonged to a different age.

A good education does not offer simply a cafeteria of study modules. There are hard questions about 'belonging', school ethos, moral education, educating the 'whole person' and not just the 'mind', and so forth. All education takes place within a culture and expresses a philosophy and value system. Children are not served by a blindness to this, or by opting for some chimera of pristine but impoverished autonomy. That way we are in danger of ceasing to exercise critical scrutiny. The delicate task is to benefit from the rich resources of the traditions and cultures in which we stand, while at the same time nurturing a proper critical engagement and independence of spirit. A cursory analysis of the literature will show that Christian social thought and Christian philosophies of education are as alert to these issues and as well equipped to deal with them as any, and better than many, even if it may not always have filtered down to Basher Street Voluntary Aided.

This is not to deny that there are also hard questions about justice in a local community when church schools through their admission policy are in danger of partisanship or impoverishing other schools in the area. There are also hard questions about funding, although it is often forgotten that current funding arrangements arose out of the fact that the church schools were originally owned and run by the Churches before the state entered into partnership. In the case of voluntary aided schools the Church contributes a percentage of running costs, and even in the case of voluntary controlled schools the Church has provided the land and building.

In society we begin where we are, not with some utopian blueprint. The purpose of these reflections is not necessarily to argue for church schools in any conceivable society. It is merely to resist an ideological demand for their removal in modern Britain. Given that we are less committed to a state monopoly in education and are moving more into a 'mixed economy' culture of partnership between state and the wider society, it is an unfounded prejudice to exclude the churches on the grounds that church schools are about making pew fodder for the next generation rather than about contributing through education to the common good. But there needs to be constant vigilance to ensure the church schools do in fact have that commitment.

These two case studies suggest that Christian engagement in the public domain should be motivated by the public good and not by a desire to impose in a totalitarian fashion a particular way of life. In the area of public debate, the churches in Britain have a creditable record.

The Mortimer commission *Putting Asunder*[22] served as a basis for the divorce law reform of 1969–71. It certainly focused on the public good, as distinct from those who might have wished the law to reflect more closely what they perceived as being specific biblical injunctions, even though they would not be widely shared in a pluralistic society. Agree with it or not, concern for the public good is manifest also in the joint *Episcopal Statement on Euthanasia*,[23] and in the Archbishop's contribution to the debate on Lord Joffe's bill (see 16.4). A commitment to the common good guides Anglican reports on *Faith in the City* and *Faith in the Countryside*, the ecumenical *Unemployment and the Future of Work*, *Prosperity with a Purpose* and the recent report *Faithful Cities*.[24] Others that could be mentioned would fill not a few shelves. Probably the best contributions of the Methodist Church over the past two decades are *The Ethics of Wealth Creation* and the *Status of the Unborn Human*.[25]

Going back earlier to the 1937 Oxford Conference on 'Church, Community and State', the papers, at worst, show a certain economic naivety in their optimism about co-operation as opposed to competition as a basis for economic life, and a similar over-optimism in their reliance on voluntary work. They, nonetheless, represent an impressive engagement with social thought and there is no hint of a desire for totalitarian control. William Temple's vision of the place of the established Church in the life of nation and empire did not imply this. The papers express deep Christian commitments to the well-being of everyone, issuing in a passion for a just and more equal society. There is a radical commitment to workers' rights, fair wages, good housing, full employment, and the raising of the school leaving age to sixteen. Extremes of wealth and poverty were declared intolerable. The papers represented an impressive concern for the common good and the same can be said of the more sober-minded Malvern Conference of 1941.

My suggestion, then, is that the Church should not use what political muscle it may have to impose a particular stance or way of life on the community, but, respecting freedom and pluralism, should particulate in public life with a view to seeking the common good.

11.4 The 'common good' – released after cautioning?

In the above section I have used rather casually the notion of the 'common good'. But what might we mean by it, and does it have dangers? The concept is the focus of much recent Roman Catholic social ethics,[26] and was used by the English and Welsh Roman Catholic bishops in a 1997 statement *The Common Good*, as well as in Anglican reports, such as *Faith in the City*.[27] What the concept stands for resonates with the commitments of many strands of political philosophy, save perhaps the market fundamentalism of the extreme right.[28] In broad terms, it expresses a vision of the well-being of the community as a whole and of every member of it. Some, however, find the notion suspicious, so it needs to be brought in for questioning.

For a start, some may contest the contrast I have drawn between a Church subscribing to the manifesto of the *Christian Britain Party* and a Church committed to the common good. The *Christian Britain Party* could insist that the common good is, in fact, served by everyone being obedient to the Christian vision for life and society which is God's will. God's will is for our good and the party knows what God's will is! My response is that this is theologically flawed for the three reasons I gave above. The very fact that this view may be advanced, however, reinforces suspicion regarding the idea of the 'common good'.

There is first, therefore, the suspicion that the notion tends to be authoritarian and oppressive. Helpful at this point is Isaiah Berlin's distinction between two very different concepts of liberty. On the one hand, liberty or freedom may mean not being interfered with by others. There must be a frontier between the public and private. On the other, there is a liberty found in one's 'true self'. The problem here is that others may claim they know what is my 'true self' better than I do. This 'true self' may be determined by the control of others with their partisan blueprint for humanity. People's 'true freedom' is conforming to the pattern of another, and if they do not understand this it is because the free choice of the 'true' self is submerged beneath the clutter of immature ideas and superficial feelings. Essentially, the individual is subordinate to state or Church and an imposed ideology. The notion of 'freedom to' becomes 'a specious disguise for brutal tyranny'.[29] My actual wishes may be ignored and I may be bullied in the name of my 'true' self or the 'true' goal of my life. Much Christian comment about homosexuality expresses a paternalism that claims to know better than people themselves what is good for them.[30]

It is for this reason that the idea of a 'common good' is, for some, highly suspect. After all, were not Stalin's programmes and the Jacobin dictatorship for the 'common good'? Judith Shklar argues that much modern liberalism is based on fear – the fear that a state committed to the common good will find itself adopting programmes that interfere too much with individual liberty.[31] One is reminded of Mill's warning concerning the 'tyranny of the majority'.[32] No wonder a fear of this can encourage a minimalist 'live and let live' philosophy. John Atherton wonders if the concept can still be appropriate on account of connotations of 'political interference in economic life and private choices' and because of nuances of 'synthesis' and 'map making'.[33] What must be absolutely clear is that if we are to use the notion it must be purged of connotations of authoritarian control, since the common good must involve a maximal honouring of individuals and their freedoms. People cannot enjoy any 'common good' unless proper quarter is given to the claims of freedom.

Anxiety might be encouraged by the ambiguity in John Paul II's understanding of the responsibility of the state to promote the common good. A stout defender of democracy and freedom, for which millions last century will have been deeply grateful, John Paul still insists upon the state's obligation to honour the truth contained in the moral law. Commitment to the 'common good' involves this recognition. On this basis he has been vocal in calling for the coercive power of the state to enact laws against abortion and patient-requested euthanasia, resisting also the extension of rights to gay couples. The 'moral value' of a democracy depends on its conformity to the 'moral law'.[34] 'The civil law must confirm to the moral law.'[35] This raises difficult questions about the relationship between freedom, democracy and truth, and the relationship between law and morals. Indeed, the call to oppose homosexual partnership is difficult to reconcile with a democracy that allows maximum freedom – a freedom affirmed in Vatican II's *Dignitatis Humanae* (1965).

Admittedly, abortion is not the best example, since if it is true that there is no difference between abortion and infanticide, then the unborn is a citizen, and the state has a duty to protect its citizens. The problem is that there is no one obviously correct understanding of the moral status of the developing unborn human (see 16.2). If issues are ethically problematical and if there is lack of moral consensus, how does a democracy respond? There seems no alternative but to hammer the matter out through the political process. This may involve a measure of honourable compromise, combined with the recognition that the relationship between statute law and what John Paul II calls moral law is complex. This is, in fact, the conclusion of the distinguished Roman Catholic moral theologian, Charles Curran.[36]

A second worry about the notion of the 'common good' is implicit in this. We live in a pluralistic society, with limited consensus as to what the common good actually involves. There is no consensus, for example, on the questions posed on page 206 above. This suggests that any notion of the common good must include the acknowledgement of conflicting interests and of pluralism alongside consensus. It is not about a sentimental vision of one big happy family of universal co-operation, but rather about struggling through pluralism and conflict to find a fairness and justice in which all as far as possible can share. The notion must not be reminiscent of a social engineering that homogenizes and subordinates the minority to the majority, or the weak to the strong. In a later book John Atherton finds the concept too heavily nuanced with a common vision that can be oppressive and giving insufficient space for difference [37]

A third difficulty follows from this, and has in fact already been alluded to. Conceptions of common good, like utilitarianism and notions of universal benevolence, may devalue complementary values. We have already instanced the value of freedom. Competition and a proper self-interest are other examples. These values are important, for instance, in the conduct of economic life.

These are serious questions and the warnings implicit need to be heeded. Because of such questions and warnings, Atherton and others discard the concept. Others, however, still allow the notion to return to our moral language, although only after a cautioning. The reality is we need a concept like the 'common good' in our moral vocabulary, and if we did not have such a concept we would have to invent one. We need some such concept to speak of our responsibility for the well-being of society as a whole and of all its members. The concept becomes a kind of portmanteau to hold together and balance the more focused concepts of liberty, justice, solidarity, subsidiarity, equality, prosperity, inclusivity, and so forth. The portmanteau concept allows these more focused concepts to be nuanced and held in creative tension. The notion of 'common good' is not a bad one, and if it has connotations that we regret then that is the case with all ethical concepts. All ethical concepts have their dangers, and need to be qualified; but we cannot do without them.

Thus, Hollenbach argues that if we have no notion of the common good we end up with a society of strangers, in which there are no common goals. Everyone is a stranger pursuing their own ends. The only agreement is that of tolerance. We cannot, however, flourish on that sparse diet alone. We need some common goals, and we need communities to which to belong. We simply cannot help but wrestle with some notion of common good since we are social animals and we cannot flourish save within society. We depend in myriads of ways upon the wider society and without some conception of the common good we retreat into the minimalism of *laissez faire*. Freedom and toleration alone will not tackle poverty, marginalization, environmental issues or provide structures for health care and education.[38] A society based simply on individual freedom and toleration will be one where the weak are dominated by the strong. This is the danger of the minimal state proposed by Milton Friedman and Robert Nozick.[39] If societies are to pursue 'freedom to' and not only 'freedom from', then decisions have to be made on the sort of questions raised above (p. 206). All these presuppose some notion of the common good. If we did not have the concept we would have to invent a replacement. That said, there is nothing sacrosanct about this particular concept. John Locke spoke of the 'public good'[40] and the traditional notion is that of the 'common weal'.[41] Indeed, Atherton implicitly invents a synonym when he uses a phrase such as 'social flourishing'.[42]

11.5 Politics and public theology

The question, however, remains: how does a pluralist and democratic society, in which there are conflicting interests, arrive at some kind of consensus? The least unsatisfactory way of proceeding is to hammer it all out through the deliberations and give and take of the political process, constrained indeed by the law, and maybe by a constitution, which together seek to safeguard basic justice. Politics is not primarily about confronting strangers from our respective citadels. It is about the testing of ideas through debate, deliberation and dialogue, finding as far as possible a shared vision. The extent of pluralism can be exaggerated. Public debate is not always about the conduct of civil war by other means.[43] There may be no consensus on the moral status of the unborn, over medically assisted suicide, penal policy, or distributive justice, but there is a wide consensus over basic human rights and the evil of racism and many forms of exclusion. Where society does disagree, there can be political debate. Through debate there may be a growing consensus, and where not, the give and take of the political process gives us an honourable compromise. It is irresponsible to withdraw from politics in order to avoid compromise or to keep our hands clean. We guard against tyrannical versions of the common good by insisting that part of what constitutes the common good is the giving of maximal freedom to people in their own lives and in their participation in the political process. This basic understanding of politics within a democracy has been outlined by writers such as Crick, Guttmann and Thompson.[44]

Christians and Church will share in the political process aimed at seeking the 'common good'. There is no vision that is *exclusively* Christian, but there may be a *characteristically* Christian one. There are clear perspectives, rooted in Christian conviction. Recent Vatican theology has spoken of a basic solidarity encouraged by the conviction that we are all together children of God. By the same token, any form of elitism is confronted, together with a one sided individualism. There is the invitation to have confidence in discovering a mutually enriching common life on an essentially egalitarian basis. This implies a deep concern about marginalization and any underclass. At the same time, the rights and sanctity of every person warn us against a communitarianism that is oppressive. This concern has led to a valuable stress in recent Vatican social ethics upon subsidiarity as arising out of belief in the freedom and dignity of every person.[45] 'Subsidiarity' may be defined as giving to the local and the individual as much autonomy as possible. For John Paul II, the complementary truths of our equal dignity and our solidarity involve a critique of the two extremes of communism and individualism. There will also be for Christians a commitment to a notion of justice as fairness, but also an openness even within social structures to a generosity that goes beyond justice. If the stance of this book is sound, the wisdom of the Christian tradition's community of memory on these matters may commend itself to those who do not share its theological underpinning. Christians may make common cause with others because this remains God's world and all people are made in the divine image.

None of this leads to geometrical precision. The world is too complex for that. As has elsewhere been noted, there is no perfect balancing of the *prima facie* values of justice, equality and freedom – however they be defined. One way of thinking of the 'common good' is as a pragmatic attempt to find the best achievable balance. Freedom is a pivotal value. Private space must be protected. But an appeal to freedom cannot be allowed to trump every counter claim. The notion of common good is further helpful because it focuses on inclusiveness, participation and justice – notions not always guarded by the notion of freedom. It speaks of the well-being of everyone in the community, and not just one class, race, age group or gender. This implies fairness, an open society, and an avoidance of polarization and social exclusion.

There is indeed a danger that when we speak of the 'common good' and of related concepts such as justice, fairness, equality and so forth, we do little more than give ourselves a soothing shower bath of abstract nouns (see 3.9). We need to ask what these concepts mean and to struggle to find how they might be expressed in a society in which there is pluralism and conflict as well as a measure of consensus. This, however, is what the cut and thrust of political debate is all about. It follows that the notion is not static. It neither ignores conflict nor simply validates the *status quo*.

My particular claim, however, is that the Church should neither thirst after control nor retreat into the private realm. The Church should rather participate in the public forum *with a view to seeking the common good*. This does not involve a 'compromise' of Christian principles. Rather, it expresses a theology. It is a theology that places high value on individual liberty, and yet within an inclusive community of justice. It is a theology that places high value on communities based on mutual respect, as well as on neighbourliness and friendship. It is above all a theology that recognizes that utopian dreams can be idolatrous and that the 'give and take' of deliberation and compromise within the forum of liberty belongs to the stuff of decent social living. We build whatever common good is possible. It is a Christian self-definition, which stresses our common humanity rather than the differences between Christians and others. All this resonates with the 'two realms' approach found classically in Augustine and Luther.[46] Broadly speaking, there is an acceptance that we live in a 'fallen' world, that we are all sinners, that human life and society are not easily perfectible, while at the same time there are always resources for renewal and reasons for hope. Christians strive in the 'realm of this world' for the most realistic and the most achievable fairness, justice and human well-being, recognizing that it is rarely the ideal. To abandon the world for this reason, however, involves a serious reneging of Christian responsibility. We cannot accept Grayling's demand that religion should be confined to the private. If Christian living and Christian vision cannot contribute to the 'healing of the nations' then Christian faith is a sham; but we need to recognize his fears about the wrong kind of participation in the public realm.[47]

Recently there has been a renewed interest in 'public theology'. The term may be a new one, but the notion is far from new. Public theology is essentially contributing to public debate out of Christian insight, but in a way that is accessible to those who do not share Christian faith. Public theology is not about control, Christendom style, but about contributing to the political and democratic processes. It has to rely on its own persuasiveness and will use a language which connects with public debate. A lot of what is expressed will have a theological underpinning for Christians, but may, nonetheless, commend itself to a wider public.[48] A public theology will commend publicly accessible truths, offering insights and challenges arising out of theology, but in a way that has coherence, rationale and persuasiveness for those who do not share the theology. A Christian public theology will, for example, challenge a society of widening extremes of wealth and poverty, a society that has a lessening commitment to equal access to education and health care, a society in which the rich put their money into private education and health, living in gated ghettos with strong security as protection against the underclass. Likewise, a Christian public theology may hold before the community the vision of a commitment to working for international justice.

The point is complicated but not invalidated by the fact that there is a plurality of 'publics'. Furthermore, public theology is not simply, or even primarily, academic theologians talking to those who have power. Good public theology comes from marginalized Christian congregations within marginalized communities, of which there are many doing sterling work rarely noticed by the media.

It is not required, nor indeed always desirable, that Christian opinion should be expressed with unanimity, and certainly no guarantee that it will never be silly. That is par for the course in public debate. Sometimes Christians will raise stimulating counter-cultural questions arising out of the Church's long tradition of reflection. An example is the submission of the Roman Catholic Bishops on *In Vitro* fertilization to the Warnock commission. The arguments did not persuade the commission – nor indeed most Christians – but the submission stimulated an interesting debate and we were all wiser as a result (see 3.10).

11.6 Civil society

So far the focus has been on the Church's participation in public debate. This is important because society cannot ignore questions of value and priority. There is always the danger that public policy will be taken over by those whose expertise is merely instrumental.[49] Sometimes there will be a stringency in this participation, as when, for example, injustice and marginalization are challenged. This may be encouraged by the influence of liberation theology. But in considering the relationship between the Body of Christ and the body politic we should not stop there. So to do might even imply that the most important thing in society is what governments do! There is also what we may call 'civil society'. Even today, the Church remains a crucial segment of civil society, strengthening communities in all kinds of ways. Lord Hurd describes the Church of England as 'the most effective collection of active citizens at work in our society',[50] although it is a pity he did not include in his observation an ecumenical or indeed multi-faith glance. The churches are places where people meet, where there is mutual pastoral care and the nurturing of neighbourliness. There is something prophetically counter cultural in the value the Churches attach to such things, rarely attracting media attention. Furthermore, both institutionally and through individual Christians, the Church is a key part of the so-called 'voluntary sector', not least through involvement in charities, many, of course, having a church foundation. Paradoxically as the Church gets weaker numerically it is more involved in community development and regeneration. The growth of church-based credit unions is one example. Grayling says it is dangerous to allow 'the major religions to jostle against one another in the public domain'.[51] It is not clear what this means, but it does prompt the question: What is his view of the Council of Christians and Jews, the Christian Muslim Forum, and scores of local inter-faith groups? In all these ways the churches and individual Christians, with people of other faiths, may help build good community relations. Both Hollenbach and Gill[52] offer firm evidence that religious communities do contribute to the public good in ways that are both peaceful and supportive of freedom.

There is evidence of a strong correlation between religious activity and political and social engagement. The churches have strengthened civil society as a domain free from the state and have so encouraged the emergence of democracy – Poland being a signal example. This resonates with Alexis de Tocqueville's classic observation that a healthy democracy depends upon the institutions of civil society.[53]

A recent study for the Rowntree Trust has identified the contribution of faith communities to 'social capital'.[54] Social capital describes a community's resource in terms of *people*, with their networks and shared values. While definitions will of course vary, the main aspects are citizenship, neighbourliness, trust and shared values, decency and integrity, community involvement, volunteering, social networks and civic participation. This theme is part of the subject of the report *Faithful Cities*, which speaks of 'faithful capital'.[55] 'Faithful capital' is the term used to speak of what might be characteristic of a faith community's contribution to social capital. It speaks of the sustained commitments of faith communities to their locality. It speaks of the values of inclusiveness, love of neighbour, care for the stranger, commitments to human dignity, reconciliation and social justice. It speaks of what may be characteristic emphases of faith communities, such as forgiveness, hope and generosity. Faith communities have also a role in bridge building and resolving conflict, not least because of their ubiquitous locations, both urban and rural, and across the social classes, having roots in all sections of the communities.

Of course, it would be outrageous to suggest that the faith communities are the only source of social and faithful capital. Again, the contribution of the faith communities is – to use traditional language – blighted by sin. It is not always benign. It is, however, neither naive or triumphalist to insist upon the very significant contribution of faith communities to social capital. The myth that religion is by nature divisive and encouraging of violent conflict needs to be exposed for what it is.

Alongside all this, there is profit in revisiting the old idea of the Church feeding Christian values into the mindset of a culture. The values of fair play, generosity, decency, altruism, justice, compassion and, above all, the rights and dignity of everyone, are not inviolable. They can easily be lost. It was the argument of the early chapters of this book that they 'stand on their own feet' but at the same time they receive powerful reinforcement within Christian belief. Over centuries Christian influence has so drip fed the mindset of cultures. In this tradition John Taylor 30 years ago was among those challenging the churches to 'raise awareness' over environmental concerns.[56] A basic fundamental equality of human beings was declared by the founders of the American Constitution to be 'self-evident'. It is not self-evident to all. It was self-evident to them because their vision derived from a mindset nourished by Christian conviction.

The tragedy is that as the Church becomes smaller it easily shoots itself in the foot by becoming more exclusive, withdrawing into its own sub-culture. Instead of 'common prayer' we often find a pattern of worship increasingly over-confident and strident, such as to frighten off anyone who is not a 'true believer'. Some within the Church of England sit lightly to the fine Anglican tradition of sharing responsibility for the well-being of the whole parish. Just as the market excludes those with no money to buy, so the Church excludes those whose wallets do not contain the currency of the required belief, thus reneging on its commitment to nurture inclusive communities. It is very 'postmodern' to emphasize distinctiveness, but is it consistent with belief that 'the earth is the Lord's and the fullness thereof'? We are all sinners, while still all bearing the divine image. This counsels a humbler approach that will give the body of Christ quieter confidence in its sharing in the 'body politic'.

It might be protested that I am here offering a reductionist understanding of the Church. This, however, is not so. This chapter has been concerned with the responsibilities of the Church within the 'body politic' and none of this implies that less weight be given to the Church's central faith and worship. On the contrary, the Church expresses and more deeply grasps that faith, and gives greater integrity to its worship, through attending to its commitments to the wider community, for, as the Psalmist says, we have seen 'the goodness of the Lord in the land of the living'.[57]

We return to the notion of 'civil society'. There is a certain vagueness about the concept, and there is no virtue in seeking a tight definition. Generally the concept refers to a kind of social jelly, which exists between the household unit on the one hand and the state and other major institutions on the other. It speaks of voluntary networks and voluntary associations. It speaks of relationships of decency and neighbourliness and mutual support. It speaks of people learning good social skills. Traditionally, civil society has focused on local communities and neighbourhoods with their networks of relationships. The Church – with its congregations in virtually every locality – has a heavy commitment to this and that is right and proper. At the same time, as technology shrinks distance, networks are no longer always local. People may be more attached to a geographically diverse network than to their local neighbourhood, thus giving a new expression to civil society.

People who live in and are formed by civil society also work for the state, in the various sectors of industry and the market economy, in health and education, in the various professions, and so forth. This, of course, includes Christians and so in addition to the institutional engagement of the Church there is the participation of Christians on a more individual basis, with at best their commitment to integrity, justice, responsibility and goodwill. This is of pivotal importance, and so we must not end with a 'clerical' emphasis on the gathered Church, important though that is. The general approach proposed here is valid also for individual Christians in their everyday lives. In all this, therefore, we need to speak both of the Church collectively and of Christians individually. The Church is not apart from the body politic, since in every sector of life Christians are present contributing out of the insights of their faith and above all integrity of life. There is truth in the old saying that the Church 'changes society by changing people'. It is not the whole truth because individual life is deeply affected by social structure and by culture. It follows that Christians have an institutional as well as an individual commitment. That said, the most crucial dimension of the Church's contribution to the common good is through the lives of each individual Christian – something deplorably neglected in the culture of clerical ecclesiastical navel gazing.

11.7 Conclusions and cautions

The argument of this chapter is that the churches and Christians have a mission within the body politic to seek the common good. This connects with belief that God's spirit is everywhere present and God's compassion extends to all. The churches, of course, are often perilously small communities in a skeletonized civil society, but that is no reason for lessening commitment or dimming a vision. If the argument of this book is sound, namely that ethics does not so depend on theology that it cannot be discussed in the public domain, many of the insights of the Christian tradition may commend themselves to wider publics even when a specifically theological framework may not be accepted.

None of this is a programme for lofty certainties. Churches have no right to enjoy the luxury of silence save when enunciating timeless truth or bland platitude. The attempt to remain secure with 'middle axioms' (general principles – but not so general as to be vacuous) perhaps has one root in such a desire (see Chapter 10). Participating in the cut and thrust of political debate is to be involved in complication and messiness, and much of the time we will get it wrong, but not necessarily more so than anyone else.

Furthermore, the Church's participation in civil society will likewise not be without its ambiguities. Here also there is the danger of a subtle social control that restricts rather than liberates people. Local communities and church communities can be oppressive. Again there has to be critical scrutiny lest the 'drip feed' into the cultural mindset becomes toxic rather than nourishing. Historically it has been both. The churches do not exist in pristine prophetic purity over and against society. They are part of society along with all the failings and ambiguities that are part of the human condition.

In modern Britain bourgeoisie success can combine with complacency about extremes of poverty and wealth, a claim to an absolute right to property, an indifference to marginalization, a low investment in local communities, and a pattern of consumption that the earth's resources may not be able to bear. Our celebrity culture swoons over youthfulness, bodily beauty and obscene ostentation. There are strands in educational philosophy that see education as doing nothing more than impart skills for the economy. There is the constant task of seeking to humanize the market. There is no shortage of areas for Christian hard thinking and sometimes costly engagement, any more than there is shortage of cause for the Church to learn and to put its own house in order. At all levels the Church and Christians can make a difference – for good or ill – and hard work, hard thinking and vigilance, and above all humility and grace are needed to ensure that as far as possible it is for the good.

Notes

1 E.g. John Stott, *Issues Facing Christians Today*, chapter on 'Should we impose our views?', London, Collins, 1990.

2 A. C. Grayling, *What is Good?*, London, Weidenfeld & Nicholson, 2003, pp. 206ff.

3 Grayling, *What is Good?*, pp. 206 and 208.

4 Even John Locke so argued in his *Letters concerning Toleration*, ed. and translated by J. W. Gough, Oxford, Oxford University Press, 1968, pp. 133ff.

5 Richard Dawkins, *The God Delusion*, London, Bantam Books, 2006, p. 319.

6 John Locke, *Letters Concerning Toleration*, especially pp. 65–80. The phrase of H. G. Wells is from chapter 10 of *Mr Britling Sees It Through* (1916).

7 John Milton, *Areopagitica*, Everyman Edition, ed. K. M. Burton, London, Dent, 1927, p. 30.

8 Karl R. Popper, *The Open Society and its Enemies*, Vol. II, London, Routledge, fourth edition, 1962, pp. 218ff.

9 Mandell Creighton, *Persecution and Tolerance*, London, Longman Green, 1895.

10 James Fitzjames Stephen, *Liberty, Equality, Fraternity*, London, 1873; Patrick Devlin, *The Enforcement of Morals*, Oxford, 1959.

11 Reinhold Niebuhr, *The Children of Light and the Children of Darkness*, London, Nisbet, 1945, p. vi.

12 John Stuart Mill, *On Liberty*, London, Dent, 1910, Everyman Edition, ed. A. D. Lindsay, p. 73.

13 Thus, Basil Mitchell, *Law, Morality and Religion in a Secular Society*, Oxford, Oxford University Press, 1967, pp. 26–7.

14 Edward Carpenter, *Archbishop Fisher*, Norwich, Canterbury Press, 1991, p. 393.

15 Owen Chadwick, *Michael Ramsey: A Life*, Oxford, Clarendon Press, 1990, pp. 145–9.

16 Church of England Moral Welfare Council, 1954. See Archbishops' Council, Church House Publishing, *Some Issues in Human Sexuality*, 2003, p. 24.

17 The phrase seems to have its origin in nineteenth-century liberalism.

18 *Book of Common Prayer* (1662), Prayer for the 'Whole estate of Christ's Church militant here on earth' in the Order for Holy Communion.

19 Mill, *On Liberty*, e.g., chapter IV, pp. 135–6.

20 For examples see Rosemary Radford Ruether, *Christianity and the Making of the Modern Family*, London, SCM Press, 2001, pp. 157ff.

21 As Basil Mitchell asked in a different context: *Law, Morality and Religion in a Secular Society*, p. 129.

22 *Putting Asunder*, report chaired by R. C. Mortimer, London, SPCK, 1996.

23 Appendix Two in *On Dying Well*, London, Church House Publishing, second edition, 2000.

24 *Faith in the City*, 1985; *Unemployment and the Future of Work*, London, Council of Churches for Britain and Ireland, 1997; *Prosperity with a Purpose*, London, Churches Together in Britain and Ireland, 2005; *Faithful Cities*, Peterborough, Methodist Publishing House and London, Church House Publishing, 2006.

25 Published by the Methodist Publishing House, both in 1991.

26 E.g. John XXIII's *Pacem in Terris* (1963), Part IV, and in John Paul II's *Centesimus Annus* (1981), the latter seeking to 'humanize' market capitalism.

27 *Faith in the City*, e.g. p. 54.

28 E.g. Anthony Giddens, *The Third Way*, Cambridge, Polity Press, 1998.

29 Isaiah Berlin, 'Two Concepts of Liberty' (1969), reprinted in David Miller (ed.) *Liberty*, Oxford, Oxford University Press, 1991, p. 43.

30 For example, *Homosexualitatis Problema*, Vatican, 1986, especially Paragraph 7.

31 Judith N. Shklar, 'The Liberalism of Fear' in N. Rosenblum (ed.), *Liberalism and the Moral Life*, Massachusetts, Harvard University Press, 1989.

32 Mill, *On Liberty*, pp. 67ff.

33 John Atherton, *Christianity and the Market*, London, SPCK, 1992, pp. 256, 265. The concept is defended, recognizing the dangers, in David Hollenbach's *The Common Good and Christian Ethics*, Cambridge, Cambridge University Press, 2002.

34 John Paul II, *Evangelium Vitae*, Vatican, 1995, Paragraph 70.

35 *Evangelium Vitae*, Paragraph 72.

36 Charles Curran, *Transition and Tradition in Moral Theology*, Notre Dame, 1979, pp. 230–50.

37 John Atherton, *Marginalization*, London, SCM Press, 2003, p. 124.

38 As argued, for example, in Hollenbach, e.g., pp. 173ff.

39 Milton Friedman, *Capitalism and Freedom*, Chicago University Press, 1962, p. 12.

40 John Locke, *Letter concerning Toleration*.

41 Meaning 'wellbeing', 'welfare', 'prosperity', 'good'.

42 John Atherton, *Marginalization*, London, SCM Press, 2003, p. 3.

43 Alasdair MacIntyre, *After Virtue*, London, Duckworth, second edition, 1985, p. 236.

44 Bernard Crick, *In Defence of Politics*, Harmondsworth, Pelican, revised edition, 1964, especially pp. 34ff. Also A. Guttmann and D. Thompson, *Democracy and Disagreement*, Massachusetts, Harvard University Press, 1996.

45 John Paul II, *Redemptor Hominis*, Vatican, 1979, paragraphs 13 ff. Also *Sollicitudo Rei Socialis,* Vatican, 1987.

46 This is in continuity with the 'two realms' notion in Augustine's *City of God*, Books 14–16, especially 14.28.

47 There has developed in Britain a tradition of 'public theology', by writers such as William Temple, Ronald Preston, John Atherton, Duncan Forrester and others. This is represented, for example, in William F. Storrar and Andrew R. Morton (eds), *Public Theology for the Twenty-first Century,* London, Continuum, 2004.

48 Storrar and Morton (eds), *Public Theology*, pp. 1–2.

49 Raymond Plant in Storrar and Morton (eds), *Public Theology*, p. ix.

50 In Stephen Platten (ed.), *Runcie: On Reflection*, Norwich, Canterbury Press, 2002, p. 27.

51 Grayling, *What is Good?*, p. 208.

52 Hollenbach, pp. 92ff.; Robin Gill, *Church Going and Christian Ethics*, Cambridge, Cambridge University Press, 1999, e.g. pp. 106ff., 193.

53 Alexis de Tocqueville, *Democracy in America*, 1834.

54 Robert Furbey *et al.* (eds), *Faith and Social Capital*, York, Joseph Rowntree Foundation, 2006.

55 *Faithful Cities*.

56 John Taylor, *Enough is Enough*, London, SCM Press, 1975.

57 Psalms 27.13.

12

Making and Sharing Wealth

12.1 The market

Christians are often vocal over the unjust distribution of wealth; and vocal also over the 'spiritual dangers' of rampant consumerism. But before wealth can damage our souls or fuel injustice, it has first to be created. We all have deep investment in the wealth of our nation, a wealth that gives us surgery and medicine, quick transport, varied and nourishing foods, and warm homes crammed with electrical gadgets. We can add books, music, films, clothes, hobbies, sports facilities, theatres and a host of other things. The nation's infrastructure – energy, water, education, health and social security – depends upon its wealth. We cannot go into the forest and gather the things we enjoy like blackberries. Wealth has to be created. But how?

Let's begin with a model, but it is only a model. The real world is immensely more complicated. One country will differ widely from another. Nevertheless, the model helps us get a handle on things. Inventors or entrepreneurs have an idea as to what people want and they go about making it. It could be Henry Ford with cars, Josiah Wedgwood with china, James Dyson with vacuum cleaners or William Hartley with jam. Maybe they borrow money to invest in their business, or maybe they invite people to buy 'shares'. The goods are made and sold and the profit is ploughed back into the business. A demand in the market is identified and the incentive of making a profit drives the inventor and entrepreneur to improve the product or devise new ones. But suppose the goods do not sell? The entrepreneur goes out of business or changes track to respond to demand. The result is an increasingly sophisticated complex for the creation of wealth, responding to the demand of the consumer. High demand pushes up the price and this encourages higher production. Low demand pushes down the price and so less is produced and resource is diverted elsewhere. The price mechanism acts as an 'invisible hand' to ensure resources are allocated according to need.[1] The market thus signals what people want and tries to respond. Competition prompts an efficient use of costly resources. There are, in fact, a number of markets – for goods and services, for labour, and for money and capital – working together.

Moreover, as Milton Friedman[2] and Michael Novak have argued, this model expresses important human values. The market honours the freedom of both entrepreneur and consumer and taps creativity and initiative. It would be outrageous if the state were to make illegal the offering of goods and services by one human being to another. It honours also the consumer's freedom to choose how to spend money. The market creates an astonishing range of choices, making life full and rich. Economic activity may thus be good *in itself.* The model is about creating wealth for the community and not only money for the few. The market creates employment, so more and more can benefit from the fruit of their labour. The market creates the wealth that gives us the resource to care for the elderly, sick and needy, and support education and the arts. Moreover, it has realism concerning the all-pervading motive of self-interest. People will naturally look to their own comfort and security. The market marshals this for the common good, as Adam Smith classically observed.[3] Again, market incentives fuel research and technological development. The market is not a modern invention. For thousands of years people have traded goods and services, even if an emerging market has often been marginal to, and has presupposed a division of labour not found in, a largely self-sufficient kinship-based agrarian culture.

What is the alternative? If we take away the right of people to operate within a market, the starkest alternative is some kind of 'command economy' where the state controls what is produced, its specification, price, and quantity. There is the common ownership of 'the means of production, distribution and exchange'. Consumers have no say through the 'market' and entrepreneurs have no freedom to find their niche. A Josiah Wedgwood would not be allowed to make and sell his own pots. He would have to persuade an official that a state-controlled factory should make a new line. Everything is decided by a state bureaucracy. This was the system tried for a time in Soviet Russia. The Kremlin decided even what kind of underwear was produced. Many commentators claim the system stagnated. The absence of a price mechanism led to an absence of discipline, and the absence of the profit motive took away motivation and incentive. The 'command economy', concerned not only with current provision, but also with future planning, involved itself in a task of absurdly unrealistic complications. The result was a stagnant domestic 'market' offering a limited range of poor quality goods. It is widely argued that there is no alternative means of wealth creation worthy of a hearing compared with a market economy. This is one of the reasons why Fukuyama claimed we are living 'at the end of history', since there is no longer any realistic debate about the best way to create wealth.[4]

Nothing, however, is perfect! The first problem concerns poverty and justice. In the wider scheme of things market capitalism alleviates far more poverty than it causes. After all, it is a powerful engine for the creation of wealth. But at the micro level the fierce competition of the market may impoverish a local community as production is taken elsewhere, or where competition drives local firms out of business. The market has no commitment to local communities and their well-being. An international company can get rich by impoverishing a whole region. When this is writ large whole nations may be impoverished. The market at best offers only rough justice, and the effects of the market's volatility through cycles, bankruptcy and unemployment, exact a terrible human toll. While this may be mitigated through the 'trickle down' and through what Schumpeter called 'creative destruction' or the 'creative churn' (profitable businesses taking the place of those closed down),[5] the fact remains that market economies may create wealth but they do not create justice.

'Justice' is a buzz word, especially in the churches, but what do we mean by it? As noted earlier (see 3.9) Robert Nozick speaks of an 'entitlement' theory of justice. The demand for justice is satisfied if what people possess has been legally acquired. Such a justice is compatible, however, with vast extremes of wealth and therefore of power. The extremes of wealth and poverty even within Britain are outrageous, and the extremes are widening. Globally, the distribution of wealth is becoming dramatically less equal and a small number of people are becoming rich in a manner without precedent.[6] Is it only *absolute* poverty that is a problem? A cleaner may be on the minimum wage, a nurse on only double, and as one goes up the economic scale there are those with obscene amounts of wealth. Some in senior positions use their power to feed their greed. It is the law of the jungle. In other words, the distribution of wealth in a market economy is not based on criteria that are *ethical*. The distribution is based on market forces. Yes, the market rewards hard work and initiative, and this may be said to be just, but the rewards, like the losses, can be out of proportion, and depend on a large amount of luck. And what of those who wish to devote their lives to, say, nursing, social work or teaching? What about the sick, disabled and the less able? Justice may not mean an equal sharing of the world's wealth, but it does mean narrower extremes. Poverty brings in its trail all kinds of social disadvantage and social exclusion. Vast differences of wealth are socially divisive. The market has no mechanism for creating a just and inclusive society. On the wider map it does not create poverty, but it does not create justice either and tends to exacerbate inequality.[7]

It follows that although the market contributes crucially to the 'common good' by creating wealth, it often damages the common good by failing to address, and indeed by exacerbating, injustice, inequality and social exclusion. There is a rat race and the swift and strong rats keep their pickings. Moreover, a concentration of wealth means also a concentration of power and of control of resources.

Furthermore, the market may nurture attitudes that are individualistic, aggressively competitive and uncaring. This seems a chillingly accurate description of *one* strand within British culture today as the rich get richer and as commitment to our common well-being seems to be weakening. The poor are no longer 'deserving'. They lack enterprise, or refuse to 'get on their bike'. The old aristocrats often had a strong sense of responsibility for their communities. The rich now erect security gates. The market tends towards individualism. Some of the rhetoric of the 'New Right', as it used to be called, so exalted the freedom and rights of the individual that there was a lack of emphasis on our common wealth, and of the extent to which we are bound together. To counter this there may be evident in Britain the influence of the American tradition of private philanthropy as mitigating some of the inequity; but justice is hardly satisfied by the largess of charity.

The market in goods and services provides a reasonably efficient mechanism for meeting demand and coping with scarcity. The 'money market', however, is in some tension with this. Computerization allows the transfer of trillions across international boundaries, sometimes reinforcing the marginalization of whole communities. Adam Smith's 'invisible hand' seems here to favour the shareholder. Value for the shareholder is not the same thing as value for the work force or the communities in which a company is set. Furthermore, people may reap where they have not sown as when through 'Hedge Funds' a profit is made through falling share prices.

Moreover, it is naive to see market capitalism as simply responding to demand. It is engaged in a subtle and even sinister stimulation of demand. If consumers will not buy the goods, then they must be persuaded. ('*You know you need it!*' says the advert, and, of course, alloy wheels promise better sex!) The result is a culture of rampant acquisitiveness fed in part by advertising that moulds our mindset so that we want more and more. Up to a point this is positive. Our lives are richer because of possibilities previously undreamt of. But at its worst a market economy creates and feeds on acquisitiveness and greedy extravagance, a 'throw away' mentality and a 'never satisfied' consumerism.

What is wrong with that? To ask serious questions about the effect of an uncritical consumerism, for those who can afford it, upon the quality and depth of human life need not imply a drab asceticism, an indifference to choice, or a denial of the amazing blessings the market brings. Our lives are damaged by want, but maybe also by an over-abundance of plenty. More immediately, the ever-extravagant consumerism of the market takes enormous risks with the environment and is in danger of stealing for ourselves resources we should bequeath to future generations. The grim fact is that the earth's resources are finite. Our spiralling consumerism is rapidly depleting many of the earth's riches. On the horizon may be the drying up of supplies of easily welled oil. Humankind's principal source of energy will be no more, to say nothing of the many by-products of this liquid gold. Yet in the airports of scores of major cities a large aircraft darkens the sky every few minutes, thus feeding our insatiable thirst for cheap air flight. It may be that our burning of fossil fuels is causing global warming; deforestation is probably having detrimental effects on climate and, in any case, can lead to soil erosion. Yet the rate of consumption is likely to speed up as large nations such as India and China further industrialize. Do we have a right to deny them what we enjoy? The market, as such, contains no robust mechanism for ensuring environmental responsibility – quite the reverse. The market incurs social and environmental costs it does not bear. The price of kiwi fruit in our supermarkets does not include the environmental cost of their transport halfway across the world. The same is the case with our cheap air tickets.

Some prophecies of doom may be exaggerated. The 'Club of Rome' report, for example, failed to take sufficiently into account technological innovation.[8] In the past predictions concerning capacity for food production have proved too cautious because things, such as the easy production of nitrogen fertilizer and other innovations, were unforeseen. Generally, we are making the best available predictions and projections on the basis of inadequate knowledge. Nevertheless, however much uncertainty there may be over the detail, it seems highly irresponsible not to take with extreme seriousness environmental concerns. It seems far too complacent to assume that the internal forces of the market will simply create the technologies that will resolve the environmental problems and find new resources to replace those depleted. Unlimited economic growth seems not to be an option in a finite world.

12.2 Managing the market: governments

We are dealing here with structures, institutions and cultures. People are, to a large extent, imprisoned by structures and formed by them. We cannot solve the problem of unjust wages, say, simply by exhorting employers to pay more. That might mean the business cannot survive and so the workers are thrown on the dole. Of course, the integrity and goodwill of the people within the system are important, but we need to tackle structures and not just people. Hence the idea of 'managing the market'.

It is perhaps unfair to criticize the market for failing to deliver justice. It was never intended to. The market is about the efficient creation of wealth and about handling the reality of scarcity. Markets, however, do not exist in a vacuum. Markets exist as part of communities and cultures, and they exist in partnership with other institutions – the most significant being governments. The role of government is crucial. All governments will manage and regulate the market. The question is by how much, in what ways, and to what ends? The 'minimal' state of Thatcherism was still involved in managing the market, even if less so or in different ways compared with other political ideologies.

Governments can legislate, regulate, control, inspect, and even subsidize. This way the market is managed so that it serves better than left alone justice and the common good. Laws banning child labour and granting employment rights are clear instances of state intervention to humanize the market. The work of the former Monopolies Commission, now the Competition Commission, is a prime example of managing the market for the wider good. Governments can supply a safety net through benefit for the unemployed and training schemes to assist their redeployment. Social security and insurance is a complex state/ private sector affair. In fact there has rarely been a totally 'free' market because government constraints have always been operative. Migration controls, in any case, restrict the movement of labour. In sum, there will be a mix between areas handled by the market and areas handled by the state, while, of course, there will be keen debate as to what in detail this mix involves. Governments also have a crucial place in managing international trade – for example, through structures for determining exchange rates between currencies.

The obvious is worth stating: the market cannot provide everything a modern society needs – 'social goods' such as the infrastructure and, in Britain, things such as education and health care. Sometimes there is no clear dividing line between what the market provides and what the state provides. Both, for example, are involved in developing 'human capital' through education and training. Governments may even 'nationalize' key industries and utilities within a 'mixed economy'. No government can be without an energy policy. Even if utilities and the rail system, say, are privatized there will be a strong *de facto* partnership with the state because no democratic society can leave such crucial areas simply to the market – in contrast, say, to a nation's supply of tin whistles and Toby jugs. And crucially important, governments must struggle to find strategies for tackling marginalization and poverty. The market will be 'taxed' in order that the government may make provision in these kinds of ways.

It must not be assumed that government involvement automatically humanizes the market and furthers justice. Political ideologies can protect powerful vested interests. Sometimes governments may yield to powerful lobbies (e.g. the arms and oil-based industries) and national governments may protect their own economy to the detriment of international justice. Protectionism, tariffs and trade wars can benefit rich nations at the expense of the poor. Western self-interest means the international market is more regulated than the domestic. Because of tariffs and other protections, we do not have free trade. The subsidy of western agriculture, for example, seriously disadvantages Third World trade. Again, the least we can learn from critics of governmental intervention, such as Milton Friedman and Robert Nozick, is that such intervention can sometimes be unwise or inexpedient, making matters worse rather than better. The whole area is one of keen debate and much uncertainty. The basic principle of governments regulating and working in partnership with the market needs, however, to be recognized. If state power checks the market, then indeed the market may also check state hegemony. It is sheer ideology to claim that the state is always synonymous with the lazy and the shoddy and the private sector with efficiency and quality. The reality tends to be more complicated.

All this presupposes that states have sufficient power. The power of a state is limited by all kinds of things, not least by what is acceptable to the electorate. The 'globalization' of our economies and the sheer power of some international companies, in economic terms greater than many states, alerts us to the concern that in many areas even states may seem impotent.[9] Such companies have, in Atherton's phrase, often become the new 'absentee landlords'.[10] Gone are the days when people like John Maynard Keynes could assume an essentially national economy. There is intense debate as to the form and extent of globalization, both in trade and in the money market, and the extent to which national governments are able to exercise control. That said, it does seem that the power of national governments to manage economies has been reduced. How markets are to be humanized and subject to moral constrains within a global economy is one of the new urgent questions for our time. At the same time, national governments need not and do not act alone. Boundaries between states are becoming fuzzier, yet governments – especially acting together – continue to have great power.[11] That said, the power of government is still limited, and not least by the fear that a nation may lose its competitiveness, thus causing a company to relocate. The British Government, for example, would not act in a way that would lose a company such as Vodafone.

All this is, admittedly, rather general. The detail has to be left to the experts. There are ranges of options rather than clear blueprints. After all, Britain has experimented with various models, from the post-war heavily managed 'mixed economy', through Thatcherism and a minimal state, to 'New Labour'. The essential *ethical* point is that pragmatically the market seems the best way to create wealth, and in many ways manifests important human values such as entrepreneurial freedom and freedom of choice. We can enjoy its amazing blessings while, through state regulation, mitigating its distortions. Markets act in partnership with and under the regulation of governments. As Preston says: It is possible to have 'indicative planning' without ... 'centralized command economies' ... 'We cannot do without markets, nor can we make do with them alone.'[12]

'The detail must be left to the expert.' Or, more accurately, the detail must be worked out with the help of the expert, subject to the political process. The ethicist has a difficult juggling act. On the one hand, ethics has to deal with the real world and be realistic and practical. On the other hand, there is difference between exploring basic value commitments and exploring how we might work towards realizing these ideals through specific social and economic policy.

12.3 Managing the market: civil society

Markets will be managed not only by the state, but also *de facto* by the cultures of which they are part. Thus, in addition to government there is also civil society – people with their values, culture and institutions. That is one reason why market economies vary considerably from culture to culture. People who work the market and those who buy goods and services are not saints; but neither are they monsters. If the market is a powerful moulder of values – some healthy, but also some not so healthy – it is not the only moulder. There needs to be a protest against any hint of a moratorium of ethical debate over the market. We all have a responsibility through our behaviour and attitude to see that 'conscience is clerk to the market'.[13] Evidence of this is in consensus concerning proper state regulation to ensure fair practice and employment rights. Evidence is found also in the increasing commitment to sustainable production, fair trade and environmental responsibility. If the market can be a powerful moulder of values, valuing competition, enterprise, risk and profit, civil society can offer checks and balances through a complementary and correcting commitment to community, and the values of caring for others. The market is a moulder of values. It prizes and rewards, and thereby encourages, the risk takers and the ambitious. It encourages competition rather than co-operation. It prizes success. None of these things should be dismissed as the gravest of vices. They have their place in the pantheon of human virtues and human goods, but none is unambiguously good. If they take over our lives we forget the values of service, altruism, community and justice. What have market values to say to those who do not succeed? Or to those who wish to devote their lives to care of the needy rather than ambition for making a large profit? What all this means is that through civil society, through culture, and through the way in which the Church and Christian vision may contribute, there needs to be a crucial engagement with the values of the market and a vigilance over the ways in which its central values may increasingly dominate the whole of society. Furthermore, a critical engagement will affect how people behave in the market. In particular, it will have an effect through the power of consumer choice.

'Business is business.' This is often said as a way of saying that the workings of the market are hermetically sealed and so invulnerable to moral scrutiny. Yes, some moral scrutiny has lacked realism and has been economically naive. But we must protest against the assumption that there can be no moral critique of the market, and that the market cannot be shaped by the culture and normative framework of which it is part. Evidence that this can bear fruit is the increasing interest in 'business ethics', 'corporate social responsibility', and the responsiveness of supermarkets to fair trade and environmental concern, together with a certain presumption in favour of using local suppliers. There is a genuine openness to this in companies such as The Body Shop, Nike and PB.[14] There appears to be a mounting public demand for 'cleaner' transport. The 'power of the consumer' has in many ways surprised us.

This will include a commitment through a responsible lifestyle, and awareness of how patterns of consumption impact on environment and structures of injustice. Traidcraft and similar groups make a valuable contribution here. Part of what this means is a simplicity of lifestyle that strikes a balance between a world renouncing asceticism and extravagance. We can certainly revisit traditional Christian warnings against the 'spiritual dangers' of riches. A frantic acquisitiveness may be rooted in the yearning for status symbols, or a desire to buttress our fragile egos. This is a mug's game, and the alternative is not a bleak austerity but a moderation that allows life to be filled with good things without a frantic possessiveness. At worst, wealth can kid people that their talents and hard work warrant it, justifying contempt for those with less. Christians need, as always, to insist on the priority of grace. Properly understood, grace does not mock or belittle talent and achievement. But it does insist that in the last analysis our dignity and self-worth do not depend on such things alone. Potentially, all this has an impact on employment by dampening demand, and lessening the impetus to technological innovation. This, however, can be managed; by contrast, it is not clear that the earth can sustain our most virulent consumerism.

That said, we should not think that those working the market are the 'bad guys' and those within civil society are the 'good guys'. We should think in terms of a partnership rather than the beauty taming the beast. Thus, John Atherton speaks of the market bearing important human values: efficiency, initiative, creativity, self-help, partnership in enterprise and so forth. These have a place in the pantheon of virtues. Values recognized by Christians are not all 'external to the market'.[15] The market may be a mixed blessing. Most blessings are. But it is a mixed *blessing*.

12.4 Managing the market: but to what end?

Governments can manage the market, but to what end? The same question can be asked of *de facto* regulation through consumer and civil society. The culture and values of society will influence profoundly patterns of production and consumption. This is recognized by the fact that through advertising the market seeks, through a counter offensive, to mould culture and its values to its benefit. Governments will manage the market in order to facilitate a successful economy. What, however, about management for the sake of justice and the wider good (see also 11.4)? What kind of justice and equality do we seek? For example, the post-war British Labour Government sought to reduce inequality by progressive taxation. Dennis Healey promised to tax the rich until the pips squeaked. A more equal distribution of wealth, imposed by the state, was embraced as an ethical ideal. It was also argued that a nation of greater equality would be good for the economy since it would empower its citizens and, thus empowered, they would contribute more to society. This quest had limited success and has been largely abandoned.[16] Equality of 'opportunity' rather than of 'outcome' is the present slogan. It is, however, more of a slogan than a reality. The 'myth of the meritocracy' exposes the fact that social and economic inequality seriously undermines equality of opportunity. Lord Young's warnings of 1958 have proved disturbingly accurate.[17] Income tax is still progressive but nothing like as punitive for the higher earners as it used to be. It is now widely claimed that if we tax too heavily the fruits of people's labour, there will be insufficient incentive to create wealth and we will all suffer. Attempts to divide the cake more equally simply make the cake grow smaller. Moreover, if the tax burden is too great, able people might leave the country and so deprive the nation of talent. As we have seen, some even question the right of a government to tax the rich in order to finance welfare programmes for the poor. The assumption here seems to be that our ownership of and access to wealth is a purely individual matter and unrelated to the wider structures of society that make it possible (see 3.9).

Suppose it is true that progressive taxation, which attempts to divide the cake more equally, makes the cake smaller? There still has to be an *ethical* decision as to what is an appropriate trade off between the benefits of greater distributive justice and a smaller cake. More generally, we cannot have all the freedom we might want along with all the justice and all the prosperity we want as well. There has to be an *ethical* judgement as to the acceptable compromise, as well as a *political* judgement as to what is achievable and how. In reality, that means society has to hammer it out through the political processes (see 11.5). Discovering the right trade off is not easy. The most efficient way of creating wealth tends to lead to injustice. The *injudicious* pursuit of greater equality invariably leads to greater poverty and therefore greater injustice. That said, we should not swallow too uncritically arguments about cakes becoming buns. There is evidence that if the poor and marginalized are not empowered, the economy and community suffer because the poor are unable to contribute fully. There are pragmatic arguments for a bit more justice! That said, there is no obvious resting place in the continuum between, on the one hand, a minimalist state that gives the market a largely free hand and, on the other, a model that stresses control, regulation, security and welfare.

In the previous chapter I looked at some of the values that might govern a Christian vision of the common good. Christian conviction, it was suggested, encourages a focus on solidarity, subsidiarity, equality, justice and inclusiveness with a complementary emphasis on freedom. Christian conviction also warns against unwarranted privilege, marginalization and exclusion. Of course, these are heavy abstract nouns and we need to ask what they mean and how they might be expressed in society. Specific to the theme of this chapter, Christian responsibility requires that through civil society, the political process and in partnership with others, we struggle to discover how this vision might be expressed over the creation and sharing of wealth. The ideal is unachievable, but we can perhaps make some steps towards it. The Methodist Church's report on the *Ethics of Wealth Creation* and the Papal Encyclical *Centesimus Annus* are examples of an approach that works with the model of a market managed and humanized by government and civil society.[18]

On a wider front, there are hard questions about the all-pervading culture of consumerism. Our minds are formed by the values of choice and consumption. Our identity is, in part, determined by our ability to consume and our freedom to choose what we consume. If the goods are not available, or if there is no money to buy, then we are impoverished. Only a moralism with its head in the clouds would deny there are positive things here. But it would be naive to deny the dangers. An uncritical consumerism can undermine a proper simplicity and a proper contentment. It can make us too much dependent on the ever-expanding abundance of our possessions. It can fuel injustice, social division and marginalization. There are large questions here for Christian ethics and Christian spirituality including many gems of insight for the Church to offer to those of the wider community who may not accept their theological undermining.

12.5 Christian socialism – a more radical alternative?

Christian socialism is highly diverse, both in its history and philosophy. In so far as we can generalize, Christian socialists have claimed the economic order must be judged by how it serves *people*, condemning exploitation and injustice. It has dreamed dreams about extending co-operation, equality, participation, and empowerment. The challenge is to put flesh on the bones of these abstract nouns and to ask how our present structures can be adapted in order, to a degree, to express them. Understood in this way there is no fundamental contradiction between so-called 'Christian socialism' and the thrust of the argument of this chapter. The market is the most efficient way to produce wealth, honouring also important values, such as freedom and creativity. We enjoy the blessings of the market while seeking to moderate its distortions and one-sidedness through government and civil society.

A more radical brand of Christian socialism wants a root and branch remodelling of how we create and share wealth. This might involve something like a 'top down' 'command' economy with the nationalization of the means of 'production, distribution and exchange'. Alternatively, it might involve a 'bottom up' remodelling of companies as co-operatives, broadly in the 'Guild Socialism' tradition. F. D. Maurice, a leader of one of the Victorian Christian socialist groups, objected to a system based on competition and self-centred acquisitiveness, claiming that economic life instead should be based on co-operation.[19] But is competition unqualifiedly evil? It is *a* good, furthering self-respect and yielding much in terms of human endeavour. Of course, it needs to be balanced with other things but balance in the 'tapestry' of moral judgement is what moral insight is about.

A tired western socialism contrasts with revitalized forms in other parts of the world, for example, through a 'liberation theology', and its influence upon the thinking of the World Council of Churches. Here I confine myself to the western context. Two major difficulties with such a radical remodelling are urged.

First – following the warnings of Karl Popper in the tradition of Edmund Burke – attempts to make root and branch changes in the structures of society are almost bound to fail. Worse, they will cause immense dislocation and suffering. Change must be gradual and piecemeal, and sensitive that much of value can so easily be swept away. This is so not least because we need to be cautious about our ability to manage change and to predict the outcome of our actions. Second, it is urged, the historical experience of command economies is not encouraging – save perhaps in providing the basic essentials. All the evidence is that the market, in partnership with the state and civil society, is the most efficient way we have of producing wealth. This is not least because it marshals self-interest and achieves some success in co-opting it for the benefit of the common good. To attempt to run society on the basis of co-operation rather than competition lacks realism about 'human nature', and the reality of conflicts of power and interests. But that is not to say we cannot bang the drum of co-operation and be confident the tune will, by some and in some contexts, be heard – including even by the drummers themselves. In truth, the market is about both co-operation and competition. There is a lot to be said for seeking a healthy tension between the two rather than the elimination of the latter.

Further to this, it is urged that the price mechanism is the most efficient means of coping with scarcity and the matching of production to demand, combined with the profit motive which prompts efficiency and innovation. What structure other than the market, it is asked, could make available the millions of goods and items of service available in a modern economy?[20]

We live in a 'fallen' world full of ambiguities. There must be realism about what is achievable, and if we try to move to the ideal in a few swift moves, we end up destroying the proximate prosperity and justice we currently enjoy. These are themes Reinhold Niebuhr powerfully developed a couple of generations ago. Socialism perhaps drank too uncritically at the well of Victorian confidence that the kingdom of God can be built on earth. At the same time, socialism's confidence that we can change things should – after a suitably cautioning – not be lost. We must leave behind any vestige of the old idea that the 'laws of economics' have the same necessity as the laws of physics.

Radical Christian socialism pays a service in challenging complacency, confronting injustice and self-interest, and dreaming dreams. But, in so far as it proposes replacing our present economic structures with totally different ones, it seems widely unrealistic. For the foreseeable future we seem stuck with what we have got, and anyway it is probably the least problematical way yet devised of creating wealth. Indeed socialist writings are stronger in their critique of market economies than in their exposition of viable alternatives. We seem better employed seeking to humanize them than dreaming of unlikely utopias.

12.6 Conclusion

I began by noting that Christians are keener on sharing wealth than on asking how it is first created. It is irresponsible to ignore the latter question, or to fail to wrestle with the dilemma of the tension between efficient wealth creation and its just sharing, so I end by stressing ambiguity. There are no perfect solutions, and there are snags with even the most sophisticated ones. We need to be released from the 'tyranny of impossible expectations'.[21] There is no perfect reconciliation possible between the efficient creation of wealth and its just distribution. There is no easy reconciliation between full employment and low inflation, between equality and freedom. The release of Third World debt will not 'make poverty history', although it may help. Neither will more aid, although some kinds of aids in some cases can help too. My gluttony does not in a straightforward way exacerbate world hunger, since (contra Malthus) there is no fixed amount of wealth to share. Christian congregations should not be made to feel guilty with sweeping generalizations about their consumption 'robbing the poor'. Only in the most carefully defined cases does this make economic sense. There is western exploitation of the 'Third World', of course, but Third World poverty is not in a straightforward way caused by western affluence. Much depends, for instance, on a nation's culture and governance.[22] None of this justifies an extravagant and complacent life, but we need to struggle with the complicated and ambiguous character of the real world and of how economies work. There is no escape from living with uncertainty and trying to make judgements over economic and political questions that explode the minds even of the experts. Where two or three experts are gathered together, there will be six opinions in the midst; but it is not their fault. Both our action and our inaction need to be judged against hard economic, political and cultural realities, and the complications are often mind-blowing. Much of the time we will get it wrong, hence the imperatives of painstaking analysis, caution, self-criticism, humility and openness. This may not be comfortable, but this is the world we live in.

Notes

1 The metaphor of the 'invisible hand' is Adam Smith's – although for him there was a measure of divine providence involved: *The Wealth of Nations* (1776), IV.II.9. Adam Smith uses the metaphor only twice in his writings.

2 Milton Friedman, *Capitalism and Freedom*, Chicago, Chicago University Press, 1962, p. 12ff. Michael Novak, *The Spirit of Democratic Capitalism*, London, IEA Health and Welfare Unit, 1982 and 1991, pp. 13ff., 82ff., 92ff.

3 Adam Smith, *The Theory of Moral Sentiments* (1759), ed. L. A. Selby-Bigge, *British Moralists*, Oxford, 1897, Volume I, pp. 320ff. Also *The Wealth of Nations* (1776), I.II and 4.II.

4 Fukuyama *The End of History and the Last Man*, London, Hamish Hamilton, 1991, pp. 44ff. where Fukuyama sees the free market as the economic manifestation of liberal democracy.

5 Joseph A. Schumpeter, *Capitalism, Socialism and Democracy*, London, Allen Unwin, 1943, pp. 81–6.

6 Eric Hobsbawm, *The New Century*, London, Little, Brown and Co., 2000, pp. 88–9.

7 There is a vast literature of such critiques in Christian thought. There is a comprehensive critique in the 1937 Oxford Conference on *Church Community and State*. The first Assembly of the WCC in Amsterdam in 1948 commented that market capitalism is strong on freedom but weak on justice.

8 *The Limits of Growth*, 1972.

9 A strong version of this thesis is in Keniche Ohmae, *The End of the Nation State*, London, HarperCollins, 1998.

10 John Atherton, *Marginalization*, London, SCM Press, 2003, p. 21.

11 Cf. essays by Malcolm Brown, Michael Taylor and Peter Sedgwick in Elaine Graham and Esther Reed (eds), *The Future of Christian Social Ethics*, London, Continuum, 2004.

12 Ronald H. Preston, *Religion and the Ambiguities of Capitalism*, London, SCM Press, 1991, p. 74.

13 The phrase is that of the Puritan Richard Steele, *The Tradesman's Calling*, 1684, quoted by R. H. Tawney, *Religion and the Rise of Capitalism*, Harmondsworth, Pelican, 1926.

14 Anthony Giddens, *The Third Way*, Cambridge, Polity Press, 1988, p. 49.

15 John Atherton, *Christianity and the Market*, London, SPCK, 1992, pp. 219–21.

16 Early scepticism was expressed by Richard M. Titmuss in *Income Distribution and Social Change*, London, Allen & Unwin, 1962.

17 Michael Young, *The Rise of the Meritocracy*, London, Thames & Hudson, 1958. The same argument is offered from the American perspective by a writer who, by coincidence, has the same surname. Iris Young speaks of the 'myth of merit': *Justice and the Politics of Difference*, Princeton, Princeton University Press, 1990, pp. 192ff.

18 Methodist Conference, *Ethics of Wealth Creation*, Peterborough, Methodist Publishing House; John Paul II, *Centisimus Annus*, 32. Also *Quandragesimo Anno*, 141.

19 Ronald H. Preston, *Church and Society in the Late Twentieth Century*, London, SCM Press, 1983, p. 19.

20 Ronald H. Preston, *Religion and the Persistence of Capitalism*, London, SCM Press, 1979, pp. 24ff.

21 Rosemary Radford Ruether, *To Change the World*, London, SCM Press, 1981, p. 69.

22 Novak, *Spirit*, pp. 272ff.

13

Violence, Peace and Justice

13.1 Introduction

Some war films in the 1950s and 60s presented World War II as something like a *Boy's Own* adventure. If people were killed, it was cleanly and off camera. If a pilot over Nazi territory entered some flak, it was a 'spot of bother'.

Films like *Saving Private Ryan, Full Metal Jacket* and *We Were Soldiers* portray war for the horror it is. Shells and grenades blow body parts into trees, bullets and shrapnel tear out in agony a man's guts. Sailors and air crew face their own particular brands of horror. Total war involves the whole population. In the fire storms created in the cities of Germany and Japan – and to a lesser extent in British cities earlier – children were victims as much as anyone else. In modern warfare more precision may be possible, but smart bombs are not always smart and in any case the other sort are cheaper. The advantage of greater precision is offset by an escalation of awesome firepower. Segments of cluster bombs will fail to explode and later blow off the leg of a child playing. Such horrific images should humble the armchair ethicist who presumes to comment on this theme.

The horror of the battlefield is only the beginning. There is the unimaginable trauma of those left behind and those who survive.

> He sat in a wheeled chair, waiting for the dark,
> And shivered in his ghastly suit of grey,
> Legless, sewn short at elbow.
>
> About this time the town used to swing so gay,
> And girls glanced lovelier as the lights blew dim;
> In the old times, before he threw away his knees.
> Now he will never feel again how slim
> Girls' waists are, or how warm their subtle hands.
> All of them touch him like some queer disease.[1]

There is the brutal destruction of historic buildings, icons of centuries of culture.[2] Whole communities may be devastated. The environmental impact can be horrific, not only in war itself but also in the development and testing of weapons. Vietnam has not yet recovered from environmental damage. Wars can create resentments and heighten antagonisms, which reap their nemesis for years, even generations. The wind of war causes the whirlwind of spiralling hatred and resentment. No wonder some have claimed the resort to war is like trying to wash blood out of a shirt in a bowl of blood.

Wars require total commitment to a life and death struggle. Propaganda moulds the mindset of 'good against evil'. Might becomes right. Ambiguities have to be set aside to maintain justification, morale and commitment. If the enemy is demonized and if right is on our side I am more willing to fight at my government's bidding. All armed services exploit the malleable naivety of young recruits. Thus, truth becomes the first casualty of war and God becomes the first recruit – in the sense that we need to be sure 'right is on our side'.

One consequence of this is that moral restraints easily become abandoned as the struggle drags on. Despite the crimes of Nazism, the German army often fought honourably on the western front in World War II. The unleashing of area bombing of German and Japanese cities, however, expressed a measure of desperation to finish the business in a way that famously caused Bishop George Bell in the spring of 1944 to warn that the allies were losing their moral claim to victory.

13.2 A just war?

In the light of these grim reflections, can war ever be justified? The majority of Christians, and indeed the majority of people who have reflected ethically on war, adhere to some doctrine of the 'just war'. The name is misleading. It might be taken to imply an easy acceptance of war. In fact, the doctrine of the just war is highly stringent. It maintains that war is a horrific evil. Provided, however, both the *resort* to war and the *conduct* of war survive the strictest moral scrutiny, a particular war may be justified. It is important to recognize that the doctrine of the just war implies many wars are emphatically not just: in intention, in conduct or both.

The tradition is rooted in classical thought, but has been developed by Christian thinkers such as Ambrose, Augustine, Aquinas and others later. It has given us a number of criteria for deciding whether or not a war is just.

For traditional criteria the *cause* of war must be just. The most obvious example – and arguably the only one – is a war to resist aggression or tyranny. This would suggest that in World War II the allies fought a just war in resisting Nazi occupation. There is usually the implication

that the aggressor should make 'the first move'. The war against Iraq
began ostensibly to prevent the use of weapons of 'mass destruction'.
Is it just to wage war by 'pre-emptive strike' on the basis of a perceived
risk? How serious does the risk have to be? Does the awesome power
of modern weaponry make a pre-emptive strike just in some circumstances and if so what are these circumstances? There is a debate as
to whether or not the just war tradition may be developed to embrace
this.

The official motives for the Iraq war displayed a chameleon quality.
When evidence for 'weapons for mass destruction' proved elusive, the
war was reinvented as one to liberate the Iraqi people from oppression.
Is a war waged against a state to liberate its people from oppression
a just war? This is not an easy question. Since World War II the inviolability of national sovereignty has been a fundamental principle.
After all, it has been so often violated in the past. What, however,
is the responsibility of the international community towards a people
languishing under tyranny? And does the international community exercise its responsibility through military intervention, which may well
make matters worse for citizens? There are other ways by which the
international community can effect change.

This leads to another criterion. Wars to be just must be undertaken
by a *lawful authority* following a formal declaration. This seems reasonable enough as a criterion. The difficulty lies in applying it. It was
difficult to apply in medieval Europe where there was often uncertainty in identifying a legitimate power. Today the question presents
itself differently. How does one legitimize the corporate action of the
'international community'. Does NATO have legitimacy in the European theatre – an issue in the Balkans war? What is the proper legal
process of international law or of the United Nations? There is a developing consensus regarding legitimate authority through the United
Nations. This, however, can be ignored or manipulated by a *de facto*
super power.

Traditional criteria also speak of the *intention* behind the war being
just. The intention must be to restore justice and peace, harmonious
international relationships and such like. The stringency of this criterion must be recognized. Wars are not about devastating a nation,
exacting revenge, imposing imperial rule or economic subjection. The
Churchillian rhetoric about magnanimity in victory and goodwill in
peace expresses something of this criterion, and certainly the allies
were extraordinarily magnanimous towards the defeated Germany
and Japan. National self-awareness and rigorous moral scrutiny are
important here. The West speaks of supporting democracy, and yet,
in reality, policy has often been guided more by the desire to preserve
access to raw material and political and economic power. Saudi Arabia

is not a democracy and has a poor human rights record, but there has been no forced regime change there.

Identifying the motive or intention of an individual is difficult enough. How do we identify the motive or intention of a nation? Do we psychoanalyse the American President? Democracies cannot resort to war without some popular support, and different groups and different people will have different mixes of motives and intentions. Apart from the declared intentions behind the Iraqi war, who can doubt that other factors were involved, at least in the motives of some, maybe in some cases covered by self-delusion? The earlier Iraqi war left unfinished business. The world's super power must act tough after 9/11. The humiliation of Vietnam needed to be absolved. Oil supplies need protecting, and so forth. Furthermore, was British support motivated in part by the desire to keep favour with her super power ally?

There must also be a well-founded *expectation of success* in achieving the just intention. The goals must be realistic and attainable, as far as we can reasonably judge. This is a troubled suggestion. Some in 1939 felt it was an expression of national self-respect and of Britain's moral responsibility to resist Nazi tyranny, however difficult the odds. Was there a reasonable expectation of success at the commencement of the Iraq war? The answer depends, of course, on how we define the war aim. If the aim was military victory, then the confident expectation was justified. The matter is unclear, however, if it was about establishing democracy. It is alarming how little thought seems to have been given to how this might be achieved, and how little cognizance given to how difficult it is, and how long it takes, for democratic institutions to take root and for a democratic culture to flourish – especially in a state divided between Sunnis, Sh'ites and Kurds.[3]

All this leads to the criterion of *proportionality*. There must be a 'proportionality' between the evil caused by war and the good achieved by fighting it. Fighting a war to resist Nazism may be 'proportional'. Fighting a war over fishing rights or the return of art treasures will not be. Moreover, moral restraints should limit the fire power to what is necessary to achieve the goal. A policy of 'scorched earth' is invariably out of proportion. One could reasonably ask if the demand of 'unconditional surrender' in World War II satisfied the criterion of proportionality, given that it must have cost scores of thousands of lives, although Max Hastings, not unreasonably, argues that, given Nazi atrocities, a negotiated surrender would have been unthinkable.[4] This criterion raises difficult questions when nations have seriously different technological capacity. The awesome military hardware of the United States has enabled it to fight wars that inflict maximum casualties while reducing their own casualties in a way beyond the dreams of World War II commanders. This criterion also includes the principle of '*non combatant immunity*'. Only those in uniform are fair targets, and yet in recent wars civilians have borne the brunt of suffering and death. The principle of proportionality is coupled with the crucial insistence that the resort to war must always be a *last resort*. All other channels for resolving conflict must first be exhausted.

The twin criteria of proportionality and non-combatant immunity are highly relevant in any assessment of recent military action in Iraq and Afghanistan – especially the former. The massive firepower, combined with heavy hardware and destructive tactics have provoked the criticism that a policy of counteracting terrorism and insurgency is being pursued like a war against a state with equivalent military power. Quite apart from the more explicit ethical issues, such a policy can easily be counterproductive, playing into the hands of the enemy, sowing the seeds of further terror, radicalizing opposition and alienating whole communities.

The just war doctrine is usually applied to the actions of states. The same basic criteria have been applied, however, to the idea of a 'just rebellion' when a tyrannical state loses legitimacy. The possibility was recognized by Aquinas.[5] The issue has been very much alive over the past century as resistance groups have challenged oppressive regimes. Christians, such as Camil Torres and Gustavo Gutiérrez, together with much 'liberation theology', have given their support, and in the former case blood as well. If there is a 'just war' it is difficult to deny that there may also be a 'just rebellion'. The criteria for a just rebellion are, however, no less stringent, and not least because the overthrow of a regime (however despotic) leaves a political vacuum. There must be a reasonable confidence it can be filled with what is better and has more legitimacy. George Orwell's *Animal Farm* presents a warning, but maybe not a veto.

The *basic principle* of the just war doctrine needs to stand out from the *detailed criteria*. This is that war is a terrible evil. The resort to war must be a last resort and acceptable only after intense moral scrutiny. As the Pastoral Letter of the United States Catholic Bishops stated in 1983: 'Are the values at stake critical enough to override the presumption against war?'[6] Furthermore, the *conduct* of war must likewise be subject to moral scrutiny and express appropriate restraint and proportionality.

World War II is a good test case. The brutalities of Nazism were unsurpassed in all human history, and were all the more evil because amplified by the technology and control available to the modern state. A. J. P. Taylor described it as a 'good war'.[7] It seems not unreasonable so to argue. The war rid Western Europe of tyranny and if Eastern Europe had to swap Nazi for Stalinist tyranny at least this was not the intention. It also rid the Far East of Japanese tyranny.

The sceptic, however, could point out that defeating Nazism and Japan cost the lives of many millions, damaged many more through emotional trauma, and caused the devastation of many cities. It led to the invention of nuclear weapons. Suppose people had sat it out through non-violent resistance? There was the reasonable hope that tyranny would mellow and crumble through its own internal contradictions. It would have taken longer – a couple of generations perhaps – but no way could it last for 1,000 years. We are thus led to a different approach to resisting oppression and tyranny – the non-violent resistance of pacifism.

13.3 Non-violent resistance and pacifism

Most pacifists insist they are not impassive in the face of tyranny and oppression. They maintain, however, that their resistance is *non-violent*. The example of Gandhi in India is an obvious one. He relied on facing down British colonialism with the defiant dignity of non-violent resistance and civil disobedience. While having different cultural and religious roots, a similar strategy was used by Martin Luther King who hoped the power of love could win over the oppressor. The oppressor is to be loved and shamed into change. This is far more effective than a violence that escalates through breeding further violence.

Stepping back from these two specific examples the basic perspective is that the aggressor or tyrant is a fellow human being. No one is impervious to the compelling vision of justice and humanity. We best defeat the aggressor by appealing to that within them which manifests the common humanity in which we share, and which can respond to the better way of love.

Questions, however, have to be asked of this approach.

First, is this *always* the right policy or only *sometimes*? No adherent of a just war philosophy would deny that this is *sometimes* a right policy. We should not polarize the 'just war' and 'pacifist' approach as if they are always straight alternatives. Non-violent resistance may have been the right strategy for Martin Luther King and Gandhi. They were both dealing with states which, whatever their faults, had deep roots in liberalism. Given, for the sake of argument, that their approach hastened change, would it have been as effective against the brutality of the regimes of Hitler or Stalin? As an appropriate strategy in some cases, especially in personal relationships, this policy may indeed be the right one. A pragmatic judgement must be made as to when it is appropriate, or how it can be mixed with other approaches.

It is worth pausing on the reference to personal relationships. Most of us face violence in our everyday encounters. It may rarely be physical violence, but it may be the violence of aggression and bullying, which easily brutalize relationships. Judgements in each case have to be made as to how to respond. That said, in many cases the evocative power of a peaceable, courteous and civil disposition is crucial.

It is, however, a bold claim to maintain that whatever the political or social context, or whatever the people or group one is dealing with, non-violent resistance is always the best strategy for defeating oppression or tyranny. Incidentally, this would not have been the position of Gandhi, who did not reject military force in all contexts. 'Just war' theory has no difficulty in supporting non-violent resistance as appropriate in some contexts. Just war theory sees war as a *last resort*. There is after all a noble history of this in the last century – in civil protest against nuclear weapons in the West and even contributing to the demise of Soviet domination in Eastern Europe. Non-violent resistance has also contributed to the overthrow of dictators, Ferdinand Marcos being an example. But is this always the right approach?

This style of pacifism is essentially a pragmatic strategy, arguing on consequentialist grounds that non-violent resistance is the best way to defeat a tyranny. Some may claim it is always the best way, others that it is sometimes the best way, depending on the context. There is, however, a more rigorous style of pacifism which claims that *whatever the consequences* non-violence is an *absolute imperative*. Stanley Hauerwas, for example, allows that peaceableness may lead to the oppressed having to suffer less protection and more injustice. Peaceableness is an absolutist moral stance, not a pragmatic policy. Sometimes this stance is based on the teaching of Jesus, although such a basis begs enormous questions as to how texts are to be interpreted and applied to radically different contexts. When Jesus said, for example, 'Resist not evil', or when he himself lived peaceably, he was not legislating for states in the twenty-first century. The problem with this style of pacifism is that by rendering itself invulnerable to pragmatic criticism through the appeal to a moral absolute, it loses touch with the reality of history and so seriously weakens its support or persuasiveness.

Let's call these two styles of pacifism 'strategic' and 'absolute'. Strategic pacifism, offered as a universal rule, in appealing to the outcome of a strategy, offers a hostage to fortune. It is weak because it cannot justify its claim that this strategy is the right one in all circumstances. In particular, it fails to justify the claim that what may be appropriate in some personal relationships is also appropriate for nations. The dynamic of how nations behave and relate is different from the dynamics of how individuals behave and relate. Absolute pacifism is weak for another reason. Rising above any consequentialist considerations, it leaves itself with no rationale to appeal to those who cannot accept its simple imperative.

As hinted above, we also have to ask if pacifism is accepted simply as a vocation of some, or offered as an imperative for states. Even Reinhold Niebuhr, a staunch critic of pacifism, acknowledged that individuals might have a vocation to offer the prophetic counter-cultural witness of pacifism.[8] The pacifist challenge encourages those who adhere to a 'just war' doctrine to apply the criterion of moral scrutiny with utmost rigour. Some pacifists have put themselves at great personal risk by being stretcher bearers on the battle field. This, however, is very different from saying that states should be pacifist.

There is another difficulty with an absolutist pacifist position. States use violence and coercion not only when they resort to war but also in maintaining law and order and the state's services. Is there a significant moral difference between the state using force to respond to a bank robbery and using force to resist a foreign invasion? May not a 'just war' be no more than citizens exercising collectively their right of self-defence? When pacifists have their homes burgled, do they call the police? Do they send their children to state schools, accept state health care, social services and benefits, even though they depend on taxation sanctioned by the coercive power of the state? These questions are asked gently and out of respect for a noble position, but their significance has not always been recognized, although they were acknowledged explicitly by writers such as Tolstoy,[9] and implicitly by Hauerwas.[10]

Critics of an absolutist pacifist stance insist that non-violent resistance, while a *prima facie* call, does not have trumps in every conceivable context. Sometimes there is a conflict between the call to non-violence and the imperative to confront tyranny and oppression. In essence, the 'just war' doctrine states we must struggle to find a balance between competing claims. By contrast, the absolute pacifist believes the imperative of non-violence always has trumps. We thus meet a specific instance of a disagreement between those who maintain moral action is about weighing and balancing competing values and claims, and those who claim one obligation or value (in this case non-violence) always has trumps (see 3.6). But how can absolute pacifism sustain its insistence that the obligation of non-violence always overrides all other claims? If we accept that moral judgement requires balancing competing claims this is a difficult position to sustain. In instances where non-violence cannot be defended on pragmatist grounds, absolutist pacifism may leave the victim unprotected. Can we justify such a disregard for the consequences of our position? There is even the danger that one might prefer the 'good conscience' and 'clean hands' of the pacifist to an end to tyranny. Furthermore, pacifism may be perceived as retreating into a sectarian unrealism, which leaves states without the moral constraints and subversive challenge of the just war tradition.

13.4 Nuclear weapons

To what extent, if at all, are the contours of the debate changed by the invention of nuclear weapons? Weaponry has been growing in sophistication ever since someone thought of attaching a stone to the end of a stick. The advent of the crossbow caused moral anxiety lest a new threshold had been breached. Are nuclear weapons merely more powerful than conventional weapons or is there a significant difference which raises fundamentally different moral issues? It could be pointed out that the devastation of Tokyo by conventional bombing was comparable to that of Hiroshima and Nagasaki. Of course, there was the serious difference in that nuclear weapons yielded radiation, but other weaponry has its own kind of deadly long-term consequences – like the unexploded bomb.

Perhaps we can get too bogged down in the 'different in kind or degree' argument. The sheer scale of nuclear weaponry makes their use practically unthinkable. The criteria of proportionality and immunity of civilians are brutally violated. Does this mean a nation is unjustified in possessing nuclear weapons and having them ready for use? We encounter here a perplexing twist in the moral assessment of the old adage: *If you want peace, prepare for war.* The idea here is that if a nation is prepared for war, a potential aggressor is deterred. Strong nations are less likely to be attacked than weak ones. This classic doctrine of deterrence applies especially, so it is argued, to nuclear weapons. It has widely been argued that the threat of nuclear retaliation kept the peace in the West during the period of the Cold War. Historians will long debate to what extent, if at all, this was true. We are thus left with the difficult moral dilemma. It is morally wrong to use nuclear weapons.[11] But might it be acceptable to possess and to threaten to use them if the intention in possessing and threatening to use them is to prevent their use and to keep the peace, and if further it is believed we best preserve the peace by so possessing and so threatening?

Even if it has merits this position is deeply uncomfortable. It is uncomfortable because of the danger of accident, or of impetuous judgements in a time of crisis. The risk is enormous. The world was on the brink during the Cuba crisis. The policy depends on bluff, and bluff is easily called. During the 'Cold War' Europe sought to protect itself from Soviet aggression through the threat of nuclear retaliation involving the United States. There was thus a deliberate escalation of risk. Moreover, there is the danger of 'horizontal escalation' as more and more nations want the protection, and status, of the deterrent. Because of the danger of escalation, it is, alas, premature to suggest that the end of the Cold War removes the danger. What moral right have some nations to belong to the nuclear club while debarring others? The greater this 'horizontal' proliferation, the greater the risk of nuclear weapons getting into the hands of a terrorist group. It is not clear that a nation needs to or can use nuclear weapons against a terrorist.

It was these ambiguities and dangers that led the influential Anglican report *The Church and the Bomb*[12] to recommend a phased and negotiated bilateral decommissioning of nuclear weapons. The details of its proposal led to much controversy but it is difficult to resist the fundamental imperative and some progress has been made, despite increasing concern over 'horizontal escalation' and Britain's controversial decision to renew its nuclear deterrent through a successor to trident.

Pacem in Terris of John XXIII likewise called for progressive nuclear disarmament.[13]

13.5 Conclusions

Pacifists of various persuasions could argue that the complications and ambiguities of international politics are such that there is a naive lack of realism in the hope that 'just war' constraints will influence nations. Far from being a last resort, war can too easily express national jingoism, pretensions of power and desire for economic gain. Once started, the 'gloves come off' and moral restraints are abandoned. Codes of chivalry in 1914 – such as the refusal to shoot down a damaged aircraft – were soon abandoned as quaint. In World War II the western allies widely used flame throwers, devastated cities, adopted strategies knowing civilians would be killed, and in some cases used torture to extract intelligence from captured officers. Furthermore, as I have noted, language about 'just intention' rarely describes the messy mix of motivations behind a nation resorting to war. Predicting the outcome of a war is a mug's game. Once unleashed the events of history unfold in ways alarmingly different from those hoped for in 'just war' calculations. Technology has given us weaponry that makes the conduct of war hideously out of all proportion to any just ends.

All this, of course, is true. But there is a difference between a troubled conscience and no conscience at all. Real life is messy and full of ambiguities. To regret these tensions, uncertainties and ambiguities is to regret the kind of world we live in. But we are stuck with this world. The challenge is to do the best we can. This resonates with a theology that refuses to identify the 'reign of God' with any human society, political structure, or state policy. We struggle with as much integrity as we can muster to build a world as just and as peaceful as possible, and sometimes this may mean using force to resist tyranny, aggression and oppression. The 'just war' doctrine does not guarantee clean hands. But it can help to limit the dirt. 'Non-violent resistance' may sometimes be the right policy, but not always. Without the resort to force, tyranny is given a blank cheque and the oppressed are unprotected. Is it morally permissible to permit tyranny when force is available to resist it? If the horrors of modern war serve as a terrifying warning, so may also the genocides of Rwanda, when the international community stood by. Therein lies one of the ambiguities with which we struggle.

It does seem difficult to resist the fundamental claim of the 'just war' tradition that as a last resort military force may be justified. To deny this is to leave the vulnerable unprotected and to give a blank cheque to oppression and tyranny. A realism about the 'fallen world' requires this. But realism requires also a stern critique of a culture that sees military action more as a first resort, feeding the pride of national hegemony and in the grip of the vested interest of the arms industry.

The realities of history are that wars have been fought under the scrutiny of moral constraints. Where there has been no moral scrutiny, we have not a 'just war' entered into with reluctance and with moral uncertainty, but rather a 'crusade'. In a 'crusade' moral constraints are forgotten. There is the rhetoric of 'good' versus 'evil'. The enemy belongs to an 'evil empire' and is dehumanized. All ambiguities are forgotten. The resort to war ceases to be an agonizingly difficult choice of the lesser evil and becomes an imperative of zeal. This idea is both evidenced and devastatingly criticized in the Hebrew Scriptures. It has, of course, many examples in western history – both 'religious' and 'secular'. The Dominican Franciscus de Victoria in the sixteenth century warned against demonizing the enemy and blindness to dirt on one's own hands.

Western nations face no serious threat of aggression on their territory. The stringent moral constraints imposed by the just war tradition are, however, no less necessary. This is so not least because of increased competition for resources – especially oil – and there might be the temptation to resort to military might to enforce economic and political hegemony. The twenty-first century could be as bloody as the twentieth if we do not find a better way. And so this leads to our final section.

13.6 Making a just peace

'*If peace is desired, prepare for war.*' This ancient principle expresses the doctrine of deterrence. Those prepared for war are more likely to be left in peace. No doubt there is truth in this *realpolitik*. There is greater truth, however, in '*If peace is desired, work for justice*'. One of the criteria of the just war tradition is that a war should be contemplated only as a 'last resort'. This has often been located within the context of the brinkmanship of final diplomacy. Wars, however, have a very long run in period. All wars have a wide economic, political and cultural background. If more attention is given to creating a 'culture of peace', then there will be fewer occasions when we need to agonize over whether or not a particular war is just. After all, war would now be unthinkable between Britain and France, or the English and the Welsh. This is so because of the development of mutual understandings, just relations, common interests and a 'culture of peace' with other means of settling disputes.

It is too simplistic to say that injustice is *the* cause of war. It is, however, a major cause, especially when we fill out the notion of injustice to embrace colonialism and its aftermath, political hegemony, unfair trade practice, economic exploitation, and such like. We best seek peace, not by fighting wars, but by tackling these issues. The soil that breeds terrorism contains many and varied constituents, but it seems that terrorism is often a protest against things such as these. Yet currently terrorism is being fought after the model of old-style wars against states. This leaves the root causes untouched. Even worse, the devastation and resentment caused by war can create the breeding ground for further terrorism. We need to struggle to find more realistic and better-informed responses to terrorism.

The direct promotion of peace with justice in many ways leaves behind the debate between 'just war' and 'pacifist' traditions. A recent church report *Peacemaking: A Christian Vocation*[14] speaks of a Christian vocation of peacemaking in key areas: the fostering of just and peaceful relationships, breaking vicious circles of hostility and fear, activity in resolving conflicts, the support of strategies for resolving violence, and engagement with the political leaders about when and how force may be used. The role of the peacemaker in a wide variety of different contexts can be costly and certainly requires courage and wisdom. Far from being naive, recent history underlines dramatically how easily military violence exacerbates conflict, division, civil disorder, resentment and poverty, and thus highlights the imperative to find alternatives to war as a means of resolving conflict. Military threats can consolidate the grip of oppressive regimes and inhibit the growth of free civil societies. The *real* naivety is in the belief that problems admit of a straightforward military solution. The reliance on provocative and counter-productive military might has often made more difficult the building of consensus and legitimacy.[15]

An earlier American Symposium, *Just Peacekeeping*,[16] had likewise explored strategies for creating a culture of peace. The international community of the churches has a key role here in prophetically challenging a culture of violence, in challenging the injustices that encourage conflict, in encouraging international protocols for peace keeping and conflict resolution, and in 'drip feeding' into cultural attitudes.

Real progress has been made through, say, the work of the United Nations and of international law. There are developing structures for international 'peace keeping' under the UN Charter. There is, however, a long way to go. The UN may be dominated or ignored by the self-interest of the most powerful nations. More needs to be done to confront the commercial self-interest fuelling the arms trade,[17] arms that easily get into the 'wrong' hands, although it is unclear which hands are the 'right' ones. The arms trade undermines a culture of peace and encourages a culture in which violence is more a first than a last resort. And in all kinds of ways money spent on arms is money stolen from the poor. Moreover, the pressure the 'arms lobby' might place upon governments in times of crisis needs to be named and confronted.

The better way is to recognize that the resort to war is a last resort, and the 'just war' criterion of 'exhausting first all other means' needs more robustly to be expanded to include building into our mentalities and culture the structures of justice and peace. One of the great contributions of the Hebrew Scriptures to humankind is precisely this challenge. We are not to 'trust in chariots' or 'build Zion in bloodshed'. Rather it is 'justice that shall yield peace'.[18] If the resort to military force is unavoidable, this is often because opportunities for peaceable ways of resolving conflict have been missed.[19]

This is not to suggest that a nation's foreign policy should be handed over to the therapists (in Henry Kissinger's metaphor) or that if only we were a bit nicer everyone will be nice in return. The world is not like that. Force has its place. But in the grand scheme of things the role of force in building peace and justice is limited.

There is nothing wrong in dreaming dreams and working towards them; the dream of greater social and economic justice, thus removing a major incitement to war; the dream of a strong United Nations, supported by international law; the dream of universal nuclear disarmament; the dream of the demise of a 'gung ho' mindset and the easy resort to war as a means of resolving conflict; the dream of strong nations leaving behind bellicose posturing; the dream of the 'arms trade' losing its grip. The distinguished Roman Catholic John Courtney Murray claims that nourished by the 'just war tradition' is the 'will to peace, which, in extremity, bears within itself a will to enforce the precept of peace by arms. But this will is a moral will; for it is identically a will to justice.'[20] To this may be added a word of F. D. Maurice: 'We must be humbled utterly in our own conceits before we can become peacemakers.'[21]

Notes

1 Wilfred Owen, 'Disabled' in *Selected Poems*, London, Bloomsbury, 1995.

2 Cf. Robert Bevan, *The Destruction of Memory*, London, Reaktion, 2005.

3 Cf. Peter W. Galbraith, *The End of Iraq*, London, Simon & Schuster, 2006.

4 Max Hastings, *Armageddon*, London, Macmillan, 2004, pp. 223–4.

5 Thomas Aquinas, *Summa Theologiae*, II-II. 42.2.

6 Washington National Council of Catholic Bishops, *The Challenge of Peace*, 1983, paragraph 92.

7 A. J. P. Taylor, *The Second World War*, London, Hamish Hamilton, 1975, p. 234.

8 Thomas Aquinas saw this as the role of non-combatant priests, II.II Q. 40. Art. 2.

9 Leo Tolstoy, *A Gospel in Brief*, Oxford, World Classics, 1940, pp. 320ff.

10 Stanley Hauerwas, *A Peaceable Kingdom*, London, SCM Press, 1983.

11 Although Paul Ramsey argued that a 'theatre' use against military targets might be justifiable. This was in *War and the Christian Conscience*, Duke University, 1961. This is reconsidered in the second edition of *The Just War*, Lanham, New York, University Press of America, 1968, pp. 211ff., 281ff.

12 The *Church and the Bomb*, London, CIO Publishing and Hodder & Stoughton, 1982, pp. 126ff.

13 John XXIII, *Pacem In Terris*, Vatican, 1963.

14 Methodist Church and United Reformed Church, pp. 65ff.

15 Robin Cook, *The Point of Departure*, London, Simon & Schuster, 2005, pp. 330–2.

16 G. Stassen (ed.), *Just Peacekeeping*, Cleveland, Ohio, Pilgrim Press, 1999.

17 On this see *Responsibility in Arms Transfer Policy*, Church House Publishing, 1994.

18 E.g. Micah 3.10; Isaiah 1.27; 32.17.

19 Methodist Church and United Reformed Church, *Peacemaking: A Christian Vocation*, 2006, p. 51.

20 Quoted by Lisa Sowle Cahill, 'Christian Just War Tradition', in M. P. Aquino and D. Mieth (eds), *The Return of the Just War*, *Concilium*, 2001/2, London, SCM Press, 2001, p. 74.

21 F. Maurice, *The Life of Frederick Denison Maurice*, London, Macmillan, 1884, Volume 2, p. 524.

14

Our Fragile Home and
Those Who Share It

14.1 Introduction

During World War II an unexploded bomb became embedded under one of the country's oldest yew trees. Would it have been worth risking a life to save the tree? Suppose the bomb had been under St Paul's Cathedral. Or, in another example, suppose mining would bring employment and prosperity to an impoverished region – but at the expense of rendering extinct a rare species. How do we resolve the tension between human need and the loss of a species?

It seems clear that we have responsibilities towards the natural world. A fundamental question, however, is whether these responsibilities boil down simply to our responsibilities *towards one another*, or whether the earth has an intrinsic value or worth *in itself*. Is it wrong to harm the environment merely because in so doing we also harm humans, or is it wrong *in itself*? In an environmental ethic, do we count only humans? Do we preserve animals of a rare species for their sake, or for ours – because they look cute in zoos? For Kant 'our duties towards nature are only indirectly duties towards humankind ... we need, of course, to pay no heed to the thing itself, but only in so far as we consider our neighbour.'[1]

If we are committed to our mutual well-being, environmental responsibilities follow at least for the sake of one another and for the sake of future generations. Oil and natural gas are finite resources. To squander them without a thought for future generations is selfish. To say the least, we need to give ourselves maximum time to develop suitable alternatives. Some have questioned this, but future generations will be like us and with similar needs. Why should the fact that they are in the future remove our responsibility? For many, this will have a personal focus. They think of their grandchildren and great-grandchildren.

Alongside oil and gas and other 'resources' there is the wider environment – clean air and water, an amenable and stable climate, fish stocks and forests, the natural wilderness to enjoy, and so forth. There seems little difficulty in saying we have a responsibility to look after all this for the sake of one another and for the sake of our children.

Such a responsibility rarely registered for former generations – and simply because the power and resource of nature seemed inexhaustible, human impact, by contrast, seemed puny. Periodic volcanic eruptions and recent tsunamis and hurricanes remind us how much we are at nature's mercy. Population growth and industrialization, however, are now having an increasingly worrying impact on the earth – hence the emergence of 'environmental ethics'. Furthermore, alienation from the natural environment impoverishes us, as does alienation from the social.

The argument seems reasonable enough so far. Matters become more controversial when it is protested that this perspective is all too 'anthropocentric'** – that is, human centred. We are seeing the earth as a commodity for our consumption. The language of 'resource' and even 'steward' implies as much. The earth and other living things do not have intrinsic value *in themselves* but only value *for us*. A lot of early writing in environmental ethics protested against such anthropocentricism. On the contrary, it was urged, the physical environment has a value in itself, making a claim upon us not to be understood simply in terms of what gives us benefit.

There is, however, more rhetoric here than conceptual clarity. Generally, it is difficult to sort out the right language to use, and we can easily be bewitched by language. Attempting to clarify our language, let us say a physical object or plant may have *instrumental value* because it gives some good for us *beyond itself*. An aspirin tablet is an example. Its value is instrumental in relieving pain. By contrast, a beautiful flower has *inherent value* because of what it is in itself, its beauty, colour and delicacy. The distinction between instrumental and inherent value is useful, even if it is a little messy. Furthermore, it may be different for different people. An enthusiastic chemist may have no interest in flowers, and yet the chemical intricacy of a drug may be a source of intense fascination and delight. For the chemist, it has inherent value. Coins and bank notes for most, have only instrumental value, that is, for what they buy. For the numismatist, however, they have inherent value as works of art. If I don't like broccoli it has only instrumental value in giving vitamins. If I do like broccoli, then it has inherent value.

Physical things have instrumental or inherent value, however, *for us*. Can we say they may also have *intrinsic value*, that is value *in themselves*? Can we make sense of this? What about the 'Last Human'** dilemma – the thought experiment in which we imagine ourselves as being the last human before the human species – along with every other sentient species – is extinct. Would it be wrong to destroy some physical object or some area of the environment before we died? There would be no sentient creatures left to suffer the loss.[2]

Can nature have a value *in itself*, a value that does not derive from our judgement? Does a beautiful orchid have intrinsic value, or only the inherent value we accord to it on account of our aesthetic sense? Suppose we run with the idea that nature has intrinsic value? We still have to ask where more specifically this value resides. For one position in ecology, value is found in living things,[3] and for the most straightforward version of this there is the advocacy of biotic egalitarianism.** In other words, all living things have *equal* value. Arne Naess and George Sessions have urged this claim.[4] Naess speaks of the 'equal right to live and blossom' of all species as being an 'intuitively clear and obvious value axiom'.[5] 'Deep ecology', for Naess, includes the view that the biosphere has intrinsic value, quite apart from the benefit it might give to humans.[6]

For some, even the physical environment has an intrinsic value and it is incumbent upon us to honour that value. In the writings of Aldo Leopold and Baird Callicott the moral community includes not only the living but also the geological.[7] Roderick Nash, likewise, suggests the natural world has inherent value in itself, even claiming rocks and rivers have 'rights'.[8] We speak here of some intrinsic moral right rather than a legal protection which is very different and generally accorded for our benefit anyway.

There are two fundamental difficulties with this kind of approach. First, value is accorded generously to all and sundry, but it is not clear what we do when there are conflicts. It is urged that all species have an equal right to flourish. Does this mean that when I weed my garden I am wrong to privilege petunias over dandelions? What do I do if there is a conflict between the right of a rat to warmth and shelter and the right of my daughter to her bedroom? It is not clear that 'biotic egalitarianism' is rationally defensible or practically realistic.

The problem arises in a different form when we consider the view that locates value in the species rather than in individual animals or plants. How do we manage a conflict between the value which resides in an individual animal and the value which resides in the survival of a species? Or suppose we locate the value, as does Aldo Leopold, more in the biodiversity of the ecosystem. The biotic collective rather than the individual is where value resides. 'A thing is right when it tends to promote the integrity, stability and beauty of the biotic community. It is wrong when it tends otherwise.'[9] It is not clear, however, on what grounds we manage conflict between the claims of biodiversity and the claims of a particular species, or individuals of that species. One problem with 'biotic egalitarianism' is that if we maximize biotic welfare, we can easily find ourselves riding roughshod over basic human needs. What do we do if there is a serious conflict between such needs and what is perceived to be the conflicting rights of the biosphere?

The problem becomes even more acute when we extend value to the non-living. Suppose I remove rock from the beach where children are playing? Suppose we divert a river so as to prevent flooding? Are we wrongly asserting our rights and needs over the integrity of the earth? No wonder Tom Regan has protested against 'environmental fascism'. The reality is, there is a misanthropy evident in some environmental ethics – when, for example, the preservation of a particular environment (for the wealthy elite?) has priority over social justice. It is evident also if biodiversity is the controlling and overriding value, or biotic egalitarianism even more so. The logic of the position requires the sacrifice of human life for the sake of this biodiversity. Such preoccupations can even be seen as luxuries for the affluent. They cut no ice for those who struggle simply to survive.

Finding a proper balance between human and non-human value, and finding inter-species justice is no easy matter.[10] Is it acceptable to cull two thousand goats to save three endangered plant species? How does one balance rarity, biodiversity and the claims of individual animals – including humans?[11] There is no way in which all this can be sorted out with anything approaching clarity and precision.

The second difficulty concerns intelligibility and coherence. Can we make sense of the notion that the non-conscious, unaware of interests, deprivation or flourishing, has intrinsic value? It is not clear that we can. The language of value resides with the language of persons, conscious of interests and capable of suffering or contentment. The non-conscious may have instrumental or inherent value for persons, but it is not clear it makes sense to say it may have *intrinsic* value in itself.

As we have seen, a lot of environmental ethics in the past has hitched a lift on the back of ideas about a self-regulating 'balance' in nature, or some 'biotic integrity', the notion of 'Gaia' being one example.[12] We have a responsibility, so it is urged, to preserve this balance and integrity. There may also be a bias in favour of biodiversity as distinct from more monochrome environments. Many of these warnings are indeed to be heeded. There are many interconnections in nature. Our impact upon the environment can set off a chain reaction. The evidence is persuasive to many that the burning of fossil fuels is contributing to global warming and thus to climate change. This might in turn affect the Gulf Stream. Similarly, the destruction of forests can affect the monsoons. The important thing to notice here, however, is that we are concerned about the impact of our activity *in so far as it affects us*. This seems perfectly reasonable, but let us not flatter ourselves that we are honouring some responsibility to care for the balance of the earth for its own sake. After all, there are many 'balances' in nature. We have simply identified those in which we have an interest. The interests of another species might focus on other balances. For slugs the 'balance' of nature is about the ready supply of lettuce. The 'earth' has no 'interest' in preserving the *status quo* as it now is, or as we sentimentally remember it as being a generation ago. The earth's history is one of gradual evolution and violent change. The earth has no investment in things as they now are. It is we that have this investment because it is our home and an all too fragile one.

Suppose we allow – but only for the sake of argument so far – that the physical earth and non-sentient life has no intrinsic moral value or status and that we have no responsibilities towards it save those that express a sense of responsibility for one another. The matter is complicated by the fact that we have to deal not only with non-sentient life and the physical landscape. There are also animals who are sentient and so capable of both suffering and contentment.

14.2 Animals

It is impossible to speak of our treatment of animals save in terms of a pragmatism as humane as feasible. There is no way in which we can tidy everything up and make it all neat and orderly. But finding a generous pragmatism through sensitivity to the needs of animals is our obligation. The alternative is inhumane exploitation and cruelty.

Some speak of the 'rights' of animals.[13] The language of 'rights' attaches most naturally to humans in society. Can we apply it also to animals? Tom Regan speaks of animal 'rights' on the basis of an analogy between animals and human beings. What, however, are the 'rights' animals are supposed to have? And which animals? It is absurd to say a hamster has a right to vote, a fox a right to freedom of worship, or a horse a right to a university education. Such animal rights as there are must be appropriate to the kind of creature an animal is. This gives the question a better focus, but it is still not clear how we answer it. Suppose we say an animal has a 'right' not to be eaten? This seems a very odd claim, given biological realities. Or is it hoped that eventually we will be able to police the forests to prevent the lion feeding on the antelope? Are carnivores in zoos to be forced to turn vegetarian? Clearly not. The claim is rather that an animal has a right not to be eaten *by a human being*. But is this right inviolable even when an animal is reared sensitively and killed humanely? Why does a rabbit have a right not to be eaten by a human, while the fox may feast with impunity?

Can we speak of animals as having a right to a 'natural' life? But, given changing habitats, how is this to be defined, and what is so significant about my cat's right to a 'natural' life when it has a healthier, more contented and longer life under my care? If still asserted may this right be overridden when captivity is an expedient to prevent extinction? Can we speak of animals having a right to medical care? Does this impose upon us the obligation to pay teams of veterinary practitioners to roam the forests? Or does the right come into play only when I place myself under an obligation, say, by requisitioning an animal as a pet? Furthermore, can we say an animal has a right not to be ridden or raced? Does an animal have a right not to be culled? And how do we balance an animal's alleged right not to be culled with the responsibility of farmers to protect their chickens? The fox is a ruthless predator.

We can hardly object to speaking in everyday conversation of the rights of an animal, but if we are trying to give our thought a bit more precision there is a strong case for confining the language of 'rights' to humans in society. Of course, the law may confer certain *legal rights* on animals, but that need not imply the appropriateness of language concerning inherent *moral rights* (see 3.4). Those, however, who deny animals have rights do not spend their spare time shooting cats, as the Oxford philosopher F. H. Bradley is alleged to have done.[14] Sceptical about the *language* of rights, we can still speak robustly of our responsibilities towards animals. We have a responsibility not to inflict suffering, to prevent it when we can, and to respect the interests of animals. This is based simply on an animal's capacity to suffer or to enjoy well-being. For Peter Singer, our responsibilities are based primarily on an animal's capacity to experience pleasure and pain.[15] John Wesley's belief that God's grace embraces the whole of creation prompted a concern for the welfare of animals, over 'all that have sense, all that are capable of pleasure or pain, of happiness or misery'.[16] There is here a stringent challenge to our complacency.

Singer insists humans and animals deserve *equal* consideration – to think otherwise is to be guilt of a 'speciesism'** as ugly as racism or sexism. Animal and human suffering are of *equal* moral concern. The good of an animal is as valuable as the good of a human. We need in our ethical thinking to 'cross the species barrier'.

Singer's argument that 'if a being suffers there can be no moral justification for refusing to take that suffering into consideration' can hardly be contested. There is a quantum leap, however, in what follows: 'No matter what the nature of the being ... equality requires that its suffering be counted equally with the like suffering ... of another being.' To discriminate on the basis of species is as wrong as to discriminate on the basis of race or gender. To favour a white person over against a black is to be guilty of racism. To favour our species over others is equally wrong.[17] On the basis of this, Singer's *Great Ape Project* campaigned for giving equality of moral status at least to the great apes.

There is a utilitarian simplicity here, which manifests both the strengths and weaknesses of utilitarianism's strict calculations. If the charge of unqualified 'speciesism' always has trumps are we being subject to an ethic of 'unreasonable demands' such as draws the protest of Simon Blackburn?[18] Furthermore, can we argue that over and against utilitarian impartiality there is nothing unreasonable in acknowledging special obligations to our own species as we have, say, to our own families (see 3.2)? The parallel between speciesism and racism and sexism is not established since it fails to recognize that there are justified as well as unjustified forms of partiality. Racism and sexism are wrong because human beings are essentially the same, despite different genders and ethnicity. Humans and animals are much more different. Suppose when walking in a wood my wife falls and badly gashes her hand? I then hear the cry of a nearby badger in pain, caught in an illegal trap. If I judge the badger's distress the greater, do I call the vet before the ambulance? Of course, I do not discount the badger's pain, but is it wrong to give my wife's distress priority? This is not to deny that we may sometimes put ourselves out, or even expose ourselves to harm, in order to save an animal. After all, the good shepherd may lay down their life for a sheep.

Furthermore, even Singer's own analysis is in danger of suffering a death of a thousand qualifications. He allows that the differences between humans and animals justify different treatments. For example, human bereavement causes longer emotional suffering than bereavement among animal pairings. 'Equal consideration for different beings may lead to different treatment.'[19] But what differences count, and for how much? We can easily end up appealing to the richness and complexity of a human life as *de facto* invalidating the charge of speciesism. And does a dog or horse count for more than Mr Mole, Mr Water Rat or even Mr Toad?

There is no straightforward ethical calculus here, and we are left with judging competing claims as responsibly as we can. But at least the claims of animals, and their interests and suffering, are part of our consideration and there is a stringent protest against the way in which we ignore animal suffering or regard the most trivial human benefit as being worth any amount of animal misery. Dean Inge remarked that if animals were able to conceptualize the devil they would envisage the devil in human form.[20]

14.2.1 Vegetarianism

Is it morally acceptable to rear and kill, or to kill in the wild, an animal for food? 'Absolute' vegetarianism would claim this is morally wrong *as such*. This can be a deeply humane creed, displaying a self-discipline one can only admire. Its theoretical basis, however, is not without its ambiguities. For many, absolute vegetarianism does not have a convincing response to the question: Given the differences between animals and ourselves – in particular their limited capacity to foresee their death – why is it wrong, given sensitive husbandry and humane killing, to eat animal flesh? Furthermore, 'absolute' vegetarianism' is not as simple as it sounds. Does it involve not drinking an animal's milk or eating their eggs? And how do we define an animal? Do we include fowl, fish or even molluscs?

Vegetarianism may instead be based on, or in its 'absolute' form be supported by, a more pragmatic argument. This takes its cue from the last paragraph: 'given sensitive husbandry and humane killing'. The literature of vegetarianism claims our meat production is such that immense suffering is often caused. Economic and commercial pressures mean we are nothing like as humane as we can and should be.[21] Vegetarianism may thus be based on the pragmatic stance that, although not necessarily intrinsically wrong, meat consumption involves acquiescing in institutionalized cruelty. One uncomfortable implication might be that the poor must be vegetarian, but the rich can buy expensive meat from carefully monitored sources.

It is difficult here to get the balance right. That meat production – and the transport and slaughter of animals probably more so – does sometimes cause suffering is beyond doubt. Some forms of intensive husbandry are vulnerable to ethical critique, although types earlier criticized have in many cases now been abandoned in the UK. Groups such as *Compassion in World Farming* do a service in challenging complacency and in helping to keep animal welfare on the agenda. We need, nonetheless, to ask how representative are the horror stories sometimes offered by single-issue pressure groups. Facts have a tiresome habit of undermining simple ideologies. It is not true that intensive systems are by definition detrimental to animal welfare, neither is it true that traditional grazing, on account of cold, foot rot and such like is always idyllic.[22] Regulations do exist, and if bad practice exists, so also does good practice. The British tradition of farming is one of humane husbandry. This is reinforced by an economic consideration. An animal badly cared for and stressed will not produce good meat. Furthermore, if animals are sometimes badly treated we should not rush to 'blame the farmer' and others involved. The consumer also has responsibilities over the economic pressures the market exerts. Practice cannot be separated from economic and social structures (see 12.3). Furthermore, not all meat comes from the farm. Some is hunted in the wild.

Vegetarianism may be reinforced by a further pragmatic consideration. It is argued that land is better used producing vegetable protein over and against animal.[23] Plant protein and other nutrients may even be lost when recycled as feed for cattle or poultry. This may be true as a broad generalization, but it does not follow that a move to arable is an economic option for each and every farm. Again, the calculation of animal/vegetable protein conversion ratios is a very complicated matter and generalizations may not accurately describe a particular context. Moreover, land used for grazing may have a certain ecological edge over arable land, and sheep can graze on and help to maintain hill land on which crops cannot be grown.

Vegetarianism is clearly vindicated as an honourable position. But are the arguments offered in its favour sufficiently coercive to make morally illicit any consumption of meat or other animal products?

14.2.2 Vivisection

Of course, there is an imperative at least to reduce to the minimum the use of animals in research, and to seek alternatives. It is right that there are strict regulations and codes of practice. There are grave concerns over inessential usage – as in cosmetics. The Body Shop has raised public awareness by selling products free of animal testing in their development. Are there, however, hard cases when we have to choose between the well-being of animals in research and the failure to develop some new drug or form of treatment such as may significantly advance human well-being? The development of genetic engineering and xenografting may well increase rather than reduce our reliance on animals, and this includes the breeding of animals, including apes, for the purposes of transplant surgery. If the choice is between the life of rats and the life of our children many will have no difficulty and no conscience about their decision. There is a belief here about the comparative value of human and animal life and a trade off between the two.

For some, this position is all too complacent. Animals are sentient creatures, and it is wrong *per se* to inflict pain and distress, however great the human benefit. If the greater human benefit justifies experimentation on animals, then it also justifies experimentation on non-consenting humans of like mental capacity, and this few would allow. To allow the former but not the latter is to be guilty of 'speciesism'. To experiment on another species is as immoral as for a Nazi to experiment on another race or the mentally challenged. We have no right to maximize human well-being whatever the cost. We should accept the costs that may follow from not experimenting on animals.[24]

In contrast to this position, R. G. Frey offers a cautious defence of animal experimentation, although subject to the stringent constraints of the 'three Rs' – 'reduction', 'refinement' and, if possible, 'replacement'.[25] Animals belong to the moral community on account of their sentience, and so suffering is not to be discounted. We cannot justify animal experimentation simply on the grounds of human benefit without allowing the legitimacy of discriminating on the basis of species alone. That said, because human mental capacity far exceeds that of animals, the quality and richness of a human life likewise exceeds it. It follows that humans may have a greater 'quality of life' than an animal. Animal experimentation may thus be justified if the consequent increase in the richness and quality of human life far exceeds the diminution of the far more limited quality of an animal life.

This defence is not without its difficulties, as Frey acknowledges in his caution. Why should animals be forced to lose their modest quality of life for the sake of human enhancement? 'To those that hath shall be given. To those that hath not shall be taken away even that which they hath.' Furthermore, as Frey concedes, if the criterion is quality of life we have no response to the classic repost: if we can experiment on animals why not on severely disabled humans who might have less mental complexity than some apes? The crucial question, urged by Singer, is: 'What is it that protects all humans while failing to protect animals?' Is the value and worth of a human life simply a function of its quality? And if not for humans, why not for animals?

It does seem difficult to justify any experimentation on animals, while at the same time protecting non-consenting humans, without incurring the charge of speciesism. Are we, however, convinced about the charge of 'speciesism' as a trump card that instantly settles any argument? After appropriate weighting, given the difference between human and animal mental life, are we so sure it is a moral imperative always to give human and animal well-being *equal* consideration? To be unsure, of course, is not to deny our solemn responsibility to take animal welfare seriously into account.

If we judge there are occasions when we can bias our own species, we must take responsibility for our decision. We must not claim too confidently some kind of special worth in the mind of God. It is better to remain humbled and troubled by ambiguity than to validate our partiality by divine permission.

There seems to be no end to the complications. Is it ethical for one nation to keep hands clean while benefiting from the research of another? Is it my responsibility to refuse medical treatment because in the past its development has depended on animal testing – even if my refusal will cause great distress to my family? It is not clear that it is possible to sort all this out. We have to be content with the most reasonable and the most humane pragmatism within our grasp.

14.3 Theocentricism?

We return to the unease many feel in the argument that we have no obligations towards the earth and other living things save those that express our obligations to one another – the only qualification being that at least some animals have their own intrinsic moral status, but on the grounds that, like us, they have interests and can feel enjoyment or suffering. For many the Kantian view of the earth as a commodity for our use does not ring true.[26] Many pages from the book of life are being ripped out before they are read.[27] Is this a tragedy simply because we can no longer absorb their riches (e.g. the medicinal potential of plants) or because they have their own moral status and a value in themselves? Many species become extinct without humanity knowing about it. To claim only the former seems reductionist, but can we make sense of the idea that the non-conscious, even less the non-living, have intrinsic value as belonging to the moral community? Or is protest against 'anthropocentricism' simply a hyperbolic but conceptually smudged way of challenging a rampant exploitation of the earth?

The rhetoric may humble our consciences, but is it coherent? The language of 'value', 'worth' and 'moral status' has its location within the realm of persons. It is persons who have intrinsic value, and things have value only for persons.[28] Some animals may be included only because they are persons of sorts. How can a physical object – or even a plant – have value, save for persons, and save as accorded by persons? It is not clear this makes sense, and yet we may still feel uneasy about anthropocentricism.

It is at this point that theology has important insights. For the theist the tension between anthropocentricism** and ecocentricism** is reconciled in a higher perspective. This is 'theocentricism'** – a God-centred view. The physical creation is God's gift, but that is not to say it is a mere commodity. It has a worth for God as creator. God's grace and love embrace all that God has made, even the fall of the sparrow. For the Psalmist, God 'preservest both man and beast' and the Hebrew Scriptures speak even of a covenant between God and all living things.[29] The earth is 'charged with the grandeur of God'.[30] Theists have no investment in denying that things may have value 'in themselves' but ultimately that value is conferred by God as creator and is secure because God values and delights in the whole of creation. Such a belief nurtures a proper sense of wonder, respect and gratitude. It guards against a strident anthropocentricism which sees the earth as simply for our benefit, but at the same time it guards against a romantic and unrealistic biotic egalitarianism which makes us feel uncomfortable if we dare even help ourselves to a blackberry.

It is thus simply not true, as some assert, that Christianity has an anthropocentric view, according to which everything is for our benefit and is subject to us. The profounder Christian vision is that God values the whole of creation. Within that creation humanity is indeed held within the divine love and grace, but not humanity alone. We can only speculate what galaxies and comets, frogs and alligators, mountains and rivers, flowers and trees, mean to God.

Such a vision will certainly emphasize the *inherent* and not merely *instrumental* value of the earth as God's creation. A stark anthropo- centricism can assume a crude instrumental view of the earth. We value it for what it gives to us. As we saw earlier, however, many things are valued *for their own sake* (3.2). Why cannot the earth and its wonders not be valued *for their own sakes*, and not simply because, in conse- quentialist fashion, some human good is served? In a similar way we value relationships of love, music, intellectual enquiry, and loads of other things *in themselves*, and not simply because of some benefit or utility they may give. Indeed, their benefit is dependent upon our rec- ognizing their *inherent* worth. This would seem to be more consistent with our own experience and to resonate with belief that the earth is God's creation and God's gift. It takes us beyond the polarized debate between 'anthropocentricism' on the one hand and 'biocentrism' and 'ecocentrism' on the other. If we want to add the concept of addi- tional *intrinsic* value, then maybe this may make better sense if we see such value as conferred through being valued by God as part of God's creation.

Creation understood in wholly deist** terms, combined with a dual- ism,** which sees the human 'self' as being other than and superior to the body, might combine with a mechanistic view of the physical world as a commodity for our benefit. A richer theology of creation, combined with a theology of incarnation, will see the earth not primar- ily as a resource for our benefit but more as that which manifests the glory of God. A God-centred cosmology will see the earth as God's and this will serve as a moral constraint upon how we regard and use it. It will encourage the language of respect, restraint, appropriate stewardship, rather than the language of resource and exploitation. As O'Donovan has put it, there is something in the relations of things to command respect.[31] Why do we speak of *conquering* Everest? Mind- blowing as the themes may be, much traditional theology has spoken of the redemption of the cosmos as intertwined with the redemption of humanity – in Paul, John and Irenaeus. God redeems humanity and the earth together.[32]

Does this help us over the hard questions? We still face difficult choices when we wrestle with a tension between human need and the claims of the earth and other forms of life. The theology I have outlined does not give us an ecological rule book or some formula for calculating trade offs. It does, however, imbibe a respect for the earth and a sense of gratitude, wonder and enchantment, which should bear fruit in gentleness and a sensitivity which can do nothing but good both for ourselves and for the earth. The granting of 'dominion' in Genesis 1.26 must surely not be understood as granting permission to dominate and exploit. 'Dominion' is to be exercised in a way that is answerable to God and which reflects God's care and respect for creation. In the words of Thomas à Kempis, 'If thy heart be straight with God, then every creature will be to thee a mirror of life and a book of holy doctrine, for there is no creature so little and so vile, but that showeth and representeth the goodness of God.'[33]

14.4 Five specific areas

I now try to be a bit more practical. The cumulative effects of economic growth, 'resource' depletion, deforestation, climate change and pollution are grave indeed. 'Wolf' may have been cried sometimes too readily, and there is much we simply do not know. We predict the future on the basis of inadequate knowledge. Decisions have to be taken and risks assessed on the basis of this limited data. Vested interests abound. That said, it is highly dangerous to be complacent. I wish to suggest that a fivefold response to our environmental responsibilities should be explored. How successful and how adequate it will be remains unclear.

First, environmental considerations cannot be separated from a commitment to justice. It is the poor who tend to live under flight paths, near power stations, waste disposal facilities, and other sources of environmental pollution. The poor bear the lion's share of the burden of environmental degradation and also the cost of resource depletion. After all scarcity pushes up prices. Furthermore, injustice – as through exorbitant debt charges – can cause environmental damage if communities are forced to rape the earth so as to maximize the production of capital crops. The global economy tends to force the poor to degrade their environment in order to survive. When industrialization downgrades a local environment, it is generally the environment of the poor. Bhopal in 1974 was a paradigmatic case. The global economy may also locate environmentally damaging industries and waste disposal in poor countries where there is less regulation and legal protection for the poor. When DDT was banned in western countries, stocks were sometimes unloaded on 'Third World' countries. 'Let them eat pollution.' There is an uncanny resonance between the protests of Isaiah and modern experience.[34] There is also, of course, colossal commercial self-interest in our current patterns of consumption – especially that of carbon fuels. Such a commitment to justice and environmental responsibility raises mammoth political and economic questions.

Second, there is the response of personal lifestyle. Just as the good life involves sensitivity to others, so also it involves sensitivity to the earth. This will involve vigilance over our 'carbon footprint', our 'ecological footprint' more generally, our energy consumption, our travelling, what we consume and the length of supply lines. It will involve appropriate recycling, and modesty in consumption. It may mean ending our love affair with cheap and frequent travel. Ecological sensitivity may involve a greater commitment to the local, as Northcott has suggested.[35] It will involve a finely tuned sensitivity even to the extent of the detergents we buy. We should not despise the contribution of seemingly simple things, like consumer sensitivity challenging unnecessary packaging. We will try to be as informed as possible economically and scientifically, lest we be carried away by naivety and sentimentality. The sheer extravagance and wastefully consumption of the richest 25 per cent – and of our corporations – can be obscene. Christian belief in the earth as God's and as God's gift should nourish an attitude of reverence and respect for nature. Lynn White's indictment of the ill effect of an interpretation of Genesis 1.26 as permitting tyranny and domination is probably exaggerated.[36] More to the point is 'eco feminism' and its critique of attitudes of exploitation, greed and plundering, although the correlation between such character traits and gender is problematical.[37] Faith communities can also play their part in 'raising awareness'. In particular, Christians, of all people, are aware that it is a mug's game to find meaning and a sense of the value of one's life in the search for ever more ostentatious wealth. It is true that simpler lifestyles lower consumption, deflate economies and create unemployment; but economies are more easily managed and redirected than is the environment. Again, mammoth political, cultural and economic questions are raised.

Third, there is the response at the level of government, in terms of policy, regulations and initiatives, and also of industry. Personal lifestyle alone will not solve problems that are largely structural. The response of lifestyle and personal commitment is, however, intimately linked with this. Government action needs popular support. Furthermore, public pressure and consumer choice can challenge the commercial self-interest of, say, oil-based industries where there might be opposition to developing cleaner alternative technologies. Government and industry cannot be 'green' without support from, and pressure from, a 'green' public when it votes, buys and in other ways makes its voice heard. The churches have a part to play here as a crucial sector of civil society.

There is thus a crucial fourth area, that of science and technology. Science can help us produce food efficiently and science can help minimize the environmental impact. Only science can deliver alternative and 'cleaner' sources of energy, and develop ways of reducing CO_2 emissions in, say, generating electricity from coal.[38] Science is needed to keep flowing the supply of clean water. This reminds us that not all economic growth is damaging to the environment. Some types are necessary to sustain it. We probably cannot do without inorganic fertilizers, herbicides and pesticides, and we rely on science to develop benign ones and solve the environmental side effects Rachel Carson alerted us to in 1962.[39] For example, Britain has banned the seed dressings to which she objected, and safer ones have been developed. As a result, sparrowhawks and magpies are returning to the arable areas where these were once used. Science is finding ways of containing carbon dioxide. Science can help us discover patterns of growth that are sustainable – sustainability defined by the United Nations as 'improving the quality of life while living within the carrying capacity of supporting ecosystems'.[40] Last, but not least, science is crucial in identifying and assessing risks, since one of the conundrums we face is that the stakes are high, and yet in our choices and policies we are acting on limited knowledge. If science and technology has helped to create the environmental crisis, then science and technology will play a major part in containing it. But again, science and technology are integrated with government, industry and civil society, and so must be given the resources and direction. Perhaps we could even steal for this purpose some of the expertise devoted to developing even smarter bombs and missiles.

Finally, all this presupposes a global perspective. We need to think globally because the impact of environmental degradation and pollution is global. Global warming knows no national boundaries. Some matters need to be tackled globally, as is evidenced by the Kyoto Protocol concerning the reduction of carbon emissions of developed countries. The Church is an international community and has served as a model for other international communities. Theistic faith inherently challenges all forms of tribalism. One of the contributions of the Church with its worldwide networks is to foster and express this global perspective.[41]

In the old myth, Adam and Eve broke faith not only with God and with each other but also with the garden. The community of the true Adam needs to attend to the earth as well.

Notes

1 Immanuel Kant, *Lectures on Ethics*, translated by Louis Enfield, London, Methuen, 1930, p. 241.

2 The 'Last Human' dilemma was introduced in 1978 by Richard Routley.

3 Paul W. Taylor, *Respect for the Living*, Princeton University Press, 1986.

4 A. Naess, 'The Shallow and the Deep', *Inquiry*, Number 16, 1973, pp. 95–100.

5 A. Naess in David Rothenberg (ed.), *Ecology, Community and Lifestyle*, Cambridge, Cambridge University Press, 1989.

6 Naess, 'The Shallow and the Deep', pp. 95ff.

7 Baird Callicott, *In Defence of the Land Ethic*, Albany, Suny Press, 1989, and Aldo Leopold, *A Sand County Almanac*, Oxford, 1968.

8 Roderick Nash advocated the ideas that everything – even rocks – has rights in *The Rights of Nature*, Madison, University of Wisconsin Press, 1989.

9 Leopold, *Sand County Almanac*, pp. 224–5.

10 See Robin Attfield, *Environmental Ethics*, Cambridge, Polity Press, 2003, pp. 44–5.

11 The example is from Michael Banner, *Christian Ethics and Modern Problems*, Cambridge, Cambridge University Press, 1999, p. 175.

12 James Lovelock, *Gaia*, Oxford, Oxford University Press, 1979.

13 E.g. Tom Regan, *The Case for Animal Rights*, Berkeley, University of California Press, 1983.

14 Richard Wollheim, *F. H. Bradley*, Harmondsworth, Penguin, 1959, p. 15.

15 E.g. Peter Singer, *Animal Liberation*, New York, Random House, 1975. Also *Practical Ethics*, Cambridge, Cambridge University Press, 1979.

16 John Wesley, Sermon Number 60, 'The General Deliverance' in *Works*, ed. A. C. Outler, Volume 2, Nashville, Abingdon, 1985, p. 437.

17 From Peter Singer, *Animal Liberation*, reprinted in Peter Singer, *Writings on an Ethical Life*, New York, HarperCollins, 2000, p. 35.

18 Simon Blackburn, *Being Good*, Oxford, Oxford University Press, 2001, pp. 47–50.

19 Singer, *Animal Liberation*, p. 29.

20 W. R. Inge, *Lay Thoughts of a Dean*, London, Knickerbocker Press, 1926, p. 199.

21 Linzey, *Christianity and the Rights of Animals*, pp. 99ff.

22 See Gordon Gatward, *Livestock Ethics*, Welton Lincoln, Chalcombe Publications, 2001, p. 15.

23 E.g. Singer, *Writings on an Ethical Life*, p. 71.

24 Linzey, *Christianity and the Rights of Animals*, p. 124.

25 R. G. Frey, 'Animals' in Hugh Lafollette (ed.), *The Oxford Handbook of Practical Ethics*, Oxford, 2003, pp. 161ff.

26 Immanuel Kant, *Lectures on Ethics*, translated by Louis Enfield, London, Methuen, 1930, pp. 239–41.

27 Rosemary Radford Ruether, *Gaia and God: An Eco Feminist Theology of Earth Healing*, London, SCM Press, 1993, p. 42.

28 Janna Thompson, 'A Refutation of Environmental Ethics', *Environmental Ethics 2*, 1990, pp. 148–60.

29 Genesis 9.8–11; Hosea 2.18.

30 The phrase is Gerard Manley Hopkins in the poem 'God's Grandeur'.

31 Oliver O'Donovan, *Resurrection and Moral Order*, Grand Rapids, Eerdmans, second edition, 1994, p. 52.

32 I develop some of these themes further in John A. Harrod, 'Wesleyan Perspectives on Ecology' in P. T. Meadows (ed.), *Windows on Wesley*, Oxford, Applied Theology Press, 1997.

33 Thomas à Kempis, *Imitation of Christ*, quoted in Linzey, *Christianity and the Rights of Animals*, p. 16.

34 Isaiah chapters 5 and 24.

35 Michael S. Northcott, *The Environment and Christian Ethics*, Cambridge, Cambridge University Press, 1996, pp. 308ff.

36 Lynn White, 'The Historical Roots of our Ecological Crisis', *Science* 155, 1976.

37 E.g. R. R. Ruether 1992. Sally McFague, *SuperNatural Christians*, London, SCM Press, 1997.

38 *Time Magazine*, 24 July 2006, p. 45.

39 Rachel Carson, *Silent Spring*, 1962, reprinted by London Folio Society.

40 Quoted by Robin Attfield, *Environmental Ethics*, p. 128.

41 An example is the World Council of Churches' document on *Justice, Peace and Integrity of Creation*, Geneva, World Council of Churches, 1990.

15

Person to Person

15.1 Personal relationships

To be human is to be in relationship. In all kinds of ways we are related to those whom we never meet, or meet only casually. Within this wider network, concepts such as 'rights' and 'justice' come to the fore. I may never meet those who deliver my milk, or those in China who make my shirt. But I recognize their rights and my obligation to honour principles of fairness and justice (see 3.4).

With others, however – although there is no clear dividing line – I am more intimately involved. They may be friends, colleagues or family. Alongside the notions mentioned, other ethical concepts readily come into play. Is it possible to map this area of personal relationship? No map can be full and complete since, in the nature of the case, each personal relationship will be distinctive. That said, there are identifiable features of the landscape.

It is a landscape full of hazards. Our personal relationships may not be heavy with agonizing moral dilemmas – as is modern medicine – but they are fraught with dangers. It is an area where the resources of 'virtue ethics' come into their own (see 3.8). Good relationships are furthered as much by the kind of people we are as by right actions, although, of course, the two cannot be separated. I noted earlier that love both gives and receives. A love that refuses to give implies we enter a relationship as a consumer, intent on what the person loved can give, but with no commitment to them. On the other hand, a love for which aggressive giving becomes almost a crusade can be paternalistic and oppressive – ultimately arrogant and even self-seeking through enjoying the moral high ground of being the one who always has the strength and resource out of which to give. Alternatively, it can betray a lack of a sense of self-worth. 'I do not deserve anything, I am very bad and my role must be simply to give.' Love is reciprocal. There is a delighting in the person loved as well as a giving to them (see 5.3.4). There is thus a need for self-awareness and judgement. Self-awareness should also alert us to the danger of manipulating people, hence our discussion earlier of gentleness (see 5.3.4). A willingness both to give and receive forgiveness, also discussed earlier, is an essential ingredient for it is rare that relationships are not sometimes hurt through what we are and do (see 8.4). A sense of humour is rarely mentioned in books on ethics, and yet it prevents us from taking ourselves too seriously and so helps to make us less unbearable to others. This touches on humility – not an obsequious self-effacement, but more like a sober and realistic assessment of oneself, combined with openness to and gratitude for others (see 5.3.4). One could, of course, go on. Helen Oppenheimer, for example, has fine discussions of 'delighting' and 'attending' in our relating.[1]

I noted earlier also the need to balance the specific obligations we have towards friends and family with our wider commitments. This balance can go disastrously wrong, when family members pamper one another but care nothing for the wider world, or when the loyal church worker, local councillor or pressure group activist, neglects their family (see 3.2).

15.2 Loyalty

We move to consider the virtue of *loyalty*, not discussed earlier. Most will feel positively about loyalty, and yet loyalty is not an unqualified good. We do not admire without qualification those loyal to their terrorist cell, or the loyalty of Himmler to Hitler. The virtue of loyalty must be qualified by the insistence that the object of our loyalty is proper. That said, loyalty is the stuff of decent human relationships. Loyalty is about being committed to the other person's well-being, even when it does not coincide exactly with my own. They show loyalty who *'sweareth unto their neighbour and disappointeth them not, though it were to their own hindrance'*.[2] Loyalty is about staying with people. It is about being reliable and trustworthy.

Loyalty is a key virtue in person to person relationships. At the same time, we may show loyalty to nations, to churches, to schools, universities, firms, regiments, and so forth. The reality is, national and institutional loyalty is much out of fashion and our modern mindset finds it difficult to find reason to be loyal beyond our intimate circle. This is understandable but our common life is impoverished as a result. Ideally, in this book I should buck the trend and address head on the question of institutional loyalty. There is not space, however, to consider every topic. Instead, I follow the trend and treat the virtue of loyalty as part of a discussion of person to person relationships. I therefore move to the paradigmatic instance of loyalty – that expressed in marriage.

A commitment to loyalty is central to the understanding of the marriage covenant expressed in Christian marriage rites, and at root Christians may see such a loyalty as reflecting God's covenant loyalty to us.

The vows of marriage involve a deliberate opting out of the mindset of the consumer, where husbands or wives are commodities delivering companionship, status, comfort, security and sex. There is rather a commitment to discovering together, through that commitment, a mutual fulfilment. It would be wrong to see loyalty as a crutch to put in the cupboard, only to be taken out to enable a failing marriage to hobble along. Loyalty is not there simply to take over when delight and sparkle fade. It is rather the covenant commitment to loyalty which feeds and nourishes the delight and sparkle. The commitment of marriage: 'I take thee, for better for worse ...' is not a threat, but a promise and a gift: 'Whatever happens we can rely on each other.'[3]

Does this mean that divorce is never possible – that the commitment of loyalty is absolute? The Roman Catholic Church's official teaching is that marriage is indissoluble. Its pastoral response to a failed marriage is either to allow separation (precluding, of course, remarriage) or to explore the possibility of an annulment. Divorce dissolves a marriage, while an annulment declares that what appears to have been a marriage never in fact was one. Practices vary, so, in fact, grounds for annulment may sometimes be more 'generous' than grounds for divorce.

Protestants have sometimes neared the position that marriage is *de facto* indissoluble. For both Catholic and Protestant traditions the argument here may be that the vow of marriage is absolute. It expresses the total and irrevocable gift of covenant love. There is, however, a certain linguistic fundamentalism in reading the vow in this way. It is difficult to see how the duty to honour a commitment to another person can be absolute in all circumstances; and if someone so regards it, it is a work of supererogation**, not an obligation. Marriage is a commitment to a *mutual* relationship. The vows are taken by *both parties*. The marriage commitment thus differs from those that are one-sided, like the commitment to repay a debt. It is crucially significant that both parties make the vow. The vow is to finding richness in life *together*. There can be no covenant without mutuality and reciprocity. If either husband or wife fails in a persistent and blatant way to honour the vow, the other party can reasonably claim to be no longer in a position to be able to keep theirs. The commitment is to a marriage relationship and it takes two to make a relationship. One party is, in effect, released from their vow because the other party has made it impossible for them to fulfil it. One is released by the death of the marriage as much as the physical death of a spouse. There remains no benefit arising from mutual devotion. All this is apart from those instances when a couple grow apart and by mutual agreement release each other from their vows. Presupposed here is an acceptance of 'irretrievable breakdown' of marriage as a ground for divorce such as is the basis for the current law in England.

Some who defend indissolubility stress the irrevocable self-gift of the partners to each other. But what about when there is no mutuality or reciprocity? What about when things turn destructive and appropriate weight is to be given to a proper self-love?

None of this suggests that divorce should be or ever is easy. It very rarely is, in terms of emotions, money, children and the wider context. Furthermore, it is not being suggested that people should up sticks at the first problem. The commitment to loyalty will prompt people to work at their relationship, and work generously. For many, there has been a poignancy about the commitment 'for better for worse, for richer and for poorer, in sickness and in health' and, as a result, life has been nobler. It remains true, however, that the commitment to loyalty cannot be absolute in all circumstances. The Church has sometimes exercised a tyranny over people with lives made miserable by a rotten marriage, demanding that they honour a commitment that is not recip-rocated. Sometimes, a person's proper commitment to their own health and happiness can come to have precedence over their vow, especially if there is abuse or violence. The Church does better to acknowledge this than to pile on the guilt.

In a society deeply moulded by consumerism, Christians can be counter-cultural and bear witness to finding in a mutual commitment a richer fulfilment than is given through serial monogamy where the focus may be more on gaining individual satisfaction. 'Whosoever shall seek their life shall lose it.' The divorce rate is indeed alarming, and may *in part* betray a mindset that sees marriage more as a provi-sional consumer choice than as a covenant. On the other hand, a lot of Christian rhetoric deploring the divorce rate is in danger of becoming shallow moralizing. The higher divorce rate is largely a function of people living longer, changing more, and having higher expectations, together with a more compassionate divorce law and an absence of social stigma. It is certainly a function of women having greater self-esteem and greater economic security. These are all positive things. Maybe our cultural mores do not support people in their marriages as they should. We dare not twitch an eyelid at the man who divorces for the sake of a younger trophy wife, owing his success to his first wife and his second wife to his success. Blatant disloyalty does exist and people are grievously let down. But it is not certain that the sum total of happiness was higher in earlier times when marriages also failed and when spouses were also abused, but with no release on account of a stricter law, a strong social stigma and, above all, the economic dependence of a wife upon her husband. It is possible there was just as much unhappiness then; but there was no means of escape.

There is a counter argument to all this, deeply unfashionable to-day. This is that where divorce is not a possibility, people live within a secure framework of expectation and are prompted to work at their marriages, and with strong social support. This will be rough for some, but overall less rough for the majority than when divorce is readily available and where there is little support for life-long marriage in the social mores. This argument receives powerful statement in Pius XI's *Casti Connubii*.[4] It is related to a very English emphasis on marriage as an 'estate', the social role subordinating the quality of the relationship.[5] Lord William Rees Mogg has offered an essentially utilitarian argument for the indissolubility of marriage. Acknowledging many marriages will be unhappy, the overall well-being of society and its citizens is, nonetheless, found within a tight structure, a structure which, not least, makes people more responsible in considering marriage and more determined to tackle difficulties. More people, and not least children, are harmed by a 'high divorce' society than are helped by the availability of release. 'Modern marriage can be a cruel thing, but mass divorce can be far, far more cruel.'[6] The argument is essentially that we cannot be trusted to treat divorce as a last resort and to accept a massive onus against it. Greater availability of divorce and the decline of social stigma undermines commitment and leads, at worst, to a spouse being easily exchanged for one more attractive and, at best, to the strains and stresses of 'serial monogamy'. All this adds to rather than diminishes human suffering.

It is reasonable to be anxious that our weaker social mores undermine the security of marriage, bringing vulnerability to some. It is certainly proper to challenge a culture in which people may view lightly vows of loyalty and personal responsibility. It is by no means proven, however, that, on the whole, people were happier under a tighter regime. Many women in particular were condemned to unhappy and even abusive marriages with no means of escape. The eulogy on the 'benefits of indissolubility' in *Casti Connubii*, while speaking some truth, betrays sentimentality and a lack of realism. Even when a society regards marriage as indissoluble, there will be the safety valve of annulment and separation. And where is the logic in allowing separation but not divorce? In modern Britain, returning to a significantly stricter law is hardly an option anyway, even if it were desirable. People will ask why they should sacrifice happiness for the sake of the 'institution of marriage', and why good marriages are helped by preserving bad ones. It seems best to try to combine, on the one hand, a strong belief in loyalty and commitment, with, on the other, a compassionate recognition that marriages fail and that people may be seriously let down. This has been the stance adopted more by the Orthodox and Free Churches in Britain. We are bound to fail, but it is not obvious we fail less through this than did our forebears under tighter legal restrictions backed up by the old stigmas.

15.3 Sexuality

Imagine a map of a valley. A glacier then travels down the valley leaving a deep imprint on the terrain. The valley is recognizably the same, but it has been radically changed. It is a moot point how valuable the old map now is. The contours of traditional Christian sexual ethics were formed at a time when the landscape was very different, but a glacier has now reshaped it.

To leave the metaphor behind, changes have taken place over the past few decades regarding our approach to human sexuality. How illuminating are the old answers when the questions are often new? Can we with integrity repeat the sexual ethic of the past without recognizing how radically new is the setting we now face? There will be much insight of the past to be appropriated. We may also be deeply critical of some contemporary approaches, the commodification of the female body, and now increasingly the male, and a communal voyeurism that offers the role model for us all in the sexual athletics of the young, slim and firm. This is not exactly pastorally sensitive to the single,[7] the widowed and people with disabilities. The sexual disadvantage of the latter is an issue in itself. That we face a new situation is hardly in doubt, and old answers do not always fit new questions.

15.3.1 Traditional approaches

The western Christian tradition is diverse and it can be perilous to make generalizations. Nevertheless, the main contours of its approaches to sexuality seem clear enough, contours imposed on deeply patriarchal terrain. First, while not inherently sinful, sexual passion tends to be disordered. This led to sexual passion and sexual pleasure being regarded somewhat negatively. Second, there is a reluctance to integrate sexuality with the person, and thus to acknowledge that sexuality may feed and nourish a relationship of love. In this suspicion of sexual passion the early Church fathers were offering little that was essentially new. They were following more the classical tradition of Pythagoras and the Stoics, neglecting the more positive view of their own Hebrew Scriptures.[8] The failure to integrate an understanding of sexuality and love is more Aristotelian than Hebraic. Incidentally, a patriarchal mindset put the emphasis more on how disordered sexual desire might damage a man, and less on how it might damage a women with whom a man has a sexual relationship.

Of course, it is sex that has kept the human race going, although it may seem deplorable that the Almighty did not come up with a more seemly way of producing the next generation! In consequence, we meet the third feature of mainstream traditional understanding. Sex is permissible for procreation and must be confined to those occasions when it is responsible to procreate. Its institutional confinement to marriage provides the context for the nurture of children, their social placement and, where appropriate, properly identifies the beneficiary of the father's estate. Marriage as a relationship is, for the well-to-do, often subordinate to the interests of property.

This leads to the fourth feature, still urged by Vatican theology. Procreation is an essential end of sexual intercourse, and we must not separate the 'procreative' from what Vatican documents generally call the 'unitive'. The preamble to the 1662 Prayer Book order for the Solemnization of Matrimony gives the game away. It speaks of sex in a very negative manner and in no way integrates it with its fine vision of 'mutual society help and comfort'. What happens in bed appears in the preamble to be an unfortunate necessity for the purposes of procreation and is not, in contrast to modern marriage service liturgies, seen as nourishing the 'mutual society'.

One legacy of this tradition is that it has encouraged us (and maybe males in particular) to think of sexuality overmuch in terms of a highly charged eroticism, the genital and the penetrative. Yet our sexuality is not just about the genital. It is also about the passionate delight that two embodied people may feel for each other. Passion aside, our sexuality connects with that part of our nature which reaches out to the other in warmth and in a desire to share. Sexuality is not just about intense physical desire, and we need not retreat into old style negativity in order to be uneasy about an exaltation of the erotic and the genital over and against covenant love and companionship, and their separation even more so.

This leads us to a deep ambivalence evident in contemporary western culture. On the one hand, the media is engaged in an exercise of mass titillation, which concentrates upon the erotic, feeding us with a constant stream of sexually charged images with the implied promise of easily available sexual ecstasy. So high now is our expectation that even images of the world's supermodels require computer enhancement. The Church should not feel too ashamed because Augustine failed to treat us to a preview of Hollywood eroticism. Unless integrated with companionship, a decent relationship and a love that sanctifies the erotic, eroticism and sexual passion can be a cruel joker in the pack of human emotions. Without a relationship of depth and decency, sexuality is the occasion of many a mocked dream, let alone exploitation, control, humiliation and abuse. The sheer *power* of our sexual passion, overt or sublimated, unleashing both destructive and life-enhancing potential, may be missed in Singer's claim that sexuality raises no unique moral problems.[9] The modern obsession with the erotic leaves us unclear as to the relationship between our sexuality and human need for companionship and secure relationships. Pornography, now instantly available through the internet, almost by definition, invites a focus on the *body*, ignoring the *person*, seeing the other as an object for sexual gratification rather than as a person to respect, cherish, honour and love.

Yet, on the other hand, contemporary culture is positive about how our sexuality may feed and nourish a relationship of companionship and mutual delight. For this reason, despite all the dangers of distortion, we see sexuality as a great gift. Few outside the Vatican and those loyal to its teaching have any serious moral qualms about deliberately separating sexuality from fertility. Many adopt an essentially *personalistic* approach, sex being about nourishing and enjoying a relationship that is special. Not only may we therefore approach the erotic positively, we must also take it seriously. It can become destructive, both of ourselves and of others whom we damage. The erotic flourishes, however, not on its own but within a relationship of decency and love. A Christian realism about sin will be alert to the pitfalls. But a Christian confidence about grace will see the possibility of a great richness through a shared desire and a shared empathy. Relationships are not inevitably abusive or exploitative. They are the principal source of our flourishing.

A 'personalistic' approach has been facilitated by the invention of reliable contraception, a change of massive magnitude. For most of human history sexuality could not be easily separated from procreation. If people had sex, the likelihood was that a baby would soon be on its way. Contraception has allowed us to separate the two, enjoying our sexuality without having to worry overmuch about an unwanted pregnancy. But traditional sexual ethics have been riveted to the inseparability of sex and fertility and the need to exercise our fertility responsibly.[10] If the two can now be separated, how much of the old ethic is still intact? Contraception, of course, has given women control over their own fertility, making it easier to combine motherhood with a career or other things, thus encouraging true mutuality and equal social power in relationships. This is why Lisa Cahill finds ambiguity in John Paul II's many and impressive protests against injustice for woman and the sinfulness of subordination to men, while at the same time insisting 'motherhood must constitute the primary identity of women'.[11]

Traditional Christian morality has widely insisted that sex must be confined to those who are married.[12] Sex before marriage is fornication – however loving and deep the friendship. The injunction 'no sex before marriage' is not quite as clear as it may sound. For a start, what do we mean if we say of a couple that they are married? Is marriage created by the wedding? Or is it created by the coming into being of a relationship of a certain kind? If so, the wedding legally and publicly ratifies what is already the case. As such, weddings, legally socially and liturgically, have a profound significance. But they do not create a marriage. It is the couple who create their own marriage by the nature of their relationship. In consequence, when we speak of 'sex before marriage' do we speak of sex before a ceremony, or of sex before the coming into being of a relationship such as to make sex appropriate? Thus, Adrian Thatcher suggests that engagement or 'betrothal', rather than the wedding, is the crucial point.[13] The fact that a significant proportion of marriages in western history have been 'common law marriages' is sufficient to show that this is a serious question.

Moreover, if we say a couple cannot have sex before marriage, what do we mean by having sex? Do we mean only penetrative vaginal sex or do we prohibit also, say, mutual masturbation and oral sex? Such subtle distinctions were debated in Washington during Bill Clinton's presidency, and upon them depended the fate of a mighty nation. And how far are people allowed to go? What about what was once quaintly called 'heavy petting'? Furthermore, talk about vaginal penetration, masturbation and oral sex, may betray a certain male perspective since orgasm has a prominence in male sexual needs, which it may not have for some women. Suppose two people 'sleep like spoons' enjoying physical intimacy? Are they 'having sex'?

It might be protested that such questions are outrageous and intolerably intrusive upon people's private lives. The matter should be left to the mature and responsible judgement of those involved. But in insisting that there be 'no sex before marriage', this is precisely what the moralist refuses to do. But with what justification?

15.3.2 Reasons for 'traditional' sexual morality

The stringency of this question is reinforced by asking why traditional Christian teaching has proscribed sex outside marriage, and if these reasons still apply today.

It seems there were at least four reasons.

The first reason is probably the most significant. It was to avoid what was called 'illegitimacy'. Now if sex could not be separated from making babies, there is a lot to be said for an ethic that confined sex to those who are legally married. It is irresponsible to bring a baby into the world without legal lineage and proper care and nurture. In particular, it is irresponsible of a man to have sex if he then deserts his partner, quite literally holding the baby. Before contraception, the hard and fast rule was arguably necessary to protect women and to protect any children who might be born as a result of people's passion. Paradoxically, the absence of contraception sometimes encouraged a double standard. Fear of unwanted pregnancy within marriage implicitly allowed men (but only men, of course) to resort to prostitutes.

It is worth commenting that if contemporary Christians defend the old ethic, they normally do so for new reasons. Traditionally, the ethic was defended as necessary to avoid illegitimacy. It is more usual today to appeal to personalistic considerations.[14] In other words, the wait until the wedding night nourishes best the relationship. This argument will have cogency for some. It is 'right for them', given how they feel and given the kind of people they are, but it is important to note that this argument, while not absent in the tradition, was invariably sub-ordinate to the argument that the rule was necessary to avoid illegiti-macy. An old ethic is thus being supported by a new reason. That is okay, as long as we acknowledge what we are doing. When we do it, however, our claim to be 'traditionalists', suspicious of those who give in too much to 'modern standards', is weakened.

The second reason has already been alluded to. The old ethic pro-tected women from irresponsible sexual predators. After all, any fleeting liaison, without aid of condoms, could lead a woman into pregnancy with a baby to support but with no man to support her. I speak, of course, of a society where women usually had little bargain-ing power and often meagre means of supporting themselves. Now people enter into relationships more as equals and with more economic independence.

The third reason has likewise already been alluded to. A mindset that was suspicious of sexual needs and discouraging of people to value sexual pleasure saw no reason to challenge an ethic that might cause considerable strain. Incredibly, until the 1960s the British Methodist Church insisted that a minister could not marry until after ordination. Suppose a couple were engaged and the man (deplorably it was only men in those days) sensed a vocation to ordained ministry. Let us sup-pose further that they both had healthy libidos. They were supposed to forgo maybe up to seven years of a sexual relationship until ordination. But this was accepted without protest in a culture that subordinated people to the rules and did not rate too highly the importance of sexual pleasure and sexual fulfilment.

A fourth reason sees sexual passion as strong and potentially dam-aging. Sexual passion needs to be channelled lest we damage ourselves and others. Its channelling is found within marriage. We find this em-phasis especially in Luther and Calvin. 'The temptation of the flesh has become so strong and consuming', declares Luther, 'that marriage may be likened to a hospital for incurables which prevents inmates from falling into a graver sin ... In this way God sees to it that the flesh is subdued so as not to rage wherever and however it pleases.'[15] No doubt the premise of this argument contains a lot of sense. It is not clear, however, that the conclusion drawn from it follows, neither is it clear the premise justifies a too easy excuse for inappropriate behaviour when people are 'carried away'. We need also to be aware of a misogynist strand in the Christian tradition, which sees women, unless they be Madonnas, as temptresses. If male sexual desire becomes incontrollable, then, of course, it is the woman who is to be blamed. It is outrageous that in the Church still the prejudice is around in some quarters that if a man behaves improperly, then it is the woman's fault for being too tempting.

15.3.3 A more personalistic approach

The above paragraphs offer a map of the territory as it was when a traditional Christian sexual ethic was constructed. But – to return to our metaphor – a glacier has driven down the valley, gouging afresh the landscape. How sound a guide is the old map?

Much contemporary Christian teaching repeats the old ethic of 'no sex outside marriage'. The British Methodist Conference in 1993 solemnly resolved (but only by a slender majority) '*Conference reaffirms the traditional teaching of the Church on human sexuality; namely chastity for all outside marriage and fidelity within it.*' This resolution is about politics as much as ethics; that is 'politics' in the honourable sense, meaning an exercise of 'give and take' which keeps people together. This offers some excuse for the deeply disingenuous appeal to the '*traditional teaching of the Church on human sexuality*'. Most modern Methodists would run a mile if they thought about what that teaching often has been. The resolution displays measured ambiguity such as is sometimes unavoidable when presented for adoption by a large body. If we are clever, we can point out (and with complete integrity) that the word 'chastity' is ambiguous. It can mean something like 'decency, sensitivity and integrity in sexual relations' rather than 'sexual abstinence'. Nonetheless, most people will interpret this as meaning 'no sex before the wedding'. A leading figure in 'Alpha', Nicolas Gumbel, likewise counsels 'no sex before marriage', by which he appears to mean 'no sex before the wedding' and even counsels a new convert in a sexual relationship to stop having sex.[16] Gumbel's approach is essentially 'Ockhamist' – we must follow the teaching of Scripture, which contains the 'maker's instructions'.[17]

There are two problems with Gumbel's approach. First, his claim that the Bible declares sex before marriage to be wrong begs mammoth questions of interpretation. Yes – there are warnings about 'sexual immorality' in the New Testament but to interpret these as condemning sex before a legal ceremony in radically different modern contexts is highly contentious to say the least. When the Bible speaks about marriage, it speaks of an institution very different from that in modern Britain. A variety of sexual expressions is often reported without embarrassment and surprise, and certainly without censure. An example is Genesis 38. Polygamy is nowhere condemned, and even commended in Levirate marriage when a man takes responsibility for his brother's widow. Even Abraham has a child by his slave without censure. This is in stark contrast to the way the prophets and the Deuteronomic history scrutinize rigorously the unjust behaviour of the kings. Often the assumptions behind biblical attitudes to sexuality are deeply patriarchal. The thrust of biblical teaching may arguably be towards an appeal in our sexual relationships to maintain honour, integrity and purity. (I say 'arguably'. It is not certain the biblical writers generally thought of a sexual relationship in personalistic terms.) But to say that the 'Bible teaches' that sex must be confined to what we call legal marriage is too sweeping. The most we can say is that it could be *implied* by a few selected texts. None of the texts Gumbel quotes says unambiguously what he wants them to say.

The second difficulty is that Gumbel adopts an essentially 'Ockhamist' approach in appealing to the authority of an ancient text (see 4.2). But suppose we insist the 'glorious liberty of the people of God' allows us to enquire ourselves into the right and the good, discovering a stance which has a rationale in terms of our mutual flourishing and appropriate relationships? Gumbel does indeed insist that the maker's instructions are 'given out of love' thereby departing from an unqualified Ockhamist approach.[18] He offers arguments for his position, but they amount to little more than warnings against irresponsibility in sexual behaviour. The question is begged when it is assumed that consensual sex before a ceremony is *always* irresponsible. He tells stories of those who have been glad they have waited for their wedding night. But who is presuming to criticize those who judge that this is right for them? To urge this as an absolute imperative for everyone is very different. There might even be a danger that the restriction encourages an unwise and premature marriage.

Gumbel is so sure of his position that he boldly warns those who disagree with him that they may be 'hurting God'. Warning that sex before marriage 'cuts us off from him' he continues: 'It is impossible to hold together a wholehearted love and service of God and disobedience in the area of sexual morality.'[19] The 'disobedience' here is sex before marriage. Many Christian couples who enjoy a sexual relationship before their wedding will protest loudly at Gumbel's presumption here.

Gumbel's arguments in favour of a universal prohibition of sex before a wedding are unlikely to persuade many who are not already convinced. The arguments read like ideology marshalled to support a position held on other grounds. Let's try another approach. Let us ask about *criteria* for *moral sex*. This coheres with the approach of this book – ethics is about discerning ourselves what manner of life is a fitting response to what we believe about God. It is further about discovering what leads to our mutual well-being, and the commitments to decent relationships that serve that well-being.

Alan Goldman asks about criteria for moral sex. In a robustly argued paper he defends 'recreational' or 'plain' sex – what at the beach party is known less politely as 'shagging'. Even the most casual of friends can enjoy a meal together or going to the theatre. The absence of a deep relationship, let alone lifelong commitment, does not make this in any way wrong. Why should sex be different? Suppose two people meet on holiday? They have healthy libidos, fancy each other's bodies and enjoy the comfort and thrill of intimacy. They enjoy sex together rather as they might enjoy a meal. Having sex and eating food are simply different ways of enjoying physical pleasure. It is simply 'no strings' sex, mutually pleasurable and by mutual consent. What is wrong with that? Goldman is not defending an 'anything goes' hedonism. He is trying to find criteria for moral sex, and he offers two.[20] I have added a third, which is I think implicit:

- Mutual consent.
- Mutual pleasure.
- No disloyalty to a third person.

There is a stringency in Goldman's criteria, writing as he is in the long tradition of 'contractual' approaches to sex.[21] The insistence upon mutual consent guards against manipulation, exploitation and abuse of power. There appears to be also an assumption of an equal relationship. A lot of sex in marriage fails by these criteria. Goldman agrees that a lifelong commitment will give a significant extra to a sexual relationship – as it would attending the Last Night of the Proms. But two people can still enjoy sex together, and also enjoy the Proms, without a deep relationship, still less a life commitment.

Are these criteria sufficient for moral sex? There is a difficulty in Goldman's comparison between enjoying a meal with a casual acquaintance and enjoying sex. Making good sex is not as easy as making a good risotto. It does not always turn out according to the recipe. Even for the well-toned sexual athletes it can go wrong, and there needs to be a relationship of tenderness and trust to avoid shame and embarrassment. But more importantly, when two people share a meal their vulnerability to each other is limited. The sharing is not total, but only as they judge appropriate to the relationship. Sex, by its nature, involves total vulnerability and total self-giving.[22] Making love betokens and expresses sacramentally that full giving and receiving. There are profound differences between having sex and having a meal, differences such as to make it appropriate only in a relationship with sufficient depth to bear it. Sex is likely to damage and hurt rather than nourish if it is for physical pleasure alone. Nothing is said about present and ongoing responsibility the partners have for each other, or a decency requiring self-discipline. Such values, along with love and fidelity, are subordinated to autonomous choice and instant pleasure. Sex, however, is about loving and cherishing; uniting persons and not just bodies. If this persuades we have a fourth criterion for moral sex. Moral sex presupposes:

- A relationship of a sufficient depth and love such as to bear it.

Many will be persuaded by this,[23] but not everyone. In the above paragraph, so it may be urged, I have not been describing sex as it is for everyone. I have been describing sex only for a particular mental paradigm. Many in the Christian tradition have been formed to see sex in this way. Essentially this is an appeal to a 'natural law' argument (see 3.10). Sex 'by nature' is not just about physical urge and physical pleasure. It is about bonding. Sex is cheapened and potentially damaging if we have the former without the latter. Here, however, we meet the stringent challenge of those strands of thinking that might be labelled 'postmodern'. Postmodernism, like existentialism, is highly suspicious of the idea that we are constrained by some 'given' in human nature, and therefore in human sexuality in particular. Of course, some people experience their sexuality as being such as to be appropriately expressed only in this kind of relationship. But not everyone has a mindset formed in that way. As Foucault argued, our sexuality is formed within a cultural context. For some there is nothing about their experience of sexuality that makes 'serial shagging' in any way damaging. Sexuality is a social construct, and different people are constructed differently. Sexuality does not have some 'essential' nature beyond its cultural construction. For Goldman, some at least have no difficulty in separating sex for physical pleasure from its personal dimensions. Sex, apart from its cultural construct, is simply a physical act and, as such, morally neutral. Sex is wrong only if it involves deceit, abuse, exploitation, and such like. But these are general moral precepts, which have nothing to do with sex as such.

Does this mean I am making a mistake similar to Gumbel's? Gumbel assumes the testimony of those who have found it good to 'wait for the wedding night' offers an imperative for everyone. Likewise, I have assumed, as an imperative for all, the idea that sex is about bonding and cherishing, and not merely physical urges. There is, however, no such thing as our 'sexual nature'. It all depends on how culture along with the mishmash of other things has formed us as we are.

This is a disturbing thought; but it gets worse. I offered above the criterion – moral sex must presuppose and express *relationships of a sufficient depth to bear it*. This, however, is deplorably, or delightfully, vague. The argument of the last paragraph is strongest when we focus on a deep and special relationship. But the deep and the special need not express a lifelong commitment. Suppose I offer a further criterion? To be moral sex must:

- Express life long commitment.

Let me not be misunderstood. There is no difficulty about defending robustly a sexual relationship expressing a lifelong commitment. There is ample evidence in human experience that such relationships yield rich joy and fulfilment and nourish people at many levels. This is even more so when there is a long-term responsibility for children. There is something deeply noble in the mutual commitment of marriage. That is not in doubt. Not in doubt also is the characteristically Christian insight – in many ways counter-cultural – that in entering into a commitment we are mining a rich seam of human experience. The act of commitment helps to create, and does not simply express, the love and bonding. None of this need be in doubt. It need not follow, however, that all sex, apart from that expressing a lifelong commitment, is *ipso facto* immoral. The reality is, many deliberately enter relationships of short-term provisional commitments. Are they always intrinsically, and by virtue of that fact, immoral? Why must morally permissible sex, when parenting is excluded, be so narrowly restricted?

There is a final criterion. Moral sex must not only satisfy the above criteria, but must also:

- Express an 'exclusive' relationship.

After all, the vows of Christian marriage services normally include a phrase such as 'forsaking all others'. This does not exclude friendships beyond the marriage. Quite the contrary, marriage relationships can become too inward looking, and to everyone's impoverishment. One of the dangers of modern marriage is that our culture can form us into expecting too much from one person. There is, however, a *sexual* exclusivity about marriage. There is no difficulty in justifying a severe condemnation of adultery as usually defined. Adultery, by definition, is clandestine and involves deceit, knowing one's partner would feel hurt and betrayed. There is disloyalty to a promise and covenant. But what about 'open marriages' where there are other relationships, although normally only with specified persons, or a specified person, with full knowledge and consent, and sometimes sharing the same household?

In western societies these can even be seen as a privatized form of poly-gamy. Is sexually exclusive monogamy an inviolable moral absolute for all people, for all times and all cultures? Thus, there are those who defend mutually consensual 'open marriages' as an option for some.[24]

It is reasonable to be deeply anxious here because we are playing with fire. Wisdom suggests a massive onus against anything other than an exclusive sexual relationship. Not many are happy about being shared at the most intimate level. The potentialities for jealousy and hurt are too great. Full consent may be professed, but there is the danger of the weaker partner being manipulated into giving it. Equality in such re-lationships will be massively more difficult to attain. As for polygamy – simple demography dictates that the strong and the wealthy will bene-fit and the poor will be left alone. The maths do not add up, although in a community where the male population has been decimated by war there may be a pragmatic case for it. To say the least, if the criterion is honouring the well-being of persons, there are massive warning signs by this particular road. But can we say that *in the nature of the case and in all conceivable circumstances and in all possible cultural con-texts all sexual relationships must be exclusive*? This is a question with which the churches in Africa, in particular, have wrestled.[25]

Moving back nearer home let us consider two young people in their late twenties who plan to marry. They want a suitable celebration and find the wedding takes about a year to arrange. By mutual consent and to the delight of both they commence a sexual relationship before the wedding and in any case they simply cannot afford separate accommo-dation. On what grounds is this condemned? Are they in the nature of the case damaging themselves and their relationship because they do not wait for the wedding? Maybe they are damaged more by Christian censure – that is if they bother to listen.

Or suppose a man and a woman are in their fifities. One, let us say, is widowed and the other single. For various reasons they do not feel it is right to marry. They do not feel that level of life and home sharing is right for them, given their situation. But they are intensively fond of each other as 'best friends'. They meet up twice a week and at least some times share sexual intimacy. It is by mutual consent. They find deep comfort in it and there is no third party to whom they are being disloyal. On what grounds – beyond appealing to an 'inscrutable ought' – can this be said to be wrong?

I have posed a series of difficult questions, and it is not clear they all admit of simple answers. Yet again we find ourselves facing ambiguity and uncertainty. But perhaps we should be unnerved by this only if we are looking for rules that are universally binding – or for that matter just one rule: no sex before a wedding. There do remain firm stand-ards, but they are standards that inform our judgement rather than lay down rules. They are standards that help us to discover mutual flourishing. Basic decency requires Goldman's criterion of mutual consent. Furthermore, despite Foucault's scepticism, many will be convinced that there is something very special about a sexual relationship. It is not only about a deep urge for physical pleasure. It is about love and cherishing at the deepest level. The special bonding requires a special relationship. Furthermore, Christians, of all people, will want to bear witness to lifelong commitments as answering a deep human need, and further to warn that an irresponsible sexual relationship can damage and impoverish us. The old rules warn us of the potential for damage. There is a proper temperance and restraint. All this adds up to a demanding and stringent ethic of decency.[26] But how different people, with different feelings and needs, and in their own differently nuanced relationships, judge how that decency is expressed will leave us with a lot of untidiness. It is not clear this is a bad thing, and it is not clear people are more damaged by this than by the old rules.

15.3.4 Social mores and conventions

All this, however, may appear far too *Guardian*. Let's see how things might look if we are *Daily Telegraph*. It might be protested that we are giving ourselves far too much freedom. It is all very well to commend decency. But does not this expect too much of people? Do people have the maturity and integrity to act responsibly? Give them an inch and they will take an ell. Does not human frailty require that we have firm social mores to protect us from ourselves? Where in a world of autonomous choice is the protection for people who want 'to wait'? What is claimed to be based on consent may, in fact, be based on conquest – an 'acquiescence rape'. Where is the protection for women, say, who do not bargain with equal social power? It is all very well celebrating the invention of good contraceptives, but people do not always use them. Teenage pregnancy is higher now than at any other time. The old rules may have been irksome, but they protected us from the worst of our follies. The sacrifice of freedom and autonomy is a price worth paying for the safeguards the old rules give us.

This counter argument brings us to a tension, which is seen perhaps most acutely over sexuality. On the one hand, it is true that the old rules and conventions did offer guidance and protection. On the other hand, however, they prevented us from enjoying the freedoms given by our hard-won autonomy. Furthermore, the rules were deeply paternalistic. Do we opt for the old rules and, for the sake of the rough and ready safeguards they offer, forgo our freedom and autonomy? Do we thereby also forgo a great deal of comfort and well-being and all that a sexual relationship, previously forbidden, can nourish? There are strengths in this position, but there are also serious weaknesses. That said, it is the position many Christians are nostalgic about, and they try to recreate it in their own Christian subculture. Indeed, in some sections of the Christian community a distinctive sexual ethic is one of the marks of being a Christian.

Alternatively, do we claim the trust to make our own judgements as to what is appropriate for us, constrained indeed by the stringent personalistic ethic outlined above, but by that alone? Mistakes will be made and people will be damaged. But people were damaged by the old rules and regulations as well. It is not clear that human well-being is served best by a paternalism, which does not trust us to judge for ourselves and to learn, including learning by making mistakes. Furthermore, teenage pregnancy is a complicated social phenomenon and is not just a function of lax sexual mores. Many other factors may be involved.

Moreover, it is not clear a return to the old rules is a realistic option. Once the genie of freedom is out of the bottle it is extraordinarily difficult to squeeze it back, even if that were right. Maybe Christians should be less nostalgic about the old rules, trusting people more, and being less censorious. Perhaps Christians have been too heavy-handed about sex, treating crimes of passion as the worst crimes in the book, when often they are among the least. At their worst (although happily they are not always at their worst) Christians can be heavy on, for example, the 'woman caught in adultery' while ignoring the failure of her husband to 'love and to cherish, to honour and to comfort and to keep', a failure which has driven her to adultery. It follows that the emphasis should be, not upon tidying up the rules, but upon nurturing qualities of responsibility, purity, loyalty and attendance to the other. When we manifest these qualities, we can be trusted to sort out our own sex lives. This also is part of what is meant by the glorious liberty of the people of God.

In Britain in the past marriage was often seen much more as an 'estate', with social functions such as nurturing children, and upheld in draconian fashion by a strict divorce law and strong social norms. Today, relationships have become more privatized, resulting in greater instability and there is mounting evidence that this is not serving well our children. This is a serious concern. Nostalgia for the past, however, solves little and, in any case, the patterns of the past brought their own brand of misery. Furthermore, the emphasis of this section on a personalistic ethic of decency, issuing in loyalty, commitment and responsibility, balks rather than fuels this trend. That said, we need more than a personal ethic. We need as a society to address the question of family policy and supportive social mores. These are not easy questions.

'Chastity' is a slippery word. The 24-volume *Oxford English Dictionary* points to two basic meanings. It may be synonymous with sexual abstinence. But the word 'chastity' may also mean something like 'maintaining honour, decency and integrity in sexual, and indeed all, relationships'. This meaning resonates more with the perspective of 'virtue' ethics (see 3.8). For this meaning, 'chastity' is not about prohibitions before a wedding and keeping to timetables. It is about approaching *all* sexual relationships with decency, responsibility, integrity and sensitivity and attendance to the other. What, however, that will mean in the infinite variety of differently and delicately nuanced relationships must be left to the judgement of the people concerned. The Methodist Conference spoke of 'chastity *outside* marriage and fidelity within', despite the fact that one of the century's key documents on Christian marriage spoke of chastity *within* marriage.[27] Furthermore, by juxtaposing 'chastity outside marriage' and 'fidelity within', it thereby stressed *sexual* fidelity, which, important though it is, neglects the wider fidelity, which loves and cherishes, honours and comforts and keeps. A more demanding ethic would speak of chastity and fidelity characterizing all our relationships.

If we get it wrong and people are damaged, then that is serious. But it is serious because people are damaged, not because of the sex. It is not clear why we should regard sex with such gravity apart from its capacity to nourish or to harm; although it has *special* capacity to cause *grave* harm. If this section has been full of ambiguities and unresolved questions we should not be too troubled. When Whitehead said God is 'somewhat oblivious as to morals',[28] he did not mean God does not care about the kind of people we are. He meant rather that the focus should be, not on rules, but on love, integrity, loyalty and responsibility in our relating. Maybe God is much more oblivious as to how we express that in our sexual relationships than are some of God's earthly representatives.

Furthermore, the Church needs massively to focus upon self-awareness and self-criticism. Sexual ethics can become a pitch on which we play the game of power politics between differing groups within the Church. Sexual need is strong and ubiquitous and in our sexual need we are deeply vulnerable. The Church needs to be aware of the temptation to exploit this as a way of controlling people. The subject can become a kind of ethical mascot, the procession of which gives us high moral ground on which to offer 'certainty' to the 'confusion' of the modern world. And a preoccupation with timetables and prohibitions can cause us to neglect the need for guidance and support for people seeking to develop wholesome relationships. Furthermore, a fixation on what people should not do *outside* marriage should not blind us to the indictment of Marxism and feminism that *within* marriage and family there can be exploitation, abuse and oppression.[29] It is deplorable how a fixation on the sin of 'fornication' has sometimes combined with blindness and complacency over how badly a husband or wife can treat their partner.

Can we summarize the theology and ethic suggested by our discussion? It sees a sexual relationship as *at one level* one type of human relationship, and the normal values of decency, sensitivity, loyalty and such like, guide us. At *another level*, however, it sees sexuality as bound up intimately with our nature as embodied. Our sexuality must consequently be treated with appropriate seriousness. Sexuality can both damage and nourish us. Sexuality nourishes when it is about bonding and cherishing as part of a covenant relationship. This theology and ethic delights in procreation where desired, but sees nothing wrong in separating the relational from the procreative dimensions of sex. Procreation aside, our sexuality will still delight in, nourish and enjoy a special relationship of fidelity and love.

15.4 Homosexuality

In a poem Studdert Kennedy laments that a beautiful woman so dominated his thoughts that he lost concentration in his prayers.[30] It is not too unkind, I hope, to express a gentle surprise that his priorities allowed writing the poem, given the social problems of his time. In a not dissimilar way it appears a scandal that sometimes the Church allows preoccupation with homosexuality to eclipse, say, addressing grave injustice. In the Bible there is only a handful of references to homosexuality, but there are hundreds concerning justice and oppression. The more scholars emphasize Paul's 'loathing ... of homosexual practice',[31] the more Paul is judged over his failure to challenge the institution of slavery. If it be protested that a challenge of the institution of slavery would have been inconceivable in his context, it is unclear why we cannot similarly relativize his alleged loathing of homosexuality.

Am I guilty of something similar in selecting homosexuality as one of the few specific issues to be addressed in this book? The subject is important, however, for at least three reasons. First, it is itself an issue of justice – justice for those who are lesbian and gay. This is a justice that allows them the same freedoms the 'straight' enjoy. Furthermore, the well-being of a significant minority within our community is no trivial matter; neither is the importance of their rich contribution to society. It is important, secondly, because the Churches are in danger of losing credibility over this issue, if they have not lost it already. That may sometimes be the cost of faithfulness to the gospel – but are we so sure this is what is involved in this case? Many will have looked upon the Church of England with disbelief when they saw the nomination of one of her ablest priests as Bishop of Reading overturned on account of a gay partnership. A report of the House of Bishops on *Human Sexuality* is gentle towards gay partnerships, while insisting they are less than the ideal. The report, however, insists gay clergy must remain celibate. The clergy are not permitted to role model good gay partnerships. For many this is a tragic and scandalous loss.[32] Official documents of other churches reflect a similar lack of consensus, generally wrestling to discover as much consensus as possible on an issue on which Christians are divided.

There is a third reason. On this issue is being contested for some the acknowledgement of the privilege and responsibility of the people of God to discern what is right for their relationships according to the criterion of human well-being, and the commitments to decency, integrity and sensitivity to others such as serve that well-being, and according also to what resonates with our vision of God. We are not subject to extraneous standards or restrictions that carry no rationale in terms of our good and that vision. By contrast, for others, on this issue is being contested the importance of obedience to Scripture's teaching, as it is judged to be, and of a prescriptive theology.

A large body of Christian opinion maintains that the same ethic that applies to heterosexual relationships applies, broadly speaking, also to those of the same sex. Given relationships that are loving, faithful and equal, gay partnerships are to be affirmed and celebrated as are heterosexual. Indeed the Churches have made a significant contribution to facilitating informed and compassionate public thinking on this matter.[33] A large body, however, by contrast, insists upon unqualified celibacy for all who are gay or lesbian, however rich and faithful a relationship. Laying aside a dislike of labels, I speak here of 'conservative' and 'liberal' positions. The issue is serious, for if the conservative position is wrong, we are guilty of injustice. If the liberal position is wrong, we are leading the Church astray. One side or the other is seriously misrepresenting the gospel.

We are concerned with people of pronounced homosexual orientation. The 'origin' of this is not the issue, and in any case the quest to discover an 'origin' can be value laden. The issue is what people do with their lives, given who and what they are. The conservative position invariably insists there is nothing sinful about the homosexual *orientation*. People cannot help having homosexual longings. What is sinful is only the *expression*. To put it crudely, gay people may 'be it' as long as they don't 'do it'. After all, all heterosexuals are celibate for part of their lives, and some for all of their lives. Why is it so outrageous to insist that all homosexuals should be celibate for the whole of their lives?

This, however, is a troubled argument. For a start, there is no real parallel. For heterosexuals there is always the possibility of a relationship, and one that society will recognize and celebrate. But for homosexuals, by contrast, celibacy is an absolute and universal requirement. Can we justify this position? According to *The Book of Common Prayer* God has given marriage for heterosexuals who 'do not have the gift of continency'. There appears to be no such gift for those who are gay – only mandatory abstinence.[34]

It is a troubled argument for another reason. The claim that homosexual feelings are not to be judged, but only homosexual 'sex', is unstable. If it is wrong to 'do', is it not also wrong to 'desire'? And if it is wrong to desire, where is the hope of redemption since we cannot help but be as we are? Moreover, the distinction between 'orientation' and 'expression' is likewise a troubled one. Our sexuality does not remain dormant until we 'have sex'. Our sexuality will nuance many of our relationships. Are gay people not to be allowed to be friends because their gay sexuality will be a factor in their friendships? Many heterosexual friendships will be expressed through the embrace, the touch on the shoulder, the kissing of cheeks. Are such expressions of affection and warmth to be denied to gay people because they express a sexual chemistry? The conservative position rarely draws this conclusion. But if this is acceptable, on what grounds do we disallow, in an appropriate relationship, sexuality's ultimate expression?

If the gay minority are to live under our prohibitions, it is incumbent upon us to make clear what is and what is not allowed. Presumably at the top of the list is anal penetrative sex between two men. But we bear false witness against our neighbour if we assume gay sex is equivalent to anal intercourse and, in any case, this is not an option for lesbians. Anal penetrative sex may be a pattern in a *heterosexual* relationship, and need *not* be the pattern for gay men.[35] What about mutual masturbation? Or suppose two people simply enjoy physical intimacy, 'sleeping like spoons'? Is this permitted? Such voyeuristic intrusions into private lives seem deeply offensive. Yet if there is a line beyond which things are prohibited, we need to know where the line is drawn. Perhaps this sense of the offensive highlights the instability of the conservative position.

The conservative position, therefore, faces a dilemma. Either it finds itself drawing an arbitrary line between impermissible and permissible sexual expression, or it finds itself rejecting homosexuals for what and who they are. If Sandra and John are single heterosexuals attracted to each other, then this attraction may have potential for great blessing. But if Rachel is gay and is attracted to another woman, then this feeling must be viewed with suspicion lest it becomes uncontrollable. Rachel is, in effect, being asked to reject not just 'gay sex', but who essentially she is and friendships that arise out of who she essentially is. It is for this reason that the often-repeated assurance that it is only the sin that is rejected, but not the sinner, will often be received as being disingenuous, however kindly meant. Rachel dare not feel, lest the feeling leads to a longing and a hope. All relationships with other women are potentially sinful.[36] It is perhaps for this reason that some conservative Christians follow the expedient of encouraging people to seek a change in orientation.[37] For most this is not an option even in cases where it might be sought.

It follows that a significant proportion of the population is, at worst, rejected for what they are. At best they are denied the nourishing comforts and joys which, subject to the contingencies of all human relationships, are in principle open to all who are 'straight'. Far too much conservative literature is focused overmuch on penetrative sex. The focus should be on the relationship. How that is expressed sexually will be nuanced by the people involved. To say, however, that they are allowed warm friendship, including physical intimacy, provided they draw the line at 'sex', as if sexual chemistry switches on only then, does not make sense.

What arguments are offered to support the conservative position?

15.4.1 The issues: (a) The appeal to Scripture

There is first the appeal to Scripture. The explicit references to homosexuality in Scripture are extremely few in number – less than a dozen.[38] Biblical scholars examine them using ever more powerful microscopes with the result that recent books on the Bible and homosexuality have extended into hundreds of pages.[39] Each book contributes to a scholarly literature that has to be reviewed by subsequent books, thus adding to their length. How can the non-specialist get a feel for all this?

Stepping back from the detail of scholarly debate, there is a twofold ambiguity in the appeal to Scripture.

To begin, there is ambiguity over the cultural and intellectual milieu of the text, as well as over interpretation. Here I simply illustrate. First, it is not certain that the biblical writers thought in terms of what we call a 'homosexual orientation', and it is further uncertain that they envisaged the serious possibility of long-term committed gay partnerships.[40] If this is so (some admittedly find it elsewhere in the ancient world, for example, Aristophanes in the *Symposium*[41]), then to that extent the Bible does not unambiguously address our question. Second, and following from that, the biblical mindset generally presupposes an understanding of sexuality as bound up with procreation and society's economic need to maintain fertility, together with a cultural need to find social placement for women. The background is also deeply patriarchal. It is not clear we are justified in lifting a condemnation of homosexuality out of that milieu and into ours without much further argument. Thus, it has been argued that Leviticus 18.22, which condemns he who 'lies with man as with a woman', should be understood against the background of a patriarchal culture.[42] When a man penetrates a women, he is taking control, such as is appropriate for the dominant sex. Homosexuality involves demeaning a man by treating him 'as a woman'; although this may have more to do with ideas concerning the created order than with any sense of personal power. The recipient partner is also allowing his masculinity to be compromised. According to Foucault, a similar anxiety was found also among the Greeks.[43] This may be one of the reasons why there is an astonishing silence in the biblical traditions concerning lesbianism. To take from this text the condemnation of homosexuality without its patriarchal and other cultural packaging seems disingenuous. It is possible, if only possible, that such ideas are in Paul's mind in 1 Corinthians 6.9–10. We simply do not know for sure what Paul meant by *malakoi autous arsenakoiti*, translated by the New Revised Standard Version as 'male prostitutes and sodomites'. That it involves homosexuality is clear, but it is not clear that it is the homosexuality that Paul condemns. It may be – but it may be that he is condemning more the exploitation of a boy by an adult, or even the feminizing of a man. The latter would resonate with Leviticus 18. if the above noted interpretation is fair. Some also argue that the treatment of homosexuality in the Hebrew Bible is related to the idea of 'purity' – a thing has its own identity and must not be confused with another. To the extent to which this is so, the condemnation of homosexuality has the same root as the condemnation of mixing cloths in Leviticus 19.19. Earlier claims that the texts are often about pederasty and prostitution[44] are currently out of favour, but the possibility that this may sometimes be a key factor remains. None of the above is immune to scholarly debate, but the point is *the text is ambiguous*. The strong and persuasive arguments of one biblical scholar will be contested by the equally strong and persuasive arguments of another. *These considerations alone render the texts highly uncertain as to how they may speak to our context.*

The second ambiguity concerns the use of the Bible in making moral judgements (see Chapter 7). Why should the exegesis of an ancient text have trumps in ethical argument today? Why should we in the twenty-first century defer to the moral specifics in the letters of Paul or, for that matter, one scholar's claim to read Paul's mind? (Which is different from allowing Paul to stimulate and inform our own judgement.) At his best Paul is magnificent, but at other times he shows he is flawed like the rest of us. Paul reminds us that there is a difference between appropriate and inappropriate sexual expression. But our judgement as to the dividing line may not be identical with his. His world is different from ours and, at the least, a process of subtle appropriation of insight is required. Is ethical decision making a matter of peering through the murky lens of the exegesis of ancient texts? Are we to adjust our morals each month according to the latest articles in *Novum Testamentum*? While the texts are ambiguous, the attempt of 'liberals' to apply a solvent to dissolve away all trace of condemnation may be misconceived. It is better to bite the bullet and acknowledge that the text may sometimes implicitly condemn our understanding of consensual partnerships, but that this does not serve as a trump card in ethical argument today. Sometimes the biblical text gets it wrong.[45] We are thus saved from the grim expedient of each 'side' appealing to the support of their chosen biblical scholar heavyweight, the 'conservatives' waving their Gagnon and the 'liberals' waving their Scroggs.

The protests of the above paragraph need to be heard – but perhaps they need to be pressed in a way that gives the conclusion with a bit more depth. We make moral judgements by enquiring into what serves our mutual well-being, and by asking what is a fitting response to our vision of God. Reading Scripture will inform and stimulate that enquiry and vision (see 7.6). The problem arises when particular texts or strands of biblical teaching fail to do this, instead diminishing it. It is precisely this dissonance that is the problem. Homosexual Christians may experience a deep conflict between what Scripture is perceived to teach, and their own experience of their relationship as a means of grace. How are we to handle this conflict? We may with complete Christian integrity judge that the experience of a relationship as a means of grace speaks more authentically of what is of God. Furthermore, and this is crucial, Scripture itself encourages us to make such a judgement and that judgement will itself be informed by other scriptural themes – such as those of love, covenant and blessing. A 'liberal' position is in this deeper sense thus more 'biblical' than the 'conservative'.

The condemnation of contraception, still maintained by the Vatican, has failed to commend itself to a large body of Christians, not only because supporting arguments fail to persuade, but also and perhaps principally because it has failed *the test of experience*. This is the experience that contraception nourishes rather than undermines a wholesome sexual relationship. This is evident in the history of the Anglican Church – the most 'conservative' of the British Protestant churches on this subject – since the 1958 Lambeth Conference reversed the more negative judgements of earlier ones.[46] Increasingly, many hope, the same is happening over the condemnation of homosexual partnerships.

15.4.2 *The issues: (b) The appeal to natural law and natural order*

What has been happening in the argument just advanced? Essentially there has been a conversation between reflection on Scripture and a theology that values as wholesome a covenant relationship of love. It is that theology which enables us to move beyond specific texts condemning homosexuality or, for that matter, intercourse during menstruation. It is rather like allowing a theology of justice and equality to confront texts tolerating slavery. But suppose there are other theologies that give a different framework?

One such theology is that of the Vatican, which appeals to 'natural law'. The idea here is that according to 'nature', sexual intercourse is directed equally towards both covenant love and procreation. These two aspects combine in an integrated whole. It follows that homosexuality is 'intrinsically evil' because nature's procreative intent for sex is thwarted.[47] Same sex relationships, while creative in many ways, in the nature of the case cannot be procreative. For this view, sex is not just about uniting two persons. The openness to procreation is an essential element as well.

We cannot indeed escape the fact that penetrative vaginal sex is necessary for securing the next generation – the occasional medical assistance aside. At the level of biology heterosexual penetrative vaginal sex has a certain privileged position. Sex, however, is also about nourishing a relationship of covenant love. Conception within the act of love making is a wonderful thing, but it seems a *non sequitur* to say it is always wrong to separate the two. What has an evolutionary origin in that which perpetuates the species may be for us also that which feeds, expresses, and enjoys a relationship of love. The 'personal' is integrated with the 'merely biological'.

Vatican theology will indeed speak movingly of the 'personal' or 'unitive' dimension of sex. Since *Casti Connubii*, the language of 'primary' and 'secondary' roles for sex has been abandoned.[48] Nevertheless, however rich the further personal dimension, the biological purpose cannot and must not be thwarted. The two must be integrated. This theology even led Aquinas to argue that while rape is, of course, a grave crime, masturbation is of a different order because at least in rape the sexual organs are used for the purposes for which they were designed.[49] For a more peronalistic approach, however, the claim that every sexual encounter must be vaginally penetrative and open to procreation does not make sense.

It is important to recognize that this argument does not rule out simply same sex relations. It rules out any sexual expression not open to procreation or where procreation is deliberately prevented. We thus reject contraception, masturbation, whether mutual or solo, oral sex, and indeed any sexual expression other than the vaginally penetrative. Vatican moral theology is consistent in drawing this conclusion.[50] It is unclear why some Protestants appeal to this natural law argument against homosexuality, while allowing contraceptives for married couples. Why is gay sex wrong because it is non-procreative, but not marital sex deliberately made infertile through contraception? The acceptance of contraception has blown a large hole in the condemnation of homosexual bondings on account of their nature as non-procreative.

There is another style of argument; it is different, but related. There are many and varied claims that the homosexual bonding is contrary to the order of creation. It would take a whole chapter to analyse and discuss these. Here I confine myself to two comments. Sometimes this is offered as a point about anatomy, even offering the observation that there is no male orifice suitable for penetration.[51] Here again we meet the assumption that male gay sexuality is primarily about penetrative sex.[52] Second, it is argued that 'creation' gives the man/woman procreative relationship a normative position, in such a way as to exclude gay partnerships.[53] There seems to be a *non sequitur* here. Of course we must be positive about the woman/man procreative relationship. But being thus positive need not imply rejecting those who are different. If anything can be derived from creation it is that creation is about the richness of diversity.

Furthermore, the theology we are considering has been subject to two qualifications. First, it has been adapted to accommodate the celibate and the single. Second, it has been adapted in Protestantism to accommodate the use of contraceptives, including the acknowledgement that a married couple may make a responsible judgement that parenthood is not their vocation.[54] As far as I am aware the Protestant version, found in the *St Andrew's Day Statement*, and implied by Michael Banner, does not question this.[55] If the normative character of the man/woman procreative relationship allows contraception, and allows others to be single, it is not clear on what grounds we still exclude gay partnerships.

Sometimes this argument is offered as a principle of biblical interpretation, in the light of which ambiguous texts may be clarified. Thus, the 'thrust' of scriptural teaching focuses upon the 'one flesh' relationship between a woman and a man as part of the order of creation.[56] Genesis 1—2, prominent at the beginning of the canon, is often quoted here. It follows that marriage and singleness are alone permitted.[57] Again, there seems to be a *non sequitur*. All these chapters tell us is that the Bible is positive about the man/woman procreative relationship. That implies nothing about those who are different. Suppose, moreover, we interpret these two chapters as speaking more generally of human beings as made for relationships? There are, however, many forms of relationship and friendship.[58] Such a reading would accommodate same sex partnerships.

Furthermore, we can with equal cogency locate other 'thrusts' in Scripture, much more affirmative of homosexual partnerships. Such thrusts point to grand biblical themes, which celebrate friendship, mutual love, covenant and fidelity. If there are 'thrusts' and 'emerging consensuses' in Scripture they are as much about these things as about any other. On these grounds those who affirm gay and lesbian partnerships are embracing a stance at least as 'biblical'. The reality is, there is no 'thrust' on this matter that can be identified by impartial exegesis. Any perceived thrust, whether 'liberal' or 'conservative', will express our appropriation of a theology from the text and we must take responsibility for our appropriation (see 7.5).

Both 'liberal' and 'conservative' positions appropriate from the text a theology of covenant love. Both, of course, will affirm the covenant of heterosexual marriage. The difference is that the conservative position insists the covenant of heterosexual marriage is the only permitted sexual relationship. For those for whom this is not an option, there is only singleness. The liberal position is baffled as to why this should be so, appealing to the belief that God's will is for our flourishing, and to the testimony of homosexuals that their partnerships are to them a source of blessing and a means of grace.

We can re-express the points in terms of 'natural law' (see 3.10). First, sex 'by nature' is about bonding and nourishing and not just physical urges and pleasure. Second, sex 'by nature' must, if moral, be open to procreation. Third, sex 'by nature' must always be heterosexual. Our argument favours the first claim, but rejects the second and third when understood exclusively. There is thus no reason why same sex covenant love must be rejected. On the contrary, there is every reason to affirm and celebrate it.

15.4.3 The issues: (c) The wider society – and people themselves

A whole clutch of arguments maintains that the general health of society would be threatened by a wider acceptance of same sex partnerships. For example, they 'undermine' marriage and family life.[59] It is certainly important that people are able to discover their sexual orientation apart from the peer pressure of a gay sub-culture. By the same token, of course, many a homosexual has been tormented by the pressure of a predominantly heterosexual culture – hence the old advice: 'Marry and it will cure you.' Sensitivity and sometimes help is required when a person is unsure as to their sexual orientation, but the norm of universal gay singleness is not the solution. Apart from this it is difficult to find any plausibility in this argument. A robust gay response might ask why the relationship of the married is to be privileged. Compared with those who are gay, it is privileged enough already! But suppose we allow it a prime status because it remains the way in which children are biologically parented, there is still a sufficient response in asking the simple question: Why should marriage and family life be threatened by those who are different? Why do differences *threaten* rather than *enrich*? Single people do not threaten marriage and family life, so why should those who are gay? Invariably, those who are gay belong to families, and many who are married and parents will testify to the generous support and interest shown by their gay friends or gay members of their families.[60] To each their own vocation.

In addition to the above, Gagnon is representative of those who offer an array of warnings regarding the consequences of tolerating gay partnerships for both society and homosexuals themselves. He cites evidence of ill-health among homosexuals and of damage to society.[61]

There is not space to consider all this in detail. I confine myself to a few comments. First, assessing and interpreting statistical correlates and other social data is a task full of perils. Even more so is identifying causal relations in society and predicting social patterns in the future. Whatever position we take, we must be aware of the temptation to mould the data to support our stance. Second, no one is claiming all is well with those who are gay and lesbian. But, to put it crudely, gay sexual orientation is a reality. If Gagnon has identified serious issues, they will not go away by stronger norms requiring universal singleness. Indeed, the likelihood is that the ill-health of gay people and issues for society are exasperated by censure and marginalization. We better address such matters by being more accepting of gay partnerships and by supporting gay people, when they wish to enter into a partnership, to discover how to build one that is wholesome and nourishing.

At the same time, a massive amount of disturbing data could easily be assembled on deep unhappiness and physical and emotional abuse within marriage, the colossal social cost of marital breakdown, the statistical correlation between single parenthood and a whole range of social indicators, and the worrying way in which the ubiquity of pornography for heterosexual men may subtly influence how women are regarded and treated and how they regard themselves. It is unjust to take a brush and tar those who are gay while neglecting all this. The reality is that our sexuality is deeply constitutive of who and what we are. Our sexuality causes both joy and pain. It may be the cause of deep unease, and of agonizingly lonely longings. Through our sexuality we can both love another person and abuse and humiliate them. That is the human condition, for both gay and straight.

There is one piece of data that is crucial. This concerns the *experience* of gay and lesbian people. There is the experience of those who are celibate, and content and whole in that state; likewise, those who are heterosexuals and single. But there is also the testimony of gay and lesbian people that they bond with others, as heterosexuals bond with others, and find their bonding to be, as do heterosexuals, a means of grace. Over and against all that is said *about* people who are gay and lesbian, there is this testimony *of them*. In a lot of conservative Christian writing, gay and lesbian people are far more often *spoken about* than *listened to*.

The prohibition which the conservative stance urges does not, for many who are gay and lesbian, find credibility within the reality of their lives. If something is experienced as a means of grace, then that is as good a reason as any to believe it is good and of God. The parallel Gagnon draws between homosexuality and incest, adultery and prostitution is outrageous.[62] The latter things cannot be means of grace because they involve abuse, exploration or betrayal. Homosexual relationships are not wrong on account of considerations extraneous to the persons involved – because of the purpose of sexual organs in natural law, because of some pattern in creation, or because the Bible is read in a particular way. They may be wholesome because they may feed and nourish. This expresses a theology. It is a theology that is positive about two human beings committed to each other in a covenant love. It is a theology that is positive about our sexuality – that part of our nature which draws two people together in a desire to express love through physical intimacy. This, in fact, copies a theology of marriage. It may not be procreative, but in other ways it may be richly creative.

15.4.4 Conclusion

Suppose a 'straight' Christian cannot feel able to affirm a gay or lesbian covenant. It does not follow they must condemn, still less work for this condemnation to be enforced by church discipline. There is a mid-position of respecting the integrity of fellow Christians as they seek to live according to their conscience and judgement. Predominantly, it is married heterosexuals who are demanding universal singlessness. But it is not they who bear the cost. The argument of this chapter is that there are no good arguments against gay partnerships and many good arguments in favour of liberty. Serious attention must be given to the testimony of gay and lesbian people, including those who are Christian, that their relationships bring great blessing. I may be mistaken, but conservative Christians may also be mistaken. Suppose there is a danger of over-confidence on both sides? Suppose the matter is ambiguous? It is difficult to justify the confidence with which conservative

Christians seek to demand celibacy of gay people. In the light of uncertainty, caution should be the norm. As Gareth Moore said: 'If unanimity fails, that is a pity. If charity fails, if we no longer listen and speak in love, that is a disaster; we deny our fundamental identity as members of the one Body and as children of the one God.'[63]

In this chapter I have been concerned with ethics, and with how our experience may inform our ethics. But on this issue as much as on any other, 'reason can be the slave of the passions'. Feelings can run high, and ethical and theological stances can be rationalizations of prejudice. We all need to be aware of this and to be self-critical.

This leaves us with human beings, some struggling to discover what their sexual orientation is, some finding their homosexuality a burden, others finding it a gift, some content to remain celibate, some longing for intimacy with someone they can love. Some will keep their sexuality to themselves, reluctant to be defined in terms of it and shying away from the 'gay scene'. Others will be more open and be glad to be known partly in terms of what is important to them. We are left with human beings with their struggles, their pains and joys, their glory and their sin. But in place of a demand for universal singleness, there should be a listening to people's testimonies and a standing alongside one another as we discover what it means to express in our relationships decency, loyalty and integrity, and to find blessing within them.

Notes

1 Helen Oppenheimer, *The Hope of Happiness*, London, SCM Press, 1983, especially chapters 7, 12 and 15.

2 Psalms 15.5.

3 Helen Oppenheimer, *Marriage*, London, Mowbray, 1990, p. 15.

4 Pius XI, *Casti Connubii*, Vatican, 1930, Boston, Pauline Books, pp. 17–21 and 43–9.

5 Expressed, for example, in G. K. Chesterton, *Selected Essays*, London, Collins, 1939, p. 259.

6 William Rees Mogg, 'Divorce? Just Say "No"', *The Times*, 23 November 1995.

7 See, for example, Donald Goergen, *The Sexual Celibate*, New York, Seabury Press, 1974.

8 Michel Foucault, *The Essential Works*, Volume 1, London, The Allen Press, 1997, p. 181.

9 Peter Singer, *Practical Ethics*, Cambridge, Cambridge University Press, 1993, p. 2.

10 Thomas Aquinas *Summa Theologiae*, II-II 154.2.

11 Lisa Cahill, *Sex, Gender and Christian Ethics*, Cambridge, Cambridge University Press, 1996, p. 205.

12 Thus, C. S. Lewis, *Mere Christianity*, Fontana, 1955, p. 86. Also Ian Gregory, *No Sex Please, We're Single*, Kingsway, 1997. Also Sacred Congregation for the Doctrine of the Faith, *Persona Humana*, Vatican, 1975, Section VII.

13 Adrian Thatcher, *Living Together and Christian Ethics*, Cambridge, 2002, especially chapters 3 and 4.

14 E.g. Gumbel who does not even mention the possibility of a pregnancy in N. Gumbel, *Searching Issues*, Eastbourne, Kingsway, 2001, pp. 41ff.

15 Martin Luther, 'A Sermon on the Estate of Marriage' in James Atkinson (ed.), *Luther's Works*, Volume 44, Philadelphia, Fortress Press, 1966, pp. 9–11.

16 N. Gumbel, *Searching Issues*, p. 47.

17 N. Gumbel, *Searching Issues*, p. 39.

18 N. Gumbel, *Searching Issues*, p. 42.

19 N. Gumbel, *Searching Issues*, p. 46.

20 Alan H. Goldman, 'Plain Sex' in Hugh Lafollette (ed.), *Ethics in Practice*, Oxford, Blackwell, 1997, pp. 224ff.

21 E.g. R. Vannoy, *Sex Without Love*, Buffalo, Prometheus, 1980.

22 On this see Karen Lebacqz, 'Appropriate Vulnerability' in J. B. Nelson and S. P Longfellow (eds), *Sexuality and the Sacred*, London, Mowbray, 1994, pp. 259–60.

23 Roger Scruton in *Sexual Desire*, London, Weidenfeld & Nicolson, 1986, pp. 322ff. insists on the importance of love for moral sex; but is ambivalent about additional requirements, such as legal marriages.

24 E.g. R. Wasserstrom, *Today's Moral Problems*, New York, Macmillan, 1975, pp. 240–8.

25 See, for example, Adrian Hastings, *Christian Marriage in Africa*, London, SPCK, 1973, especially pp. 72ff.; and Benezeri Kisembo, Laurenti Magesa and Aylward Shorter, *African Christian Marriage*, Dublin, Geoffrey Chapman, 1977, pp. 63ff.

26 Marvin Ellison has spoken of an ethic of decency in 'Common Decency: A New Christian Sexual Ethics' in J. B. Nelson and S. P. Longfellow (eds), *Sexuality and the Sacred*, London, Mowbray, 1994, pp. 236ff.

27 Pius XI, *Casti Connubii*, Vatican, 1930.

28 A. N. Whitehead, *Process and Reality*, Cambridge, 1930, p. 485.

29 There is truth as well as exaggeration and rhetoric in F. Engels, *The Origin of the Family, Private Property and the State*, 1884, and in Catherine MacKinnon, *Feminism Unmodified*, Harvard University Press, 1977.

30 G. A. Studdert Kennedy, poem 'Temptation', *The Unutterable Beauty*, London, Hodder, 1927, p. 15.

31 C. K. Barrett, *Romans*, London, A. & C. Black, 1971, p. 39.

32 Despite the 'official' stance there remain many excellent gay clergy who live with partners and with the knowledge and even support of their bishops. See Stephen Bates, *A Church at War*, London, Hodder & Stoughton, 2004.

33 The Wolfenden Commission was set up in part as response to the recommendation of the Church of England's Moral Welfare Council.

34 Gareth Moore, *A Question of Truth*, London, Continuum, 2003, p. 202.

35 Norman Pittenger, *Time for Consent*, London, SCM Press, 1970, p. 72.

36 I am indebted to Gareth Moore OP in developing this argument.

37 See Rosemary Radford Ruether, *Christianity and the Making of the Modern Family*, London, SCM Press, 2001, p. 275 n. 59

38 Leviticus 18.22, 20.13; Romans 1.18–32; 1 Corinthians 6.9–10; 1 Timothy 1.8–11; Jude 7.

39 E.g. Robert A. J. Gagnon, *The Bible and Homosexual Practice*, Nashville, Abingdon, 2001.

40 John Barton, *Ethics and the Old Testament*, London, SCM Press, 1998, p. 52.

41 Plato, *Symposium*, 198d ff. p. 32 in the Everyman Edition, ed. Tom Griffin, London, 1986.

42 This was the argument of Derrick Sherwin Bailey in his classic *Homosexuality and the Western Christian Tradition*, London, Longmans, 1955, pp. 31ff. It has persuaded many writers since, e.g. Moore, *A Question of Truth*, pp. 77, 109.

43 Michel Foucault, *The Essential Works*, Volume 1, London, Allen Press, 1994, p. 152.

44 Thus, Robin Scroggs, *The New Testament and Homosexuality*, Fortress Press, 1988, *passim*, especially pp. 125ff.

45 Diarmaid MacCulloch, *Reformation: Europe's House Divided*, London, Allen Lane, 2003, p. 705.

46 *The Family in Contemporary Society*, London, SPCK, 1958, is an Anglican report which documents this change.

47 Paul IV, *Humanae Vitae*, Vatican, 1968, especially Paragraphs 11–12 and 13; and John Paul II, *Veritatis Splendor*, Vatican, 1993, Paragraph 80.

48 Pius XI, *Casti,* Vatican, 1930, Section 2.

49 Thomas Aquinas, *Summa Theologiae*, II.II Q. 154 Art 12. Aquinas here considers the objection that 'the unnatural vice is not the gravest sin' since 'adultery, seduction and rape' are 'injurous to our neighbour'. In consequence 'the more a sin is contrary to charity the graver it is'. This objection, however, he rejects.

50 Vatican, *Persona Humana*, 1975, Paragraphs 19–20.

51 E.g. Gagnon, *Bible and Homosexual Practice*, p. 254.

52 On this see Moore, *Question of Truth*.

53 Karl Barth, *Church Dogmatics*, 3.4, pp. 44–5. See also, for example, pp. 154, 163, 168ff. Also House of Bishops, *Some Issues in Human Sexuality: A Guide to the Debate*, London, Church House Publishing, 2003, 4.4.53. Also John Paul II, *Homosexualitatis Problema*, Vatican, 1986.

54 See the 'Root' Commission, *Marriage, Family and the Church*, SPCK, 1965, para 45.

55 T. Bradshaw (ed.), *The Way Forward?*, London, SCM Press, 2003, pp. 5f. Michael Banner, *Christian Ethics and Contemporary Problems*, Cambridge, Cambridge University Press, 1999, pp. 252–309.

56 E.g. John Stott, *Issues Facing Christians Today*, p. 344. Also Simon Vilbert, 'Divine Order and Sexual Conduct', pp. 115ff. in Bradshaw (ed.), *The Way Forward*.

57 This is the position of 'The St Andrew's Day Statement', reprinted in Bradshaw (ed.), *The Way Forward*.

58 Michael Vesey, *Strangers and Friends,* London, Hodder & Stoughton, 1995, pp. 49ff.

59 Thus, Gagnon, *Bible and Homosexual Practice*, p. 480.

60 I wish to pay tribute to the support a dozen or so gay friends have given to me in my role as husband and father.

61 Gagnon, *Bible and Homosexual Practice*, p. 471. Also John Paul II, *Homosexalitatis Problema*, Vatican, 1986, Paragraph 7.

62 Gagnon, *Bible and Homosexual Practice*, p. 489.

63 Moore, *Question of Truth*, p. 3.

Life and Death

16.1 Medical ethics

When Moses approached the burning bush he did not playfully flick twigs into it; neither did he roast toffee apples. He took off his shoes in fear and trembling. We need to approach issues in medical ethics in a like manner. Here we face agonizing dilemmas and the hard edge of human tragedy. We need all our resources of knowledge, clear thinking and compassion, but often all we can manage is a difficult judgement based on the most responsible deliberations we can muster. This will rarely exorcise the sting of dilemma and the pain of the tragic.

At least since Hippocrates in the fourth century BC, medical care has been the subject of ethical reflection, the focus traditionally being on the commitments and values of physicians. The mind-blowing potential of modern medicine and surgery has shifted the focus to medical care itself. The ethical dilemmas are equally mind-blowing. The success, not the failure, of medicine means there is an unavoidable gap between demand and resource. On what basis do we allocate health care resources? How many hip replacements is a new kidney dialysis machine worth? What code of confidentiality does a doctor follow with a minor? In revealing a prognosis to a patient, how does a doctor balance truthfulness, sensitivity and an obligation to steer clear of patronizing paternalism? Does a parent have a right on religious grounds to refuse their child a blood transfusion? Does patient autonomy have limits? Is it ethical to experiment on human embryos? Is there a kind of 'genetic engineering' that is permissible and, if so, for what purpose and according to what code of practice? Is a right to treatment lessened by lifestyle and, if so, what lifestyle indicators are to be taken into account? Is it ethically permissible for parents to seek to determine the sex of their child and, if so, in what circumstances and for what reason? Should a state adopt an 'opt in' or an 'opt out' policy over the use of organs of cadavers for transplant? Should a woman with severe learning difficulties be given a hysterectomy to prevent pregnancy? What code of practice should guide a failed abortion leading to a live birth? Is it permissible to withhold an operation on a Down's syndrome baby to reopen the oesophagus, thus offering only 'caring to die'? Should the carriers of certain hereditary diseases have children and, if so, which diseases? Should a pregnant woman who has become brain dead be kept physiologically alive in order for her baby to grow to term? The list of questions seems endless.

In this chapter I confine myself to discussing two central issues. The second is currently the subject of keen debate in Britain, and the first in America given that a number of states – partly because of right-wing Christian pressure – are reconsidering the position adopted by the definitive Supreme Court case of 1973, *Roe versus Wade*, which gave a woman a *de facto* right to self-determination over abortion in the first two trimesters of a pregnancy.

16.2 Abortion

Over the ethics of abortion there are deep uncertainties. All responses have a measure of ambiguity. The subject is a paradigmatic ethical dilemma. No subject in ethics has been more exhaustively discussed but there seems no prospect of agreement.

Suppose a woman has two pre-school children. She is pregnant again and her partner leaves her. The child she is carrying is identified as having some disability requiring special care. The woman feels she does not have the resources to cope alone, and that she cannot give what her new baby will need. For that reason, and also for the sake of the other two children, she decides to have an abortion. Most will respond with profound sympathy – especially in a society that often leaves people alone and isolated, without support networks. Maybe only a few will be prepared to say that she acted wrongly. Yet many will also see ambiguity because a potential life has been taken. Maybe also there is unease over the insinuation that those with disabilities have a weaker claim upon life. But suppose she decides to allow her baby to grow to term? Then other ambiguities become evident. Has she sufficiently attended to her own proper needs, as well as those of the two children she already has? Is it right to bring into the world a baby whose quality of life may be low?

The ambiguities and uncertainties are found in at least three areas.

16.2.1 *The ambiguous moral status of the unborn*

The language we use is a problem. Language can be value laden and can influence how we see things. No language is without its difficulties, but here I speak of the '*unborn human*' to describe simply the physiological reality of the growing embryo or foetus. I use the phrase '*moral status*' to speak of that judged to attach to the '*unborn human*' such as to demand of us the respect and protection we accord to a fellow human being.

There is a deep ambiguity over the moral status of the unborn human. This ambiguity derives from the biological fact that human life does not come into existence instantaneously, but rather gradually. We confuse the issue if we say 'when life begins'. Separate biological life begins with conception – or at least differentiation – but nothing unambiguously follows from that regarding moral status. The more fruitful question to ask concerns *the moral status of the unborn human*, but the issue is ambiguous precisely because the human is *developing*.

Suppose we try *to fix a point* when we accord to the unborn human full moral status, thus demanding of us all the protections we accord to a fellow human. And suppose we fix that point at conception. There is thus no difference between abortion in the womb – however early – and murder in the cot. This is a position many hold, but at the same time many are not persuaded. To many it seems counter-intuitive to give full moral status to totipotent** cells invisible to the naked eye. At this early stage it makes no sense of speak of consciousness, awareness of interests and the capacity to feel pleasure or pain. These, however, are among the principal criteria of personhood. Furthermore, there appears to be no 'point' of conception – the exchange of genetic material takes about 24 hours. Again, until the possibility of twinning has passed some two weeks later there is some ambiguity about speaking of the beginning of one particular human life.

Suppose, by contrast, we fix that point not at conception, but later in the development of the embryo or foetus. The difficulty is knowing how to identify that point. And do we say that before this point there is only tissue? And what criteria do we use? There is, in fact, no point in the development that bears unambiguously the weight of being a clear morally significant dividing line. Again, we trip up over the biological reality. Human life develops gradually. If the process is gradual there is no point along the way that has the moral significance we are looking for. There is a continuum without any critical dividing line. Not unreasonably, those who look for a fixed point often play safe and go back to conception.

Let's try another possible approach. Instead of fixing a point when moral status is accorded, we say that right from the beginning the unborn human has the potential to become a member of the human community, and so deem the unborn to have full moral status by virtue of that potential. What has potential should be treated as if it is already actual. Full moral status is accorded from conception on account of potentiality. This can be seen as offering a neat way of granting full moral status from conception while avoiding the problem that human life develops gradually. There is a lot going for this approach, but again it does not persuade everyone. It is not obvious that the worth we attach to the actual should be accorded also to the potential. For example, we do not accord to the potential of an acorn the same regard we attach to a venerable oak.[1]

Do we, however, have to adopt an 'all or nothing' approach? In other words, do we have to say the potential either has or does not have full moral status? Singer discusses this option as if we have to choose between two stark alternatives.[2] Suppose instead, however, we claim that the potential still evokes a sense of respect and reverence, although not as fully as the actual? The growing foetus does not have full moral status but, because of the potential, is not to be treated simply as physiological tissue. This suggests another possibility – that which uses the concept of *the gradual.*

The advantage of the gradualist approach is that it takes seriously the difference between the developing human and the developing oak. The difference is that each human individual has a value and significance we do not accord to the individual oak tree. Ronald Dworkin has expressed this by using the concept 'sacred'. The nascent human life is sacred in a way in which an acorn is not – because each nascent human life has potential to become a unique individual human person.[3] An oak tree, however magnificent, is a replaceable instance of its class. We cannot say this of a human person.

The above two approaches fall down because of the biological fact that human life develops gradually. If the fact of gradual development is the problem, can we turn it into our advantage by weaving it into a different kind of approach? Suppose we say that there is no single point when moral status is accorded? Instead, we say that moral status grows as the embryo or foetus grows. That which is in the process of growing into a human being imposes upon us a strong *prima facie* claim but a claim that is not as strong as that imposed by the actual. In other words, moral status grows gradually as the embryo or foetus grows. Instead of looking for a fixed point we embrace gradualism.

Perhaps gradualism, although troubled, is the least problematical position. It takes seriously the fact of biological development. As the unborn human grows in the womb, so also does the moral status and thus the claim the unborn human places upon us. We can accord to the embryo or foetus – indeed to the fertilized ovum right from the beginning – a moral status appropriate to the stage of development. It follows that early abortions are less problematical than later ones. At the same time, no abortion is as ethically unproblematical as a tonsillectomy. Current English law presupposes such a 'gradualist' position in that experimentation on embryos is allowed for the first two weeks after conception, but not afterwards. At this stage, there is differentiation and so the cells are no longer totipotent. Furthermore, abortion is normally not allowed after 24 weeks, *roughly* equivalent to viability. *Roe versus Wade*, the American Supreme Court ruling in 1973, was gradualist in allowing abortion in the first two trimesters, but granting the unborn human protection in the third. The gradualist position is hardly precise. We cannot say the claim of the unborn of six months' gestation is exactly double that of the unborn of three months. We cannot expect that kind of mathematical precision. A gradualist position, however, does allow a perspective for making judgements that, while often troubled, express as much rationality as we can expect in this area.

The debate so far has assumed two fixed boundaries. We have discussed the moral status of the unborn human between conception and birth. On what grounds, however, do we accord these two events such moral significance?

Suppose we base our argument upon potential. We accord full moral status to the unborn because of what the unborn is to become. What has potential is treated as if already actual. If, however, this is our position, why do we begin with conception? If the zygote, or the early embryo, has potential to become a viable living human, then so has every ovum in the ovary. These exist at birth, stored up and ready for release. They all have potential to become a new human being. Why accord such moral significance to fertilization? Like it or not, the according of full moral status on the ground of the potential of the embryo or foetus gives conception a significance that is only pragmatic and, in so doing, this position betrays its own ambiguity. Moreover, this is as much a difficulty for those who regard conception as the point when full moral status is accorded.

Suppose, by contrast, we adopt a gradualist stance. What is odd about gradualism is that at birth it changes tack – or if not birth, the possibility of surviving birth, hence a rough estimate of viability. The gradualist ceases to be gradualist once the child is born, or capable of a live birth, whatever the gestation date. This is the actual point at which finally full moral status is accorded. It is almost as if the unborn human has been gradually pumped with moral status in the womb, and with birth declared to be full. But from a gradualist perspective it is difficult to justify seeing birth as so significant, especially as birth can occur prematurely. If infanticide is murder and punishable as such, why do we allow abortion with impunity only a few weeks earlier? Or suppose a child with a disability is born prematurely. Why is it a capital offence to murder that child but permissible to abort a child with a like condition and a like gestation age?

Mary Anne Warren defends abortion on the grounds that the moral status of the unborn is ambiguous. For her, moral status depends on consciousness of interest. In the case of the unborn human about to be aborted, there is no conscious person with conscious interests and thus aware of what is shortly to be taken away. Whose interests or aspirations are being frustrated if there is an abortion, since the foetus is not yet aware of interests and aspirations?[4] We must not think of the unborn as persons already living in some shadowy parallel space, longing to be born, and experiencing grief if we refuse entry.[5]

These are strong arguments. One problem, however, is that they can be applied also to the new-born infant. Consciousness of interest has not yet developed. The born child has indeed independent existence. This has some significance since by virtue of this fact the potential for conflict between the rights of the unborn and the well-being of the mother is lessened. It is not clear, however, that these considerations justify the moral significance we give to birth when trying to assess the moral status of the growing human.

There seem to be three possible responses to this difficulty.

The first response is to avoid the difficulty by insisting full moral status attaches at conception. There is, however, one difficulty this position does not avoid. That is the difficulty of rendering itself convincing. To claim full moral status attaches to a fertilized ovum (or at the latest the early embryo) is to ignore biological reality. Human life develops gradually. There is *moral significance* right from the beginning, but many are not persuaded there is, right from the beginning, *full moral status*. If there is full moral status from the beginning, then an abortion of the tiny fertilized ovum is murder and so even a 14-year-old girl who has been raped must bring her baby to term. That seems to be the position of John Paul II's *Evangelium Vitae*.

The second response is that of Peter Singer. We bite the bullet and deny birth has such significance. Singer – along lines similar to Mary Anne Warren – argues moral status depends on conscious life and awareness of interests. This has not yet developed in a new-born baby. Infanticide may therefore be an ethical option in the case of a severely disabled baby declined by the parents and for whom adoptive parents cannot be found.[6] This, he suggests, might be up to 28 days after birth. He admits this is fairly arbitrary, but some point has to be fixed.[7] For Singer there is no compelling reason for allowing abortion, but not infanticide, for infants of the same gestational age.

The third response is perhaps the most persuasive. There is no point that can be fixed with *compelling* moral argument. Life is not always neat and tidy, but law and medical codes of practice do require the fixing of boundaries. The points are fixed on the basis of a reasonable pragmatism simply because there is no other basis. Current British law and medical practice give significance to birth, to the statutory gestation limit to abortion based very roughly on viability, and two weeks for embryo research, based on cell differentiation. There are reasons for these boundaries, but they are at most only persuasive. They do not give us indubitable certainty. Singer acknowledges the same with the boundary he proposes. In effect, Singer's argument is that there are compelling reasons for law and medical practice fixing the point in defined cases of disability after birth. This is partly out of compassion for parents who feel their lives are devastated by the birth of a seriously disabled child.

There are some pieces of wood so rough in the grain that however sharp the blade they will not plane smooth. The biological reality is that human life does not come into existence cleanly and instantaneously. The process is vulnerable and uncertain. However sharp the cutting edge of our analytical tools we cannot make it smooth. We adopt a position as responsible as we can find, but the whole question of the status of the unborn is ambiguous and sometimes tragic. Ethicists support people more if they acknowledge the anguish of the ambiguity rather than by claiming a clarity and certainty that is not there.

16.2.2 The well-being of the mother

There is another biological reality we must take seriously, and an exclusive concentration on the moral status of the growing human can easily ignore this. Another human life is involved. Human life comes into being through a unique and demanding relationship with the mother.

In the past it was often assumed that a married woman had a prime responsibility to produce children. Women have often been defined primarily as mothers in a way men rarely, if ever, have been defined as fathers. Children, after all, were important for the economy, and society had a strong interest in producing as many babies as possible. Many died before reaching maturity and it was important to ensure factories, fields, armies and navies, were not short of labour. This societal need became internalized and little truck was given to any suggestion that women might have needs, rights or aspirations, inconsistent with serial and indeed life-threatening child bearing.

It is interesting to speculate whether or not this argument, now strongly contested, might begin to reappear. The birth rate in the West is falling, and also in 'developing' nations more rapidly than expected. A population scare is gradually being replaced by a concern that we are not producing enough children for the health and wealth of our nations. In contemporary Britain, babies have to be produced at a rate of about 2.2 per woman to maintain the population. The average is now down to about 1.7. That is why many argue immigration is essential to our economy. But the world could soon run out of countries with excess population to export. Will we then find social mores changing in order to reassert a 'duty' to produce children?

That is perhaps for a future generation. The fact is that there has been a massive rebellion against the idea that women are destined by nature to be serial child bearers. Paradoxically, this may have led to our valuing children more rather than less. The children we have are more likely to be wanted and cared for. Increasingly, however, we recognize the right of women to choose whether or not to have children, how many and when. Their role as mothers is chosen and not predetermined for them by nature and culture. Hence, contraception has been such a force for liberation.

Over and against the developing claims of the growing child, then, we have to consider the well-being of the pregnant woman and her right of control, at least *prima facie*, over her own life. In the past the wrongness of abortion may not have been questioned simply because the rights of women were not recognized. Moreover, the moral tradition was formulated primarily by males, even celibate males. The issues seem to boil down to how we resolve the tension between the *prima facie* claim of the growing child and the *prima facie* claim of the mother.

One response which is passionately argued is that the mother's judgement is always overriding. This is the position of Judith Jarvis Thomson.[8] She allows that the growing child does indeed assert a growing claim upon us. An abortion is never as ethically unambiguous as, say, a tonsillectomy. Nonetheless, the *developing* claims of the growing child can never be stronger than the *actual* right of the woman to self-determination. After all, the child is not yet aware of interests or aspirations. It is asking an enormous amount of a woman to require her to carry, give birth to, and nurture a child against her will. We are not justified in demanding this of any woman. The right of the woman to choose always has trumps. It follows that ethically a woman has an absolute right to abortion. The pivotal *Roe versus Wade* Supreme Court ruling in 1973 declared the protection of a foetus during the first two trimesters to be unconstitutional because it violated the rights of the mother.

Judith Jarvis Thomson is not against motherhood. She recognizes that many women wish to have children – accepting pregnancy as a joy and a gift. Her point is that we have no right to demand this of any woman. Choice and self-determination cannot be overruled. Mary Anne Warren adopts a similar position: 'A foetus, especially in the early stages of development, satisfies none of the criteria for personhood. Consequently it makes no sense to grant it moral rights strong enough to override the woman's right to liberty, bodily integrity, and sometimes life itself.'[9] In the nature of the case the rights of an *actual* person outweigh the rights of a merely *potential* person. Foetal rights, although acknowledged, are always subordinate to maternal rights.

This need not mean that maternal rights are asserted lightly or callously. Where they are so asserted, there is no reverence for the developing human. It is treated as nothing more than tissue or as an intrusive stranger. This, however, is not to say an abortion is always wrong. It is, though, to say that the decision should never be made casually and that the element of the tragic cannot be eliminated.

Something distinctive about this argument has to be noticed. This position says that the rights of the mother have trumps *only if she so decides*. A woman may choose to have an unplanned child, giving weight to the strong *prima facie* claim made by the miracle of new life within her. It is, however, her judgement. No one has a right to force a woman to have a child against her will. Again we come up against the facts of biology. Human life comes into existence through an integral, unparalleled and demanding relationship with a mother.

This position, of course, does rest on an important assumption. It presupposes the moral status of the unborn is sufficiently ambiguous or insecure such as to warrant leaving the matter to the judgement of the mother. After all, we do not permit parents to murder their child if they decide that they no longer wish to be parents. The state has a duty to protect its citizens, and in allowing abortion the state is assuming the unborn is not yet a citizen. This is why the issue is currently so contentious in the United States, the attempt being made to take away the right of choice given by *Roe versus Wade*. The Supreme Court ruling judged that the moral status of the unborn in the first two trimesters is sufficiently ambiguous to give the claim of the mother trumps. The scales tip only in the third trimester, after a rough identification of the beginning of viability. So-called 'Pro-Life groups are challenging this. But given lack of public consensus on this, do those who believe the unborn has full moral status have a right to impose their views through the law on those not persuaded?

We are thus led to the third question: *Who decides?*

16.2.3 *Who decides?*

One straightforward answer is that the mother decides. Her right to self-determination at this crucial point is inviolable. After all, she is to carry the risk, responsibility and cost of child bearing and, invariably, child care. No one has a right to overrule that right. However strong the *prima facie* claim of the unborn child the rights of the mother in the nature of the case are paramount. Thus, Ronald Dworkin argues that the 'investment' of a mother's life is in the nature of the case higher than the 'investment' of a child in the womb since the child has no conscious interest and so cannot regret its imminent non-existence. It follows that the mother has a right to give priority to her own investment in her life.[10] Dworkin thus resists the idea that the growing child has a stronger claim because of 'vulnerability' or a longer expected life. There is not yet a conscious subject to which these notions may attach.

The position in English law, expressed mainly in the Abortion Act of 1967, is officially different. Strictly speaking, the decision is not made by the mother or allowed to the mother. In addition to allowing abortion in the case of foetal abnormality, the state permits an abortion only when two doctors can certify that the bringing of a baby to term would damage the physical or psychological health of the mother. Ever since the Bourne case of 1938, English law has allowed 'preserving the life of the mother' to be permissible of the interpretation 'preserving the mental health' of the mother, and not simply protecting her from death.[11] Dr Alec Bourne had been prosecuted for performing an abortion on a woman who had become pregnant as a result of gang rape, but he was not convicted. If, however, the decision is in the hands of the representatives of a paternalistic state – the two doctors under current English law – then it may be asked what right has anyone *to force a woman to have a child against her will*? And if it is *a man* who does the forcing, or a culture or law dominated by males, is this another instance of patriarchal oppression? We may deplore the decision of a woman who seeks an abortion for trivial or self-indulgent reasons, but does that mean the state should intervene and require her to carry the baby to term against her will? Moral disapproval is one thing. A separate case has to be made for enshrining it in criminal law or clinical practice. That said, although formally paternalistic, the law in practice gives a *de facto* right of choice since it is normally possible to find two doctors willing to certify that the denial of choice will damage the mother's emotional health.

Michael Banner appears to view all abortions as morally wrong, but this unambiguous position is arrived at by concentrating on the status of the foetus, while giving insufficient weight to the counter claims of the mother.[12] He rightly points out that a too easy appeal to 'pastoral considerations' can be patronizing, failing to honour the fact that women are moral agents who may accept an obligation to their growing child. He powerfully challenges a too confident urging of 'rights' and 'choice' pointing to the Christian call to have our minds 'remade and our whole nature transformed'. Such a 'remaking' of our minds will include receptivity to the gift of new life, instead of seeing the unborn as a threat or stranger.

All this is true; but it is in danger of becoming a prescription for every woman rather than an invitation, which some or most, but not necessarily all, will accept as compelling. The victims of rape, the young student, or the pregnant mother of three abandoned by her mate, may be women of profound moral seriousness who weigh carefully the issues, but who in the end judge, not selfishly, or stridently asserting self-indulgent rights, but rather responsibly, that nature is placing upon them too great a demand. Barth, in fact, in such cases allows that different women may judge they have different 'vocations'.[13]

It does not follow that if one rejects Banner's clearer position the only alternative is a complacency that sees an abortion as nothing more than the removal of tissue. There may be instead an agonizing and responsible balancing of competing claims. The whole point is that there are deep ambiguities in this area. We cannot flinch from the real dimension of the tragic.

Beyond the mother, what if the father's wishes differ? Moreover, does the state have a legitimate role in watching over patterns of fertility with a view to the common good? A more rigorous control of abortion would lead to children born disproportionately to households needing support in their upbringing; possibly even leading to an increase in crime.[14] Is society prepared to bear the cost? And is this a legitimate consideration in assessing the ethics of abortion?

16.2.4 A Christian perspective?

Is there a characteristic Christian perspective? The Vatican has sympathy for surgery such as to remove a cancerous womb, even if the woman is pregnant, since appeal may be made to the 'double effect'** (see 16.4). Nonetheless, there is evident over the last century a certain 'hardening' of attitude, since traditional theology did make distinctions within the process of gestation, often giving a significance to 'quickening' or to the notion of 'ensoulment' – the idea that the soul connects with the body at a certain time after conception.[15] In terms of the biology of the day, this expressed a gradualist position.

The current Vatican position is either that abortion is equivalent to infanticide, or that that which has potential must be treated as actual.[16] *Apostolicae Sedis* (1869) of Pius IX seems to represent the decisive shift towards regarding conception as the decisive point. According to a classic statement: 'However much we may pity a mother whose health and even life is gravely imperilled in the performance of the duty allocated to her by nature, nevertheless, what could ever be sufficient reason for excusing ... the direct murder of the innocent?'[17] John Paul II describes abortion as murder, an 'unspeakable crime' because it involves the elimination of a weak, defenceless and innocent human being.[18]

There are two and related problems with John Paul's argument. First, it begs the question of the moral status of the unborn. It has to be said that this is simply asserted and not argued for in *Evangelium Vitae*. Second, the assumption that abortion is equivalent to murder justifies ignoring any counter claims of the mother. This encyclical does not even mention the possibility that the rape of a minor may be an exception; neither does it settle uncertainty over the Vatican position on ectopic pregnancies. A lot of Christian writing likewise is overconfident about the moral status of the unborn, and insufficiently cognizant of the dilemma faced when there is conflict between the claims of the unborn and the reasonable claims of the mother.[19] John Wyatt, for example, writes movingly and persuasively of the reverence we should have for the new life in the womb, but he does not address difficult questions about moral status, and does not allow the force of this appeal to be tested in 'hard cases' save that of the 12-year-old child made pregnant through rape. But if some 'hard cases' elicit sympathy, why not some others? Richard Hays objects to discussing the question in terms of the language of 'rights'. Life, he insists, is rather a gift of grace.[20] Of course it is, and this claim should be urged, but what when, after agonizing consideration, it cannot be perceived as a gift?

It could be urged that the ambiguity over the moral status of the unborn is resolved by claiming that the growing child has a worth conferred by God. As a ground for giving the growing child the 'benefit of the doubt' and a strong *prima facie* claim, this is a reasonable position for a Christian to take. But that is far from saying it has trumps over the prospective mother who cannot perceive the matter in this way. However strongly we affirm the dignity and sacredness of human life in the eyes of God, we still have to make hard judgements as to the moral status of the unborn human; in other words, concerning when that dignity and sacredness is accorded. Theology cannot ignore the biological reality that human life develops gradually.

While the decision to have an abortion is an individual one, abortion always takes place against a social and cultural background. Christian nurture will certainly commend a responsible expression of our sexuality, such as to reduce the number of unwanted pregnancies. Christians will want to encourage networks of support for parenting within church and civil society. Adoption may in some cases be an alternative, but that will depend on a woman's consent to being *de facto* a surrogate mother. Christians will also encourage responsible fatherhood, since the absence of a father adds to the pressure upon a mother. There will be a critique of a male resort to abortion as a means of escaping responsibility in sex. That said, it seems too harsh to say to a woman that if she consents to sex she thereby consents to pregnancy, thus foreclosing the option of an abortion.[21] This is so not least because the notion of consent is problematical and related to a whole range of social and cultural factors that may undermine the proper autonomy of women. As Ann Loads has argued, a women's willingness to 'appropriate the grace of pregnancy' is related to whether or not society supports parenting and permits proper self-governance for women and gender justice.[22]

There is no Christian wisdom on this issue that delivers us from ambiguity. A Christian demeanour will indeed bring to the topic a generous commitment to the vulnerable, and a receptivity to the gift of new life. The nascent life is not lightly to be treated as an intrusion or threat, but as a gift to be cherished and inviting the noble vocation of parenting.[23] Furthermore, as Rosalind Hursthouse has argued, moral language that stresses the 'right' of a woman to self-determination should be balanced against the encouragement to nurture a virtue and wisdom that values child bearing and parenting, the 'value of love and family life and our proper emotional development through a natural life cycle'.[24] If we prematurely assert our right to self-determination, we are in danger of diminishing our lives through failure to be receptive to this gift. For Christians, the onus against abortion will be as strong as for anyone. But that is not to say abortion is never justified. A lot of Christian (normally male) writing on abortion lacks realism because it ignores the facts of biology. Human life comes into being in a way that is gradual and vulnerable, and through a unique and unparalleled relationship between a woman and the foetus. This relationship is wonderful when the pregnancy is wanted, but when not it is simply impossible to give equal weight to the claims of a woman and those of the unborn. No Ethical Knight Errant is able to slay the dragons of dilemma, ambiguity and tragedy and the attempt so to do can only add to the human costs. Of course, many women and their partners will accept a child as a blessing and a gift, nobly accepting the demands alongside the joys. Many, if not most, will weigh seriously the moral dimensions, acknowledging the growing child has a *prima facie* claim to protection. The emotional and physiological considerations will be weighed alongside the ethical. Given, however, that the developing claims of the unborn are more precarious than the actual claims of the mother it seems difficult to resist the argument that a woman has an overriding right to make the considered and responsible judgement that a particular pregnancy is for her an unreasonable burden to bear.

16.3 The beginning of life

There is a further range of issues that can hardly be separated from the question we have just discussed, although here we can indicate them only briefly. The moral status of the unborn human is relevant not only to the question of abortion, but also to 'reproductive technology'. *In vitro* fertilization involves fertilization and thus the bringing into being of human embryos (sometimes called zygotes or pre-embryos) outside the human body. An embryo may then be implanted in the womb. *In vitro* fertilization involves the production of 'spare' embryos, which may be used for research or which may be discarded. The research may lead to improved techniques for this kind of assisted reproduction, but may also open up other possibilities as well.

The starting point seems fairly straightforward. If we judge that the embryo has full moral status, on the basis of either actuality or potentiality, then research on embryos, thereby forfeiting their life, is unacceptable. *In vitro* fertilization is likewise unacceptable because of 'spare' embryos that are sacrificed. The Vatican's opposition is consonant with its claim that the embryo has full moral status right from conception. For various reasons, a similar position is adopted by the protestant Paul Ramsey.[25]

Suppose, however, we claim that moral status is attained gradually? Only modest moral status attaches in the early stages. It could then be argued that the benefits of overcoming a couple's distressing infertility, and of related research, outweigh the unease we have about experimentation and the discarding of embryos arising out of *in vitro* fertilization. This, in fact, was the conclusion of the Government Committee of Inquiry into Human Fertilization and Embryology, leading to the 'Warnock' report which is now the basis of English law and medical practice. *In vitro* fertilization is permitted, as is research on embryos up to 14 days. This is the time of 'differentiation' with regard to the grouping of cells, some to develop into the foetus and others the placenta. It is also the time of twinning, should twinning occur. Although not arbitrary, there is certain pragmatism in deciding that this is the point.

In vitro fertilization opens the door to research on embryos with a view of bettering the success rate of the treatment. But other avenues of research are opened up as well. There is, for example, the possibility of research into genetics. Suppose some debilitating disease is discovered to have a genetic origin. An embryo carrying the gene could be identified early on and elimination would be no more problematical than a later abortion for the same reason. It could be less problematical since the elimination is earlier. Alternatively, there is the possibility of some genetic manipulation or genetic replacement therapy. In this way the propensity for the disease may be eliminated without eliminating the embryo.

Many will be content with the stance of Warnock. The moral status of the pre-embryo, merely a group of totipotent cells, is sufficiently modest to permit the benefits outlined. It appears medical science has many hurdles to surmount before more substantial possibilities are opened up. Genetic intervention and manipulation is a risky business and we must proceed with caution. The risks need to be identified.

For instance, there is the danger that some genetic engineering might have a serious 'knock on' effect not initially apparent. Genes associated with some diseases may have other effects that are beneficial. For example, the gene associated with sickle cell anaemia appears to give some immunity to malaria.

Are there ethical issues arising out of *in vitro* fertilization itself? We have already considered one objection, and suggested it is not persuasive (3.10). But are there others? Does assisted reproduction heighten the risk of a child suffering from disability or serous illness? Are patients sufficiently apprised of the risks and low success rate? The desire of a disappointed couple to have a child can be immensely powerful. How can medical advice be sensitive to this without being paternalistic? What are the issues when the technique involves surrogacy and egg or sperm donation? Is surrogacy to be seen as a gift relationship, or is it acceptable on a commercial bias? What value do we attach to biological connections and are there issues here for the self-understanding of the person born? Is a child born from expensive private IVF to carry an unreasonable burden of parental expectation? In allocating health care resources, what priority is to be given to infertility? Should reproductive technology be filtered on the basis of the 'suitability' of the mother (with or without a partner) for parenthood and, if so, what are the criteria? Can this be justified, given that parents have total freedom over normal reproduction? Are there issues – especially regarding the well-being of the child – if the mother is beyond normal child-bearing age?

These are not the kind of questions that suggest there is anything inherently wrong with *in vitro* fertilization, merely that there are issues to be addressed so that couples longing for a child may fully benefit, and so that everything that can be done in the child's best interests is done. Medical ethics is not about tormenting people, erecting unreasonable prohibitions, or finding out what is happening in order to stop it. It is rather about helping one another to flourish as much as possible within the context of respect for the value and dignity of life.

Moving away from *in vitro* fertilization, what about the wider possibilities of genetic research, genetic manipulation and gene replacement? Research is advancing rapidly. Who can say what might be possible in ten years' time? We are talking, of course, about a person's genetic imprint only. We are not determined by our genes. A 'cloned' human being (if such becomes a possibility) is not identical to the parent, merely one with the same gene profile, a kind of delayed twin. Many of our most valuable characteristics as human persons appear not to be genetically determined, although they may be gene related. Genes are only one factor in that mishmash that makes us what we are.

Many express an unease about 'designer babies' – parents choosing say the gender, hair and eye colour of a child. There will be greater unease about manipulating genes that predispose the child to be this kind of person rather than that, although that prospect is probably fanciful. Suppose we are able to eliminate serious diseases or disability – is there a line to be drawn between this and babies 'made to order' either by their parents or by a mad dictator? Beyond eliminating identifiable disability, disease or disease propensity, what good reason might there be to engage in gene manipulation or replacement? Sex selection is an obvious example. Is sex selection justifiable – save where a disease or disability is gender specific? Is it compatible with belief in gender equality? Does a sex preference imply a culture of prejudice or discrimination against a particular sex? Furthermore, widespread choice in this area would run the danger of unbalancing a population's sex ratio.

Suppose it is possible through gene manipulation to reduce the possibility of a child being born with a propensity to homosexual orientation. Do parents have the right to make such a decision on behalf of their child yet to be born? Does the decision betray a deplorable heterosexual prejudice? Do we thereby deprive our communities of the rich contribution of those who are gay?

It is reasonable to ask if there are choices it is unwise to give ourselves. The more we control, the less a child is a gift. This is not to indulge in sentimentality, but to recognize that the dignity and self-worth of our children depend largely on the fact that in their difference they are given to us; they are not designed to our specifications. The flourishing of our human race depends on this in all kinds of ways, and not only because of a rich gene pool. Are there boundaries we should not cross – for our sake and for the sakes of our own children? It seems that there are.

It is difficult to identify those boundaries with absolute precision. As in the case of abortion, ethical reflection cannot always draw lines clearly, but the law can. In other words, political debate and decision making draw lines that are enshrined in law and medical practice. These lines are not arbitrary but they make a judgement over ambiguities. We have no option sometimes but to step on slippery slopes. There is no reason, however, why we cannot find a foothold. In this kind of area the law's function is to define clearly what ethical judgement is bound to find more ambiguous.

16.4 Medically assisted dying

There is no single thing that is described by phrases such as 'medically assisted dying' or 'voluntary euthanasia'. Different legal frameworks may put in place different procedures and safeguards, different grounds may be allowed, and boundaries may be located in different places. In the case of 'voluntary euthanasia' (VE) a person's death will be intentionally brought about by a medical third party, but in any civilized society there will be at least two conditions. First, this will be at the patient's request, or with the patient's presumed consent, because the quality of life is no longer acceptable to them. Second, strict procedures will be followed and there will be safeguards to prevent abuse.

Lord Joffe's recent bill on assisted dying (AD), defeated in the House of Lords in May 2006, proposed the legalization of medically assisted dying, but only within carefully defined limits. It applied to the terminally ill only, and then only to those able to make and express an informed judgement. Furthermore, self-administration by the patient was essential. A whole series of safeguards was to be put in place to ensure vulnerable members of society were not put at risk.

The subject is high on the current agenda for at least two reasons. First, people in the West increasingly demand the right of self-determination, and this combined with an emphasis on the quality of life, which sometimes conflicts with its duration. Second, there is the fear that the benefits of modern health care are such as sometimes to extend life beyond the time when its quality is acceptable.

Happily, the majority will die naturally, with pain controlled and with reasonable dignity. Palliative care for those suffering terminal illness can be excellent and no exponent of VE/AD would wish to deny it to those who opt for that route. The issue is whether the law should be changed to allow, in carefully identified cases and with the safeguards of protocols, a positive response to a request for voluntary euthanasia or medically assisted dying.

16.4.1 Theological arguments

Christians sometimes offer specifically theological arguments against VE/AD. Essentially they challenge the right of autonomy and of a person to judge that their future, on account of illness, pain or failed powers, is such that the prospect of living through that future fills them with dread.

First, there may be an appeal to a theologically based belief in the value and sacredness of life. This is not in question; but it is a *non sequitur* to derive from that premise, without further argument, the insistence that it is never appropriate to take steps to relinquish one's life. On the contrary, it could be held that precisely because life is sacred and of value there may be occasions when existence is such a travesty of the quality and richness we seek that we demonstrate belief in life's sacredness when sometimes we take steps to relinquish it.

Second, Christians may appeal to the argument: 'Life is a gift from God and only God can take it away.'[26] Again this seems a *non sequitur*. Life is indeed a precious gift from God. But it does not follow that there cannot, in principle, be occasions when it is a responsible judgement that the time has come to relinquish it. The gift of life ceases to be a gift when it becomes an intolerable burden. Moreover, presupposed in this argument seems to be the notion of God as like a swimming pool attendant who directs us out of the pool when our time is up. It seems, however, a credible understanding of God must envisage God as through creation relinquishing control, allowing creation to work according to its own patterns. It follows that God does not decide when we die. The time of our death is rather a function of a whole web of factors that make us what we are. Furthermore, the God who has given us the gift of life has also given us responsibility and choice. Why should it be disallowed to take steps to relinquish life, but not to take steps to prolong it or better its quality? Why is the former but not the latter encroaching on God's preserve?

A third argument insists that a Christian spirituality will seek to face confidently whatever life offers, assured that the grace of God will be sufficient. With the right attitude, no situation is without its redemptive potential. Suffering and deprivation may even be embraced as learning experiences, furthering personal and spiritual growth. If suffering cannot be avoided, then, by God's grace, we should look for some redemptive potential within it. Thus, John Hapgood speaks of the faith that God can redeem and make bearable even the most desperate situations.[27] Likewise, Rowan Williams, debating Lord Joffe's bill, claimed 'there is no stage of human life, and no level of human experience, that is intrinsically incapable of being lived through in some kind of trust and hope'.[28] It seems, however, a *non sequitur* so to premise a total rejection of VE/AD. This statement expresses a profound Christian conviction, and it challenges a superficial hedonism, which can sometimes regard a pain-free life as a fundamental right. Pain and suffering are realities, and where unavoidable may by the grace of God have a redemptive dimension. Such considerations may need to be urged, but they do not preclude the responsible judgement in some cases that the time has come to relinquish life back to God. Moreover, this argument questions whether God's grace, and this redemptive potential, are sometimes manifest precisely in the deliberate relinquishing back to God of a life that has come to its end. Maybe in some circumstances life becomes so bleak and suffering so intense that the 'redemptive potential' of which the Archbishop speaks is to be found only in death.

We must also resist the claim that what may be appropriate for one must be appropriate for all. Christian literature sometimes holds up the example of those who have heroically lived through the gravest suffering and illness. They are to be honoured, but one person's vocation is not everyone's vocation. To offer the invitation is one thing, but there can be a subtle tyranny in denying to people the option of VE/AD if they judge it right for them.

We leave behind specifically theological considerations and enter the arena of public debate. Sometimes a parallel between animals and humans is drawn. It seems odd, so it is argued, that we are prosecuted for assisting the dying of a human on account of suffering, while if an animal suffers we are prosecuted for not ending it. Why does an animal deserve better treatment than a human?[29] This argument, however, is not decisive since there are important differences between humans and other animals that may justify different treatment. For example, the thorny problem of creating a culture where the vulnerable may be subject to emotional pressure to consent to VE/AD is not an issue for animals, neither do we worry overmuch about what constitutes animal 'consent'.

16.4.2 Law and morals

Suppose the above considerations persuade us that it is morally wrong to seek VE/AD, or, more circumspectly, wrong for Christians. Do we thereby have a right to take away that option from others who judge otherwise? There may indeed be the invitation to see that there is 'no stage of human life ... that is intrinsically incapable of being lived through in some kind of trust and hope' but this is no ground for the continued illegality of VE/AD for those not so persuaded. The relationship between law and morals is complex. Fundamentally, law is concerned with defending liberty and protecting the exploited, the defenceless and vulnerable. No one is proposing VE/AD be mandatory – merely that it be an available option in appropriate circumstances. We need arguments in addition to those so far considered if this is to be opposed. Otherwise we take away the freedom of those who see things differently.

16.4.3 The central tension

I wish to argue that the fundamental issue is difficult because of a tension between competing claims. It is a tension not easy to resolve.

On the one hand, there is the *prima facie* right of self-determination. I am losing my sight, and a stroke has rendered me incontinent and virtually immobile. I have severe arthritis. Widowed, there is no one who would be devastated by my death. My circle of friends and family might even welcome the end of my suffering. Life no longer has quality. I wish to take steps to end my life with dignity NOW. On what grounds am I compelled to follow an ethic I do not believe in? On what grounds does the state compel me to live against my will? Pastorally, it is difficult not to have enormous sympathy here, and ethically, it is difficult to resist the claim that a person has a strong *prima facie* right to self-determination. This right may not be absolute. The responsible person will take into account the networks of relationships of which they are part. And a supposed right to die does not impose obligations on anyone – including medical personnel – to act contrary to their conscience. But the *prima facie* right to self-determination remains strong. Michael Northcott's protest at the 'utilitarian prioritization of the minimization of suffering over all other moral good' seems unfair. The balanced and considered judgement that VE/AD may be appropriate in some circumstances need not imply such a shallow ethic.[30] Many object that medical opposition to VE/AD is expressive, at worst, of a paternalism bordering on tyranny. It is almost as if one is told, 'The doctors know what is good for you. How dare you be dissatisfied with our drugs and palliative care?'

On the other hand, there is a proper concern for the good of the wider society. Let us suppose VE/AD is legalized. Would the vulnerable, the impressionable and those with low self-esteem, anxious about being a burden on family or health care resources, be subject to subtle emotional pressure to allow themselves to be put away? Would relatives with an eye to inheritance think VE/AD is the preferred alternative to expensive residential care, and so impose subtle pressure?

> They bumped old granny off you know, she had a cold.
> Her suffering, they told the court, was dreadful to behold.
> The judge was kind; besides, he said, she was getting rather old.
> So they left the court and went away to share old granny's gold.

Would we create a culture which expects the elderly to think it selfish to hang on? Would a right to die become a duty to die?[31] And would this lead to a right to end the life of another? Would health care accountants favour VE/AD as the most cost-effective way of handling terminal or chronic illness? And (granted that no doctor be required to act against their conscience) what effect would a change have on the medical profession and how we regard it? Would budgets for more expensive palliative and geriatric care be reduced? Would life become 'cheaper', and the legal acceptability of the practice lessen society's reverence for the inviolability of human life? Speaking of the 'worthwhileness of life', we may ask 'Do we, by legally accommodating the mental suffering of some, debase the currency for all?'[32] Few fail to take seriously these concerns, but not everyone is convinced they have trumps. Why should providing an option in carefully defined circumstances have these grave consequences? Vigilance and codes of practice can hold these dangers at bay. Obviously, there need to be clear codes of practice. A patient's request must be fully informed, clear and repeated. The patient must be convinced there is no reasonable alternative, given the suffering and poor quality of life. Similarly, vigorous criteria must be in place for the comatose.

The heart of the dilemma, then, is how to resolve the tension between the *prima facie* right of individual self-determination and the *prima facie* duty of the state to seek the common good and the protection of the vulnerable. It may not be unreasonable for the state to continue to restrict the right of the individual for the sake of the wider good. Few rights are absolute. They need to be balanced against other claims.

People come to different judgements as to how this tension is to be resolved. Simon Blackburn plays down the danger to the common good. Describing as the 'most serious argument' the anxiety that there are people who will profit by another's extinction, he remarks: 'The evil seems small and controllable, compared with the painless termination of many of the worst kinds of dying.'[33] Brad Hooker comes to a similar conclusion: 'Any law allowing euthanasia would need to be very carefully drafted. And the law would have to be rigorously policed to prevent abuse. Though not certain, I am confident these things could be done. And undeniably the benefits, mainly in terms of the decrease of suffering and the increase in autonomy, are potentially enormous.'[34] It may be urged also that if there are dangers in changing the law, a change would have the advantage of allowing comfort and assurance to those who with advancing health problems and declining powers dread a lingering end.[35]

By contrast, the churches have tended officially to be less confident. It is not impossible this is partly because the churches are pastorally more in touch with vulnerable people than are the liberal intelligentsia among whom support for VE/AD is stronger. A joint statement of the Anglican and Roman Catholic bishops argued, not unreasonably, that to justify a 'change in the law it would be necessary to show that such a change would remove greater evils than it would cause'.[36] One of the evils it would cause is that some patients would be 'under pressure to allow themselves to be put away'. Anglican moral theologian Gordon Dunstan was firm in his opposition a generation ago.[37] Even stronger opposition is found in John Paul II's eleventh encyclical, *Evangelium Vitae*. It speaks of the incomparable worth, sacred reality and dignity of the human person and has hard hitting things to say about injustice and exploitation. But just as this belief rules out 'subhuman living conditions, arbitrary imprisonment, deportation, slavery', etc., so also it rules out euthanasia even when requested by the patient. The cumulative case laid out against what is called a 'culture of death'[38] is essentially the cumulative case summarized here.[39]

The question is essentially: How confident can we be that having stepped on the 'slippery slope' we will not end up in a heap at the bottom? The slippery slope argument is a serious one, but it need not have trumps. In all kinds of contexts we cannot help but step on slippery slopes. There is no inevitability that we slip. We can find secure footholds. Yes, we may slide a bit and make mistakes, but no moral stance or practice on this issue is without its ambiguities and dangers. Much of life is about struggling on slippery slopes. There is rarely a firm cliff of moral certainty.

Sometimes the British experience of the law on abortion is cited as a warning. A law intended to permit abortion in carefully identified circumstances led to a practice far more permissive than intended. Abortion is *de facto* available on demand since it is normally possible for a woman to find two doctors who will testify that a baby will damage her emotional and mental health. If VE/AD is permitted for the terminally ill who clearly wish it, will the result be that the elderly will soon feel pressured not to continue their lives at the expense of the young? Thus, Robin Gill expresses the fear that a change for compassionate reasons may create a society less compassionate.[40] So significant is this concern, that it is dignified with its own academic jargon. People talk of 'procedural deterioration' and 'unintended consequence'. Others, however, cite the evidence of the Dutch Remmelink Commission as reassuring as far as the experience of the Netherlands is concerned.[41] Furthermore, Lord Joffe argued that eight years after Oregon's *Death with Dignity* act there is no 'credible evidence of abuse'.[42]

Oddly, the issue resolves itself as one that is as much sociological as ethical. Can we with confidence predict what effects a change in the law would have on the culture and values of our society?

16.4.4 Further issues

The matter is further complicated by three more thorny questions.

The first concerns the nature of consent. Let us assume no one is to be helped to die against their will. Euthanasia must be voluntary. But how do we determine the 'real' will? Suppose someone requests medically assisted suicide at a time of depression or acute pain? Does this express their 'real' desire? Or suppose the request is rooted in a desire not to be a burden? In other cases the desire is 'real' but rooted in a sense of low self-worth. Or suppose the 'presenting' issue is the request for VE/AD but the 'real' issue is the fear of uncontrolled pain. And what of those unable to answer for themselves? On what basis do we presume consent? What right does anyone have to decide this on another's behalf? Or suppose a patient signed in the past a 'living will' or an 'advance directive' but, on account of unconsciousness or dementia is unable to confirm their earlier wish. Does the wish expressed then express the wish now?

This is a real can of worms. Those having responsibility for care must wrestle with the tension between the 'presenting' and the 'real'. But if we say the 'presenting' is never the 'real' we are guilty of a paternalism bordering on tyranny. Perhaps the least problematic way of resolving this issue is to follow a code of practice that requires fully informed consent, repeated over a period of time, and when the patient is 'of sound mind'. Not to respect that is unacceptable paternalism.

The difficulty is just as acute when patients are unable to answer for themselves. Suppose someone is permanently comatose. Is it ethically justifiable to terminate such a life, even if the 'person' appears no longer to be there? Where there is no consciousness and no prospect of consciousness are we in fact ending the life of a 'person', or only a body manifesting some of life's functions? Suppose we have no way of determining what their wish would be. Do we have a right to terminate the life? Is termination supposed to be 'good for them', or is it really good for health care budgets?

The second difficulty concerns the troubled distinction between things we *do* and things we *merely permit*. In this instance the distinction is between the acts of terminating life and acts of letting die. The law allows us to let people die. There is no legal obligation to preserve life to the limit of medical ability. A patient may refuse treatment, therefore hastening their passing. If the patient is unable to express consent one way or the other, there are protocols that permit the withdrawal of treatment. 'Thou shalt not kill but needs not strive officiously to keep alive.'[43] The distinction between 'killing' and 'letting die' is conceptually coherent and central to medical practice upheld by the law. But is there a significant *ethical* distinction? Where is the coherence in respecting a person's right to refuse treatment but not their request for VE/AD? It seems a very fragile distinction upon which to build the edifice of current medical practice upheld in draconian fashion by the law. In withholding treatment we are acquiescing in avoidable death through an act of omission.

Related to this is the so-called principle of the 'double effect'.** This principle points out that many actions have more than one consequence. We are not, however, responsible for an unavoidable consequence if some other consequence is our laudable intention. Many analgesics have 'double effects'. They relieve pain, but they may also hasten death. Death is thus hastened by our practice. The death, however, is not intended. The relief of suffering is the intention.

It is a deeply troubled argument. It is based on the principle that we have no responsibility for a *known consequence* of our action provided that known consequence is not our *direct intention*. This is a very difficult principle to justify, and it is difficult to think of comparable instances when we would allow such a defence. Death as a secondary is known beforehand. Although not directly intended, it is known to be part of the package. The reality is that in such cases *a decision is made to reduce suffering by allowing a hastening of death*. The alternative of not relieving the pain has been rejected. There may be a 'double effect' but one is responsible for both effects, even if one's prime intention is the one rather than the other. A compromise between the duration of life and the relief of suffering has been accepted.

To allow this but not VE/AD is to live with a troubled distinction. Present law and medical practice seek to ignore the known consequence of an act and instead focus on the intention behind it. The most one can say for this is that the line that is drawn is one of a workable pragmatism. Sometimes workable pragmatism is the best we can hope for, but the fact remains we are already on the slippery slope and there are other footholds no less secure a little further down.

There is a third difficulty. If VE/AD is to be permitted, we must ask for what reason. The most likely candidate is terminal illness involving pain and the distress of failing powers. Lord Joffe's bill related to terminal illness only. But what of illness that is chronic but not terminal? What of loss of sight or hearing? What of loss of a limb? Where do we draw the line? Most proponents of VE/AD draw the line fairly sharply under terminal illness although some will include the gravest chronic conditions. But how grave must they be, and if some conditions are allowed, why not others? Do we end up allowing medically assisted euthanasia 'on demand' for those tired of life? What of those who have no chronic or terminal illness but who wish an end to '*the slings and arrows of outrageous fortune ... the heartache, and the thousand natural shocks that flesh is heir to*'?[44]

The debate will continue until such a time as the law is changed and, if and when it is changed, the debate will shift into ensuring our protocols and procedures are robust enough to enable us to enjoy the benefits while avoiding the pitfalls.

Notes

1 Simon Blackburn, *Being Good*, Oxford, Oxford University Press, 2001, p. 61.

2 Peter Singer, *Practical Ethics*, Cambridge, Cambridge University Press, 1993, p. 155.

3 Ronald Dworkin, *Life's Dominion*, London, HarperCollins, 1993, pp. 68ff., 74–5.

4 Mary Anne Warren, 'On the Moral and Legal Status of Abortion' in Hugh Lafollette (ed.), *Ethics in Practice*, Oxford, Blackwell, 1997, pp. 79ff.

5 The image is that of Ronald Dworkin in *Life's Dominion*, p. 77.

6 Peter Singer, *Rethinking Life and Death* p. 217. See also Helga Kuhse and Peter Singer *Should a Baby Live?* Oxford, Oxford University Press, 1985.

7 Singer, *Practical Ethics*, pp. 169ff., 181ff.

8 Judith Jarvis Thomson, 'A Defence of Abortion' in Lafollette (ed.), *Ethics in Practice*, pp. 69ff.

9 Warren, 'On the Moral and Legal Status', p. 80.

10 Dworkin, *Life's Dominion*, pp. 84ff.

11 Church Information Office, *Abortion: An ethical discussion*, 1965.

12 Michael Banner, *Christian Ethics and Contemporary Moral Problems*, Cambridge, Cambridge University Press, 1999, pp. 119ff.

13 Karl Barth, *Church Dogmatics*, III.4, pp. 421ff.

14 Some have suggested a correlation between lower incidence of crime and the absence of a cohort of adults consequent upon Roe versus Wade. E.g. Steven D. Levitt, *Freakonomics*, London, Allen Lane, 2005.

15 This for Aquinas was 40 days, but only for a boy! Girls had to wait until 90 days: *Summa Theologiae*, 1a 118a 2.

16 Pius IX, *Apostolicae Sedis* (1869). See also the Vatican, 1974, *Declaration on Procured Abortion*.

17 Pius XI, *Casti Connubii*, Vatican, 1930, Section IV.

18 John Paul II, *Evangelium Vitae*, Vatican, 1995, especially Section 58.

19 A notable exception is the report adopted by the British Methodist Conference in 1990, *The Status of the Unborn Human*, especially paragraphs 1.3.2 and 4.5.

20 Richard Hays, *The Moral Vision of the New Testament*, Edinburgh, T&T Clark, 1996, p. 454.

21 John Stott, *Issues Facing Christians Today*, London, Marshall Pickering, 1990, p. 313.

22 Ann Loades, *Feminist Theology: Voices from the Past*, Cambridge, Polity Press, 2001, p. 69.

23 Loades, *Feminist Theology*, pp. 38 ff.

24 Rosalind Hursthouse, 'Virtue Theory and Abortion' in Roger Crisp and Michael Slote, *Virtue Ethics*, Oxford, Oxford University Press, 1997, p. 223.

25 Paul Ramsey, *Fabricated Man*, New Haven, Yale University Press, 1970.

26 This is the argument of John Paul II in *Iura et Bona*, Vatican Sacred Congregation, 1980, Section I. It is found also in Thomas Aquinas, *Summa Theologiae*, II-II 64.5.

27 John Habgood, *A Working Faith*, London, Darton, Longman & Todd, 1980, p. 143.

28 Rowan Williams, *House of Lords Hansard*, 12 May 2006, column 1196.

29 Blackburn, *Being Good*, pp. 71–2

30 Michael Northcott in Robin Gill (ed.), *Euthanasia and the Churches*, London, Cassell, 1998, p. 73.

31 Letter signed by the Chief Rabbi and the Archbishops of Canterbury and Westminster, *The Times*, 13 May 2006.

32 Rowan Williams, *House of Lords Hansard*, 12 May 2006, column 1198.

33 Blackburn, *Being Good*, p. 71. The argument was also offered by Leslie D. Weatherhead in *Why do Men Suffer?*, London, SCM Press, 1935, p. 125.

34 Brad Hooker, 'Rule Utilitarianism and Euthanasia' in Hugh LaFollette (ed.), *Ethics in Practice*, Oxford, Blackwell, 1997, p. 51.

35 P. H. Nowell-Smith, 'The Right to Die' in Paul Badham, *Ethics on the Frontier of Human Existence*, New York, Paragon, 1992.

36 Church Information Office, *On Dying Well*, second edition, 2000, p. 73.

37 Gordon Dunstan, *The Artifice of Ethics*, London, SCM Press, 1974, pp. 88ff.

38 John Paul II, *Evangelium Vitae*, Vatican, 1995, Section 64.

39 John Paul II, *Evangelium Vitae*, Section 66.

40 Robin Gill (ed.), *Euthanasia and the Churches*, London, Cassell, 1998, p. 27.

41 Thus Paul Badham in Gill (ed.), *Euthanasia and the Churches*, p. 56.

42 Lord Joffe, *House of Lords Hansard*, 12 May 2006, column 1184.

43 Arthur Hugh Clough, 'The New Decalogue'.

44 Shakespeare, *Hamlet*, Act 3, Scene 1.

Postscript: Comfortable Words[1]

The fundamental claim of this book is that ethics is about discovering together what serves in and through our relations with one another our mutual well-being or flourishing. This is a robust and even defiant humanistic ethic. Humanity is not, as Cupitt says – rather mysteriously and with much caricature of the Christian tradition – 'constrained or directed by exalted and invisible entities of rather obscure status'.[2] Any moral claim has to attest its credentials in terms of our well-being. This is true of even the most venerable of biblical texts. Indeed, such a humanistic ethic has a strong claim to resonate with the biblical tradition for which God's will is again and again stated to be *for our good*. It follows that the good life is not about a minimal keeping to the straight and narrow. It is positively and imaginatively about creating value.[3]

The notion of human well-being or enhancement puts ethics in the public realm. Ethics can be sensibly discussed because human beings have so much in common. We can discuss together in the public realm what serves the enhancement of our lives. The notion, nonetheless, discourages ethical colonialism because it allows different people in different contexts to discover what flourishing means for them. It carries the nuances of justice, inclusiveness and respect for freedom, and so escapes the 'hermeneutic of suspicion', which sees ethics as in the pay of the powerful. Above all, it responds to widespread moral convictions about what ethics is about. There can be no final and finished blueprint for human flourishing. A stress on human well-being gives a large place to individual freedom since enjoying such freedom is part of what our good involves. It will resist the clench-fisted bullying which is all too common in some writings on 'Christian ethics' where we are told 'on authority' what we can and cannot do.

We have developed, however, a particular form of humanism – a Christian humanism which claims that human life is valued and nourished all the more when seen within the context of the love and redeeming grace of God. To the 'secular' focus on human well-being the Christian adds the additional focus of asking what manner of life is a fitting response to our vision of God. If for those made in the image of God the good life is about responding to the grace of God, and in so doing to find salvation, then ethics must be rooted in the nature of things. We have also seen that such a humanistic ethic does not exclude – indeed it requires – a proper regard for animals and the earth.

But is this a book on *Christian* ethics? This question prompts another: What *constitutes* a Christian ethic? I have rejected the kind of Christian ethic that is so all pervadingly theological or even ecclesial that there can be no participation in the forum of public debate. The ethic defended in this book remains a theological ethic – but it is the kind of theological ethic that honours our capacity simply as human beings to engage with ethical issues. The 'earth is the Lord's and the fullness thereof' and all people bear the stamp of the divine image. There is a divine 'kenosis'** (that is 'self-emptying') in the giving of worth and autonomy to creation and its life. 'We see the goodness of the Lord in the land of the living.'[4]

The study of ethics can be a deeply disturbing experience. The study properly confronts our prejudices, our complacencies, and the narrow limits of our compassion and sympathy. But it is disturbing in another way. We are presented with agonizingly perplexing dilemmas, not amenable to simple solutions. When Britain eventually lost the final decisive battle in the American Wars of Independence it took three weeks for the news to reach London. Today in our global village all news is instant news and that is one reason why the world is now an immensely more complicated place. There is something almost objectionable to modern readers in the way in which H. A. Prichard and David Ross in the 1930s gave the impression that ethics is simply about the general obligations of promise keeping and truth telling in the privileged world of pre-war Oxford.[5] We cannot get away with that now.

The second part of this book has illustrated the intractable nature of many of the dilemmas we face. It goes without saying we wrestle with them as responsibly as we can, and with all the resources we can muster. But how do we cope with the sense of dislocation, perplexity, inadequacy and failure? It helps to remember the classic Christian insistence that we live, not by 'works' but by 'grace'. A 'work' may be a life of moral rectitude. A 'work' may be some achievement or some deep understanding of a particular issue. A 'work' may also be some moral discernment. It is important not to despise 'works'. We rightly value our achievements, our gifts and our creativity. Human genius and goodness are as much a reality as are human frailty and evil. The claim that we are not 'saved' or 'justified' by our 'works' is not to be taken as despising or devaluing 'works'. But in the last analysis our self-respect and standing before God do not depend them. Our standing depends on being upheld by grace. We need to remember this when we are successful as much as when we are failures. We live by grace.[6]

The knowledge that, in the last analysis, we live by grace saves us from clambering for the good 'works' of a perfect moral insight, which can easily express a zeal that lacks humility and gentleness. When it comes to moral judgement – to repeat a metaphor used earlier – the anchor may be reasonably secure, but the chain is long and slack and the sea is stormy. As has been amply illustrated in the third part of this book there are many ethical issues so intractable that no response is without ambiguity. The most we can hope for is to struggle to find as much integrity and responsibility as possible. This suggests that ethics has to be more exploratory and less prescriptive, more humble and less judgemental, than it often is. It also means we indulge in less fantasizing about our own moral insight and rectitude. The arrogance and the hypocrisy of the moralist can be just as obnoxious as that of the 'know-all' religious believer.

Many in the churches long for 'clear teaching' and a 'strong moral lead'. The trouble is, such calls are usually made, not where they are justified, as in confronting racism or blatant injustice, but in areas where we have found genuine ambiguity. We have to live with this ambiguity. Christian faith is not about giving us all the certainties we might long for. On the contrary, it more authentically confronts this longing as often rooted in a pride which takes ourselves too seriously. Instead, it resources us to live with uncertainty. It can be immensely liberating to realize that we are not heavily guilty if we cannot always see with clarity what is right or wrong. For the book of Job, 'wisdom' in its fullness is not available to us. For us, the heart of wisdom is 'the fear of the Lord' and 'departing from evil' is understanding.[7] Our quietness of mind is not found in our grasp of ethical wisdom. Our quietness of mind is found in seeking to live with as much integrity, wisdom and compassion as we can muster in our complicated world. If we fail, or rather *when* we fail, we remember that we live not by our wisdom or achievements but by grace. This connects with the insight that the heart of the good life is not knowledge of right doing, but a firmer grasp of right being, in which we love mercy, do justly and walk humbly before our God.[8]

Notes

1 The phrase is from Cranmer's Liturgy for Holy Communion in the 1662 *Book of Common Prayer.*

2 Don Cupitt, *The New Christian Ethics,* London, SCM Press, 1988, p. 1.

3 Cupitt, *The New Christian Ethics,* pp. 4 and 22.

4 Psalms 27. 13.

5 W. David Ross, *The Right and the Good,* Oxford, 1930; *The Foundations of Ethics,* Oxford, 1939; H. A. Prichard, 'Does Moral Philosophy Rest on a Mistake' (1912) in *Moral Obligation,* Oxford, 1968.

6 On this see Hans Küng, *Justification,* London, Burns & Oates, 1964, p. xxvi.

7 Job 28.28.

8 Micah 6.8.

Glossary

Many of the notions listed below are ambiguous, require delicate nuancing, and are often given quite complicated conceptual analysis. This glossary does not attempt a strict analysis but simply gives indicative explanations that enable the reader to follow the text where these notions are used.

Anonymous Christians
The term used by the Roman Catholic theologian Karl Rahner to describe people of other faiths. Their devotion to God and purity of life is understood to express an implicit desire for fulfilment in Christianity. They are thus 'anonymous Christians'. The idea has been widely criticized. People of other faiths have a right to be self-defining. The notion expresses a subtle Christian colonialism and an implicit denial that the Spirit of God is active outside the sphere of Christianity.

Anthropocentric
Human centred. An ethic which gives priority to human need over and against an independent regard for the earth. It implies also a subordination of animal welfare to human need.

Autonomy of ethics
In outline the view that ethical demands and values do not derive from beliefs about God, or facts concerning the human condition, but are rather 'autonomous' of any considerations beyond themselves. Likewise, the human person may have 'autonomy' when exercising freedom to make a moral decision in contrast to being subject to some moral authority. The notion of autonomy – applied both to moral values and to persons – is subject to many differently nuanced definitions.

Biotic egalitarianism
The idea that all living things have equal value and an equal claim.

Consequentialism
The approach to ethics which judges an action in terms of the consequences of its performance.

Deism
Basically, a theological perspective which sees God as respecting the autonomy and natural process of the world, allowing the world to run according to its own patterns and regularities.

Demythologize
The attempt to restate in more direct speech that which is expressed in terms of myth, poetry or metaphor.

Deontological
An approach to ethics which centres on the ethical analysis of *an act itself* apart from its consequences.

Double effect
All actions have more than one consequence or effect. The appeal to the principle of the 'double effect' argues that the agent is not culpable for an undesirable consequence of an action, on account of another consequence which is desirable and effected only through the action, and where this consequence, rather than any other, is the intention behind the action.

Dualism
When speaking of 'mind' and 'body' – the idea that the 'self' and 'consciousness' are totally separate from the physical body. This contrasts with a more holistic view which sees selfhood and consciousness as 'emergent' properties in nature, coming into being through the development of life.

Ecocentric
An approach to ethics that centres, not upon the human, but on the natural environment within which human life is played out.

Eliminationist
The name given to describe the claim that a single insight, resource or approach is sufficient in ethics. In consequence, all other possible resources or insights may be eliminated. An example is the claim that in ethics 'all we need is love'.

Erastianism
A state of affairs in which the Church is – to whatever degree – controlled or governed by the secular state.

Eschatological
A perspective beyond and not simply continuous with that of the historical, cultural or natural 'here and now'.

Existence precedes essence
The invitation of existentialism to assert our freedom to discover our own 'existence' as individuals, derived primarily from our free choices,

decisions and judgements; thus minimizing any constraints imposed by notions of the 'essence' of what it is to be human. More generally the suspicion of any attempt to restrict overmuch human freedom by appeals to the naturally given. Presupposed here is the assumption that much claimed to be 'naturally' given in fact derives from culture.

Hedonism
The idea that pleasure or happiness alone has intrinsic value. More generally, an attitude of favour towards pleasure or happiness.

Hermeneutic
An interpretation of a text.

Hermeneutic of suspicion
The perspective on a text (especially a text offered as authoritative) that is suspicious of the text's cultural and historical relativity, and especially its collusion with structures of power and oppression.

Kenosis
'Self emptying'. The word has a Greek root, and is used classically in Philippians 2.5–8.

Last human dilemma
A thought experiment in which we imagine ourselves to be the last human, and often also the last animal of similar sentience and similar need.

Non sequitur
A false argument in which a conclusion is assumed wrongly to follow from a particular premise.

Ockhamist
Used in this book to describe an approach to ethics that sees ethics as simply obedience to the command of God, this command being seemingly arbitrary and having for us no rationale, being unconnected with our nature or what serves our flourishing. There are passages in the writings of William of Ockham that imply this.

Patriarchy
Dominance and oppression of women by men. Also a culture structured in this way.

Polytheism
Belief in more than one god or a number of gods.

Postmodernism
A term often used very loosely and with a variety of meanings. Usually it describes a mindset that has lost confidence in the 'modern' quest for that which is true in the sense of corresponding with reality, or

fitting *per se*. Instead, the emphasis is on the differing perspectives of differing people depending on their culture, language and mindset. It follows there is an emphasis on style and distinctiveness rather than upon a quest for that which is universally appropriate and universally true. A rejection of 'grand narratives', claimed to be universally true, in terms of which we see the world, a rejection often fed by the suspicion that these are both culturally relative and ideologies serving the powerful.

Prima facie
At first sight. Expressing an initial onus.

Proportionalism
The view that descriptions of acts such as lying, promise breaking, adultery, and such like, are only general or indicative descriptions (sometimes spoken of as 'analogous') since the character of a lie, broken promise or of some marital infidelity is always nuanced by the specific act and its context. In consequence, there can be no final moral judgement prior to an analysis of the specific act in its specific context.

Sacramental
The capacity of the 'physical' to feed and nourish the 'personal' and 'spiritual.'

Secular
The word can be used to describe an attitude which is anti-religious or anti-Christian. The word can also be used in a theological context to describe sectors of life and experience which, belonging to God's creation, are given by God a certain independence and separateness. It is in this latter sense that the word is generally used in this book.

Social contract
Generally, a thought experiment in which we envisage human beings as existing 'before' society and agreeing the terms on which they enter society or the type of society they wish to construct. Examples are to be found in the work of Thomas Hobbes, John Locke and John Rawls.

Speciesism
The view that it is wrong to discriminate or privilege on the basis of species just as it is wrong to discriminate or privilege on the basis of gender or race. Speciesism generally acknowledges that there are morally relevant differences between humans and animals that justify differing treatments.

Supererogation
A work of supererogation is doing more than is required. Going the 'extra mile'. Going beyond the call of duty.

Theocentric
God-centred.

Thought experiment
A mental exercise in which we envisage a situation constructed in order to clarify a question – often by excluding in our construct the kind of complicating factors usually encountered in real life.

Totipotent
Having potential to become more than one thing. Cells formed after conception are totipoent in the sense that they may form either embryo or placenta.

Utilitarianism
The philosophy that laws and public policy – and even individual moral decisions – should be judged by whether or not our actions lead to the 'greatest possible happiness of the greatest possible number'.

A Sample of Questions to Ponder

What virtues do you admire, and what vices do you deplore, and in what situations? And why? *'Our virtues would be proud if our faults whipped them not'*. How can 'virtues' become faults?

Is there both a Christian critique and a Christian appreciation of the values of contemporary British culture? What values should the Church bear witness to, and so 'drip feed' into the mindset of a culture?

Looking to the past, has this Christian 'drip feed' on some matters been more toxic than wholesome? And what of the contemporary churches?

How can the Church collectively, and Christians individually, make a contribution towards humanizing the market? And in what ways should we seek to humanize the market?

Some give limited moral status to the unborn child because moral status is focused on consciousness of interests over time. Such consciousness of interests has not yet developed in the unborn. But is consciousness of interests the only or the main criterion for determining moral status? What, for example, about the potential to *develop* into a human person? And how is this consideration to be balanced against other claims?

'The *developing* rights of the unborn are always less secure and less robust than the *actual* rights of the mother. The mother's actual rights must always have priority over the developing rights of the child. It follows a woman has an absolute right to an abortion if she so chooses.' What is your estimate of this statement?

Many issues in medical ethics cannot be settled conclusively by appeal to ethical argument. Law and codes of practice, however, have to determine clear guidelines – informed but not determined by ethical considerations. Are the current benchmarks determined by law over abortion, embryo research and medically assisted suicide, pragmatically the most acceptably or is there a case for change?

Can the values of a 'consumer society' adversely affect the qualities of our personal relationships?

What are your reflections on discussing moral issues with people of other faiths, and people of no faith? If you have no such experience could you consider building relationships in the course of which such conversations might take place?

What has the Church to learn from the value commitments of modern western culture?

Imagine a person becomes a committed Christian, having been before quite outside the community of faith. How might his or her new found faith affect their understanding of moral issues and the good life? Are there dangers that a misguided theology might render this sometimes less than wholesome?

What method does a Christian adopt, and what resources are available in making moral judgements? What difference does belief in God make to our understanding of morality?

What is your assessment of Peter Singer's claim that sexuality raises no special ethical issues, and that issues in sexuality can be faced adequately by appeal to general values and obligations such as guide our human relationships?

Consider Anthony Grayling's claim that religion should be confined to 'private observance only' and given no quarter in the 'public domain'.

Is discriminating on the basis of species as morally objectionable as discriminating on the basis of gender or ethnicity?

Was the invasion of Iraq a just war?

Is the British Government right in deciding to renew the nuclear deterrent?

Should the state give me the legal right to request medically assisted suicide when the quality of my life is no longer acceptable to me?

'Chastity for all outside marriage. Fidelity within.' Is this an adequate summary of Christian sexual ethics?

What are the strengths and weaknesses of an approach to ethics based on *consequences* of actions, an approach based on human *rights,* and *an approach based on the nature of the act itself*?

Are there basic 'givens' in 'human nature' and the 'human condition' that guide and constrain our moral choices?

In what ways do we exercise our environmental responsibility?

And many more!

Some Further Reading

The range of literature available is immense. The following is an indicative selection. Many basic books will include bibliographies – and the reader may refer also to the notes at the end of chapters.

Some basic introductions

Simon Blackburn, *Being Good*, Oxford, Oxford University Press, 2001.
Harry J. Gensler, *Ethics: A Contemporary Introduction*, London, Routledge 1998.
Peter Singer, *Practical Ethics*, Cambridge, Cambridge University Press, second edition 1993.
Peter Singer, *Rethinking Life and Death: The Collapse of our Traditional Ethics*, Oxford, Oxford University Press, 1994.
Peter Singer (ed.), *Applied Ethics*, Oxford, Oxford University Press, 1986.
Peter Singer (ed.), *A Companion to Ethics*, Oxford, Oxford University Press, Blackwell 1991.
Mary Warnock, *An Intelligent Person's Guide to Ethics*, London, Duckworth, 1998.

Those from a theological perspective

D. J. Atkinson and D. H. Field, *New Dictionary of Christian Ethics and Pastoral Theology*, Leicester, Inter-Varsity Press, 1995.
Richard Bauckham, *The Bible in Politics*, London, SPCK, 1989.
James F. Childress and John Macquarrie (eds), *A New Dictionary of Christian Ethics*, London, SCM Press, 1986.
John Elford, *The Ethics of Uncertainty*, Oxford, One World, 2000.
Elizabeth Frazer, et. al. (eds), *Ethics: A Feminist Reader*, Oxford, Blackwell, 1992.
Robin Gill (ed.), *The Cambridge Companion to Christian Ethics*, Cambridge, Cambridge University Press, 2001.
Robin Gill (ed.), *A Text Book of Christian Ethics*, Edinburgh and London, T&T Clark and Continuum, third edition, 2006.
Stanley Hauerwas and Stanley Wells (eds), *The Blackwell Companion to Christian Ethics*, Oxford, Blackwell, 2004.
Bernard Hoose (ed.), *Christian Ethics: An Introduction*, London, Continuum, 1998.
George Newlands, *Christ and Human Rights*, Aldershot, Ashgate, 2007.
Helen Oppenheimer, *The Hope of Happiness*, London, SCM Press, 1983.

Esther Reed, *The Genesis of Ethics*, London, Darton, Longman & Todd, 2000.

Cyril S. Rodd, *Glimpses of a Strange Land*, Edinburgh, T&T Clark, 2001.

Joseph Runzo and Nancy M. Martin (eds), *Ethics in the World Religions*, Oxford, One World, 2001.

Keith Ward, *Is Religion Harmful?*, London, Lion, 2007.

J. Philip Wogaman, *Christian Ethics: An Historical Introduction*, London, SPCK, 1994.

J. Philip Wogaman, *A Christian Method of Moral Judgment*, London, SCM Press, 1976.

Some books specifically on the themes of Part 3

An excellent collection of papers on many of the themes is:
Hugh LaFollette (ed.), *Ethics in Practice*, Oxford, Blackwell, 1997.

The themes of Chapter 11
John Atherton, *Marginalization*, London, SCM Press, 2003.

John Atherton, *Public Theology for Changing Times*, London, SPCK, 2000.

Faithful Cities, Peterborough, Methodist Publishing House and London, Church House Publishing, 2006.

David Fergusson, *Community, Liberalism and Christian Ethics*, Cambridge, Cambridge University Press, 1998.

Elaine Graham and Esther Reed, *The Future of Christian Social Ethics*, London, Continuum, 2004.

David Hollenbach, *The Common Good and Christian Ethics*, Cambridge, Cambridge University Press, 2002.

William F. Storrar and Andrew R. Morton (eds), *Public Theology for the Twenty-first Century*, London, Continuum, 2004.

Jim Wallis, *God's Politics*, San Francisco, Harper, 2005.

The themes of Chapter 12
John Atherton, *Christianity and the Market*, London, SPCK, 1992.

Malcolm Brown and Paul Ballard, *The Church and Economic Life*, Peterborough, Epworth 2006.

John Elford and Neville Markham (eds), *The Middle Way: The later thought of R. H. Preston*, London, SCM Press, 2000.

Employment and the Future of Work, London, CTBI, 1997.

Prosperity with a Purpose, London, CTBI, 2005.

The themes of Chapter 13
Maria Pilar Aquino and Dietmar Mieth, *The Return of the Just War*, Concilium, 2001/2, London, SCM Press, 2001.

Richard Harries, *Christianity and War in a Nuclear Age*, London, Mowbray, 1986.

John Kleiderer et. al., *Just War Lasting Peace*, Maryknoll, New York, Orbis, 2006.

Peacemaking: A Christian Vocation, Methodist Church and United Reformed Church, 2006.

The themes of Chapter 14

Robin Attfield, *Environmental Ethics*, Cambridge, Polity Press, 2003.

Celia Deane-Drummond, *A Handbook in Theology and Ecology*, London, SCM Press, 1996.

Sallie McFague, *Super, Natural Christians*, London, SCM Press, 1997.

Michael S. Northcott, *The Environment and Christian Ethics*, Cambridge, Cambridge University Press, 1996.

The themes of Chapter 15

Simon Blackburn, *Lust*, Oxford, Oxford University Press, 2004.

Timothy Bradshaw, *The Way forward: Christian Voices on homosexuality in the Church*, London, SCM Press, 1997.

Lisa S. Cahill, *Sex, Gender and Christian Ethics*, Cambridge, Cambridge University Press, 1996.

Andrew Linzey and Richard Kirker (eds), *Gays and the Future of Anglicanism*, Winchester, O Books, 2005.

Gareth Moore, *A Question of Truth: Christianity and Homosexuality*, London, Continuum, 2003.

James B. Nelson and Sandra P. Longfellow, *Sexuality and the Sacred*, London, Mowbray, 1994.

Helen Oppenheimer, *Marriage*, London, Mowbray, 1990.

Adrian Thatcher, *Liberating Sex*, London, SPCK, 1993.

The themes of Chapter 16

Terrence F. Ackerman and Carson Strong, *A Casebook of Medical Ethics*, Oxford, 1989.

Ronald Dworkin, *Life's Dominion*, London, HarperCollins, 1993.

Tony Hope, *Medical Ethics: A Very Short Introduction*, Oxford, 2004.

Helga Kuhse and Peter Singer (eds), *Bioethics*, Oxford, Blackwell, 1999.

Hans Küng and Walter Jens, *A Dignified Dying*, London, SCM Press, 1995.

Neil Messer (ed.), *Theological Issues in Bioethics*, London, Darton, Longman & Todd, 2002.

Neil Messer, *Selfish Genes and Christian Ethics*, London, SCM Press, 2007.

Michael M. Uhlmann, *Last Rights: Assisted Suicide and Euthanasia debates* Grand Rapids, Eerdmans, 2005.

Index of Subjects

Main reference, where appropriate, given in bold type

Index of Names